A view of Swindon towards the end of the Broad Gauge era.
(F. Moore's rail photos)

From left to right, No 6000 King George V, *No 5010* Restormel Castle *and No 4004* Morning Star *pose at Old Oak Common*. (W.J. Reynolds)

GREAT LOCOMOTIVES OF THE GWR

O.S. Nock

Haynes
PSL
Patrick Stephens Limited

First published in 1990

British Library Cataloguing in Publication Data
Nock, O. S. (Oswald Stevens) *1905*
Great locomotives of the Great Western Railway.
1. England Railway services: Great Western
Railway. Steam locomotives, history
I. Title
625.2610942

ISBN 1-85260-157-4

Patrick Stephens Limited, a member of the Haynes Publishing Group, has published authoritative quality books for enthusiasts for more than twenty years. During that time the company has established a reputation as one of the world's leading publishers of books on aviation, maritime, military, model-making, motor cycling, motoring, motor racing, railway and railway modelling subjects. Readers or authors with suggestions for books they would like to see published are invited to write to: The Editorial Director, Patrick Stephens Limited, Sparkford, Nr Yeovil, Somerset, BA22 7JJ.

Note
At the time the GWR ceased to exist in January 1948, and became part of British Railways, the art of railway photography in colour had barely started. The colour pictures in this book were all taken after this change and show GWR locomotives either in their working days in post-nationalization colours or restored to their former glory on some of the country's many preserved railways.

Typeset by Burns & Smith Limited, Derby

Printed in Great Britain by The Bath Press, Bath, Avon

10 9 8 7 6 5 4 3 2 1

Contents

	Preface	4
1.	Lingerings of traditionalism	6
2.	Dean's greatest years	17
3.	The advent of Churchward	25
4.	Persisting foreign influences	34
5.	The magic 'hundred'—the saga of the Ocean Mails	40
6.	The grand conception, and its fulfilment	49
7.	Churchward's all-line policy	62
8.	Finalization of pre-war engine design	72
9.	The Great Western locomotive status *in toto*	79
10.	The war years: a time for reflection	89
	Great Locomotives of the GWR in colour	93
11.	Churchward's retirement: the new team, and engine tests	113
12.	The 'Castle' storm centre	123
13.	New smaller engines	132
14.	'Saints' and 'Stars'—the Golden Years	140
15.	Design and introduction of the 'Kings'	153
16.	'A machine of precision'	160
17.	Engine testing: new advanced practices	169
18.	Maximum performance in the later 'thirties	176
19.	Mixed traffic units, large and small	187
20.	Hawksworth's years—Phase 1	196
21.	Hawksworth's years—Phase 2	206
22.	Dissolution	216
	Appendix I: Preserved locos of the GWR	226
	Appendix II: Out of the shadows—the 1952 saga of the 'Manors'	229
	Bibliography	230
	Index	231

Preface

I suppose it is a little strange to say that I am approaching the writing of the fourth and last of these books on the pre-nationalization locomotives of the railways of Great Britain with somewhat mixed feelings. In the past 30 or 40 years I have written more about the Great Western and its locomotives than of any others, and one might imagine that there would be little or nothing new to write about it. At the outset, however, I ought to now make clear how I came, apparently, to be so partial to the products of Swindon. At the time of nationalization, when the various executives were being set up, it was apparent that the Great Western had got something of a 'raw deal'. It was represented on the Railway Executive by no more than a not very eminent commercial man, whereas the engineering and operating departments were powerfully represented by former officers of the LMS and the LNER, and the Chairman came from the Southern. Not until many years later did I learn of the antagonism with which the whole process of nationalization was viewed by the top management of the Great Western Railway, and but for this attitude both the Chairman of the new organization and the Chief Civil Engineer would have been GWR men had not both turned down flat the invitation.

In the 'raw deal' atmosphere, which I found shared by very many railway enthusiasts whom I met at gatherings of the Stephenson Locomotive Society and other kindred bodies, I became the mouthpiece of an unofficial 'GWR supporters club', and inevitably found myself writing about Swindon locomotives more than all the others. Added to that, with my post-war business activities involving regular journeys between Bath and Paddington, my travelling log-books became full to overflowing with Western Region runs. How thoroughly I had apparently become indoctrinated is shown by an amusing incident when I had to lecture to the railway society of Leeds University, and the Chairman introduced me thus: 'We all know that Mr Nock is a Great Western fan. When he was at Imperial College, whenever his prof wanted him they used to send a messenger across to Paddington to collect him'! On a more serious note, in 1946, when the Transport Bill had just been launched in the House of Commons, I was advised by the celebrated bookselling firm of W. Heffer and Sons of Cambridge that because of the impending nationalization of the British railways they were going to publish a memorial volume on each of the 'Big Four', and would I write the one on the Great Western. Needless to say I jumped at the opportunity. Who the other writers were that Heffer's approached I have no idea; but in the event mine was the only one that got off the ground. In any case it was a long time coming, for whereas the manuscript and all the illustrations and maps were complete and sent off by midsummer of 1948, the book itself did not appear until three years later.

Coming to the present book, I was at first in some difficulty at which date I should start. The earlier volumes in this series had sagas stretching well back into the nineteenth century, and not only the memories and sentiments of engineers like William Adams, the Drummonds, Webb, H.A. Ivatt and Bowen Cooke remained through the Grouping age, but also many of their locomotives were to be seen, if not on actually first class duty, nevertheless on worthwhile revenue-earning service. With the Great Western it was very different. When E.L. Ahrons wrote his famous series of articles for *The Railway Magazine*, 'Locomotive and Train Working in the latter part of the Nineteenth Century', and notched up no fewer than ten meaty contributions on the Great Western Railway, there was scarcely a mention of the Dean express passenger engines that carried the railway into the twentieth century, and none at all of the mixed traffic and goods classes. In the immediate post-war years publicity literature from Paddington did not seem to acknowledge anything that had not a tapered domeless boiler. On the other hand, in addition to the engines lovingly described by Ahrons, because he was a GWR man and knew many of them intimately, there were others introduced between the final demise of the Broad Gauge and the turn of the century which certainly deserve the term 'great'. So in this book I shall begin the story in 1892, though taking a farewell look at the once famous engines of the Broad Gauge.

In the cold light of history, the Crimean War would not appear to be one of the most distinguished episodes in the annuals of the British War Office, but the gallantry and fortitude of the troops themselves and the devotion of Florence Nightingale and her nurses aroused a tremendous amount of fervent patriotism at home, and it was not surprising that some of the latest of Daniel Gooch's 8-foot 4-2-2 engines were named *Alma*, *Balaklava*, *Inkermann* and *Sebastopol*, while others were named *Crimea* and *Eupatoria*, which was the old and little-known name of the Black Sea. At the time when the 'Battle of the Gauges' was on, in 1845, and for a few years after, Daniel Gooch's 8-ft 4-2-2 locomotives were unequalled for power and speed anywhere in Great Britain, though with the isolation of the Broad Gauge they were not developed, and it was the men of the standard gauge engineering centre at Wolverhampton who came to the fore, except when the South Devon railway was absorbed and G.J. Churchward came to Swindon.

In twentieth-century Great Western locomotive history, Churchward indeed dominates the scene both as a father figure and a colossus in engineering. The principles and precepts of the great development, which had begun even before he had finally succeeded Dean in the chair at Swindon, were all established in no more than a dozen years, and they provided for modern powerful and highly efficient standard designs for express passenger, mixed traffic, suburban passenger and heavy goods and mineral traffic, which lasted for the rest of the life of the Great Western Railway. Because of steadily increasing demands of traffic, some enlargements were necessary, though not to the wheel arrangement of passenger engines; but the precepts of design remained absolutely the same. It was fascinating to see how this was done in producing such famous and successful locomotives as the 'Castles' and 'Kings', introduced by C.B. Collett. The last Chief Mechanical Engineer of the GWR, F.W. Hawksworth, was also a Swindon man by training and life-long experience, but when he succeeded to the chair in 1941 the whole complexion of railway working in Great Britain was changing, and he had to make some changes to the precepts of Churchward, devoted admirer as he had always been of the 'Old Man'.

In writing this book I must express my thanks to the chief officers and staff of the Great Western Railway and the Western Region of the nationalized British Railways. It is not only to Hawksworth and his successors, K.J. Cook and A. Smeddle, that my thanks are due, but to all on the strength, Works Managers, Assistant Engineers, Divisional Superintendents, Draughtsmen, Locomotive Running Inspectors and, in my footplate work, very many drivers and firemen, all of whom made me so welcome on all their engines. But above all I am indebted to Sam Ell and his dedicated team of testing engineers for many occasions in the stationary testing plant and out on the line in the dynamometer car.

I began this Preface by expressing certain mixed feelings, and indeed I am ending the book itself with many more of them. I was working on the 21st chapter when there arrived through my letter-box a finely produced 28-page newspaper entitled 'Swindon Industry News'. Apparently this publication incorporates the 'Bristol Business News and the Bath and West Wilts Business News'; but as its present title signifies, it is predominantly concerned with Swindon, and where industry is concerned I was not surprised that from end to end of the paper there was not one mention of railways. Many other railway centres have changed in the last 50 years, but nowhere else has there been so complete and utter a finale as that experienced at Swindon. This book is thus not merely a scientific and a nostalgic look at past achievements of Great Western locomotives, but is also a memorial to the great works where they were born, now so silent save for the relatively small enclave allocated to the National Railway Museum for exhibition purposes, and for the repair of certain units to maintain them at the high standards demanded by law for any steam locomotives running passenger trains today.

Regarding preserved Great Western locomotives, when writing Chapter 12 of this book I suggested that in connection with the visit of the LNER 'Pacific' *Flying Scotsman* to Australia, it might have been an idea to move *Pendennis Castle* temporarily to Perth so that the one-time rivals could meet again. This, in fact, did take place, but in the event the significance of the juxtapositioning of the two British locomotives was all but submerged by the media publicity accorded to *Flying Scotsman*'s new record for the longest non-stop run in steam locomotive history. Actually, of course, Gresley's celebrated No 4472 was not in any way concerned in the Locomotive Interchange Trials of 1925, when *Pendennis Castle* did so well in hauling heavy LNER expresses between King's Cross and Doncaster. Her rivals then were 'Pacifics' stationed at King's Cross Top Shed, while No 4472 was then shedded at Doncaster.

O.S. Nock

1. Lingerings of traditionalism

Having every regard for the esteem in which the Broad Gauge was held by railwaymen in the West Country, I feel it would be graceless to ignore it in a book about Great Western locomotives, even though the main-line engines working between Paddington, Bristol and Newton Abbot in those last years had long since ceased to be anything like 'great' in their performance on the road. Much as they were revered at Swindon, and indeed by the hierarchy at Paddington, they were really hopelessly out of date by the later 1800s. Some of them had been replaced by entirely new engines of the same design, and while all of them eventually carried boilers working at 140 lb psi instead of the original 110, despite those large boilers having a heating surface far greater than any other express passenger locomotives of the 1800s, they had a nominal tractive effort much below that of their more advanced contemporaries. It is interesting to set down their leading dimensions alongside those of some celebrated rivals on other railways, as in the table below.

From the prestige point of view, much store was set at Paddington by the fact that the 'Flying Dutchman' and the 'Zulu' had one of the fastest start-to-stop runs anywhere in the world at that time, being booked to cover the 77.3 miles from Paddington to Swindon in 87 minutes, 53.3 mph average. Furthermore, on the Bristol and Exeter section, the trains, hauled by fresh engines, went on to cover the 44¾ miles from Bristol to Taunton in 51 minutes, a further good average of 52⅓ mph. But from such contemporary accounts that have been passed down to us, these Broad Gauge expresses kept very poor time, certainly on the fastest booked sections. E.L. Ahrons was trained in the Locomotive Department at Swindon and did much footplate riding on both Broad Gauge and standard gauge express locomotives. The trouble with the Broad Gauge 8-footers was that even with the relatively light trains of six or seven eight-wheeled coaches, they seemed incapable of exceeding 60 mph at the very most between Paddington and Swindon, and losses in time on the 87-minute schedule up to nearly 4 minutes were the usual thing. No one seems to have made any detailed recordings of the way the Bristol-based 8-footers performed on the fast schedules between Bristol and Taunton.

The tabulated details of the various typical express locomotives reveal how deficient the Broad Gauge 8-footers were in nominal tractive effort. This was understandable, for they were really quite out of date, but on the other hand they had boilers providing heating surface that was enormous for the day, amounting to around 2,000 ft on the boilers fitted to the latest rebuilds and renewals. One might have thought that with such boilers the drivers would have been inclined to push their engines along in a more enterprising manner, despite the lack of tractive effort resulting from cylinders no larger than 18 in by 24 in. But pure dimensions do not by any means represent the potentiality of a steam locomotive for speed or pulling power. The form of the valve gear and its setting would be all-important, and the speed-worthiness of certain contemporaries of the Great Western 8-footers, on the LNWR, the Midland and the Caledonian, which reached the high 80s frequently, bears this out. In 1846, when scheming out the design of his 8-footers, Daniel Gooch used a form of link motion that was his own. It was criticized by certain later students of locomotive engineering, notably by Pettigrew in his celebrated 'Manual', first published in 1899. Even so, the Gooch link motion survived through the entire life of the Broad Gauge 8-footers.

Although the South Wales main line, together with the connecting line from Swindon to Gloucester, had been converted to standard gauge in 1872, and there were prospects of heavier traffic due to the development of ocean steamship services via Milford Haven, no

Some typical express locomotives of the 1880s

Railway	Engineer	Type	Class	Wheel diameter (ft in)	Cylinders, diameter × stroke (in)	Boiler pressure (psi)	Nominal tractive effort (lb)
LNWR	Webb	2-4-0	'Precedent'	6 9	17 × 24	150	10,870
NER	Tennant	2-4-0	'Tennant'	7 0	18 × 24	160	12,570
LB&SCR	Stroudley	0-4-2	'Gladstone'	6 6	18¼ × 26	140	13,190
Midland	Johnson	4-4-0	'1740'	7 0	18 × 26	160	13,600
South Eastern	J. Stirling	4-4-0	'F'	7 0	19 × 26	140	13,190
Caledonian	D. Drummond	4-4-0	'60'	6 6	18 × 26	160	14,650
GNR	P. Stirling	4-2-2	8-footers	8 0	18 × 28	160	12,830
GWR	Gooch	4-2-2	—	8 0	18 × 24	140	9,600

Broad Gauge 8-ft 4-2-2 Emperor, *one of the first six of the 'Iron Duke' Class originally built in 1847 and seen here in its final form in the old station at Exeter St Davids.* (BTC Archives)

A Rev A.H. Malan photograph of Broad Gauge 4-2-2 Sebastopol *at Newton Abbot in 1890.* (Rev A.H. Malan, BTC Archives)

other express passenger locomotives other than the 2-2-2 type were built for the increasingly important standard gauge services. Admittedly the traffic authorities at Paddington in those last years of the Broad Gauge made sure that no standard gauge train was timed so fast as the Broad Gauge 'Flying Dutchman', the 'Zulu' and the 'Cornishman'; but the standard gauge 2-2-2s were in themselves very good engines, and when they got beyond Swindon there was some hard work for them, climbing up to Sapperton Tunnel.

In readiness for the final conversion of the gauge, Dean built some very large 7-ft 8-in single-wheelers of the 2-2-2 type, and eight of them, Nos 3021–3028, were built as 'Convertibles' working with the Gooch 4-2-2s in the same Broad Gauge links from 1891. What the old drivers thought of them is not recorded, but the Rev A.H. Malan, to whom we are indebted for so many fine photographs of Broad Gauge engines at speed and on the sheds, was not amused. He was an out-and-out Broad Gauge enthusiast and had no time at all for the newcomers, comparing their top-heaviness with the massive stability of the Broad Gauge 4-2-2s.

The origin of what eventually became a very celebrated class of Great Western locomotives actually dates back to 1886 when Dean built a 2-2-2 for the standard gauge with 7-ft 8-in driving wheels, engine No 10. This was important as the prototype of the entire range of Dean's later locomotive designs. The novel feature of engine No 10 so far as Swindon was concerned lay in the positioning of the slide valves underneath the cylinders. The arrangement originated on the Brighton, with Stroudley, and had the advantage that the valves dropped off their faces when steam was shut off and, by the elimination of this item of sliding friction, the engine was enabled to coast freely. On the other hand, the exhaust passages were lengthened considerably as compared with those of an engine having valves on top of, or between, the cylinders. Dean did not adopt this arrangement direct from Stroudley, as it were, but more probably through the influence of James Holden, who had been principal assistant at Swindon. When Holden went to the Great Eastern in 1885 to succeed T.W. Worsdell, he adopted the Stroudley valve arrangement on his excellent 'T19' Class 2-4-0s, the first of which came out in the same year as Dean's No 10 on the GWR. The difference was that Holden went straight ahead with a large class,

Left *The westbound 'Flying Dutchman' at Worle Junction.* (Rev A.H. Malan, BTC Archives)

Below *No 3017, one of the Dean 7-ft 8-in singles, as originally built as a 2-2-2 and before naming; it was later named* Prometheus. (Rev A.H. Malan, BTC Archives)

Below right *Dean 7-ft 8-in 2-2-2 No 3009* Flying Dutchman. (W.J. Reynolds)

whereas at Swindon the application was experimental until the '30XX' Class was turned out, from 1891.

The first version of the '3000' Class of 7-ft 8-in singles had the abnormal cylinders dimensions for a 2-2-2 of 20 in diameter by 24 in stroke. The boiler was very large, providing a total heating surface of 1,466.73 sq ft, and a grate area of 20.8 sq ft. With a working pressure of 160 psi, the nominal tractive effort was far in advance of that of the Gooch 8-ft Broad Gauge singles, but whether or not any of the eight convertibles operated in the prestigious links that worked the 'Flying Dutchman', the 'Zulu' or the 'Cornishman' is not recorded. Apart from the 'Convertibles', the remainder of the first 30 of the class were built as ordinary 2-2-2s. While Dean did not adopt Patrick Stirling's method of steadying the front end by placing the axle of the leading wheel immediately beneath the smokebox and chimney, he provided 2 in lateral play in the axleboxes of the leading wheels. Whether this feature contributed to the alarming mishap to engine No 3021 *Wigmore Castle* was not disclosed in the subsequent investigation; but the engine sustained a broken leading axle travelling at full speed in the middle of the Box Tunnel. Fortunately there were no casualties—except, probably, a rise in blood pressure for those on the footplate! As a result of this, Dean decided to fit leading bogies to all engines of the class.

This was easier said than done. One of the conventional type with a centre pin carried on a stretcher between the frames would have made it extremely difficult to remove the steam chest covers and to obtain access to the port faces below the cylinders, but the problem was solved by a modification of the Dean carriage bogie of the suspension type. For this, four pillars were fixed to the inside frames, two on each side between the bogie wheels. Two transverse cross-bars, carried on the bases of pillars on opposite sides, were connected at mid-length by a box containing the centre block for the bogie pin, which had a limited amount of side play. The bogie frame had a cross stay on which an inverted

centre pin was fixed. The weight of the engine was transferred to the bogie by four long suspension bolts anchored at the outer ends of the two crossbars. By removing the nuts at the bottom of the four pillars, the entire bogie and its carriers could be run out on lifting the front end of the engine, leaving the underside of the cylinders clear. The engines of the class that had originally been built as 2-2-2s had the springs of the trailing pair of wheels underhung, and when they were rebuilt as 4-2-2s this feature was for a time continued. But when the new batch beginning at engine No 3031 was built, the trailing springs were above the frames, and the cab reduced in width to permit this.

Eventually all 80 of those beautiful engines were named. The first eight, built as 'Convertibles', had no room for a nameplate, and they were among the very few engines running on the Broad Gauge to have numbers. Early photographs also show that some of the 2-2-2s of the class built for the standard gauge had no names. The chronology of the first 30 engines of the class was as follows:

No	Name	Date first built
Built as 'Convertibles' (name when standard gauge)		
3021	*Wigmore Castle*	April 1891
3022	*Bessemer*	May 1891
3023	*Swallow*	July 1891
3024	*Storm King*	July 1891
3025	*St George*	August 1891
3026	*Tornado*	August 1891
3027	*Worcester*	August 1891
3028	*Wellington*	August 1891
Built for standard gauge as 2-2-2s		
3029	*White Horse*	November 1891
3030	*Westward Ho*	December 1891
3001	*Amazon*	January 1892
3002	*Atlanta*	January 1892
3003	*Avalanche*	February 1892
3004	*Black Prince*	February 1892
3005	*Britannia*	February 1892
3006	*Courier*	March 1892
3007	*Dragon*	March 1892
3008	*Emperor*	March 1892
3009	*Flying Dutchman*	March 1892
3010	*Fire King*	March 1892
3011	*Greyhound*	March 1892
3012	*Great Western*	March 1892
3013	*Great Britain*	March 1892
3014	*Iron Duke*	April 1892
3015	*Kennet*	April 1892
3016	*Lightning*	April 1892
3017	*Prometheus*	April 1892
3018	*Racer*	April 1892
3019	*Rover*	April 1892
3020	*Sultan*	April 1892

Referring to the building dates for engines completed in 1892, it is evident that a tremendous drive must have been made in the erecting shop at Swindon to turn out eight new express passenger engines in one month, March, and another seven in April. Doubtless this was due to the imminence of the final change of the gauge on the West of England main line, and the withdrawal of all the Broad Gauge 8-ft singles. Certainly on this special occasion Swindon succeeded in stepping up its new express engine output to something like Crewe's normal standards. Many of the names of these new standard gauge 2-2-2s were taken from the Broad Gauge 4-2-2s that they replaced; but it was significant that the names associated with events in the Crimean War were not used again.

I have been unable to find any notes of the performance of these engines in their 2-2-2 condition. There was so much excitement on the lines northward from Euston and King's Cross in the years following the abolition of the Broad Gauge that it was understandable that those who made a hobby of timing fast trains concentrated their attention on the brilliant running of the London and North Western and of the Great Nor-

Left *Up express milk train near Langley, Bucks, hauled by 4-2-2 No 3001* Amazon. (Author's collection)

Right *Dean 7-ft 8-in 4-2-2 No 3031* Achilles. (GWR postcard)

thern rather than the somewhat pedestrian efforts of the Great Western. The tune was to change dramatically in a few years' time. Even so, many of Charles Rous-Marten's earlier articles in *The Railway Magazine* seemed couched in terms to emphasize how inferior the work of the Dean singles was compared to that of the four-coupled 'Atbara' Class 4-4-0s, even though by that time all the earlier 7-ft 8-in singles had been converted to 4-2-2s and 50 additional 4-2-2s had been built at Swindon between March 1894 and March 1899. One can see, over many years of reading railway literature, a trait with journalists whose training has not been in any of the mechanical sciences, to latch on to anything that is new to the apparent disadvantage of what has gone before, while as far as Swindon was concerned, orders for 7-ft 8-in 4-2-2s were still being passed to the works while all the 20 6-ft 8-in 4-4-0s of the 'Badminton' Class had been completed. The 'Atbaras', as will be described later in the book, followed immediately after the last batch of 7-ft 8-in singles had left the erecting shop.

The 50 7-ft 8-in engines built new as 4-2-2s included some very attractive names. Some came from the Broad Gauge 8-footers, others from Queen Victoria's family and its numerous associations, while others stemmed from the West Country, including J.N. Maskelyne's favourite, *Lorna Doone*. Some had their names changed later, as when *St George* became *Saint George* and was used on a new 4-6-0 of the 'Saint' class; likewise *Shooting Star*, which was transferred to one of the new four-cylinder 4-6-0s. After these alterations, attractive new names were found for the single-wheelers. The second of the '3031' Class, as the 50 built as 4-2-2s were sometimes called, No 3032 *Agamemnon*, was the subject of a magnificent folding lithographic plate in the January 1896 issue of *The Railway Engineer*. The full list of these engines as originally built with the dates of their construction are shown in the following list, which shows that never again did Swindon touch the rate of production achieved in March 1892, though there were several months when five new engines of the class were turned out.

Below *Down 'Flying Dutchman' passing Bedminster hauled by 4-2-2 No 3047* Lorna Doone. (L&GRP No 12214)

The '3031' Class

No	Name	Date built
3031	*Achilles*	March 1894
3032	*Agamemnon*	July 1894
3033	*Albatross*	July 1894
3034	*Behemoth*	July 1894
3035	*Beaufort*	July 1894
3036	*Crusader*	Sept 1894
3037	*Corsair*	Sept 1894
3038	*Devonia*	Sept 1894
3039	*Dreadnought*	Sept 1894
3040	*Empress of India*	Sept 1894
3041	*The Queen*	Oct 1894
3042	*Frederick Saunders*	Oct 1894
3043	*Hercules*	Jan 1895
3044	*Hurricane*	Jan 1895
3045	*Hirondelle*	Jan 1895
3046	*Lord of the Isles*	Jan 1895
3047	*Lorna Doone*	Feb 1895
3048	*Majestic*	Feb 1895
3049	*Nelson*	Feb 1895
3050	*Royal Sovereign*	Feb 1895
3051	*Stormy Petrel*	Feb 1895
3052	*Sir Walter Raleigh*	March 1895
3053	*Sir Francis Drake*	March 1895
3054	*Sir Richard Grenville*	March 1895
3055	*Trafalgar*	March 1895
3056	*Timour*	March 1895
3057	*Tartar*	April 1895
3058	*Grierson*	April 1895
3059	*Voltigeur*	April 1895
3060	*Warlock*	April 1895
3061	*Alexandra*	May 1897
3062	*Albert Edward*	May 1897
3063	*Duke of York*	June 1897
3064	*Duke of Edinburgh*	June 1897
3065	*Duke of Connaught*	July 1897
3066	*Duchess of Albany*	Dec 1897
3067	*Duchess of Teck*	Dec 1897
3068	*Duke of Cambridge*	Jan 1898
3069	*Earl of Chester*	Jan 1898
3070	*Earl of Warwick*	Feb 1898
3071	*Emlyn*	Feb 1898
3072	*North Star*	June 1898
3073	*Princess Royal*	June 1898
3074	*Princess Helena*	June 1898
3075	*Princess Louise*	July 1898
3076	*Princess Beatrice*	February 1899
3077	*Princess May*	February 1899
3078	*Shooting Star*	February 1899
3079	*Thunderbolt*	March 1899
3080	*Windsor Castle*	March 1899

In this day and age, when enthusiasts with long memories recall the long saga of the Swindon 4-6-0 pursued by Churchward, Collett and Hawksworth, it is indeed hard to imagine how hard the Broad Gauge tradition died on the Great Western Railway, with Dean still building single-wheelers for the heaviest main-line traffic between Paddington and Newton down to the year 1899, when on the Caledonian McIntosh had progressed to his third series of 'Dunalastairs', H.A. Ivatt on the GNR had built the first of his 'Klondikes', and on the Lancashire and Yorkshire Aspinall had the first series of his 'Highflyer' 'Atlantics' running.

Soon after the abolition of the Broad Gauge, under the aegis of the new General Manager, Mr, later Sir Joseph, Wilkinson, some very fine new trains were put on, one of them indeed making the longest daily non-stop run anywhere in the world at that time, from Paddington to Exeter, 193¾ miles in 3 hr 43 min, an average speed of 52 mph. Then there was the 'Flying Welshman' non-stop over the 143.5 miles from Newport to Paddington, via Bath, in 177 minutes, an average of 48.7 mph. In 1897, when these two trains were put on, the Dean 7-ft 8-in 4-2-2s were the standard engines for the West of England east of Newton Abbot, and for the new Welsh train two of them were

Left *Swindon nearing the end of the Broad Gauge era, with standard gauge 2-2-2s in evidence.* (F. Moore's rail photos)

Right *An up West of England express near Dawlish when the line was still single tracked; engine No 3067* Duchess of Teck. (L&GRP No 21403)

allocated to Ebbw Junction shed. Each with a specially selected crew, they worked the train on alternate days, the second engine standing pilot at Newport until the 'flyer' had got away. Then this second engine had an easy day of it working no farther than Gloucester and back with an all-stations stopping train. These long non-stop runs, though timed on considerably lower average speeds than we came to know on the Great Western in the twentieth century, were no sinecures for single-wheelers; while on the Exeter run there was only the Whiteball bank to trouble the engine and crew, from Newport after climbing out of the depths of the Severn Tunnel there was still the heavy ascent through the single-line Patchway Tunnel, and after descending to the outskirts of Bristol there were still the steep climbs through Box Tunnel and the ascent of the Dauntsey bank.

The very first number of *The Railway Magazine*, in July 1897, included a long account of a footplate ride on No 3006 *Courier* working this train, but unfortunately the writer gave no details at all of the engine working other than that the start from Newport was 3 minutes late, that they were 5 minutes early passing Swindon, and despite a signal check to 'walking pace' at Uffington, they arrived in Paddington 3 minutes early. So far as the 'Cornishman' was concerned, Rous-Marten logged the up train, as per the accompanying tabulation. The checks in the Taunton area cost about 9 minutes between them, but that at Reading no more than a single minute. Though this was not a very exciting run in itself, the net time of 221 minutes showed an average speed of 52.6 mph. The start from Exeter up to Whiteball summit was excellent, although Rous-Marten appeared to omit taking the time at the summit signal box, which would have been about a minute later than at Burlescombe station. The down 'Cornishman' got some publicity in the December 1899 issue of *The Railway Magazine* in the form of a handsome colour plate 7 in by 22 in showing the train running at

Up 'Cornishman', 1897

Load Six corridor coaches, about 145 tons
Engine 4-2-2 No 3013 *Great Britain*

Distance (miles)		Actual time (min	sec)	Average speed (mph)
0.0	EXETER	0	00	—
14.9	Tiverton Junction	19	37	45.7
19.2	Burlescombe	25	03	47.7
23.7	Wellington	30	20	50.9
28.8	Norton Fitzwarren	35	09	68.0
30.8	TAUNTON	38	00	
—				sig stop
		40	12	
33.6	Creech Junction	45	20	
—				sig stop
		46	19	
42.3	Bridgwater	58	03	—
48.6	Highbridge	64	33	58.2
63.6	Yatton	80	31	64.2
74.5	Bedminster	92	00	57.5
76.6	Bristol East Depot	95	30	36.0
87.7	BATH	109	12	46.0
92.7	Box	116	12	49.0
96.3	Corsham	122	18	44.2
100.6	CHIPPENHAM	127	12	52.3
111.7	Wootton Bassett	139	48	53.4
116.3	SWINDON	146	31	47.8
122.0	Shrivenham	152	23	57.8
127.1	Uffington	157	24	61.3
133.2	Wantage Road	163	18	62.4
140.5	DIDCOT	171	04	56.8
—				sigs
157.6	READING	192	02	48.9
162.6	Twyford	198	11	49.2
175.1	SLOUGH	211	40	55.3
180.4	West Drayton	216	57	60.2
187.9	Ealing	224	47	57.2
193.6	PADDINGTON	230	58	—

speed near Bathampton. Produced by the lithographic process, the colours were a trifle garish, but as a final souvenir of nineteenth-century magazine production it is one of my treasured items.

My late friend R.E. Charlewood was a good deal more fortunate than Rous-Marten in securing good runs with the 7-ft 8-in singles, and three of his runs made in 1900 are tabulated herewith. The non-stop timing of 88 minutes for the 75.6-mile run from Exeter to Bristol had some very uneven point-to-point bookings intermediately. To pass Whiteball summit in 26 minutes required some hard work. Although it is only in the last two miles that the gradient steepens to 1 in 115, the collar work is continuous from Exeter. The

GWR: 3.7pm Exeter–Bristol, 1900

Run No			1		2		3	
Engine No			3065		3055		3063	
Engine name			*Duke of Connaught*		*Trafalgar*		*Duke of York*	
Load (tons full)			165		165		185	
Distance (miles)		**Schedule (min)**	**Actual (m s)**	**Av speed (mph)**	**Actual (m s)**	**Av speed (mph)**	**Actual (m s)**	**Av speed (mph)**
0.0	EXETER	0	0 00	—	0 00	—	0 00	—
3.5	Stoke Canon		7 20	—	6 50	—	7 15	—
8.4	Hele		13 55	44.6	13 10	46.5	13 10	49.7
12.6	Cullompton		18 50	51.3	18 11	50.3	17 37	56.6
14.9	Tiverton Junction	19	22 00	43.6	21 25	42.5	20 17	51.7
19.9	*Whiteball*	26	29 25	40.4	28 45	41.0	26 31	48.1
23.7	Wellington		33 20	58.3	32 53	55.1	30 15	61.0
28.8	Norton Fitzwarren		37 20	76.5	37 30	66.5	34 17	75.9
30.8	TAUNTON	38	39 00	72.0	39 40	55.5	36 08	64.8
36.6	Durston		44 30	63.3	45 45	57.1	42 07	58.1
42.3	BRIDGWATER	52	50 05	61.2	51 50	56.2	47 51	59.6
48.6	Highbridge		56 05	63.0	58 25	57.4	53 57	61.9
51.4	Brent Knoll		—	—	—	—	56 39	62.2
55.9	*Uphill Junction*	66	63 00	63.3	65 55	58.3	61 00	62.1
63.6	Yatton		70 15	63.7	73 50	50.8	68 40	58.8
			pws	—	—	—	*eased*	—
69.6	Flax Bourton		77 15	—	80 40	52.7	75 39	—
			—	—	—	—	*sig stops*	—
75.6	BRISTOL	88	84 25	—	88 25	—	85 35	—
	Net times		83½		88½		82½	

brief descents past Hele and Tiverton Junction give no respite, and merely enable a driver to gain a little speed to help him on the next stretch of climbing. Then comes the anomaly of 12 minutes allowed for the 10.9 miles of real racing ground down to Taunton, while the ensuing 25.1 level miles on to Uphill Junction were allowed 28 minutes. In these circumstances it is not surprising that the drivers of single-wheelers were inclined to take things quietly up to Whiteball, knowing that they could easily regain a few lost minutes afterwards.

Engine No 3065 *Duke of Connaught* had not then achieved immortality in the locomotive world by her performances on the Ocean Mails, but on the run detailed in column 1 she put up some fine running. Things were taken easily to Whiteball following a punctual start, but there was some really fast work down the Wellington bank. No maximum speed is quoted, but with an average of 76½ mph from Wellington to Norton Fitzwarren, the top speed must have been very near 80 mph, if not in excess of it. From being 3½ minutes down at Whiteball, the train was 2 minutes early on passing Bridgwater. Good steady running at 60 to 64 mph continued over the long level stretches of the Somersetshire coastal flats, and despite a permanent way slack between Yatton and Nailsea, Bristol was reached 3½ minutes early.

As shown in column 2, No 3055 *Trafalgar* did not do nearly so well. Exeter was left a minute late, but although the immediate start was better than that of *Duke of Connaught*, and similar up to Whiteball, the subsequent work was not in the same class at all. Charlewood makes no mention of the weather on this trip. A crosswind can be a serious hindrance over the completely exposed stretch of line from Durston to Flax Bourton, while a wet rail would set up that imperceptible slipping that could be a great handicap to a single-wheeler. Anyway, from whatever cause it may have been, *Trafalgar* barely held her own, and I have included the run as an example of the less brilliant side of the Dean 7-ft 8-in singles. The load was by no means excessive, and in any case the engine did quite adequately on the section where the load would have the greatest effect.

The last run in the table, with engine No 3063 *Duke of York*, was a brilliant performance, with the heaviest load of the three. First of all, the hard booking up to Whiteball was practically kept, and the final minimum speed of 37¾ mph was first class for a single up 2 miles of 1 in 115. Speed then rose to 77 mph down Wellington bank, and despite a slight easing through Taunton the train was 4¼ minutes early passing Bridgwater. Although things were then so well in hand, this driver continued in good style to the outskirts of Bristol, and even after two signal stops he was still 2½ minutes early on arrival. This splendid run shows the Dean 7-ft 8-in singles at their very best, with a good paying load. The actual train consisted of seven clerestory corridor bogies, and Charlewood records that as usual with this train it was very full. The train hauled so well by *Duke of Connaught* in run No 1 consisted of six corridor bogies and one six-wheeler. In connection with the work of this class I am only sorry that I can find no details of down runs from Bristol to Exeter, which would include the harder taks of climbing from Norton Fizwarren up to Whiteball summit.

At the turn of the century the fastest non-stop runs were made on the Birmingham service, via Oxford of course at that time, when the allowance was 140 minutes for the distance of 129.3 miles, an average speed of 55.5 mph. This was equal so far as average speed is concerned to the much publicized two-hour runs of later years on the Bicester route, though the latter, with permanent speed restrictions at Old Oak Common and High Wycombe, together with heavier gradients, was a harder run. The older route had only the slight slack at Didcot, and a heavier one through Oxford. Both runs tabulated opposite were entirely without checks, and the drivers of *Fire King* and *Grierson* brought their respective trains into Snow Hill almost exactly on time. Intermediately there was a considerable difference between the running of the two engines. *Fire King* on a rough January day had to contend with a strong side wind and heavy rain all the way from Slough to Oxford. Things were distinctly better

An Eastbound Broad Gauge express picking up the mails at Cullompton in 1891. (Rev A.H. Malan, BTC Archives)

GWR: Paddington–Birmingham (via Oxford)

Run No			1		2	
Engine No			3010		3058	
Engine name			*Fire King*		*Grierson*	
Load to Leamington (tons full)			155		170	
Load to Birmingham (tons full)			135		130	
Distance (miles)		**Schedule (min)**	**Actual (m s)**	**Av speed (mph)**	**Actual (m s)**	**Av speed (mph)**
0.0	PADDINGTON	0	0 00	—	0 00	—
1.3	Westbourne Park		3 18	—	3 11	—
5.7	Ealing		9 07	45.4	9 13	43.9
9.1	Southall	12	12 49	55.1	13 03	53.2
13.2	West Drayton		17 26	53.4	17 33	54.7
18.5	SLOUGH	21½	22 57	57.7	22.48	60.6
24.2	Maidenhead	27½	29 20	63.5	28 45	57.5
36.0	READING	39	42 00	56.0	40 46	59.0
41.5	Pangbourne		47 51	56.5	46 18	59.7
48.5	Cholsey		54 44	60.8	53 15	60.4
52.8	*Didcot East Junc*	57	59 13	57.5	57 40	58.4
56.1	Culham		62 38	57.8	60 56	60.7
58.3	Radley		64 53	58.7	63 10	59.1
63.4	OXFORD	68	69 51	61.5	68 10	61.2
66.3	*Wolvercot Junction*	72	73 27	48.3	71 18	55.3
69.0	Kidlington		76 19	56.5	74 05	58.2
71.0	Bletchington		78 26	56.8	76 20	53.4
75.1	Heyford		82 28	60.8	80 40	56.9
78.0	Somerton		85 13	63.3	83 41	57.8
80.2	Aynho		87 18	63.3	85 57	58.5
86.1	BANBURY	91	92 52	63.7	91 52	59.8
89.7	Cropredy		96 32	58.9	95 47	55.3
94.8	Fenny Compton		101 53	57.2	101 27	54.1
99.8	Southam Road		106 24	66.5	105 54	67.4
105.9	LEAMINGTON	113	112 25	60.9	111 34	64.7
107.9	Warwick		115 07	44.5	114 01	49.0
112.1	Hatton		121 04	42.3	119 35	44.2
116.3	Kingswood*		126 10	49.4	124 35	50.4
118.8	Knowle		128 59	53.4	127 27	52.3
122.2	Solihull	132	132 40	55.3	131 11	54.5
125.0	Acocks Green		135 16	64.6	133 50	63.5
127.0	Small Heath		137 03	67.1	135 39	66.2
128.0	Bordesley		138 05	58.1	136 42	57.2
129.3	BIRMINGHAM	140	140 03		138 34	

* Later Lapworth

afterwards with the wind behind the train, and speed averaged 60 mph from Oxford to Leamington. Here the line is rising steadily from Kidlington to the summit point at Claydon Crossing, midway between Cropredy and Fenny Crompton, after which there is a fast run down into Leamington.

Grierson, although running on a June day, fared no better for weather. It was wet, with a bad rail, and between Oxford and Banbury the engine was much hindered by hail and a heavy side wind. Because of this the general work north of Oxford was below that of the previous run, and speed fell to a minimum of 50½ mph beyond Cropredy. But this driver was evidently a pretty resolute type, as he took his engine hard down to Leamington, touching 75 mph after Southam Road, and passed Leamington ½ minute early. The slack through the station was severely enforced on both runs, and the usual quick recovery followed on the

Broad Gauge 4-2-2 Bulkeley *at Didcot.* (Author's collection)

favourable mile to the crossing of the River Avon before Warwick. Then comes Hatton bank, with its 3 miles of 1 in 108-103-110, not to mention the sharp approach gradients. *Fire King* fell to 33 mph on this severe incline, but although the loads were now reduced to 130–135 tons, *Grierson* did well to climb the bank at a minimum of 38 mph. After that both engines ran well on the final gradually downhill stretch into Birmingham, and that villainous quarter-mile at 1 in 45 up through Snow Hill tunnel was rushed smartly.

2. Dean's greatest years

Despite the esteem and affection in which they were held on all hands in the Locomotive Department of the GWR, there is really no doubt that the Dean 7-ft 8-in 4-2-2s provided something of a false start to twentieth century locomotive practice at Swindon. When those engines for a time became the regular engines east of Newton Abbot, a new type altogether was designed for the heavy gradients of the West Country. The first of the new type, appropriately named *Duke of Cornwall*, was completed at Swindon in 1895. In the light of what had gone before it had some unusual and unexpected features. It was the last Great Western passenger locomotive design that could be described as pure Dean, and in view of the heavy uphill work that was required in the West Country, it might at first sight have seemed strange that having used 20-in diameter cylinders on his high-speed 4-2-2 and 4-4-0 engines, there should have been a reversion to 18 in on the 'Dukes'. It is probable, however, that some considerable restriction in axle loading was imposed over Brunel's timber trestle viaducts. In any case, the boiler was much smaller than that of the earlier eight-wheeled tender engines, having a total heating surface of 1,398.18 sq ft against 1,561.33 sq ft on the Armstrongs, and the maximum axle load was 15.35 tons, against 15.9 tons. The load on the bogie was 17.5 tons against 19.3 tons.

The boiler was unique in the range of inside cylinder 4-4-0s covered by the present study, in having a flush round-topped firebox and a huge extended smokebox. It is strange that Dean should have abandoned, in one of his last designs, the form of firebox with the top raised above the level of the boiler barrel, because the feature was so advantageous in providing additional steam space above the water line, thus minimizing any tendency to prime. But with such an enormous dome, the provision of extra steam space above the crown of the firebox was evidently thought to be unnecessary. The huge and aggressive-looking extended smokebox was to provide for a diaphragm plate and netting for spark arresting, and could be discerned as the very first evidence of Churchward's influence in locomotive design at Swindon. At the time the first 'Dukes' were built in 1895, Churchward was Manager of the Carriage Works, but his keen interest in locomotive work and his familiarity with current practice in the USA suggest that the adoption of such characteristic features of American practice as the long extended smokebox and the diaphragm plate was probably made at his instigation.

Another striking feature of the first batches of the 'Duke' Class was the use of Mansell-pattern wood-centred coach wheels for the engine bogie and for the tender. The first 40 engines and the first 25 tenders were so equipped. The tenders were extremely short, having a wheelbase of no more than 11 ft 0 in. It must be recalled, however, that prior to the abolition of the Broad Gauge, the line west of Newton Abbot had been worked exclusively by tank engines, and the turntables were appropriately short. Even with their very short tenders, something of a contortionist act was necessary at some sheds to turn the 'Dukes'. The tenders had to be jacked up because their rear ends extended beyond the length of the turntable and the rearmost wheels

The first of the 'Duke' Class 4-4-0s in photographic grey, No 3252 Duke of Cornwall, *built at Swindon in 1895.* (British Railways)

A train from Didcot approaching Southampton, headed by No 3265 St Germans. (D.S.M. Barrie)

needed to be lifted clear of the rails.

The 'Dukes', which in their early days were also known variously as the 'Pendennis Castle' Class and also as the 'Devons', had a long and diverse career, involving many changes of boiler. These began after the first 40 of the class had been built, up to March 1897. These first batches had charming names, nearly all connected with the lore, history and legends of the West Country:

Original number	Name	Built
3252	*Duke of Cornwall*	1895
3253	*Pendennis Castle*	1895
3254	*Boscawen*	1895
3255	*Cornubia*	1895
3256	*Excalibur*	1895
3257	*Guinevere*	1895
3258	*King Arthur*	1895
3259	*Lizard*	1895
3260	*Merlin*	1895
3261	*Mount Edgcumbe*	1895
3262	*Powderham*	1896
3263	*Sir Lancelot*	1896
3264	*St Anthony*	1896
3265	*St Germans*	1896
3266	*St Ives*	1896
3267	*St Michael*	1896
3268	*Tamar*	1896
3269	*Tintagel*	1896
3270	*Trevithick*	1896
3271	*Tre Pol and Pen*	1896
3272	*Amyas*	1896
3273	*Armorel*	1896
3274	*Cornishman*	1896
3275	*Chough*	1896
3276	*Dartmoor*	1896
3277	*Earl of Devon*	1897
3278	*Eddystone*	1897
3279	*Exmoor*	1897
3280	*Falmouth*	1897
3281	*Fowey*	1897
3282	*Maristow*	1897
3283	*Mounts Bay*	1897
3284	*Newquay*	1897
3285	*St Erth*	1897
3286	*St Just*	1897
3287	*St Agnes*	1897
3288	*Tresco*	1897
3289	*Trefusis*	1897
3290	*Torbay*	1897
3291	*Tregenna*	1897

Although there was 'system' in their naming, there was none of the interminable tedium of the systematized class naming that imposed a positive strangehold on

Great Western locomotive nomenclature from the 1930s onwards. These first 40 'Dukes' contained in their names a happy mixture of geography, personalities, legends, and even West County saints, with which latter there was no confusion with Churchward's '2900' Class 4-6-0s. In Swindon terminology, St Agnes, St Anthony, St Germans and St Michael would never have been regarded as Saints any more than Sir Lancelot would have been confused with the Knights. Then look at such lovely names as *Armorel*, *Chough* and *Tre Pol and Pen*, and it can be realized with what good taste and artistic feeling the titles were chosen. Even the geographical ones like *Eddystone*, *Tintagel* and *Mounts Bay* had none of the adherence to 'system' that sometimes made ridiculous the same technique, used elsewhere with less imagination—*Portland Bill* for example!

'Duke' Class Dimensions

Cylinders
  diameter 18 in
  stroke 26 in
Boiler barrel
  length 11 ft 0 in
  distance between tube plates 11 ft $3\frac{1}{4}$ in
Smokebox, length 5 ft $0\frac{7}{8}$ in
Firebox, length 5 ft 10 in
Heating surfaces (sq ft)
  Tubes 1,285.58
  Firebox 115.27
Grate area 19.11 sq ft
Boiler pressure 160 psi
Adhesion weight $28\frac{1}{2}$ tons
Total engine weight 46 tons
Total tender weight 24 tons
Nominal tractive effort at 85% boiler pressure
  17,000 lb

Left *A right-hand-side view of No 3289* Trefusis. (O.S. Nock collection)

Right *A view of No 3291* Thames *showing the later type of boiler with Belpaire firebox, top feed and superheater.* (Stanley J. Rhodes)

The boiler was an excellent steam-raiser. The deep-set narrow firebox was easy to fire, the tubes were of large diameter in relation to their length, and from the detail drawings it could be seen how simple and direct were the passages from the exhaust ports to the blast pipe, the cap of which had a diameter of no less than 5 in. A feature that was a little curious by later practice was that there was no definite choke in the chimney—in fact, the diameter at the base, 1 ft 1 in, was actually larger than that at the top, 1 ft 0 in. It is evident that the chimney was proportioned so that the cone of exhaust steam from the blast pipe cap just filled the chimney at the top. Taken all round, one gains the impression of an excellently designed, well-balanced locomotive, ideal for the heavy intermittent work of the West Country.

Until the introduction of the 'Dukes', Great Western locomotives has carried their names on the driving wheel splashers, in cast raised letters on a plate of appropriate radius. But on the 'Dukes', the smaller diameter of the coupled wheels and the use of overhung springs left no room in the traditional place, especially as many of the new names were long; so horizontal plates were fitted extending forward from the boiler band central with the dome, to a point just in the rear of the large clack boxes of the boiler feed. These plates were made the same length irrespective of the length of the name, so that while *Duke of Cornwall* had the letters neatly and compactly spaced, names like *Amyas*, *Chough* or *Merlin* were strung out to fill the plate. The numberplates were placed high on the cab sides in line with the nameplates.

The elaboration of the finish was considerable, with the frames in crimson lake, the double lining-out of the boiler bands, and the profusion of polished detail work on the bogies, spring hangers and clack boxes, quite apart from tremendous features like that dome; the overall effect was to make them extraordinarily impressive engines, small though they were.

Because of the shortness of the tenders, the usual Great Western painting style with three panels was not used, and the elaborately intertwined scroll letters 'GWR' were set in the middle of a single panel. In passing, one could hardly imagine a detail more typical of the Victorian era of railways, and especially of the Great Western, than that scroll. It did not take Churchward very long to discard it. The cab fittings could not be simpler, though the shelter itself was narrow to give plenty of room within the structure gauge for an engineman to climb out along the running plate when necessary. Dean used only a single water gauge glass, a feature followed in all Great Western engines through Churchward's, Collett's and Hawksworth's days.

At Swindon in 1899, as soon as the last four 7-ft 8-in singles had been completed, the erecting shop was switched at once on to another 19 4-4-0s. Fifteen of them were the same as the 'Dukes', except for having spoked wheels for the bogies and the tenders instead of the Mansell pattern; the last four also had raised Belpaire fireboxes. Because of these variations from the original 'Dukes', the series, originally numbered 3313 to 3331, was sometimes referred to as the 'Cotswold' Class. Their names and numbers were as follows, all built in the early months of 1899:

3313 *Cotswold*
3314 *Chepstow Castle*
3315 *Comet*
3316 *Guernsey*
3317 *Jersey*
3318 *Jupiter*
3319 *Katerfelto*
3320 *Meteor*
3321 *Mercury*
3322 *Mersey*
3323 *Mendip*
3324 *Quantock*
3325 *St Columb*
3326 *St Austell*
3327 *Somerset*
3328 *Severn*
3329 *Thames*
3330 *Vulcan*
3331 *Weymouth*

Before the Works had embarked upon the 'Cotswold' series of 4-4-0s, there had been an isolated 5-ft 8-in engine, which had at first been regarded as prototype, but which turned out to be forerunner of something quite different. This was engine No 3312 *Bulldog*, a 4-4-0 with a very much larger boiler than the 'Duke' Class; furthermore it has the same medium raised Belpaire firebox that had been introduced into Swindon practice on the 'Badminton' Class of 4-4-0s in 1897, of which there is much to tell later, but *Bulldog* as originally built had a vastly larger firebox, with a grate area of no less than 23.65 sq ft. This was considerably greater than that ultimately standardized in the Churchward No 4 used on the 'Cities', 'Counties' and eventually the swarm of '43' Class 'Moguls'. I cannot recall ever having seen a technical comment on the first 'Bulldog' boiler, nor any notes on the working of the engine itself. It was evidently one of those things best forgotten in the Swindon records—why, I cannot imagine.

Some years before the final gauge conversion, in 1883 in fact, William Dean produced for the standard gauge section of the line a new standard 0-6-0 goods engine, No 2301. It was apparently so 'ordinary' and so lacking in distinctive features that in his monumental series of articles 'Locomotive and Train Working in the latter Part of the Nineteenth Century', E.L. Ahrons never even mentioned it. By that time in the series one could not complain of editorial restrictions limiting the content, as when the London and North Western instalments precluded any reference to such celebrated engines as the Webb 17-inch 'Coal engines', or the 18-inch 'Crested goods', as the 'Cauliflowers' were then known. Altogether the Great Western got ten instalments of Ahrons to a paltry *four* to the LNWR! Yet as readers of more modern railway literature know well enough, the 'Dean Goods' had become one of the 'immortals' of British steam railway history. How this came about will be told in one of the final chapters of this book, but in the meantime I must revert back to what Hamilton Ellis once called 'The Stately Days of Dean'.

The first batch of these famous engines would have been unrecognisable to modern eyes, for they had domeless boilers of the 'straightback' variety that Dean was then using on his 2-2-2 express engines for the

standard gauge routes. The domeless boiler vogue did not last long on the 'Dean Goods', and after the first 20, subsequent batches had domes on the first barrel ring and smokeboxes made flush with the boiler clothing. Construction continued until 1898, by which time there were 260 of the class. Twenty other 0-6-0s built in 1885-6 differed from the '2301' Class in having double frames and larger cylinders. This was an insurance policy in case the need arose for additional Broad Gauge 'convertible' engines at about the time when many of the old engines were being scrapped. Actually, the 2361-2380 series of 0-6-0s were never adapted to run on the Broad Gauge. The standard '2301' Class, even when built, were no more than moderately powered engines. Their basic dimensions make an interesting comparison to those of their famous contemporaries on the North Western, thus:

Left *The experimental 4-4-0 No 3312* Bulldog *as originally built in 1898.* (Loco Publishing Co)

Below left *One of the earliest of the 'Dean Goods' 0-6-0s, No 2481, with the dome on the first ring of the boiler.* (F. Burtt, National Railway Museum)

0-6-0 Express goods engines

Railway	Great Western	LNWR
Designer	W. Dean	F.W. Webb
Cylinder diameter × stroke (in)	17 × 24	18 × 24
Driving wheel diameter (ft in)	5 1	5 1½
Total heating surface (sq ft)	1,192.7	1,079.8
Grate area (sq ft)	16.4	17.1
Boiler pressure (psi)	140	140
Weight of engine (tons)	33	33¼
Value gear	Stephenson	Joy

Right *No 2513, a later example of the 'Dean Goods' but still retaining the polished brass dome cover.* (Author's collection)

The 'Cauliflowers' were the first built, in 1880, and there were eventually 310 of them. Their longevity matched that of the 'Dean Goods', because about the time that one of the latter was getting haloes for itself by its performances on the Swindon stationary testing plant, I was making some footplate trips on some of the 'Cauliflowers' in regular passenger service on the Cockermouth, Keswick and Penrith line. Apart from having boilers with Belpaire fireboxes, the 'Cauliflowers' were more or less in their original condition, whereas most, if not all, of the 'Dean Goods' had then been superheated. This important development had followed Churchward's experiments with superheating on certain of his 4-6-0s, and will be referred to in a later chapter. Attention to the 'Dean Goods' came in the wholesale treatment of the 'second line' tender engines, 4-4-0s and 0-6-0s alike, following the finalization of the design of the Swindon No 3 superheater in 1909. Such was the programme that some 270 4-4-0s alone had been treated by the end of 1913.

The 'Dean Goods' proper, the '2301' Class, were numbered 2301 to 2360 and 2381 to 2581 consecutively, and were not renumbered at any time in their long lives. The last ten, built at the end of 1897, had Belpaire fireboxes, and these became standard for the whole class early in Churchward's time. Then the boiler and firebox proportions were thus:

'Dean Goods'—Belpaire fireboxes

	Non-superheated	Superheated
Heating surfaces (sq ft)		
Tubes	1,091.38	960.85
Superheater	—	75.30
Firebox	106.32	106.45
Total	1197.7	1142.60
Grate area (sq ft)	15.45	15.45
Boiler pressure (psi)	180	180

When, during the First World War, the battle front of the British Army in France and the Low Countries became almost stabilized in a frightful deadlock, the British home railways were asked to lend locomotives to work ammunition, supply and leave trains to and from the 'forward' regions, and the Great Western at first lent a large number of 'Dean Goods'. Later, in 1917, when more standard Churchward 2-6-0s of the '5301' Class were made available to the Railway Operating Division of the British Army, some 'Dean Goods' engines were shipped to Salonika to assist in the battles on the Grecian Front with Bulgaria. I append herewith the numbers of those which completed all their war service on the Western Front, and those which were subsequently transferred to Salonika.

Engines wholely used on Western Front

2303, 2306, 2309, 2311, 2313, 2316, 2317, 2330, 2332, 2338, 2339, 2348, 2349, 2355, 2357, 2383, 2403, 2415, 2430, 2446, 2452, 2457, 2458, 2461, 2463, 2469, 2470, 2473, 2476, 2480, 2484, 2489, 2514, 2517–2520, 2522, 2528, 2531, 2535, 2549, 2566–2578, 2580 Total 56

Engines transferred from Western Front to Salonika

2308, 2318, 2322, 2327, 2329, 2334, 2336, 2387, 2420, 2453, 2454, 2488, 2533, 2542, 2557, 2563 Total 16

Seven of those used in Greece never returned to the GWR, namely Nos 2308, 2334, 2387, 2420, 2453, 2543 and 2563. The saga of this very celebrated class of locomotives is continued in a later chapter of this book.

The next class to feature in this gallery of great locomotives of the GWR takes the story back into Joseph Armstrong's time. The 'Metro tanks' originated as long ago as 1869, but with successive modernizations the stud, eventually numbering 140 units, lasted through Dean's time, through Churchward's and so far into Collett's regime that when I was commuting from Ealing Broadway in the late 1920s, they were still our regular engines on the business trains to Paddington and Bishops Road. By the time Joseph Armstrong died in 1878, 80 engines of the class had been built, not all alike, because improvements were incorporated in all successive batches. But the basic dimensions remained the same, cylinders 16 in diameter by 24 in stroke, coupled wheels of 5 ft 1 in diameter and boiler pressure at first 140 psi and later 160. On the face of it these would not appear to be the ingredients of a 'great' 2-4-0 tank locomotive; but Dean already appreciated the sterling worth of these little engines, and between the years 1882 and 1894 he had added 60 more of them, all the time taking care to keep the older units up to concert pitch. They needed to be, because the work that they were required to do on the London suburban services was severe for such relatively small engines. While the earlier engines of the class weighed no more than 33 tons, the successive improvements with longer frames

and higher boiler pressure brought them up to $38\frac{3}{4}$ tons.

They were most attractive to behold, especially in the Dean era, when they had polished copper tops to their chimneys, a polished brass dome of elegant proportions, and a polished brass safety valve cover. In those days they had no cabs, merely a weather-board to protect the men on the footplate. With the Dean improvements there were numerous changes in the detail dimensions, but as they entered the twentieth century, and all of them eventually received boilers with Belpaire fireboxes, the final dimensions were as follows:

Boiler	
Length between tube plates	10 ft 6 in
Maximum diameter	4 ft 3 in
Tubes, number	221
Tubes, diameter	$1\frac{5}{8}$ in
Heating surface	
Tubes	1,008 sq ft
Firebox	91.5 sq ft
Total	1,099.5 sq ft
Grate area	14.6 sq ft

The valve gear was the Stephenson link motion, but for engines with such small cylinders the valve travel was exceptionally long, $4\frac{1}{2}$ in, and this undoubtedly was the main cause of their being such free-running engines. Despite having coupled wheels no larger than 5 ft 1 in, they regularly ran up to speeds of 60 mph—sometimes a good deal more! Their controls were of the simplest. They had lever reversing gear and in the many months I travelled behind them each morning from Ealing Broadway to Bishops Road, I always made for a seat in one of the leading coaches. Then I could hear clearly how the engine was started up—full gear for the first 100 yards or so, then regulator shut while the lever was notched up, then away in earnest.

Before the electrification of the Metropolitan line from Bishops Road through Westbourne Park to Hammersmith, the GWR 'Small Metro' tanks worked this line in addition to the suburban services of the main line together with the branches to Windsor, Henley and so on. At that time, before the introduction of the new Churchward 4-4-2 tanks, practically the whole stud of 140 were in the London area. The Birmingham and Black Country area, which had been under the sway of George Armstrong at Wolverhampton, was served mainly by 0-4-2 tank engines. The London engines at one period had to make some fairly long non-stop runs, for diminutive tank engines that is, for example from Paddington to Maidenhead. Naturally in the Churchward era they lost some of their nineteenth-century glitter, with the domes and safety valve covers painted green and the running plates and valances painted black; but when I was commuting from Ealing Broadway, all of them I saw, stationed at Southall, were kept looking smart. It is remarkable that Dean, in the early evening of his career at Swindon, should apparently have been so impressed with the usefulness of these engines as to bring out a slightly larger version, in 1899. They had the same cylinder dimensions and boilers, but had larger fireboxes with a grate area of 16.44 sq ft. All of them, like the smaller 'Metro tanks', began their careers without cabs. These 20 1899 engines were numbered 3581–3600.

In those commuting days I found it convenient to travel by one of the through trains to the City, proceeding through to King's Cross without needing to change at Paddington. The Great Western tank engines always ran bunker first in the up direction, and although by then they had received cabs, these were of such a scanty nature as to afford not the slightest protection from the weather when running in this manner. When I went to live in Ealing I was engaged on the preparation of a Paper that I had been asked to read before the Graduates Section of the Institution of

Far left *'Dean Goods' No 2513 as modified in the Churchward era, in plain green with a Belpaire firebox.* (M.D. England, National Railway Museum)

Left *A 'Dean Goods' on the Bristol Taunton main line in the final form, with the boiler having a Belpaire firebox and a Swindon superheater.* (G.H. Soole, National Railway Museum)

Right *One of the small 'Metro tanks' as originally built and lovingly polished up: No 1492.* (F. Burtt, National Railway Museum)

Above *A small 'Metro tank' with cab added and less ornate livery, though retaining the polished brass joint at the smokebox; engine No 470.* (M.D. England, National Railway Museum)

Left *The last form of the 'Metro tanks', with a boiler having a Belpaire firebox and no adornments; No 975.* (M.D. England, National Railway Museum)

Mechanical Engineers. One part of it was to describe the technique of spacing automatic colour light signals to provide the minimum headway between succeeding trains when accelerating from station stops. Naturally I had in mind multiple unit electrics, but after a few weeks of travelling on my regular business train to King's Cross, always announced at Ealing as for 'Acton, Bishops Road and City', I realized that with those old Armstrong 2-4-0s I had an absolutely classic example of precision suburban train performance. It did not matter which of them was on the job; the running was as regular as clockwork. I am only sorry that I did not keep the numbers of the many engines of the class that did us so proud. I have kept a diagram which was part of the data I included in that very amateurish paper read when I was about 24 years old, and it is startling indeed.

The six-coach close-coupled articulated trains, the maximum length that could be accommodated on the Metropolitan tunnel section, were no light weight when fully loaded with passengers, but yet the diagram that I prepared, and which represented the standard performance of these remarkable little engines, shows that in 2 minutes from the Acton start they were 0.71 miles on their way, and in 2½ minutes 1.15 miles. At that time the speed had risen to 53 mph. Such daily exuberance could not last for long, because they had to slacken off to take the junction on to the Metropolitan line east of Westbourne Park. At Bishops Road, of course, they came off and were replaced by a Metropolitan electric locomotive. In his beautiful book *Some Locomotives I have Known*, J.N. Maskelyne tells of some very fast running by these engines on the outer suburban trains; one, indeed, when No 3586, on a train that ran non-stop from Reading to Slough managed to attain a speed of 68 mph between Taplow and Burnham Beeches—not bad for a 2-4-0 tank engine with 5 ft 1 in coupled wheels!

3. The advent of Churchward

G.J. Churchward, born at Stoke Gabriel beside the River Dart, received his early training at Newton Abbot, and when the South Devon Railway was absorbed by the Great Western in 1876 he was transferred to Swindon. He was then 19 years of age, but such was his subsequent progress that by 1881 he had been promoted to be assistant to James Holden, who was then Carriage Works Manager, and when in 1885 Holden went to the Great Eastern Railway, Churchward got the job. Eleven years later he was further promoted to Locomotive Works Manager, and a year later he was appointed Assistant Locomotive, Carriage and Wagon Superintendent while retaining his existing appointment.

It was an unusual assignment, but the circumstances that led up to it were unusual, too. Those who have studied Great Western locomotive practice in any detail have remarked upon the evidence, particularly from 1898 onwards, of Churchward's influence while Dean remained in the chair. It might have been imagined that this was a pleasant case of a distinguished elder statesman of the engineering profession giving scope to a brilliant assistant to develop his own ideas, but this was unhappily not the case. It was, on the contrary, no more than a few outward and visible signs of a great human tragedy. By 1896 it was becoming evident to the Locomotive Committee of the Board, to whom he reported directly, that Dean's mental capacity was beginning to fail, and that the outstanding success with which he had managed his large department hitherto was likely to be seriously impaired. But he was still expecting to remain in office for a number of years, and the way the Board dealt with this difficult situation was a monument of kindly, psychological understanding of human nature. It was have been easy enough to have given him a 'golden handshake' and relieved him of all his duties, and the result in so difficult a case would have been bewilderment for Dean, bitterness, and an earlier end to his life. They were, however, supremely fortunate in having such a man as Churchward to put in as assistant, for quite apart from his ability as an engineer, Churchward had a warmly human side to his character, and for five years played the delicate part confided to him with consummate tact and unerring judgement.

That he did so well in handling the great human problem put to him was in large measure due to the nature of his own genius as an engineer. He could not be ranked among the great inventors, and the features of Great Western locomotive practice of later days that were uniquely his own were very few. His genius lay not only in recognizing a good thing when he saw it, but in the skilful application of it to his own particular problems. He was far removed from an egoist, and like many distinguished men of strong personality he was ready to listen attentively to the views of his staff, even down to the level of draughtsmen, works chargehands, drivers and firemen. By the year 1896 he had become very interested in American locomotive practice, particularly in the development of very large boilers. When this delicate task was assigned to him, with the definite idea that one day he would succeed Dean, he began, with the covert approbation of the Board, to make plans for the complete modernization of the locomotive stock. At the same time, out of human considerations it was necessary to avoid giving any outward impression that the reins were gradually being taken out of Dean's hands. In beginning his great development of the Swindon boiler, two features of past history favoured the impression that some of it was a logical development of Dean's earlier work, and indeed that of Daniel Gooch. A firebox raised above the level of the boiler stemmed from Broad Gauge days, while not only Gooch, but also Dean himself, had built locomotives with domeless boilers.

The hand of Churchward first became apparent in the design of the 'Badminton' Class of express passenger 4-4-0s, the first of which, No 3292, was completed at Swindon in December 1897. This was originally conceived as a 6-ft $8\frac{1}{2}$-in version of the 'Armstrongs', with smaller cylinders, a boiler with a high-raised round-topped firebox, and the extended smokebox of the 'Dukes'. The 'Armstrongs', by the way, were those very beautiful 4-4-0s, only four of them, which looked like a coupled-wheel version of the Dean 7-ft 8-in 4-2-2s. In their original form they were not very successful. But from his studies of American practice Churchward had become convinced of the advantages of the Belpaire type of firebox, in the greater

The first of the 'Badminton' Class, No 3292, built in 1897 and not named until April 1898. (British Railways)

steam space afforded above the water line, and in the simpler arrangements of staying the inside firebox, and so, at a late stage, the design of the 'Badmintons' was changed to include a Belpaire firebox. The result was a locomotive that so far as appearance went was something of a misfit.

Looks apart, the 'Badmintons' were splendid locomotives in traffic. Their early work is fortunately well documented, but before discussing details of individual runs, reference must be made to two further essays by Churchward in domed boilers with raised Belpaire fireboxes. These were the isolated No 3312 *Bulldog*, completed at Swindon in October 1898, and the last four of the 'Duke' Class, Nos 3328–3331, built at Swindon in July-August 1899 (see page 19). Details of these three types of boiler were as follows:

Domed boilers, raised Belpaire fireboxes

Type	**'Badminton'**	**'Bulldog'**	**'Dukes' Nos 3328–3331**
Tubes			
Number	244	290	244
Outside diameter (in)	$1\frac{5}{8}$	$1\frac{5}{8}$	$1\frac{5}{8}$
Heating surfaces (sq in)			
Tubes	1,175.32	1,395.62	1,174.25
Firebox	121.58	124.41	115.60
Grate area (sq ft)	18.32	23.65	18.37
Boiler pressure (psi)	180	180	180

Right *'Camel' Class 5-ft 8-in 4-4-0 No 3416* Bibby, *showing the earlier form of curved nameplates.* (P.J.T. Reed)

Below *No 3310* Waterford, *the experimental engine with domeless boiler, high raised firebox and combined number and nameplate.*

The boiler used on *Bulldog* is generally considered as the first prototype of Churchward's Standard No 2, which was followed by the first domeless variant on No 3310 *Waterford* of the 'Badminton' Class, built in January 1899.

No 3292 was evidently regarded as a prototype, and it remained the only one of the class for nearly five months. During that time it was also nameless. But when production began in earnest, the next 11, Nos 3293–3303, were turned out in three months. In July 1898, Swindon, at one per week, was almost rivalling Crewe's rate of locomotive production. The pioneer locomotive was named *Badminton* in April 1898 and gave its name to the class, while the production 11 had a varied collection of names, thus:

3293	*Barrington*	3299	*Hubbard*
3294	*Blenheim*	3300	*Hotspur*
3295	*Bessborough*	3301	*Monarch*
3296	*Cambria*	3302	*Mortimer*
3297	*Earl Cawdor*	3303	*Marlborough*
3298	*Grosvenor*		

The names were mostly connected with the directorate, Earl Cawdor then being Chairman, while Nos 3299 and 3302 had the Christian names of their owners added later, othewise No 3302 might have been mistaken for a station name. The last eight locomotives of the class were turned out from Swindon between September 1898 and January 1899, and it was the last but one of these that had the special domeless boiler.

3304	*Oxford*	3308	*Savernake*
3305	*Samson*	3309	*Shakespeare*
3306	*Shelburne*	3310	*Waterford*
3307	*Shrewsbury*	3311	*Wynnstay*

Nos 3304 and 3307 had their names removed in the 'purge' by the Traffic Department, but *Badminton, Marlborough* and *Savernake* escaped. Why, it is hard to explain, when as told earlier in this book remote Cornish village names were removed because it was feared they might confuse the travelling public. One might equally have said the same about the name of No 3310, when the Waterford Boat Express was one of the high prestige trains leaving Paddington. On a point of detail, they were the first Great Western locomotives to have curved nameplates carried above the splashers, except in the case of *Waterford*, which for some reason had a large combined number and numberplate carried on the cab side.

Personalia apart, the Badmintons' were excellent locomotives in traffic. They were allocated to the fast express routes which had gradients that the single-wheelers found trying, such as London-Wolverhampton via Worcester, and the West-to-North route via the Severn Tunnel. Their machinery was apparently the same as that of the 'Armstrongs' with the inside and outside cranks in line, and the same arrangement of the slide valves beneath the cylinders. But there was a 'something' in them that made them just as fast as the 'Armstrongs' were sluggish. They had ample port openings, and a direct exhaust from the valves between the cylinders and upwards straight to the blast pipe, and they used to attain speed well in excess of 80 mph.

First of the domeless-boilered 5-ft 8-in 4-4-0s, No 3352 Camel. (W. Beckerlegge)

Rous-Marten went down to Exeter to log the 12.05 pm up non-stop to Paddington. There seems no doubt that a special show was put on for his benefit, for the train arrived in Paddington just 15 minutes early, and could have been much more had not the driver eased down very much after passing Didcot. A detailed log is shown on the next page, not as an example of everyday running, but to indicate what these fine engines could do. A maximum of $83\frac{1}{2}$ mph was attained down the Wellington bank, and a good steady speed on the level between Taunton and Bristol. There was also some particularly free running between Didcot and Swindon. Rous-Marten estimated that another 8 minutes could have been cut from the schedule if the effort had been sustained eastwards from Didcot; but a possible arrival in Paddington 23 minutes early was a little too much to expect!

The varying boiler dimensions of Churchward's first locomotives show the extent to which experimenting was in progress. I have previously quoted the dimensions of *Bulldog's* original boiler, but at one time the heating surface was considerably larger, by the use of 286 tubes of $1\frac{7}{8}$ in diameter, giving a tube heating surface of 1,589.5 sq ft. But this arrangement was evidently found to be too crowded, and to give nominal heating surface at the expense of a reduced volume for circulation of the water; the later arrangement, with

290 tubes of $1\frac{5}{8}$ in diameter, was the same as on *Waterford*, even though the latter had the domeless barrel. *Waterford*'s boiler proved no more than the penultimate stage in the development of the parallel version of the Swindon Standard No 2, which appeared in its final form on No 3352 *Camel* in October 1899. The barrel was the same size as that of *Waterford*, but had 277 tubes of $1\frac{7}{8}$ in diameter and the total heating surfaces were tubes 1,538.06 sq ft and firebox 124.96 sq ft, while the grate area was reduced to 21.45 sq ft against 23.65 sq ft. *Camel* (which was named after the river, and had nothing to do with war in the desert) was followed between November 1899 and March 1900 by 20 more, Nos 3332–3351, which could quite correctly have been described as 'Dukes' with domeless boilers. They had the same shape of outside framing, handsomely curved over the coupled wheel axle-boxes, and had the same bogies, cylinders and motion. The wheelbase was also the same. The boilers had the circular drumhead type of smokebox, supported on the curved-sided saddle that became such a characteristic feature of Great Western inside-cylinder 4-4-0s. There was still indecision as to how to display the names, and all the 21 'Camels' with curved outside frames had oval combined number and nameplates on the cab sides, making the names a little difficult to recognize when running past at full speed. *Camel* itself had additional numberplates on the centre-line of the smokebox. The 20 locomotives of this first batch carried the following names:

3332	*Avalon*	3342	*Orion*
3333	*Brasenose*	3343	*Pegasus*
3334	*Eclipse*	3344	*Pluto*
3335	*Etona*	3345	*Perseus*
3336	*Glastonbury*	3346	*Tavy*
3337	*Kenilworth*	3347	*Tregothnan*
3338	*Laira*	3348	*Titan*
3339	*Marco Polo*	3349	*The Wolf*
3340	*Marazion*	3350	*Swift*
3341	*Mars*	3351	*Sedgemoor*

A 'Camel', No 3332 Avalon, *on an up West of England express on the single line section between Teignmouth and Dawlish.* (L&GRP)

GWR: 12.05pm Exeter–Paddington

Engine 'Badminton' Class 4-4-0 No 3298 *Grosvenor*

Load 165 tons

Distance (miles)		Actual (m s)	Average speed (mph)
0.0	Exeter	0 00	—
3.5	Stoke Canon	6 17	—
7.2	Silverton	10 27	53.2
8.4	Hele	11 53	50.3
12.6	Cullompton	16 15	57.4
14.8	Tiverton Junc	18 59	49.1
19.9	Whiteball box	25 26	47.3
23.7	Wellington	29 16	59.5
28.8	Norton Fitzwarren	33 04	80.5
30.8	Taunton	34 48	69.1
36.6	Durston	41 16	53.3
42.3	Bridgwater	46 40	63.4
44.9	Dunball	49 10	62.4
—		pw slack	—
48.6	Highbridge	55 12	37.0
55.3	Bleadon	62 06	58.3
58.8	Worle Junc	65 18	65.7
63.6	Yatton	69 56	62.1
67.5	Nailsea	73 44	61.6
69.9	Flax Bourton	75 57	64.9
74.5	Bedminster	80 26	62.1
75.2	Pylle Hill Junc	81 56	27.9
77.9	Bristol East Box	86 26	36.0
80.1	Keynsham	89 59	37.1
82.5	Saltford	92 45	52.2
87.0	Bath	97 23	57.8
89.3	Bathampton	100 48	40.2
92.0	Box	103 56	51.8
95.6	Corsham	108 46	46.4
99.9	Chippenham	113 52	38.8
106.2	Dauntsey	119 24	68.4
111.0	Wootton Bassett	124 56	52.0
116.4	Swindon	130 59	53.5
122.1	Shrivenham	136 32	61.6
127.2	Uffington	141 00	68.3
129.8	Challow	143 18	67.8
133.3	Wantage Road	146 12	72.3
137.2	Steventon	149 29	71.6
140.6	Didcot	152 16	73.2
—		slack	
152.2	Pangbourne	165 22	53.1
157.7	Reading	171 17	55.9
—		slack	
169.5	Maidenhead	185 47	49.0
175.2	Slough	191 09	63.8
184.6	Southall	200 13	62.2
188.0	Ealing Broadway	203 24	
193.7	Paddington	209 56	

Nos 3336, 3337, 3338 and 3347 lost their names in one of another of the Traffic Department 'purges'. Presumably *Laira* was considered a snare to guileless enginemen, tempted to hitch a lift back to their home shed: how stupid can officialdom get!

After the completion of No 3351 *Sedgemoor* in March 1900, there was a pause of two months in the building of 5-ft 8-in 4-4-0s during which the first of a new class of 6-ft 8-in engines appeared, No 3373 *Atbara*. With these locomotives the flowing curves of Great Western types, which had begun to disappear with the 'Badmintons', went for ever, because the 'Atbaras' had a straight-topped running plate that extended unbrokenly from the footplate to a point level with the rearward bogie wheel.

Furthermore, when construction of the 'Camels' continued in May 1900, it was seen that they too had the straight-topped frames. Production of the two classes continued almost simultaneously during the rest of the year 1900, as follows:

Month	'Atbaras'	'Camels'
April	4	–
May	6	1
June	–	4
July	3	–
August	5	–
September	2	–
October	–	4
November	–	8
December	–	3

After that 'drive', in which 40 new passenger locomotives had been turned out in nine months, there was a pause before the second large batch of 'Atbaras' began to issue from Swindon. But while the new 6-ft 8-in engines, and the 5-ft 8-in type from No 3353 onwards, looked very much alike, and had the same boiler, the 'Atbaras' had the same crank arrangement as the 'Badmintons' whereas the 'Camels' had that of the 'Dukes'.

One can be a little curious as to why Churchward retained double frames, when he was clearly so partial to American practice in other respects. Although by the year 1900 he was becoming more and more in charge of affairs at Swindon, one feels that the general introduction of domeless boilers was enough in the way of major change while Dean was still there. His major development was centred on the boiler, and the double-frame arrangement was well tried, familiar to the shops and needed little or no drawing office work for the new locomotives. The bogie afforded little interference to

Left Atbara — *a portrait at Westbourne Park shed.* (W.J. Reynolds)

Below Atbara *still in express work in the 1920s on a Wolverhampton-South Wales express on the North Warwickshire line.* (L&GRP)

Left *An 'Atbara' with a name that could be misconstrued — No 3390* Terrible *(actually that of a contemporary warship!).* (L&GRP)

Below *An 'Atbara', No 3374, originally* Baden Powell *but decorated and specially named* Britannia *for the Royal Train workings in 1902.* (British Railways)

access to the slide valves once the bogie itself had been run clear. The actual valve dimensions were standard on all the inside-cylinder 4-4-0s while they retained slide valves. Both 'Camels' and 'Atbaras' had much wider cabs than the 'Dukes' and 'Badmintons', so much so that the overhung springs of the rear coupled wheels passed inside the cab. By comparison with older Great Western engines the cabs were quite roomy, though the shelter they provided was scant. As originally built they had steam-operated reversing gear. The nominal tractive effort with 180 psi boiler pressure was no greater than that of the 'Badmintons', and considering the moderate loads of the principal express trains, which will be more apparent when I come to some actual details of their running, their coal consumption was not particularly light. In 1901 it was reported that the average consumption of those in the link at the Paddington old shed was 32.6 lb per train mile.

The naming of the 20 'Atbaras' built at Swindon in 1900 followed popular sentiment of the day, and included names that were on everyone's lips. But like many of the Crewe names bestowed in comparable circumstances, the significance of a number of them faded with the years; while few would continue to have doubts about *Baden Powell, Kitchener* or *Roberts, Powerful* and *Terrible* might conjure up thoughts far removed from the armoured cruisers that played a part in the South African campaign. It is interesting to see that names chosen from both the Sudanese and South African wars were grouped together and applied more or less alphabetically, with one or two 'outsiders', as it were, interspersed:

3373 *Atbara*
3374 *Baden Powell*
3375 *Conqueror*
3376 *Herschell*
3377 *Kitchener*
3378 *Khartoum*
3379 *Kimberley*
3380 *Ladysmith*
3381 *Maine*
3382 *Mafeking*
3383 *Kekewich*
3384 *Omdurman*
3385 *Powerful*
3386 *Pembroke*
3387 *Roberts*
3388 *Sir Redvers*
3389 *Sir Daniel*
3390 *Terrible*
3391 *Wolseley*
3392 *White*

The 'Atbaras' differed from the 'Badmintons' only in their boilers, and it was not surprising that they proved equally fast runners. Rous-Marten made a number of trips specially to see what could be got out of them, and claimed on one occasion a maximum of 97 mph. On another, Driver David Hughes, who had such a distinguished record of achievement with the 2-2-2 No 162 *Cobham*, put on a special show with the pioneer No 3373 *Atbara* on the morning Paddington-Birmingham non-stop, which was then allowed 143 minutes for the 129.3 miles via Oxford. With a load of 180 tons the train passed Leamington, 106 miles, in 107 minutes 35 seconds despite four signal checks and a dead stand lasting 3 minutes in Radley station. Although he was getting far ahead of time, the driver continued to press on vigorously, only to experience more signal checks,

and finally a dead stand lasting 6½ minutes at Bordesley. The train eventually drew into Snow Hill in 141½ minutes from Paddington. The net time was 119½ minutes, representing an average of 65 mph. On the strength of this there was much talk of a two-hour schedule, via Oxford.

The outstanding event of 1902, and undoubtedly the pinnacle of fame achieved by the 'Atbara' Class locomotives, was of course the Royal visit to Devonshire in March, in the course of which the longest non-stop runs yet attempted on the Great Western Railway were successfully made. The down train, on 7 March, was run non-stop over the 228.5 miles from Paddington to Kingswear, while on the return, on 10 March, the special was worked non-stop over the 246.4 miles from Millbay Crossing to Paddington. The five coaches of the train had a tare weight of 126 tons, and were worked on both the long non-stop runs by No 3374, specially renamed *Britannia* for the occasion, with Driver Burden in charge. Scheduled time for the down journey was 285 minutes, but with King Edward taking great personal interest in the running of the train, and having no inhibitions about speed, the train was allowed to run somewhat ahead of time, and reached Kingswear more than 20 minutes early. It will be seen from the accompanying table that a notably steady average of around 60 mph was maintained on the open stretches of line, and that the average from Paddington to Exeter of 56 mph was much the same as that of service runs made with the down 'Cornishman'. The Royal party continued to Plymouth the same day, No 3374 worked the train back to Newton Abbot and from there, after reversal of direction, the engine was a 'Camel', No 3357 *Exeter*, renamed *Royal Sovereign* specially for the occasion.

GWR: Royal Train, 7 March 1902

Engine 4-4-0 No 3374 **Britannia**
Load 126 tons

Distance (miles)		Actual (min)	Average speed (mph)
0.0	Paddington	0	—
31.0	Twyford	34	54.8
36.2	Reading West Junc	39	62.5
53.1	Didcot	56	59.7
77.3	Swindon	80	60.6
106.9	Bath	110½	58.2
118.4	Pylle Hill Junc	127	41.8
137.75	Uphill Junc	146	55.2
162.85	Taunton	171½	59.1
193.6	Exeter	206½	52.9
213.8	Newton Abbot	234½	43.3
228.5	Kingswear	262½	31.5

On Monday 10 March, the return journey to London was made, and the times run are shown in a further log. Again very steady speed was maintained throughout, and the average of 52.2 mph from Millbay to Paddington was an excellent effort in train operation, although not involving any exceptional locomotive work. In assessment of the performance it must be recalled that at that time severe speed restrictions were called for through Exeter and Taunton stations, in addition to the slacks for single-line token exchange on the South Devon line between Dawlish and Teignmouth. Furthermore, at His Majesty's request, the train slowed down passing Swindon Works so that he could see better, and acknowledge the acclaim of the vast numbers of railwaymen who had been allowed briefly to leave their duties in the works and see the Royal Train go by.

GWR: Royal Train, 10 March 1902

Engine 4-4-0 No 3374 *Britannia*
Load 126 tons

Distance (miles)		Actual (min)	Average speed (mph)
0.0	Millbay Crossing	0	—
32.6	Newton Abbot	47	41.5
52.8	Exeter	75	43.3
83.6	Taunton	109½	53.5
108.7	Uphill Junc	137	54.8
129.5	Bristol East Depot	159½	55.5
139.5	Bath	172	48.5
169.1	Swindon	203	57.1
193.4	Didcot East	227	61.0
210.2	Reading West Junc	245½	55.5
215.4	Twyford	251	56.8
246.4	Paddington	284	56.3

By way of anticipation I may add that when the 'Cornish Riviera Express' was put on in 1904 the timing from Plymouth North Road to Paddington was 265 minutes, with a running time of 195 minutes for the 193.6 miles up from Exeter. Although the new 'City' Class engines were then available, the 'Atbaras' took their turn on this celebrated train, and with the moderate loads first conveyed the running of the two classes of 4-4-0 was indistinguishable. I have tabulated the journal times of three down journeys made during the first month the train ran. On the first of these it will be seen that *Pembroke* drew gradually ahead of time after Reading, and ran between 2 and 3 minutes early all the way to Plymouth, without any exceptional running. *Ladysmith* ran fast in the early stages, passing Bath 4 minutes early, but easing down thereafter, while in the last column *Malta* was badly checked by adverse signals between Slough and Reading, and passed the latter station 6 minutes late. After that, however, the lateness was reduced to 5 minutes at Swindon, 3 at Bath, 2 at Taunton, and 1 minute early by Exeter, through an obviously very fine effort from Taunton, and a time of only 31 minutes for the 30.8 miles, including the climb from Norton Fitzwarren to Whiteball box. On this run the average speed over the 157.6 miles from Reading to Exeter was 61.3 mph, while the net time of 259 minutes throughout from Paddington to Plymouth is equal to 57 mph.

GWR: 'Cornish Riviera Express, 'Atbara' Class locomotives

Load 6 coaches, 146 tons tare

Locomotive No		3386	3380	3407
Locomotive name		*Pembroke*	*Ladysmith*	*Malta*
Distance (miles)	**Schedule (min)**	**Actual (min)**	**Actual (min)**	**Actual (min)**
0.0 Paddington	0	0	0	0
18.5 Slough	20½	20	20	21
–		–	–	sigs
36.0 Reading	36	36	37	42
53.1 Didcot	53	51	53	58
77.3 Swindon	77	75	76	82
106.9 Bath	106	104	102	109
118.7 Pylle Hill	120	118	117	123
137.7 Uphill Junc	139	137	134	142
162.8 Taunton	163	161	158	165
193.6 Exeter	197	194	192	196
213.7 Newton Abbot	222½	220	220	221
245.6 Plymouth	267	264	266	265

One of the later 5-ft 8-in 4-4-0s No 3450 Swansea, *leaving Penzance with the very first up 'Cornish Riviera Express'.* (James Gibson)

The 20 straight-framed 'Camels' of 1900 had names that were nearly all connected with the West Country, and inevitably some of the topographical ones were fated to disappear in later years. The 20 engines were:

3353	*Blasius*	3363	*One and All*
3354	*Bonaventura*	3364	*Pendragon*
3355	*Camelot*	3365	*Plymouth*
3356	*Dartmouth*	3366	*Restormel*
3357	*Smeaton*	3367	*St Aubyn*
3358	*Godolphin*	3368	*Sir Stafford*
3359	*Kingsbridge*	3369	*Trelawney*
3360	*Launceston*	3370	*Tremayne*
3361	*Lyonesse*	3371	*Tregeagle*
3362	*Newlyn*	3372	*Torquay*

All these locomotives had the oval combined plates on the cab sides, and had the standard domeless parallel boiler, with high-raised Belpaire firebox. The last batch of 'Camels' to be turned out new with this boiler was numbered 3413 to 3432, and entered service between December 1902 and May 1903. It was on this batch that new styles of nameplates were first seen. Nos 3413 to 3420 had the first form of what was to be the new standard type. Whatever the length of the actual name, the plate itself was carried in a complete arc of a circle, from running plate to running plate, but because of the presence of the overhung springs it was spaced at some distance radially outwards from the splasher.

The engines from 3421 onwards had the new standard nameplates from the time of construction. The last batch of 4-4-0s to be built new with the domeless parallel boiler, the first Standard No 2, consisted of 20 'Atbaras' all named after cities of the British Empire. They had the new type of nameplate, extending from running plate to running plate, but because of the larger diameter of the coupled wheels there was no need to have the spacer piece between the nameplate and the top of the splasher. These 20 locomotives were:

3393	*Auckland*	3398	*Colombo*
3394	*Adelaide*	3399	*Dunedin*
3395	*Aden*	3400	*Durban*
3396	*Brisbane*	3401	*Gibraltar*
3397	*Cape Town*	3402	*Halifax*
3403	*Hobart*	3408	*Ophir*
3404	*Lyttleton*	3409	*Quebec*
3405	*Mauritius*	3410	*Sydney*
3406	*Melbourne*	3411	*St Johns*
3407	*Malta*	3412	*Singapore*

Engine No 3410 *Sydney* was a special favourite of mine, since in the year 1913 my father presented me with a Gauge 1 Bassett-Lowke model of the engine and a three-coach train of bogie clerestory roofed coaches to run with it.

An 'Atbara', No 3381 Maine, *at Fishguard Harbour with the mail special from the first call of the* Mauretania *in August 1909.* (British Railways)

4. Persisting foreign influences

In the early summer of 1902 Dean, by the kindest of suggestions, had been prevailed upon to retire, although he was then no more than 62 years of age. He left Newburn House and the Company found a quiet retreat for him at Folkestone. But before he went, in March of that same year, Swindon Works had turned out the first Great Western express passenger 4-6-0, No 100, which was afterwards named *William Dean*. Although the technical press, and particularly Rous-Marten in his most exhuberant mood, bestowed on him all the honours for his innovation, in due course it was learned that the entire conception and actual execution of the design was Churchward's. The design provides an interesting study. The boilers of the 'Atbara' Class 4-4-0s had steamed freely, and in designing the pioneer express 4-6-0 the much larger boiler needed was a straight enlargement of the 'Atbara'. It had the same type of high-raised Belpaire firebox, and a barrel that was larger in diameter, longer, but entirely parallel. The comparative dimensions were:

Engine	'Atbara'	No 100
Length of barrel (ft in)	11 0	14 8
Diameter (ft in)	4 5	5 0
Firebox length (ft in)	7 0	9 0
Grate area (sq ft)	21.28	$27\frac{3}{4}$
Total heating surface (sq ft)	1,664.28	2,400
Pressure (psi)	180	200

The tube heating surface of the 'Atbaras' was provided by 277 tubes of $1\frac{7}{8}$ in outside diameter, and with a distance between the tube plates of 11 ft $3\frac{13}{16}$ in, gave a heating surface of 1,540.18 sq ft. The larger diameter of the boiler of the 4-6-0 engine enables 300 tubes to be accommodated, and brought the tube heating surface up to 2,252.94 sq ft.

The special constructional feature of the front end merits particular attention. The cylinders, together with their associated piston valves, were made in two identical castings, each with a half-saddle, and bolted together on the engine centre-line. This allowed for easily arranged exhaust passages, which were simplified to obviate the need for separate exhaust piping and numerous joints, all of which would have to have been made steamtight. Some years later Churchward, questioned as to why he had adopted the long piston stroke of 30 in, said that it was the only way he knew of making a simple engine equal to a compound, in thermal efficiency. From this it would seem that he saw the challenge of the compound locomotive some little time before the importing of the De Glehn 'Atlantics'. The piston valves were of the double-ported type of $6\frac{1}{2}$ in diameter, actuated by Stephenson's link motion through an arrangement of rocking levers.

Four years later Churchward read a most absorbing paper to the Institution of Mechanical Engineers on 'Large Locomotive Boilers', and the text and the accompanying illustrations showed how thoroughly he had studied American practice, though not to the extent of abandoning the Belpaire firebox, which was a Belgian invention and already widely used in France and Holland. The idea behind the taper boiler, which was derived directly from contemporary American practice, was to obtain free circulation of the water in the hottest part of the boiler and to avoid the abrupt transition in cross-sectional area from the square-sided Belpaire firebox to the parallel diameter of the barrel. The evolution of the tapered barrel had begun even before Dean had been retired. The first engine to have this form of boiler that was to become historic was one of the double-framed inside-cylinder 2-6-0s of the 'Aberdare' Class, No 2662. This was quickly followed

Below left and above *The first GWR express passenger 4-6-0, No 100 built in 1902, and later named* William Dean. (British Railways)

Right *The first GWR engine to have a tapered boiler, No 3705* Mauritius, *seen here as later superheated with top-feed.* (W.J. Reynolds)

Right *A 'Badminton' Class 4-4-0 rebuilt with a taper boiler; No 4102* Blenheim, *on a Bournemouth train with Great Central stock, passes Tilehurst.* (M.W. Earley)

by its application to an 'Atbara', No 3405 *Mauritius*. The design was not quite finalized on these two locomotives, for while they had the tapered barrel, the firebox was straight-sided in its upper half and the curves at the top were relatively sharp, as in the 'Atbaras' and the 5-ft 8-in 'Camel' Class 4-4-0s. The top surface of the firebox, also, was horizontal.

When Churchward came to apply the same principles of design to further new engines, the fireboxes were tapered towards the back, both at the sides and on top, to give increased space all round at the forward end. Churchward spent a great deal of time personally on the development of the curvature of the side plates of the firebox, not only to secure the good circulation he considered essential, but also to ensure minimum stay stresses from the relative expansions of the firebox and the casings. Direct staying for all surfaces was employed. The Standard No 1 boiler bore an almost uncanny likeness to one introduced on the Illinois Central Railroad in 1897 in all the finer points of its detail, except that the American used a steam dome on the tapered rearward portion of the barrel. The drawing office records at Swindon show that the American drawing was booked in on 19 August 1902, when the design of the Standard No 1 was being finalized. The firebox of the Illinois Central boiler was 9 ft 9 in long, and the barrel 13 ft long. The grate area was 27.18 sq ft, almost exactly the same as the Great Western's.

While Churchward was feeling his way, as it were, with the big engines, he evolved what became known as the Standard No 4 boiler, and in its non-superheated form, applied first to the 'Atbara' Class 4-4-0 No 3405 *Mauritius*, the boiler was coned for two-thirds of its length, increasing from 4 ft 10¾ in at the parallel front ring to no less than 5 ft 6 in at the firebox tube plate. In one respect, however, the final form was not reached on *Mauritius*. The upper part of the firebox had vertical parallel sides, as on the 'Camels' and standard 'Atbaras'. Apart from this, No 3405, reboilered thus in September 1902, was the true prototype of the most famous range of boilers in locomotive history. The basic details of the 'Atbara' and Standard No 4 boilers were as follows:

	'Atbara'	**Standard No 4**
Tubes		
Number	277	350
Outside diameter (in)	1⅞	1⅝
Heating surfaces (sq ft)		
Tubes	1,540.18	1,689.82
Firebox	124.10	128.30
Total	1,664.28	1,818.12
Grate area (sq ft)	21.28	20.56
Boiler pressure (psi)	180	200

It was possible to have a greater number of tubes on the No 4 not only because they were of smaller diameter, but because the forward ring of the barrel was of a 4 ft 10¾ in diameter outside, against the 4 ft 5 in of the parallel boiler of the 'Atbaras'. It is interesting to find that Churchward increased the boiler pressure in the No 4 to 200 psi and this brought the nominal tractive effort from 16,010 lb to 17,790 lb. The raising of the pressure caused some shaking of heads, particularly as some other railways were doing their best to get pressures down in order to lessen boiler maintenance charges. It was therefore all the more interesting to hear what H.C. King, Locomotive Works Manager at Swindon, had to say about it:

> The design illustrated in the Paper [Churchward's classic of 1906] with the increased water surface, the conical barrel, and the improved area through which the water could very freely circulate, through the sides and back plates of the firebox, had produced for his company, whatever that pattern may have produced elsewhere, nothing but unqualified satisfaction. He could therefore state with the use of the higher pressures, the steady rise from 150 lb to 165 lb, then to 180 lb, and now 200 lb with 225 lb as a limit, had not produced that measure of increased difficulty which some people had anticipated would vary as the arithmetical ratio of the pressure. Of course there were difficulties—no one using locomotive boilers was free from them—but there were no special difficulties incidental to the higher pressures. He was not going to say that that measure of satisfaction had been produced without constant and unremitting care on the part of all those in the boiler shop and in charge of the construction; everybody was aware that boilers were being built from which great things were expected, and he could say truthfully that the difficulties had not been proportional to the increased pressure.

I think that this last sentence is the crux of the whole matter: 'everyone was aware. . .' It was the same with the running inspectors on the footplate. Churchward was carrying the whole department—Drawing Office, Works, and outdoor staff with him—in a combined, well co-ordinated drive to 'great things'. It was on the 'City' Class, of which No 3433 *City of Bath*, completed at Swindon in March 1903, was the first, that finality was reached in the shape of the Belpaire firebox, with the sides curved very slightly inwards towards the top, and a much larger radius used in the transition from the sides to the flat top. Also, the top was not horizontal along the line of the boiler, but sloped down slightly towards the cab. In this respect Churchward was following American practice on many of the large boilers illustrated in his paper. Although it was the boiler that was the outstanding feature of *City of Bath*, it must be added that in these locomotives the Stroudley

method of balancing was abandoned, and the outside cranks were placed diametrically opposite to the inside, in the conventional way.

Quite apart from technicalities, the 'Cities' were much finer-looking than the 'Atbaras'. The larger boiler, with its centre line pitched 3 in higher, and the tapered rear portion rising to meet the outline of the firebox, gave a balanced elegance that was absent in the angular functional aspects of the 'Atbaras'. In a further respect opinions may differ, but I think they looked their best with the tapered cast iron chimneys, especially those with the raised cowl at the front. The later large-diameter 'copper tops' and such additions as top feed, certainly gave them a 'standard' appearance, but I prefer the older version.

There were some curiosities about the naming. As will be seen from the list the first nine were neatly in alphabetical order, and it looked as though Exeter had been forgotten and was put in at the last minute! Then there is the inclusion of Winchester, reached only by a sparsely used branch line, and Worcester omitted. It looks as though No 3442 was to have been *City of Worcester* and that the name was discarded in favour of *City of Exeter*. The GWR already had one of the 7-ft 8-in singles named simply *Worcester*, so presumably honour was satisfied. The class, as completed, was as follows:

3433	*City of Bath*
3434	*City of Birmingham*
3435	*City of Bristol*
3436	*City of Chester*
3437	*City of Gloucester*
3438	*City of Hereford*
3439	*City of London*
3440	*City of Truro*
3441	*City of Winchester*
3442	*City of Exeter*

In 1901, while Dean was still in the chair, in the most private conclaves of the Locomotive Drawing Office at Swindon there was produced a diagram showing in outline six new locomotives the like of which had never been seen before on the GWR. They represented Churchward's forward thinking for locomotive standardization. Few people even in the upper echelons of the department knew of these proposals, and certainly they were not for the eye of enterprising and persistent technical journalists like Charles Rous-Marten. His lengthy dissertation when the first essay of one of the proposed new standard designs, No 100, took the road in 1902 was largely 'off the beam', particularly his attributing the entire conception of the design to Dean. Even in 1903 the production of a further prototype 4-6-0 and the unusual step of purchasing a De Glehn compound 'Atlantic' from France did not seem to point the way Swindon was ultimately going; and while the first 4-6-0s were in regular service, and *La France* was already doing good work, Churchward was well enough aware that for several years the 'Atbaras' and 'Cities' would be the backbone of the top-line motive power stud.

To provide a clear assessment of the maximum capacity, a test was made with No 3435 *City of Bristol* and the new dynamometer car in July 1903. It seemed as if an attempt was made to determine the 'all-out' capacity of these locomotives. I was able to study the actual dynamometer car record, and from it I have prepared the log overleaf. The ascent of the steepest part of the Wellington bank was quite exceptional for the period. The load would have been considered on the heavy side for a top-class Great Western express of that period, and for the speed not to have fallen below 40 mph over the last mile to Whiteball Tunnel involved some very hard work. In fact, the cylinders were very definitely 'beating the boiler'. After the immediate start from Taunton, No 3435 was worked to Wellington in 38 per cent cut-off with the regulator three-quarters full open. This brought the boiler pressure down from the rated 200 to 160 psi. Here the engine was exerting a drawbar pull of no less than 2.2 tons at 53 mph. On the

Above left *The first of the 'Cities', No 3422* City of Bath, *at Westbourne Park shed.* (Loco Publishing Co)

Left *A 'City' Class 4-4-0, No 3702* Halifax, *on an Oxford-Paddington express near Tilehurst.* (M.W. Earley)

Right *An up Worcester express east of Twyford, hauled by No 4716* City of London. (H. Gordon Tidey)

final ascent, when one mile short of the tunnel entrance (milepost 172), cut-off was advanced to 48 per cent and although boiler pressure fell still further, to 150 psi the 1 in 80 gradient was topped at 38 mph, and on the mile at 1 in 127 through the tunnel the speed dropped no more than 1 mph. The actual drawbar pull on entering the tunnel was no less than 3 tons, and the equivalent drawbar horsepower, on level track, no less than 920. This was an outstanding effort at such a speed as 38 mph, but it was clear that it could not be sustained for long.

For test purposes a stop was made at Tiverton Junction, prior to which there had been a fast descent from Whiteball. From the restart the locomotive was worked in 26 per cent cut-off and regulator one-half open, and made fast time down the gently falling gradient from Cullompton to the outskirts of Exeter. When *City of Truro* was restored to working condition in 1957, and I had the pleasure of riding on the footplate, I noted that the locomotive ran beautifully in 26 per cent cut-off, though at that time it was superheated and the original slide valves had been replaced by piston valves. That, however, is a later part of the present story.

GWR: Dynamometer car test run, 27 July 1903

Engine No 3435 *City of Bristol*
Load 240 tons

Distance (miles)		Actual (m s)	Average speed (mph)
0.0	TAUNTON YARD	0 00	—
0.8	Milepost 164	2 40	—
1.8	Milepost 165	4 08	40.9
2.8	Milepost 166	5 19	50.7
3.8	Milepost 167	6 28	52.2
4.8	Milepost 168	7 36	53.0
5.8	Milepost 169	8 44	53.0
6.8	Milepost 170	9 52	53.0
7.8	Milepost 171	10 09	53.7
8.3	Milepost 171½	10 44	51.5
8.8	Milepost 172	11 23	46.2
9.3	Milepost 172½	12 06	41.9
9.8	Milepost 173	12 51	40.0
10.8	Milepost 174 (Whiteball)	14 27	37.5
11.8	Milepost 175	15 40	49.3
12.8	Milepost 176	16 35	65.4
13.8	Milepost 177	17 24	73.5
14.8	Milepost 178	18 12	75.0
15.8	Tiverton Junc (179)	20 00	—
1.0	Milepost 180	3 01	—
2.0	Milepost 181	4 15	48.7
3.0	Milepost 182	5 15	60.0
4.0	Milepost 183	6 12	63.2
5.0	Milepost 184	7 06	66.7
6.0	Milepost 185	7 58	69.2
7.0	Milepost 186	8 51	67.9
8.0	Milepost 187	9 44	67.9
9.0	Milepost 188	10 34	72.0
10.0	Milepost 189	11 24	72.0
12.0	Milepost 191	13 03	73.5
14.9	EXETER	16 30	—

Reverting to foreign influences, while it has been shown that the Belpaire firebox came originally from Belgium and the taper boiler from the USA, the French connection, which began in 1903, had one very significant sequel, far from any ideas of Great Western compounds, that eventually persisted through the remaining life of steam locomotives at Swindon and, through Stanier's influence, spread far and wide on the LMS as well. One important feature of 4-6-0 design was in an embryo stage at the time when *La France* arrived. On his larger express passenger engines, Dean had used Stroudley's arrangement of having the slide valves accommodated beneath the cylinders and driven by direct acting Stephenson's link motion. When it became necessary to change from 2-2-2 and 2-4-0 types to bogie engines, the presence of the valve chests immediately below the cylinders made it extremely awkward to provide the customary mounting for a bogie, and as we have seen Dean designed an adaptation of his centreless carriage bogie for his larger locomotives, in which all the weight was taken on side supports, and no more than a light framework was used to provide a guide for the bogie pivot, which took no weight. This could not have been adapted to an engine with large outside cylinders, so Churchward turned again to American practice. In these the loads were applied to the axle-boxes by equalizing bars, and the bogie was connected to the engine frame by swing links. These latter proved troublesome, however, and experiments were made to obtain more satisfactory wear from their pivots. Concern was also expressed at the amount of flange wear that began to develop on the leading coupled wheels. While the swing links allowed freedom of lateral movement of the bogie, and consequently at the front of the engine, in so doing it caused the leading coupled flanges to do a considerable part of the work of guiding the engine into curves. The beautifully smooth riding of *La France* provided some food for thought in the Swindon Drawing Office.

When *La France* was first put to work on the Great Western Railway, the interest of Churchward and his men was concentrated upon all the factors contributing to power output. The drawbar pull was what mattered. But then other points began to intrude. The organization of the locomotive department, as it was also on the majority of English railways in pre-grouping days, kept

Above *The first French compound, No 102* La France. (British Railways)

Right La France *on the first Plymouth non-stop passing Westbourne Park engine sheds.* (Loco Publishing Co)

the Locomotive Running Inspectors closely in touch with the inside staff. They were the eyes and ears of the Drawing Office, and they were frequently called into consultation by Churchward himself.

The fact that men marked for promotion were given spells of intermediate responsibility at the out-stations, in addition to time in Main Works or the Drawing Office, was an indication of the extent to which all aspects of locomotive design, maintenance and running were co-ordinated in Churchward's time, and the Running Inspectors as a body were relied upon to keep the chief informed as to how the locomotives were doing. Their opinions were carefully and sympathetically considered, and these men, regularly and critically riding on *La France*, reported that she was the sweetest riding engine that had yet run on Great Western metals. Part of this was immediately attributed to her having four cylinders with the drive divided between the two coupled axles; but these experienced observers began to realize that there was more to it than the arrangement of the machinery.

La France was working in the London-Plymouth link, with a very sharply curved stretch of line west of Newton Abbot, and it became noticeable that she entered the curves and reacted to the frequent successions of reverse curves much more smoothly than the Great Western engines. These observations were in due course transmitted to Churchward, and eventually he decided to give the French bogie a trial. It was of quite different design from that used on the first three Great Western express passenger 4-6-0s and continued on the ten-wheeled engines built in 1905, to be mentioned later. In the De Glehn design the weight of the engine was transmitted to the bogie through sliding flat surfaces. The lower surface was on the bogie frame and the weight was applied to the upper surface by hemispherical cups, which allowed angular movement of the bogie relative to the engine frame. The side bearers by which the weight was transmitted downwards can be seen in the photograph of *La France*.

Meanwhile, the bogie centre pin on the engine frame engaged a centre block on the bogie, but lateral movement of the block relative to the bogie frame could take place under the control of springs. Movement of the bogie relative to the engine frame applied a force through these springs which tended to lead the engine frame into a curve. It was noticed also that the action of these springs tended to reduce any tendency of the front end of the engine to oscillate. Churchward did not adopt the French bogie in its entirety, but retained the equalizing bar arrangement of wheel springing. The blend of Swindon and French practice that resulted was extremely successful; it was not, however, until the year 1908 that it was adopted as standard in all large bogie engines, though all ten-wheeled engines built previously were in due course modified. On the four-cylinder engines built prior to 1908, with the outside cylinders roughly in line with the rear pair of bogie wheels, one could see whether the bogie had been modified because the side bearers would be clearly visible. On the two-cylinder engines, they would be concealed behind the cylinders.

5. The magic 'hundred'—the saga of the Ocean Mails

From top to bottom *Track of the Ocean Mails: Whiteball Summit with an up express putting off its pilot engine.* (Author's collection); *the down 'Cornish Riviera Express' hauled by an 'Atbara' leaving Parsons Tunnel, Dawlish* (L&GRP); *and Uphill Cutting, with the down 'Flying Dutchman' hauled by an unidentified 7-ft 8-in Dean 4-2-2.* (Author's collection).

From quite early days in Great Western history, Plymouth had been a railway port of some consequence. Mails and passengers from Australia, India and the Cape had been regularly handled and special trains run to Paddington as required. It was, however, the decision in 1903 of the North German Lloyd and the Hamburg-America companies that henceforth all their express steamers should call at Plymouth that gave such a fillip to the traffic. Liners of these fleets had wrested the Blue Riband of the Altantic crossing from British steamers, and the Great Western Railway in accepting the traffic from these crack German ships found itself in strong competition with the London and North Western Railway, and the London and South Western. Some American mail was put ashore at Queenstown, and conveyed via the GS&WR to Kingstown for transference to the 'Irish Mail' route, while other mail was put ashore at Liverpool. At the same time the London and South Western received other incoming mail at Southampton. But by reason of its geographical position, Plymouth was the most favourably situated of all the main ports, and the Great Western was able to participate in working the fastest services between New York and London. Up to the end of 1903, the GWR had a monopoly of this traffic and the special trains carried both passengers and mails. A typical train consisted of five corridor 'firsts', two brake 'seconds', two dining cars, two mail vans, and a bullion van. Very often two 'City' Class engines were used.

The significance of the 1903 decision by the two German steamship lines was not lost upon the London and South Western management. At once extensions and improvements to their own terminal facilities at Stonehouse Pool were put in hand, and with their extensive experience in the working of similar traffic at Southampton, the new Ocean Quay station was magnificently equipped. The outcome of this splendid enterprise on the part of the South Western was an agreement to divide the incoming traffic; the Great Western would take the mails, and the South Western the passengers, and very soon the two companies were engaged in a speed competition that bid fair to eclipse anything that had occurred on the northern lines in 1895.

In the early months of 1904 the Great Western had made several quite fast runs, but the true zero hour proved to be 2 am on Saturday 9 April when the Great Western and South Western mail tenders cast off, and in the blackest hour of the 24 set out on their short voyages to the breakwater protecting the entrance to Plymouth Sound. The American Line's vessel SS *St Louis* was expected, and three hours later the railway race was on. The Great Western were away at 4.59 am from Millbay Crossing with the mails, and the South Western special with the passengers left Stonehouse Pool at 5.3 am. That morning the Great Western won handsomely, as the mail reached Paddington at 9.17 am, 19 minutes ahead of the South Western arrival in Waterloo. But the South Western were new to the game. On 9 April it was evident that they were treating the new traffic very seriously, and both Mr Henry Holmes, Superindendent of the Line, and Mr Dugald Drummond, Locomotive Superintendent, travelled with the train. The Great Western run that morning was not quite their own record for the up journey, but it was a very fine one, seeing that 12¼ minutes out of the journey time of 4 hr 18½ min were spent standing at stations, and that 10 minutes were lost through other checks. But on Saturday 23 April the South Western broke all records with an overall time of 4 hr 3 min from Stonehouse Junction to Waterloo. This record lasted exactly one week, for on the following Saturday the Great Western made the hitherto unprecedented time of 3 hr 54 min on a run which included, moreover, two

GWR: Ocean Mail specials in 1904

Date	9 April	18 April	23 April	30 April	2 May	7 May
Vessel	*St Louis**	*Kaiser Wilhelm II*†	*St Paul**	*Philadelphia**	*Kaiser Wilhelm der Grosse*†	*St Louis**
Time of Departure (Millbay)	4.59 am	4.21 pm	3.55 pm	6.1 pm	12.21 pm	8.27 am
Load from Plymouth (vans)	5	5	5	4	5	5
from Bristol (vans)	3	3	3	2	3	3
Engines						
Plymouth–Exeter	*Wolverhampton*§	*City of Exeter*	*City of Exeter*	*City of Exeter*	*City of Gloucester*	*City of Exeter*
Exeter–Bristol	*City of Exeter*	*City of Exeter*	*City of Exeter*	*Sir Richard Grenville*	*City of Gloucester*	*City of Exeter*
Bristol–Paddington	*Duchess of Albany*	*Brisbane*‡	*Wilkinson*	*Duke of Connaught*	*City of Gloucester*	*City of Exeter*
Distance (miles)	**Actual (min)**	**Actual (min)**	**Actual (min)**	**Actual (min)**	**Actual (min)**	**Actual (min)**
0.0 Millbay Crossing	0	0	0	0	0	0
24.0 Totnes	34	34	30½	28	28	30
32.7 Newton Abbot	47	45	41	37	37	40
52.9 Exeter	72	68	66	60	58	61
	—	—		—		
—	0	—	—	0	—	—
83.7 Taunton	28	97	96	31	88	90
95.2 Bridgwater	37	107	106½	41	99	100
127.8 Pylle Hill Junction	—	—	—	68	128	128
—				—	—	—
128.5 Temple Meads	66	138½	136	0	0	0
	—	—	—	—	—	—
—	0	0	0	—	—	—
41.4 Swindon	44	40	41½	39	39	41½
65.6 Didcot	64	60	63	57½	60	63½
82.7 Reading	77	77	78	71	74½	77½
118.7 Paddington	108	109	112	99	106	110½
Total time	4 hr 18 min	4 hr 13 min	4 hr 12 min	3 hr 54 min	3 hr 56 min	4 hr 1 min
Average speeds						
Plymouth–Exeter	44.0	46.7	48.1	52.9	54.7	52.0
Exeter–Bristol	68.7	64.1	64.9	66.0	64.1	67.1
Bristol–Paddington	65.7	65.1	63.3	72.0	67.2	64.3

* American Line † North German Lloyd Line § 'Camel' Class ‡ 'Atbara' Class

changes of engine. There was also a significant change in the working arrangements east of Bristol in that the special ran via Bath instead of Badminton, and so avoided all the engineering slacks on the new line.

So far as the Great Western is concerned details of six runs between 9 April and 7 May may be summarized as in the accompanying table. The drivers were:

Engine No	Name	Driver
3052	*Sir Richard Grenville*	Killock
3056	*Wilkinson*	Burt
3065	*Duke of Connaught*	Underhill
3066	*Duchess of Albany*	Edwards
3396	*Brisbane*	Lee
3437	*City of Gloucester*	Millard
3442	*City of Exeter*	Warren
3452	*Wolverhampton*	Uren

The well-known drivers Millard and Warren, and no less Driver Clements, who later handled *City of Truro* on the fastest run of all, were all Exeter men. The fact that these drivers then worked through expresses over the entire distance from Plymouth to London is a commentary in itself upon the rostering that existed before the opening of the shortened route.

Of the engines concerned, the 'Camel' Class was a 5-ft 8-in 4-4-0 later included in the 'Bulldog' Class; *Brisbane* was an 'Atbara', and of the remainder those not named after cities are Dean 7-ft 8-in singles. The loads were never more than five vehicles, and of these at least one was cut off at Bristol. On the fastest run of the above series, on 30 April, the load was one of four vans from Plymouth to Bristol, and only two beyond. The fine performance of the single No 3052 *Sir Richard Grenville* will be specially noted in running the 75.6 miles from Exeter to Bristol in 68 minutes start to stop.

The first day, 9 April, was in many ways a special occasion, and while Mr G.A. Sekon, editor of *The*

Left *Maker of one of the fastest runs to Bristol, engine No 3442* City of Exeter. (Author's collection)

Below *'Bulldogs' were occasionally used on the racing trains west of Exeter; this is No 3743* Seagull *on a London-bound express.* (Author's collection)

Railway Magazine, travelled by the LSWR train, the Rev W.J. Scott rode with the GWR mail special. An abbreviated log of this running between Exeter and Bristol is given below:

GWR: Ocean Mail Special

Engine No 3442 *City of Exeter*
Load 5 vans, 150 tons full

Distance (miles)		Actual (min sec)	Average speed (mph)
0.0	EXETER	0 00	—
1.3	Cowley Bridge Junc	2 40	—
14.9	Tiverton Junc	15 02	66.0
19.9	Whiteball Box	19 30	67.1
23.7	Wellington	23 02	64.7
30.8	TAUNTON	27 55	87.1
55.9	Uphill Junc	47 24	77.2
74.5	Bedminster	62 30	74.3
75.6	BRISTOL	65 24	

There was some magnificent running on this trip. Scott records that the speed was 71 to 72 mph over the easy rising gradients between Hele and Cullompton, and after taking the two miles at 1 in 155 before Tiverton Junction, the maximum of 72 mph was renewed at the spot where Sampford Peverell station then stood. With the impetus from such an exceptionally fast approach, Whiteball summit was cleared at a minimum of 60 mph. Down the steepest part of the bank the engine would seem to have been much restrained, but once through Wellington, the driver piled it on with a vengeance. Scott writes with a tantalizing evasiveness about the speed on this stretch, saying 'we ran smartly, but not faster than on other occasions', and making no mention of the maximum speed. But the average from Wellington to Taunton was 87 mph and this was followed by the still more commendable average of 77.2 mph over the 25.1 miles from Taunton to Uphill Junction, almost entirely dead level road. With this demonstration of what was necessary to make the Bristol-Exeter run in 65½ minutes, it would have been most interesting to have had more details of the run of 30 April, when the single-wheeler *Sir Richard Grenville* made the run in 68 minutes. Unfortunately nothing more than the journal time has been handed down to us.

But all these earlier runs, splendid as they were, proved no more than a leading up to what Mr Cecil J. Allen has called 'the colossal feat' of 9 May. Quite apart from the railway aspect this was a momentous occasion in many other ways. The North German Lloyd steamer *Kronprinz Wilhelm*, eastward bound from New York, was carrying an exceptionally heavy mail. She was also carrying bullion representing the American payment to France on account of the price of the Panama Canal, and there was thus a special incentive to convey the mail and specie to London as quickly as possible.

By this time the Great Western had reduced every feature of the mail working to a fine art, from the navigation of the tenders in Plymouth Sound to the changing of engines at Bristol; and on the morning of 9 May 1904, they surpassed themselves. The mail was at rest in Paddington station 5 hr 10 min after the *Kronprinz Wilhelm* dropped anchor! The mail engine from Plymouth was *City of Truro*, with Driver Clements and Inspector G.H. Flewellen of Newton Abbot on the footplate. The driver's Christian name was Moses, but so far as biblical names are concerned it might more appropriately have been Jehu, son of Nimshi!

Many years later, Inspector Flewellen recalled the instructions given to him by Mr Churchward regarding the running of these Ocean Mail specials. At first he was definitely restricted, while the permanent way was being fettled up, and the traffic officers were building up the organization. He had several encounters with the latter in the early days. Churchward's orders were brief and characteristic: 'Withhold any attempt at a maximum speed record till I give the word—then you can go and break your b— neck'! The progressively faster running of the 'specials' between Plymouth and Exeter was one of the phenomena of this particular railway race. The South Devon Line is one of the most difficult express routes in the British Isles. Quite apart from such exceptional gradients as Hemerdon, Rattery and the two sides of Dainton, the curves are exceptionally severe; and in 1904 the coastal stretch was complicated by single line working between Teignmouth and Dawlish. From the journal records of the runs of 30 April, 2 May and 7 May, with their times of 60, 58 and 61 min from Plymouth Millbay to Exeter, it was evident that some exceptional work was necessary, and Rous-Marten's detailed timing on the morning of 9 May throws a good deal more light on what must have been a set of hair-raising experiences.

In his original description of that day's run, in *The Railway Magazine* of June 1904, Rous-Marten quotes no maximum and minimum speeds over the South Devon line; but it is evident that the minimum speed on the 2 miles of the 1 in 41 of Hemerdon Bank must have been between 25 and 30 mph and this was followed by an average of 60 mph up the rising grades from Cornwood to Wrangaton. Only those who have ridden over the South Devon line on the footplate, however, and seen the curves as they appear through the cab glasses, will appreciate what average speeds of 68.8 mph from Wrangaton to Brent, and again from Brent to Totnes, must have meant. The top speed down the Rattery incline was 77 mph and it will be seen from the averages of 57.5 and 58.0 mph on either side of it that the Dainton 'gable' was taken as if it did not exist! Thus the almost incredible time of 33 min 35 sec was made from passing North Road to passing Newton Abbot—an average speed of 56.9 mph; yet this performance must have been closely paralleled on 30 April, on 2 May and on 7 May! It is significant of the exceptional running made over the South Devon line that the tablet slacks at Teignmouth and Dawlish, and the permanent way slack at Starcross, proved a far greater hindrance than Dainton bank, and the average speed from Newton to Exminster was only 53 mph.

Having passed Exeter in the splendid time of 59 min 2 sec from Millbay, the succeeding time to Whiteball was actually slower than that of *City of Exeter* on 9 April; for whereas No 3440 took 19 min 29 sec, pass to pass for the 19.9 miles, No 3442 took 19 min 30 sec from *start* to pass. Moreover, the respective average speeds from Tiverton Junction to the summit were 60 and 67 mph. But while *City of Exeter*, passing Whiteball at 60 mph, was run easily down the first part of Wellington bank, *City of Truro* was just let fly. The story of how her 100 mph dash down the bank was checked by some platelayers remaining in the 'four foot' until the last minute might be called a classic, or a 'chestnut', according to one's own inclinations; but this performance is

GWR: Ocean Mail record run, 9 May 1904, Plymouth–Bristol

Engine 4-4-0 No 3440 *City of Truro*
Load 5 vans, 148 tons loaded

Distance (miles)		Actual (m s)	Average speed (mph)
0.0	MILLBAY CROSSING	0 00	—
0.9	NORTH ROAD	3 07	17.3
1.2	Mutley	3 36	37.2
4.9	Plympton	7 31	55.2
7.6	*Hemerdon Box*	11 54	36.9
9.3	Cornwood	14 05	46.6
11.7	Ivybridge	16 29	60.0
15.0	Wrangaton	19 48	59.8
17.2	Brent	21 43	68.8
24.0	Totnes	27 39	68.8
28.8	*Dainton Box*	32 40	57.5
32.7	NEWTON ABBOT	36 42	58.0
37.9	Teignmouth	41 59	59.0
40.7	Dawlish	45 54	42.9
44.4	Starcross	50 14	51.2
—		pw slack	—
48.2	Exminster	54 09	58.3
52.1	Exeter St Thomas's	57 49	63.8
52.9	EXETER ST DAVID'S	59 02	39.5
56.4	Stoke Canon	62 54	54.4
60.1	Silverton	66 26	62.9
61.3	Hele	67 33	64.5
65.5	Cullompton	71 13	68.8
67.8	Tiverton Junction	73 32	59.8
72.1	Burlescombe	77 43	61.6
72.8	*Whiteball Box*	78 31	53.5
73.8	*Milepost* 173	79 26	65.7
74.8	*Milepost* 172	80 08	85.7
75.8	*Milepost* 171	80 45½	96.0
—		brakes	—
76.6	Wellington	81 18*	89.2
81.7	Norton Fitzwarren	85 19	76.5
83.7	TAUNTON	86 51	78.2
89.5	Durston	91 42	71.6
95.2	BRIDGWATER	96 10	76.5
101.5	HIGHBRIDGE	101 09	75.7
116.5	Yatton	113 01	75.9
122.5	Flax Bourton	118 11	69.7
127.4	Bedminster	122 19	70.9
127.8	PYLLE HILL JUNC	123 19	—

* Adjusted time: original published figure 81 min 38 sec.

GWR: Ocean Mail record run, 9 May 1904, Bristol–Paddington

Engine 4-2-2 No 3065 *Duke of Connaught*
Load 4 vans, 120 tons loaded

Distance (miles)		Actual (m s)	Average speed (mph)
0.0	PYLLE HILL JUNC	0 00	—
1.7	*Bristol East Depot*	3 39	27.9
4.9	Keynsham	7 21	51.9
7.3	Saltford	9 32	65.8
11.8	BATH	13 38	65.8
14.1	Bathampton	16 00	58.4
16.8	Box	18 28	65.8
20.4	Corsham	22 01	60.8
24.7	CHIPPENHAM	25 48	68.1
31.0	Dauntsey	30 49	75.5
35.8	Wootton Bassett	35 06	67.2
41.4	SWINDON	39 37	74.5
—		pw slack	—
41.8	*Bridge at 76m 74c*	40 31	26.6
47.1	Shrivenham	45 19	66.8
52.2	Uffington	49 17	77.1
58.3	Wantage Road	53 47	81.3
65.6	DIDCOT	59 08	81.9
70.2	Cholsey	62 35	80.1
73.9	Goring	65 21	80.6
77.1	Pangbourne	67 52	76.5
82.7	READING	72 09	78.3
87.7	Twyford	76 00	78.0
94.5	Maidenhead	80 58	82.2
100.2	SLOUGH	85 03	83.7
105.5	West Drayton	88 53	81.5
109.6	Southall	92 04	77.3
113.0	Ealing	94 35	81.1
117.4	Westbourne Park	98 01	76.8
118.7	PADDINGTON	99 46	—

Slack at Bridge 76m 74c to 5 mph

analysed and discussed fully later in the chapter. After Taunton *City of Truro* was slightly slower than *City of Exeter* on to Bedminster, the respective averages over this length of 43.8 miles being 75.3 and 75.9 mph. Both, of course, were superlatively fine performances, and showed, more than any brief spurts at 100 mph, the quality of Mr Churchward's engines. On 9 May the stop was made at Pylle Hill Junction and the time of 123 min 19 sec from Millbay is a record which has never been surpassed, though *City of Exeter* on 9 April was a full minute faster between Stoke Canon and Bedminster.

So we come to the culmination of it all. After the experience of running through from Plymouth to Paddington with the same engine and crew on 2 May and 7 May, when the times from Pylle Hill were 106 and $110\frac{1}{2}$ minutes with 'City' Class engines, the mail train of 9 May was worked forward from Bristol by a fresh engine, No 3065 *Duke of Connaught*. This engine had already been credited with a run from Bristol to Paddington in 99 minutes on 30 April, albeit with a train of only two coaches, but on 9 May Rous-Marten recorded the wonderful run detailed herewith. Despite the difficult start, round the many sharp curves of the Bristol avoiding line, despite the regular speed restriction at Bath and the subsequent ascent through Box tunnel, 'even time' had been reached by Dauntsey, and the average speed of 74.5 mph over the rising stretch from Wootton Bassett to Swindon showed a standard of running even higher than that of the 'City' Class engines. Then came the underline bridge slack, to walking pace, at the Cricklade Road; following recovery from this hindrance, there came the performance that the Great Western Railway did not surpass until 1931. Between Shrivenham and Reading the running was such as one might have expected from a 'star' engine, after what had previously occurred in the race: a speed of slightly over 80 mph on the gradual descent past Wantage Road and Steventon, tailing off slightly on the dead level east of Cholsey. But after Reading the engine must have been given a little extra, for between Twyford and West Drayton, on level road, she averaged no less than 82.9 mph. Such a feat, with a load not much below those of the sharpest-timed passenger trains of the day, marks the very zenith of performance of the Dean singles—and indeed of any single-driver express locomotive that has ever been run in Great Britain.

Thus 9 May 1904 marked a climax, almost unbelievably brilliant, in the race with the Ocean traffic from Plymouth. There is no doubt that the authorities were a little apprehensive of the speeds run, and Rous-Marten was asked to withhold publication of the most sensational item of all, the maximum of 102 mph down Wellington bank. Nevertheless, the Ocean Mails continued to be run at very high speed, and in *The Railway Magazine* for 1906 Rous-Marten records a run with a 'City' Class engine and 150 tons on which the time was 4 hours exactly from Millbay to Paddington, inclusive of a 2-minute stop in Bristol. The same engine worked

Left *One of the heroes of the Race — No 3440* City of Truro, *an official portrait.* (British Railways)

Below *Another hero of the Race — the Dean single No 3065* Duke of Connaught *at Exeter.* (P.J.T. Reed)

Ideal work for a 'City': No 3711 City of Birmingham *on a Wolverhampton-London express passing Fenny Compton in 1923.* (L.J. Thompson)

through, and she reached 95½ mph on the descent of Wellington bank. But for the Great Western Railway, the years 1900–4 formed merely a prologue to the remarkable chain of development that was to follow, and which was to manifest itself little by little in the daily running of the trains. In the meantime the success with which Inspector Flewellen had handled the locomotive working of the Ocean Mails led to his transfer from Newton Abbot to Swindon, in 1908. Subsequently he was appointed Chief Locomotive Inspector of the GWR, a position he retained till his retirement from the service in the summer of 1926.

The running of the Ocean Mails in 1904, and no less that of the advance section of the 'Cornishman' in July 1903, pointed clearly to a new standard of express train speed on the Great Western. While hitherto 60 mph on the level had been considered the hallmark of an express train, the 'City' Class engines with loads of about 150 tons had shown themselves capable of 70 to 75 mph as long as the level stretches extended, as, for example, Taunton to Nailsea. In comparing their loads with those of the present day, it is most important to realize that the rolling resistance of coaching stock is not nearly so high as it was 50 years ago. Early tests with the present GWR dynamometer car indicate that the resistance of stock at 60 mph was then around 12 lb per ton, whereas now it is no more than 8 to 9 lb. Thus on the level a train of 1904 having a dead weight of 150 tons would pull roughly equal to about 200 to 210 tons of modern stock. The work of running the 150-ton mail trains at 75 mph on level track would be equivalent to about 500 drawbar horsepower. *City of Exeter* considerably exceeded this on her record ascent from Exeter to Whiteball on 8 April—indeed, there is every indication that between Tiverton Junction and Burlescombe she was developing over 1,000 dhp. With such a boiler, an output of this magnitude could be no more than transitory, and this may explain why she was eased down Wellington bank, to restore boiler pressure and water level.

It was the boiler that so distinguished the 'Cities' from the 'Atbaras', and in the 'City' boiler Churchward had come very near to finality in basic design. As we have seen, the barrel was coned and the firebox tapered towards the back, both in plan and elevation. Moreover, the sides of the firebox were very carefully curved. To secure increased efficiency, a longer range of expansion was desirable, and consequently higher boiler pressures; these in turn brought higher temperatures, and unless the freest possible circulation took place, local heating would be liable to occur, with possible failures of stays and tubes. By coning the barrel Churchward provided considerably increased water space at the hottest part of the barrel, while the high Belpaire firebox gave additional steam space above the water line and so reduced the risk of foaming. The dome, with its large hole in the barrel, is always a point of weakness in a boiler. It had already been shown with the experimental engine *Waterford*, of the 'Badminton' Class, that if sufficient space was allowed above the water line in the outer firebox, there was no necessity to use a dome as a safeguard against priming, and in both 'Atbaras' and 'Cities' the dome was omitted. The new boilers steamed very freely, and the basic design formed the pattern which Great Western practice was to follow for the next 40 years. Churchward certainly counted upon the availability of good Welsh coal. Fifty years ago the output from the South Wales pits was prodigious, and its cost relatively low. At that time there seemed no likelihood of any serious interruption of supplies, nor deterioration in quality.

Quite apart from the boiler, which was a milestone in British locomotive design, there was the extraordinary capability for speed of the 'City' class engines. The readiness with which they ran up to speeds of 95 and 100 mph was a tribute to an excellent design of valves and steam passages. One may be very sure that the drivers never attempted to force them to such velocities, particularly when so much was at stake on the Ocean Mail trains. It may be pointed out that the 'City' speeds on dead level track were less than that of the single-wheeler *Duke of Connaught*; but the piston speed of the single doing 87 mph around Burnham was no more than that of a 'City' doing 75 mph, and it is the ability or otherwise of an engine to get steam in and out of the cylinders that governs maximum speed in the normal way. The 'City' doing 100 mph was making 411 revolutions per minute, while the single at her maximum of 87 was making no more than 318. But then the critics may ask: 'Did *City of Truro* ever really attain 102 mph?' That is a point to which I have given a great deal of thought, with very serious regard to the discrepancies that undoubtedly exist in the figures Rous-Marten has handed down to posterity. But one of the most remarkable features about the great run of 9 May 1904, upon which Rous-Marten himself commented, was the entire absence of report on the record in the popular daily press of the day. The censorship deemed necessary at Paddington was evidently most successful. But it did have one most unfortunate result. There can be no doubt that Rous-Marten's co-enthusiasts, the Rev W.J. Scott, Norman D. Macdonald and others, discussed details of the record very closely with him; but they, too, abided loyally by the Paddington request for silence, and so the discrepancies brought to light in 1935 were never cleared up in the lifetime either of Rous-Marten himself, or of Scott.

I have now attempted a reconstruction of what actually happened in the descent of Wellington bank, using as much as possible of Rous-Marten's original data. The speed at Whiteball summit was about 52 mph and then from Milepost 173 onwards successive quarter-mile timings gave speeds of 81.8, 84.9, 88.2, 90.0, 91.8, 95.7, 97.8 and 102.3 mph. These have been plotted on the accompanying graph, and with the exception of the very last they lie on a perfectly reasonable and fair curve. I am quite prepared to believe that Rous-Marten may have been one-fifth of a second out on the last quarter, reading 102.3 mph instead of the dead '100'; but then came the check. How everyone concerned must have cursed those platelayers! Every time Rous-Marten had occasion to refer to the episode in subsequent writings, he finds adjec-

City of Truro *preserved and mounted in the original Railway Museum at York in 1935.* (O.S. Nock)

A reconstruction of the GWR Ocean mails Run on 9 May 1904
Engine 3440 *City of Truro* **Load** 148 tons

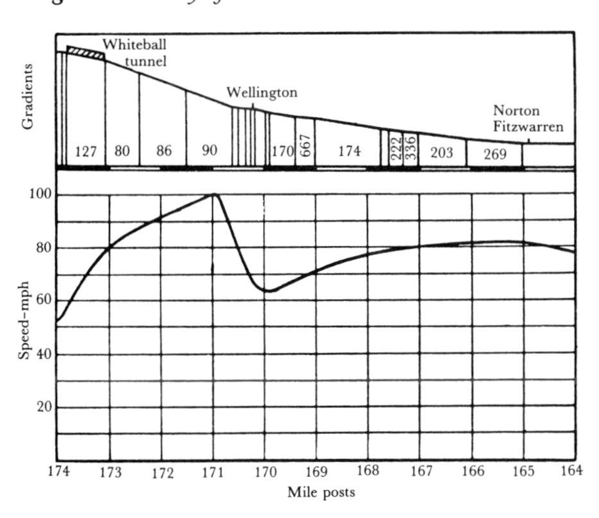

City of Truro *rejuvenated in 1957, at Kingswear working a special excursion train from Swindon; on the return journey a speed of 84 mph was attained descending the Wellington bank.* (O.S. Nock)

tives ever more scathing by which to describe them: 'foolish', 'stupid', 'dawdling', 'loafing', 'idiotic', accompanied by varying degrees of scorn! But I wonder if it really was the platelayers that caused steam to be shut off, and the brakes applied? Rous-Marten as usual tells a highly colourful story of how they loafed in the four-foot until the very last minute, despite prolonged whistling of the engine; but a first-class driver must have known that no application of the brakes at the last minute could possibly have saved the men had they persisted in remaining on the line, and I feel it is much more likely that the driver, realizing the terrific speed at which he was travelling, shut off steam deliberately and eased the train over the reverse curves through Wellington station. In the graph I have plotted what would be the effect of a heavy brake application with the brake apparatus then in use, with the brakes released again just after passing Wellington.

In previous discussions of this episode there was more than a suggestion that those on the footplate were going for an 'all-out' record. The ascent from Exeter to Whiteball hardly bears this out, for the times on that stretch were consistently and markedly slower than with *City of Exeter* on the earlier Ocean Mail run. I feel that *City of Truro* was merely allowed to run from Whiteball, probably with little change in the working conditions, and that the very high speed was an incidental feature rather than a deliberate attempt at a world record, despite Churchward's homely words to Inspector Flewellen! How locomotives can accelerate on such a descending gradient was shown in a run I clocked from the footplate in the autumn of 1953 when a 'King', hauling 500 tons on the up 'Dutchman', passed Whiteball summit at 46 mph. The working was then changed from main regulator and 17 per cent cut-off to first valve and 15 per cent, and we reached a maximum speed of 92 mph. The one major item published by Rous-Marten that does not fit in with the reconstruction shown graphically is the passing time at Wellington station. In many years of speed recording, however, I have found it is extremely easy to jot down a station passing time 20 or 30 seconds out. When subsequently checking times against speeds, the error readily comes to light, but in the case of the *City of Truro* run, a censorship had been imposed upon the speeds, and in the original published records it is probable that no exhaustive check was made. If the passing time at Wellington is adjusted from 3 min 7 sec after Whiteball to 2 min 47 sec, all the other details fall into place. In his first published account of the run in *The Railway Magazine* for June 1904, Rous-Marten says that the check occurred near Wellington station; in my reconstruction the lowest speed due to the brake application took place about a quarter of a mile after passing the station, this corresponding with a note in a log published in *The Engineer*. But in the discussion that took place in *The Railway Magazine* during 1934 and 1935, some confusion was caused by reference to a letter to *The Times* written by Locomotive Inspector Flewellen many years after the event, in which he states that speed was reduced near Bradfield Crossing—that is half-way between Wellington and Norton Fitzwarren. This, however, is very much at variance with the details originally published by Rous-Marten immediately after the run, in which he states that the 'hurricane descent' of the Wellington bank 'was nearly spoiled, however, by a check near the station through some foolish platelayers calmly staying on the "four-foot" when the lightning special was close on them. . .' Although we shall never know precisely what happened, my own conviction is that with the one exception of the Wellington passing time, Rous-Marten's published figures were accurate. I feel that a maximum of at least 100 mph may be accepted on *City of Truro*'s behalf.

6. The grand conception and its fulfilment

It was in 1901, while Churchward was still Assistant Locomotive Carriage and Wagon Superintendent, that the diagram was prepared showing the six standard types of locomotive that were envisaged as meeting the main line requirements of the whole railway, thus:

1 Heavy main line express passenger, 4-6-0, 6 ft 8½ in wheels
2 Express passenger for heavily graded routes, 4-6-0, 5 ft 8½ in
3 Heavy goods and mineral traffic, 2-8-0, 4 ft 4½ in
4 Heavy shorter-distance goods and mineral traffic, 2-6-2 tank, 5 ft 8½ in
5 Lighter express passenger, 4-4-0, 6 ft 8½ in
6 Shorter-distance express tank, 4-4-2, 6 ft 8½ in

All six classes were to have the same sized cylinders, 18 in diameter by 30 in stroke, and the same valve motion, while originally only two sizes of boiler were provided for, the first for classes 1, 2 and 3 and the second for the remainder. This was no pipe dream as far as Churchward was concerned, because the pioneer engines of five out of the six classes were running by the end of the year 1905, as follows:

Engine No	Type	Boiler pressure (psi)	Date
98	4-6-0	200	1902
97	2-8-0	200	1903
99	2-6-2T	195	1904
3473	4-4-0	200	1904
2221	4-4-2T	195	1905

Exercising hindsight, some connoisseurs of the history of British locomotive practice have queried the wisdom of including the 4-4-0s of the '3473' or 'County' Class, even though the original scheme of standardization was conceived as relatively long ago as 1901. It was considered that the 'Atbaras' were an adequate and indeed excellent second line express passenger power unit. The question was raised again as recently as 1950 when K.J. Cook read his paper on 'The late G.J. Churchward's Locomotive Development on the Great Western Railway' before the Institution of Locomotive Engineers. Sir William Stanier was present on this occasion, and referred to the building of the 'Counties' in a jocular vein. But I must be pardoned for questioning whether he had got *all* his facts right.

According to Stanier, Churchward when he prepared his standard engine diagram of 1901 was proposing to use his big new 4-6-0s on the West to North route between Bristol and Shrewsbury, and as the line north of Hereford was jointly owned by the GW and LNW railways, the latter company had to be consulted on matters of locomotive utilization. Whether this was actually the case around 1901 is very doubtful, but according to Stanier there appeared to have been some difference of opinion, for Stanier said that Churchward 'was not going to be told what he could, or could not do, by old Webb', so he designed the 'Counties', which had the same tractive effort as the 4-6-0s. When they were first built, in 1904, Webb had in any case retired, and the first batch of them, numbered 3473 to 3482, were used almost exclusively between Paddington and Plymouth, on the principal West of England expresses.

In view of the experimentation being extended to the large ten-wheeled express locomotives and the purchase of two further De Glehn compound 'Atlantics' from France, it is interesting to review the production rate of new engines from Swindon between 1903 and 1907 as it affected the new standard designs covered on the 1901 diagram. The dates quoted below are those of the completion of the respective Swindon 'Lots'.

Date	Engine No(s)	Description
1903		
February	98	4-6-0 express passenger
June	97	2-8-0 heavy goods
September	99	2-6-2T goods
October	102	French compound 4-4-2
December	171	4-6-0 express passenger *Albion*
1904		
October	3473–82	'County' Class, first 10
1905		
February	172	4-4-2 express passenger
March	3111–3120	2-6-2T goods
April	173–8	4-6-0 express passenger
May	179–180	4-4-2 express passenger
June	3121–3130	2-6-2T goods
June	103–4	French compound 4-4-2
September	181–190	4-4-2 express passenger
October	2801–10	2-8-0 heavy goods
December	2811–20	2-8-0 heavy goods

Thus at the end of 1905, so far as the standard engines were concerned, Churchward had eight 4-6-0s, 17 4-4-2s, three of the French compounds, ten 'Counties',

21 2-6-2 tanks, and 21 2-8-0s. Construction of the 4-4-2 'County' tanks had begun, but the authorized batch of ten engines, 2221–30, was not completed until October 1906. It was evident that Churchward's mind was not fully made up about his big engines in those formative years, as witness the preponderance of 'Atlantics' over 4-6-0s, only eight of the latter against 14 Swindon-built 4-4-2s including *Albion*, converted from a 4-6-0, together with the three French compounds. In contrast to this hesitation he had gone ahead with two successive batches of 2-6-2 tanks of the '3111' Class, a first batch of 'Counties', and two batches of 2-8-0 heavy goods engines. Furthermore, in the very next year 20 more 'Counties' were built and 20 more 2-6-2 tanks. In the maximum power category, the year 1906 saw the production of the 'Lady' series of 4-6-0s, and yet another 'Atlantic', the four-cylinder simple, No 40 *North Star*. At this stage it seems a good moment to list the names of the new standard engines built at Swindon up to the end of 1906, although it was not until the end of this last mentioned year that most of the ten-wheeled engines built in 1905 were named.

'County' Class, 1904 batch

3473	*City of Middlesex*	3478	*County of Devon*
3474	*County of Berks*	3479	*County of Warwick*
3475	*County of Wilts*	3480	*County of Stafford*
3476	*County of Dorset*	3481	*County of Glamorgan*
3477	*County of Somerset*	3482	*County of Pembroke*

'County' Class, 1906 batch

3801	*County Carlow*	3811	*County of Bucks*
3802	*County Clare*	3812	*County of Cardigan*
3803	*County Cork*	3813	*County of Carmarthen*
3804	*County Dublin*	3814	*County of Chester*
3805	*County Kerry*	3815	*County of Hants*
3806	*County Kildare*	3816	*County of Leicester*
3807	*County Kilkenny*	3817	*County of Monmouth*
3808	*County Limerick*	3818	*County of Radnor*
3809	*County Wexford*	3819	*County of Salop*
3810	*County of Wicklow*	3820	*County of Worcester*

'Atlantics'

171	*The Pirate*	184	*Guy Mannering*
172	*The Abbot*	185	*Peveril of the Peak*
179	*Quentin Durward*	186	*Robin Hood*
180	*Coeur de Lion*	187	*Bride of Lammermoor*
181	*Ivanhoe*	188	*Rob Roy*
182	*Lalla Rookh*	189	*Talisman*
183	*Red Gauntlet*	190	*Waverley*

4-6-0s

98	*Ernest Cunard*	175	*Viscount Churchill*
100	*William Dean*	176	*Winterstoke*
173	*Robins Bolitho*	177	*Robertson*
174	*Lord Barrymore*	178	*Kirkland*

The sixth class in Churchward's diagram of 1901, the

5-ft 8-in 4-6-0, was presumably conceived at the time when all West of England expresses, brought down from Bristol by single-wheelers, changed engines at Newton Abbot; but with the introduction of the powerful new 'Atbara' Class 4-4-0s, through working to Plymouth became practicable. The availability of the new dynamometer car made possible some competitive trials in June 1905 to see how the 'Atlantics' would perform on the very severe gradients of the South Devon line. The 4-4-2 engine No 172, originally named *Quicksilver*, was matched against 4-6-0 No 178 *Kirkland*, and the upshot was that the 'Atlantics' were regularly used west of Newton Abbot, including the non-stop 'Cornish Riviera Express' to and from Paddington in the days when it ran via Bristol. There was thus no immediate need for the 5-ft 8-in 4-6-0 included in Churchward's original proposals. One of the immediate results of the standard engine building of 1904–5 was the prowess of the 'County' Class 4-4-0s used turn and turn about with 'Atlantics' and 4-6-0s on the most prestigious express passenger workings, even including the 'Cornish Riviera Express' after the shortened route to the West of England had been opened in 1906.

Some dynamometer car trials had been carried out with engine No 3473 *County of Middlesex* in December 1904, and one of the points under investigation was the smoothness of the engine working when running with a fully opened regulator and 18 per cent cut-off in contrast to part regulator and 25 per cent cut-off. The reports gave no comment on this, but studying the actual dynamometer graphs, the rolls show a very much smoother pull on the drawbar at 25 per cent cut-off than at 18 per cent, or less when it was tried. Rous-Marten went down to Exeter to record the running of what was then colloquially called the 'Torquay Diner' which ran at 12.7 pm non-stop to Paddington via Bristol. With a load of 305 tons, No 3474 *County of Berks* made an excellent run, particularly in its vigorous start up to Whiteball Tunnel, and in the fast running on to Bristol. Despite a severe slowing for permanent way work north of Bridgwater, they passed Bedminster, before the long slowing over the Bristol avoiding line, in 77 min 34 sec for the 74.5 miles from the start at Exeter. The log on page 53 shows the details of the running. Beyond Bristol, with the train well on time, there was not so much need for haste, and the train was checked by signals several times; but the overall net time of 197 minutes for the 193.6 miles from Exeter, with its average speed of 59 mph, was an excellent performance for a 4-4-0 locomotive hauling a load of 305 tons.

The working of the 11.25 am non-stop express from Paddington to Birmingham, via Oxford, involved some interesting running, even though the loads were usually lighter than on the West of England trains. The 11.25 am slipped a coach at Leamington, in 113 minutes for the run of 105.9 miles from Paddington, an

Left *Engine No 3478* County of Devon *at Laira shed, with the original copper-capped chimney.* (P.J.T. Reed)

Below left *One of the Irish 'Counties', No 3808* County Limerick. (British Railways).

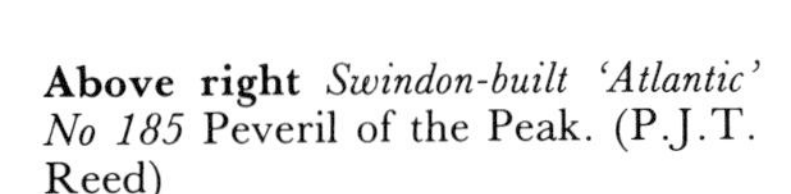

Above right *Swindon-built 'Atlantic' No 185* Peveril of the Peak. (P.J.T. Reed)

Right *One of the first batch of two-cylinder 4-6-0s, No 173* Robins Bolitho *at Laira sheds.* (P.J.T. Reed)

Top *'Atlantic' No 190, afterwards named* Waverley, *on a West of England express at Old Oak Common.* (Author's collection)

Above *One of the first batch of 'Counties', No 3474* County of Berks, *with tapered chimney.* (P.J.T. Reed)

average speed of 56.3 mph, and with a normal load of 200 tons they got away in great style passing in no more than 8 seconds over 'even time'. The engine was appropriately No 3479 *County of Warwick*, and she had averaged 67 mph from Slough to Reading. In spite of a bad signal check at Tilehurst, Didcot East Junction, 52.8 miles, was passed in 53 min 5 sec and Oxford, 63.4 miles, was passed in exactly even time. There were moderate permanent way slacks at Culham and Aynho, and Banbury, 86.1 miles, was passed in 86 min 26 sec. With a maximum speed of 75½ mph down the Southam Road bank, the 103 milepost was passed in 101 min 48 sec, but because of traffic operations at Leamington, a station stop had to be made instead of slipping, after a signal delayed approach. Even so, the arrival was nearly 4 minutes early, in 109 min 9 sec from Paddington.

After the opening of the shortened route to the West of England, the up 'Cornish Riviera Express' made a passenger stop at Exeter and one day in 1907 Rous-Marten went down to try one of the new 4-6-0s of the 'Lady' series on the three-hour non-stop run up to Paddington. But he was disappointed, because when the train arrived from Plymouth it appeared that the 'Lady' in question, No 2908 *Lady of Quality*, had been showing some very unladylike traits on the way up, and at Exeter she was taken off the train. No 3820 *County of Worcester* was commandeered at a moment's notice, but Rous-Marten was so disappointed at not having his 'Lady' that he took very little detail of what must have been a very fine run. The summary details are shown in the accompanying table, alongside details of a run with the same engine which had worked from Plymouth with a load of 200 tons. Despite having to take a very much increased load of 290 tons from Exeter, the two runs tied to within a single second to Whiteball, although on the first one should make some allowance for the engine not being immediately ready for top class express duty when it was suddenly substituted for the wayward *Lady of Quality*. This first run of the *County of Worcester* was badly delayed by adverse signals at Taunton, so it had not drawn level with the more heavily loaded second run until Castle Cary. The sharp gradients between that junction told somewhat on the 290-ton trip, but from Westbury both engines covered the remaining 95.6 miles to Paddington in 95½ minutes—splendid work.

GWR: 'Cornish Riviera Express', 1907

Loads (tons full)		**190**		**290**	
Distance (miles)		**min**	**sec**	**min**	**sec**
0.0	Exeter	0	00	0	00
19.9	Whiteball Box	23	46	23	45
30.8	Taunton	34	46	33	45
35.8	Cogload Junction	39	01	38	00
58.4	Castle Cary	61	24	61	25
78.1	Westbury	81	50	84	40
173.7	Paddington	177	20	180	20

The run on which *County of Worcester* worked the 'Limited' through from Plymouth to Paddington, with a load of no less than 290 tons from Exeter, can well be set down as one of the maximum achievements of the class in its non-superheated condition, seeing that the boiler pressure was 200 psi against 225 on the 'Atlantics' and 4-6-0s, and the grate area was only 20.56 sq ft.

GWR: 12.07 pm Exeter–Paddington

Engine No 3474 *County of Berks*
Load 305 tons full

Distance (miles)		Actual (min sec)	Speed (mph)
0.0	EXETER	0 00	—
3.5	Stoke Canon	5 40	37.1
7.2	Silverton	9 49	53.5
8.4	Hele	11 11	52.8
12.6	Cullompton	15 43	55.7
14.9	Tiverton Junction	18 28	50.2
19.9	Whiteball Box	24 58	46.2
23.7	Wellington	28 54	57.5
28.8	Norton Fitzwarren	33 05	73.1
30.8	TAUNTON	34 42	74.3
36.5	Durston	39 43	68.4
42.3	BRIDGWATER	45 27	60.6
		pws	
48.6	Highbridge	52 46	43.5
58.8	Worle Junction	62 31	63.1
63.6	Yatton	67 46	66.3
69.6	Flax Bourton	73 18	65.0
74.5	Bedminster	77 34	68.9
76.6	Bristol East Junction	82 02	—
86.7	BATH	93 46	—
99.6	CHIPPENHAM	109 43	—
105.9	Dauntsey	115 42	63.0
110.7	Wootton Bassett	121 17	51.5
116.3	SWINDON	127 26	54.8
137.1	Steventon	146 29	69.0
—		sigs	—
140.5	DIDCOT	151 17	—
157.6	READING	168 02	—
—		sigs	—
175.1	SLOUGH	184 47	—
—		sigs	—
184.5	Southall	194 15	—
193.6	PADDINGTON	204 22	—

Net time 197 minutes

* Speed restriction

Of course the 'Counties' had 10-in diameter piston valves and the long valve travel that had been standardized after the building of the 4-6-0 engine No 98; but for a 4-4-0 with no more than 20,000 lb tractive effort, the sustained performance of *County of Worcester* over more than four hours, most of it at an average speed of all but 60 mph, must have been very near the limit. Two further points about the 'Counties' in those early days: the first batch at the outset had the straight copper-capped chimney as fitted to the 4-6-0s and 'Atlantics', but soon these were changed to the shapely cast iron type used on the 'Cities' and 'Atbaras'; the 1906 batch all had cast iron chimneys from the outset.

The second point concerns the names. It was significant of the interest the top management of the GWR was then taking in the development of business and tourist traffic to Southern Ireland, via Fishguard, that the first ten of the 1906 batch should be named after Irish Counties (see page 50).

While the 'Atbaras', 'Cities' and 'Counties' were carrying the bulk of the most important express work east of Plymouth, Churchward and his men in the Drawing Office, with the valuable assistance of the running inspectors, were busy sizing up the relative merits of the 'Atlantic' versus the 4-6-0 type, and no less those of the three French compounds against the indigenous

Swindon products. When in Alfred Smeddle's time at Swindon I had the privilege of studying the dynamometer records and other Drawing Office archives, I was surprised to find that apparently no records had been preserved of the running of the three French compounds. *Albion* and certain of the other early Churchward ten-wheelers were there in full measure, yet from what Churchward said at the memorable meeting at the Institution of Mechanical Engineers in 1904, when he spoke at some length in the discussion on M Edouard Savage's paper 'Compound Locomotives', it was evident that he was already in possession of some highly important data regarding the performance of *La France*. For the big engines he had set himself a target that they should be able to sustain, continuously, a drawbar pull at the back of the tender of 2 tons at 70 mph. He told the members of the Institution of Mechanical Engineers in 1904 that already the GWR had one or two locomotives capable of doing that, and *La France* was one of them. Another of them, Churchward said, was his 4-6-0 No 98, which was then working at a boiler pressure of 200 psi against 227 on *La France*. With the later 4-6-0 *Albion*, working at 225 psi, he hoped to get the 2-ton drawbar pull at 75 mph working at a shorter cut-off than 25 per cent.

The comparisons with the French engines were continued to the extent of converting *Albion* to an 'Atlantic', and then, in 1906, building a new 'Atlantic' as a four-cylinder simple. The French influence at Swindon was already profound. The compound 'Atlantics' ran with exceptional smoothness, and as mileage increased they were not subject to the roughness that develops almost inevitably in a locomotive with two outside cylinders. One can think of many other famous designs outside the GWR that were rough and uncomfortable to ride upon, such as the 'King Arthurs' of the Southern, Stanier's 'Black Fives' and the whole range of British standard locomotives. The two-cylinder engine is ideal for general-purpose work, but in long-distance express passenger traffic, such as was being actively developed on the GWR in the early 1900s, the desire for a smooth-riding engine was more than a mere question of comfort on the footplate. To lessen vibration and knocking, enginemen will work with longer cut-offs and partly-opened regulator; and this, in limiting the range of expansion of the steam, would defeat the very object on which Churchward had so fixedly set his sights, in his adoption of high boiler pressure, and long-lap, long-travel valves.

In planning his four-cylinder 'Atlantic' engine, Churchward gave particular attention to the valve gear. Previous British four-cylinder engines had not been very successful, notably Webb's compounds of the 'Jubilee' and 'Alfred the Great' Classes on the LNWR, and Dugald Drummond's first 4-6-0s on the London and South Western. On the Great Western the

Top La France *at Stafford Road sheds, Wolverhampton.* (Author's collection)

Above *The second de Glehn compound 'Atlantic', No 103* President. (British Railways)

use of inside cranks combined with the generous size of axle-box and crankpin which Churchward employed, left insufficient room for inside Stephenson valve gear. Churchward was impressed by the Walschaerts gear of the Frenchmen, but he thought it very light, and described it as a 'watchmaker's job'. In his two-cylinder engines he had used a massive valve gear with generous bearing surfaces. The gear would not deflect under the heaviest loads, and would suffer little wear between general repairs; it ensured that the valve setting was maintained with little deterioration, in sharp contrast to the behaviour of the locomotives of some other railways. As Churchward proposed to use two sets of valve gear for four valves, the valve gear of the four-cylinder engine must therefore be at least as massive as that of the two-cylinder machines and he considered that there was insufficient room within the loading gauge for an outside gear with links of the requisite size.

Yet another objection to an outside valve gear was that Churchward's outside connecting rods had solid-bush big-ends, so that an outside valve gear would have had to be partly dismantled to allow the removal of a connecting rod (this in fact had to be done on thousands of locomotives on other railways). It was thought that, provided that the valve gear could be made as durable as that of the two-cylinder engines, the big-end would need to be taken down more frequently than the valve gear. With an outside gear behind the cylinder and a rocking lever ahead of it, some part of the valve gear would have had to be disconnected before an outside valve could be removed. On top of all these technical objections was Churchward's aesthetic objection to any unnecessary outside fittings. Whatever the critics might dislike in his early locomotives, they must have agreed that only the bare essentials of the mechanism were visible.

A study of the characteristics of the Stephenson and Walschaerts gears, designed with the same steam lap, port size and valve travel, showed that at short cut-offs, although the maximum opening of the valve to steam was the same for both gears, the tendency of the valve with Walschaerts gear to 'dwell' at the end of its movement caused it to admit more steam to the cylinder whilst it was open. As it was expected that the four-cylinder engine would be capable of doing much of its work at 15 per cent cut-off, which gave the maximum possible expansion ratio in the cylinder, the Walschaerts gear offered an advantage.

W.H. Pearce, the draughtsman who had designed the Churchward Stephenson gear, began to sketch a Walschaerts gear for the four-cylinder engine, and hit on the idea of simplifying this gear further by eliminating eccentrics altogether. He proposed to use the crosshead of one inside cylinder to provide the equivalent of the eccentric of the other inside cylinder. In the Walschaerts gear the final drive to the valve is compounded of two motions, one taken from the crosshead of the cylinder concerned, and the other from an eccentric or return crank at 90 degrees to the crank of the cylinder. This second component can alternatively be taken from the crosshead of the other cylinder, since the cranks of the two cylinders are at 90 degrees. There was some geometrical complication in fitting two gears of this type between the two sets of slide-bars, but the arrangement eliminated eccentrics, and left the crank axle unencumbered. This gave two advantages: it reduced the unsprung weight on the crank axle, and it also removed a weakness of all gears in which a drive is taken from an eccentric or return crank—that in any position of the axle in which the eccentric rod is inclined to the horizontal, movement of the axle on its springs causes a small displacement of the valve.

Pearce made a wooden model of this gear in June 1905, and submitted it to Churchward, who ordered the gear to be fitted to the engine. The wooden model is still in existence. This same idea had previously occurred to a number of other engineers, both locomotive and marine, but Pearce was quite unaware of this when the idea came to him. R.M. Deeley is said to have designed a gear of this type when he was an assistant to S.W. Johnson on the Midland Railway at Derby. He showed the scheme to Johnson, who would have nothing to do with it; but when Deeley himself succeeded Johnson he revived the idea for his large 4-4-0 No 999. On 11 August 1905 he applied for a patent for the gear, which was granted in June 1906. In the meantime No 40 had appeared from Swindon fitted with Pearce's gear, which from the shape of the expansion link levers earned the name of 'scissors' gear.

It was said at Swindon that a strong letter arrived from Deeley accusing Churchward of using the Deeley gear without acknowledgement. There was no difficulty in establishing that the Swindon gear was designed before Deeley applied for his patent, and that Churchward had every right to use it. In its characteristics, the scissors gear was similar to the Walschaerts, that is the lead was constant at all positions of cut-off. The Stephenson gear, as used in the two-cylinder locomotives, has the characteristic that the lead decreases as cut-off is increased, and it therefore makes an engine better at starting and at hill climbing at low speed.

The gear fitted to No 40 had a disadvantage, however. If a defect developed in one cylinder, motion, or valve gear of a two-cylinder locomotive, involving dismantling of the connecting rod, the locomotive had a good prospect of moving itself off the running lines, or even of reaching a shed, on the surviving cylinder. With the cross-connected gear, the disconnection of one connecting rod automatically immobilized the valve gear of the other cylinder, and the locomotive could not move itself. For this reason the scissors gear was not used on subsequent four-cylinder engines, but it remained in No 40 until 1929, when the engine was rebuilt as a 'Castle'. The valve gear of the subsequent Great Western four-cylinder locomotives incorporated a detail which made it easy to fasten one pair of valves in their mid-position in an emergency, so this requirement was evidently important to Churchward.

The four-cylinder 'Atlantic', No 40, later named *North Star*, immediately preceded a further batch of two-cylinder 4-6-0s, the 'Ladies', which were completed by May 1906. It seemed as if Churchward was satisfied with his two-cylinder engines as a general-purpose express passenger type, while he was developing the four-cylinder variant for the long-distance high-speed runs. It should be remembered that in the early

Top *An official view of the pioneer four-cylinder simple 'Atlantic' No 40* (British Railways); *and* **above**, *still unnamed, on the down 'Cornish Riviera Express'.* (Loco Publishing Co Ltd)

Below *'City' No 3408, originally named* Ophir *but renamed* Killarney *for the first day excursion run from London to Killarney in 1907.* (British Railways)

1900s Plymouth was not the only goal of such runs. The development of Fishguard as a packet station not only for the burgeoning Irish traffic but also as a rival to Liverpool for transatlantic business loomed large in the forward planning at Paddington. A 'City' Class 4-4-0, appropriately named *Killarney* for the occasion, had made the first ever non-stop run from Paddington to Fishguard with the first day excursion from London to Killarney. In the meantime, observation of the five specially earmarked 'Atlantics', 102, 103, 104, 171 and then No 40, continued during 1906, and at the end of that year Churchward's mind was evidently made up. In 1907 he built the ten four-cylinder 4-6-0s of the 'Star' class, and later in that same year 20 more two-cylinder 4-6-0s, named after Saints.

It has always seemed to me that not a little pride, and perhaps even a little conceit, went into the naming of the Churchward 4-6-0s. In all my footplate work, not only on the Great Western but much farther afield, I have often heard enginemen refer to a good or favourite engine as 'a real lady', and this affectionate term may well have led the folks at Swindon to introduce a class of 'Ladies', but whether engine No 2905 could historically qualify for this is doubtful. Then, if the ladylike quality of these engines was not enough, the next batch, of 20, bore the names of 'Saints'. As a foil to the names of Nos 2901–2910, it was noticeable that with engines Nos 2911–2930 male saints heavily predominated. In this, however, I have always felt that Swindon missed a trick by not including Saint Christopher, the patron saint of travellers. The first production batch of four-cylinder 4-6-0s revived the names bestowed on the Broad Gauge 2-2-2s built by Robert Stephenson & Co following the acclaim with which the original *North Star* was greeted when it arrived on the Great Western Railway. Following the Churchward 'Stars' in 1907 it was evident that the 'upper crust' atmosphere of Swindon-built 4-6-0s should be maintained by naming them after some of the distinguished Orders of Knighthood. It was with one of these latter, working the up 'Torquay Diner' in April 1908, that Churchward's target performance of a 2-ton

Right *4-6-0 No 2918* Saint Catherine *as originally built, non-superheated.* (P.J.T. Reed)

Below *One of the first batch of four-cylinder 4-6-0s, No 4002* Evening Star. (P.J.T. Reed)

drawbar pull at 70 mph was more than consummated.

Before discussing the detail of what was a very impressive run, reference must be made to the changes in valve gear on the 'Stars' from the original layout used on *North Star*. The arrangement of the reversing gear linkage was similar to that used in No 40, in that the reversing rod from the cab was connected to a reversing shaft extending across the locomotive. There was an individual auxiliary reversing shaft for each valve gear, connected by an auxiliary reversing rod and crank to the main reversing shaft. A short link was provided near each auxiliary reversing shaft by which the auxiliary reversing arm could be attached to a bracket on the engine frame if it was necessary to immobilize one cylinder. The auxiliary reversing shaft of the defective side was disconnected, leaving the other valve free to be operated by its own auxiliary reversing rod. This arrangement of the reversing gear made it a simple operation to put one side of the engine out of action in an emergency, but had the arrangement not been necessary in No 40 for the scissors gear, a simpler arrangement might have been devised for the Walschaerts gear. The valves had a steam lap of $1\frac{5}{8}$ in, a lead of $\frac{1}{8}$ in, and a travel of $6\frac{7}{8}$ in at the maximum cut-off to $76\frac{1}{2}$ per cent. A small but significant difference from No 40 was an inspection hole in the framing opposite the inside slide-bars. This gave a useful means of access to the slide-bars and the front part of the valve gear, and mitigated the inaccessibility of the inside motion.

As has been mentioned, the scissors gear fitted to *North Star* remained until the engine was rebuilt as a 'Castle' in November 1929, and I had a thrilling example of what the engine could do in May 1927 when of course it had long since been converted to the 4-6-0 type and superheated. I joined the second portion of an up West of England express at Reading one Saturday and was pleased to see *North Star* was on the job. We got a bad start from a lengthy permanent way slack right into Sonning; but once clear of this we went like the wind averaging 72 mph over the 23.6 miles from Twyford to Hanwell, and attaining a maximum of $77\frac{1}{2}$ mph at Slough. The load was 270 tons.

Apropos of the scissors valve gear, no more than a few weeks later I had my last run with one of the Deeley '999' Class Midland 4-4-0s fitted with it on the night express from St Pancras to Edinburgh as between Leeds and Carlisle. With a substantial load of 290 tons the engine climbed well and ran freely downhill and we were in good trim to complete the 76.8 miles from

Hellifield to Carlisle in 87 minutes, when perforce we had to join the early Saturday morning queue waiting to get into the Citadel station and spend about 15 minutes outside. The '999' Class engines, non-standard by current LMS reckoning, were scrapped soon afterwards.

GWR: 12.5 pm Exeter–Paddington: Dynamometer Car test run, 28 April 1908

Engine No 4013 *Knight of St Patrick*
Load 368 tons tare, 390 tons full

Distance (miles)		Schedule (min)	Actual (min sec)	Speed (mph)
0.0	Exeter	0	0 00	—
3.5	Stoke Canon		6 46	48
7.2	Silverton		10 58	56
8.4	Hele		12 13	58
12.6	Cullompton		16 21	63
14.9	Tiverton Junction		18 40	56½
15.9	Milepost 178		19 40	63
19.9	Whiteball box	25	23 57	47
23.7	Wellington		27 30	78½
27.9	Milepost 166		30 48	75
—			slight sig check	—
30.8	Taunton	35	33 50	55
35.8	Cogload Junction	40	38 55	62
38.8	Athelney		41 59	57/61
42.7	Curry Rivel Junction		46 05	59
46.8	Milepost 127		50 21	50
48.0	Somerton		51 46	63
51.3	Charlton Mackrell		55 05	59
53.5	Keinton Mandeville		57 12	71
58.4	Castle Cary	64	61 40	64
62.0	Bruton (post 126)		65 15	55
65.25	Milepost 122¾	73½	69 11	41
70.0	Milepost 118		74 04	69
72.4	Frome		76 24	27 (slack)
77.0	Milepost 111		83 14	63
78.1	Westbury	87½	84 45	32 (slack)
82.3	Edington		90 31	53
86.8	Lavington		95 13	61
92.6	Patney		101 50	48½
94.8	Woodborough		104 22	60
			pw slack	9
98.4	Pewsey		108 33	—
103.6	Savernake	114	118 36	41
107.3	Bedwyn		122 32	64
112.2	Hungerford		126 52	66½
115.2	Kintbury		129 29	71
120.6	Newbury	130	134 10	67
124.1	Thatcham		137 16	70
127.0	Midgham		139 44	71
132.5	Theale		144 28	69
135.8	Southcote Junction		147 35	—
137.7	Reading	148	151 16	24 (slack)
142.7	Twyford		157 56	58
149.5	Maidenhead		164 15	68

Distance (miles)		Schedule (min)	Actual (min sec)	Speed (mph)
155.2	Slough	166	169 15	69
160.5	West Drayton		173 59	65½
164.6	Southall	175	177 48	64½
168.0	Ealing Broadway		180 52	67
172.4	Westbourne Park		185 18	—
			sigs	
173.7	Paddington	185	189 58	

Knight of St Patrick, Engine No 4013, was used on a dynamometer test run on 28 April 1908, and I compiled the accompanying log of the journey direct from the test chart. It is shown in more than the usual detail because of the importance and significance of the occasion. From the test chart I was able to compute details of the engine working and some of the more notable drawbar pulls:

Engine working: No 4013, 28 April 1908

Location	Regulator	Cut-off (per cent)
Milepost 192 to Whiteball	Full	25
Whiteball to Curry Rivel Junction	Part-open	12½
Curry Rivel to Bruton	Full	20
Bruton to 122¾	Full	25
Milepost 122¾ to 116½	Half	15
Recovering from Frome slack	Full	20
Milepost 94½ to 76	Full	20
Recovering from Pewsey check	Full	35
Milepost 74½ to Savernake	Full	20
Savernake to Southcote Junction	Part-open	15
Reading to Milepost ¾	Full	20

High drawbar pulls: engine 4013, 28 April 1908

Location	Speed (mph)	Cut-off (per cent)	Pull (tons)
Tiverton Junction	63	25	2.8
Langport	56	20	2.4
Keinton Mandeville	69	20	2.1
Milepost 122¾	41	25	4.3
Patney	51	20	2.4
Taplow	69	20	2.2

It will be seen from the log that the train was nearly 3 minutes early passing Westbury, but the permanent way check at Pewsey was a very severe one and cost at least 5½ minutes in running. After Reading came the climax of the performance with a steadily maintained drawbar pull of 2.2 tons at a speed of 69 mph between Maidenhead and Slough, when the engine was working with full regulator and 20 per cent cut-off.

When the shortened route to the West of England via Castle Cary was first opened, the two-cylinder 4-6-0s were used turn and turn about with the four-cylinder, and truth to tell there was nothing to choose between their maximum efforts, both classes being non-superheated at the time. I have tabulated a run on

GWR: 3.30 pm Paddington–Exeter

Load (tons) to Westbury : 414 tare, 440 full
to Taunton : 339 tare, 360 full
to Exeter : 265 tare, 283 full

Engine 4-6-0 No 2903 *Lady of Lyons*

Distance (miles)		Schedule (min)	Actual (m s)	Average speed (mph)
0.0	Paddington	0	0 00	—
5.7	Ealing		8 47	38.8
9.1	Southall	11	12 13	58.7
18.5	Slough	20	20 43	66.3
31.0	Twyford		32 24	64.2
36.0	Reading	37	37 20	61.0
37.8	Southcote Junction		40 38	33.3
40.0	Milepost 40		43 05	53.5
53.1	Newbury	56	56 18	59.2
70.1	Savernake	73½	73 32	59.2
95.6	Westbury	97½	97 02	65.1
101.3	Frome		103 38	45.6
108.5	Milepost 112¾	113½	112 01	51.1
—			pws	
115.3	Castle Cary	120	118 43	—
—			pws	
137.9	Cogload Junction	144	142 20	—
142.9	Taunton	149	147 40	55.8
158.8	Whiteball Box	161	160 25	51.1
—			sigs	
173.7	Exeter	180	181 58	—

Top *Two-cylinder 4-6-0 No 2903* Lady of Lyons *at Exeter,* (P.J.T. Reed)

Above *'Atlantic' No 188* Rob Roy *outside the original station at Exeter St Davids.* (P.J.T. Reed)

the 3.30 pm from Paddington from Mr A.V. Goodyear's collection with engine No 2903 *Lady of Lyons*. It will be seen that with a gross load of no less than 440 tons, strict sectional times were kept to Westbury, and one would be interested to know what the drawbar pulls were on the level to Reading and on the long upward pull to Savernake. Goodyear recorded that the train consisted of 15 coaches, many of them doubtless of the older clerestory-roofed type, which pulled considerably 'heavier' than their tare weight might have suggested, and it was very fine work to average exactly 60 mph over 24 miles of the gradual rise up the Kennet valley, and to clear Savernake summit at 51½ mph. Passing Savernake on time, the rest of the journey was relatively easier, with the load reduced by slipping coaches at Westbury and Taunton. Having passed Whiteball summit slightly ahead of time, the driver ran very easily down to Exeter, and a concluding signal check made the actual arrival there nearly 2 minutes late.

Although the Swindon-built 'Atlantics' proved to be no more than a transition stage in Churchward's locomotive development, there is no doubt that they did some fine work on the West of England expresses, though they suffered from lack of adhesion weight when weather conditions were adverse. I am glad to be able to include in this chapter a fine example of 'Atlantic' performance from Mr Goodyear's collection, once again on the up 'Torquay Diner', and the accompanying log makes an interesting comparison with that of *Knight of St Patrick* on the dynamometer test run. The load was even heavier, and as so often the case in that era of Great Western history, a bank engine was provided up to Whiteball summit. Exeter was then a major depot for main-line express motive power, and with locomotive utilization not intensive there were usually quite a few express engines available for odd spells of duty such as piloting expresses up to Whiteball. It is on record that on one occasion a Dean 7-ft 8-in single working an important train from Newton Abbot to Bristol required a bank engine from Exeter and was provided with a new 4-6-0, *Lady Macbeth*. More's the pity there was no photographer on hand to record this remarkable case of double-heading. No such incongruous combination was made on Goodyear's journey, albeit the bank engine itself was a celebrity of the first magnitude, none other than No 3440 *City of Truro*. In partnership with the first of the type built new as an 'Atlantic' in 1905, and originally named *Quicksilver*, they made short work of the Whiteball ascent, and then as the log shows No 172 *The Abbot* did well on to Paddington. Significantly, however, on the steep uphill lengths, as from Castle Cary to Milepost 122¾ and up the bank to Milepost 82, the 'Atlantic' did noticeably slower work.

GWR: 12.5 pm Exeter–Paddington

Engine 4-4-2 No 172 *The Abbot*
Load 13 coaches, 390 tons tare, 415 tons full
Assistant engine to Whiteball No 3440 *City of Truro*

Distance (miles)		Schedule (min)	Actual (min sec)	Speed (mph)
0.0	Exeter	0	0 00	—
3.5	Stoke Canon		5 47	54
8.4	Hele		10 42	64
12.6	Cullompton		14 31	67½
14.9	Tiverton Junction		16 45	60
19.9	Whiteball	25	22 00	stop
			23 54	start
23.7	Wellington		29 52	76
30.8	Taunton	35	35 38	73
35.8	Cogload Junction	40	39 52	55
42.9	Curry Rivel Junction		—	59
48.0	Somerton		51 49	53
53.5	Keinton Mandeville		57 30	60
58.4	Castle Cary	64	62 24	57
65.2	Milepost 122¾	73½	71 31	30
72.4	Frome		79 05	slack
78.1	Westbury	87½	85 57	slack
85.7	Milepost 88		94 56	61
91.7	Milepost 82		102 02	44
98.4	Pewsey		109 54	55
103.6	Savernake	114	115 40	53½
107.3	Bedwyn		119 10	69
120.6	Newbury	130	130 05	76
127.0	Midgham		135 11	73
135.8	Southcote Junction		142 55	slack
137.7	Reading	148	146 10	25
142.7	Twyford		152 30	61
149.5	Maidenhead		158 45	68
155.2	Slough	166	163 48	66½
164.6	Southall	175	172 36	63
—			sigs	
168.0	Ealing Broadway		178 32	
171.7	Milepost 2		183 17	
—			sigs	
173.7	Paddington	185	187 59	

Net time: 183½ minutes

7. Churchward's all-line policy

During the first decade of the twentieth century, construction of new locomotives at Swindon, and the reboilering of others which could still be classed as 'nearly new', provides one of the prime paradoxes in British railway history. One might think that Churchward, having established what I termed in Chapter 6 as 'the grand conception', would have concentrated on building none but the standard types, with the one isolated variation of the smaller 2-6-2 tank engine, which proved a very popular unit; but down the year 1908 he was still building inside-cylinder engines with double frames, not just perpetuations of existing designs, but also modified ones which clearly had involved some new Drawing Office work. To the historian this period naturally affords a fascinating study, particularly as it was contemporaneous with the building of *The Great Bear*.

One important double-framed class has so far escaped mention, the heavy freight 2-6-0s of the '2600' Class, the 'Aberdares'. There were eventually 81 of them, and by their longevity and the esteem in which they were held by the running department they certainly deserve to be included in the 'greats', though non-standard as far as Swindon of Churchward's day was concerned. The 'Aberdares' had a strange beginning. The prototype, if it can be called so, was an ungainly outside-framed inside-cylindered 4-6-0 with a large domed boiler built by Dean in 1896. It was intended for working heavy mineral trains through the Severn Tunnel. Three years later it was joined, through Churchward's influence no doubt, by another outside-framed 4-6-0, but with an 'Atbara'-style domeless parallel boiler and an enormously high Belpaire firebox, the forward part of which was projected into the boiler barrel. The boiler mountings, with the copper-capped chimney dwarfed by the size of the polished brass safety valve column, did not add to the generally unpleasing effect, but to crown all was the huge sandbox, sited halfway between the chimney and the safety valve cover, as one journal termed it, 'similar in shape to a small saddle tank'. The ensemble could easily be described as the ugliest engine ever built, and the men and the locomotive 'buffs' were not long in naming it after the national enemy of the hour, 'Kruger'! Although this monstrosity was completed at Swindon at the end of 1899 it was not until a year later that a picture of it, hauling a goods train near Taplow, appeared in *The Locomotive Magazine*.

The 'Aberdares' proper, the '2621' Class, were first built in 1901. They could be described as a 2-6-0 version of the 'Camel' Class, with cylinders of 18 in diameter by 26 in stroke and 4-ft 7-in coupled wheels. All the same it appeared that Swindon had not finished with the 'Krugers', and in 1901 a second engine was built, with the 2-6-0 wheel arrangement but retaining the unprepossessing outline. These engines, eight more of which were built in 1902–3, were always known as the 'Krugers' though the object of national enmity had been removed from the South African scene by then. They were rebuilt to conform to the 'Aberdare' Class in 1905–7. The first of these latter, which was originally given the prototype number 33, was built in 1900, and 60 more, Nos 2621–2680, followed in three batches of 20 each in 1901–2. The final batch, numbered 2611–2620, had taper boilers of the type fitted to the 'City' Class 4-4-0s, and were completed by August

Below left *Prototype of the 'Aberdares', one of the 'Kruger' series of 2-6-0s built in 1902–3.* (Author's collection)

Above *An 'Aberdare', No 2666, in original condition.* (National Railway Museum)

Right *An 'Aberdare', superheated and with standard top-feed, No 2678.* (National Railway Museum)

Below right *One of the earlier 5-ft 8-in 4-4-0s fitted with the Standard No 2 taper boiler, No 3722 (original numbering) on an up Cornish express.* (Loco Publishing Co Ltd)

1903. The prototype engine No 33 was renumbered 2600, and with the rebuilding of the 'Krugers' the class was up to its full strength by 1907. Eventually all 81 engines had Standard No 4 taper boilers and were superheated, but this phase of their history is dealt with in the following chapter. Superheating or not, the 'Aberdares' proved an extremely useful tool of operation, especially in South Wales. While the nimble 0-6-2 tanks of the Taff Vale, Rhymney and Barry railways trundled their loads to the ports for shipment overseas, the Great Western '2600' Class humped vast tonnages of coal up the hillside from Mountain Ash southwards, through the tunnel in the mountainside, crossing the Taff Vale main line at high level at Quakers Yard, and so by devious ways to the GWR main line at Ebbw Junction. From there the coal went to almost every other point of the compass.

The last batch of 'Camel' Class 4-4-0s with the parallel domeless boiler, Nos 3425–3432, came out in May 1903, and their numbers immediately preceded in chronological order those of the 'Cities'. Then there was a pause of four months, and in September a new standard boiler made its appearance. This was the first version of the taper-barrel Standard No 2, and was fitted to the first of a new batch of 'Camels', No 3443 *Birkenhead*. It will be noted that the number followed that of the last of the 'Cities'. The new boiler was not, however, primarily intended for the 'Camels'. Churchward's celebrated diagram of January 1901 showing his six proposed standard classes included only two sizes of boiler; a 15-ft 0-in barrel with a 9-ft 0-in firebox for the ten-wheeled locomotives, and a smaller one with an 11-ft 2-in barrel and an 8-ft 0-in firebox for the 2-6-2 tank, the 4-4-2 tank and the 4-4-0 express

passenger. Both boilers were originally planned with a 5-ft 0-in diameter barrel, so as to permit of maximum interchangeability of details and tooling. However, weight restrictions made it necessary to develop a lighter edition of the proposed boiler with the 8-ft 0-in firebox. This had, in any case, been shortened to 7-ft 0-in for the Standard No 4, but the lighter version, which did not permit of the use of the same flanging plates as the big No 1, became known as the Standard No 2, and was designed primarily for the prototype 2-6-2 tank No 99, which was completed at Swindon in September 1903.

Be that as it may, Churchward had in commission at the time 39 'Atbaras' and 60 'Camels' with the parallel version of the No 2 boiler, and the advantage of having a taper-barrel version interchangeable with the older one was no doubt irresistible. Like the rebuilding of the 'Atbara' Class locomotive *Mauritius* with the prototype No 4 taper boiler, it was another step towards the integration of the main standardization programme with the equipment of the older inside-cylinder locomotives. The firebox of the taper-barrel Standard No 2 was 7 ft 0 in long, 4 ft 0 in wide at the bottom, 5 ft 3 in wide at the upper portion of the throat plate, and 4 ft 9 in wide at the back plate. The grate sloped downwards 1 ft 0 in, and the width of the waterways at the foundation rings was uniformly $3\frac{1}{2}$ in, a dimension that was carried generally through the entire range of Great Western standard boilers. The barrel of the Standard No 2 was 11 ft 0 in long as originally planned, but the rear barrel section tapered over a length of 5 ft 6 in from 5 ft $0\frac{1}{2}$ in at the throat plate to 4 ft $5\frac{1}{8}$ in at the front. Such were the elements of what was sometimes called the 'half-cone' boiler, to distinguish it from the later No 2 in which the tapering extended for three-quarters of the length of the barrel. The Standard No 4 used on the 'Cities' had the same length of firebox as the No 2 but was larger in the barrel.

As compared to the domeless parallel boilers used on the first 'Camels', which had 277 tubes of $1\frac{7}{8}$ in diameter, a tube heating surface of 1,538 sq ft and a grate area of 21.45 sq ft, the 'half-cone' Standard No 2 had 289 tubes of $1\frac{5}{8}$ in diameter, a tube heating surface of 1,396.58 sq ft and a grate area of 20.35 sq ft. As on the No 4 boilers fitted to the 'Cities', the boiler pressure was raised to 195 psi. It was fitted to 30 5-ft 8-in 4-4-0s built between September 1903 and April 1904. The class, which by the latter date mustered 91 locomotives, were still known variously as 'Camels', or sometimes as 'Avalons', and were named as follows:

3443 *Birkenhead*
3444 *Cardiff*
3445 *Ilfracombe*
3446 *Swindon*
3447 *Newport*
3448 *Paddington*
3449 *Reading*
3450 *Swansea*
3451 *Taunton*
3452 *Wolverhampton*
3453 *Dominion of Canada*
3454 *New Zealand*
3455 *Australia*
3456 *Albany*
3457 *Tasmania*
3458 *Natal Colony*
3459 *Toronto*
3460 *Montreal*
3461 *Ottowa*
3462 *Winnipeg*
3463 *Vancouver*
3464 *Jamaica*
3465 *Trinidad*
3466 *Barbados*
3467 *Empire of India*
3469 *Madras*
3470 *Bombay*
3471 *Queensland*
3472 *Columbia*

In 1906 a further batch of 30 5-ft 8-in 4-4-0s was completed at Swindon, having the long, or three-quarter coned boiler, and by that time it was evident that the inspiration for naming was drying up, because the whole batch was originally put into traffic unnamed. Their numbers were 3701 to 3730, and the personal names added later, as under, were mostly those of directors:

3701 *Stanley Baldwin*
3702 *John G. Griffiths*
3703 *James Mason*
3704 *A.H. Mills*
3705 *George A. Wills*
3706 *John W. Wilson*
3707 *Francis Mildmay*
3708 *Sir Arthur Yorke*
3720 *Inchcape*
3724 *Joseph Shaw*

Sir Arthur Yorke was Chief Inspecting Officer of Railways of the Board of Trade. Two others came in for topographical names, 3712 *Aberystwyth* and 3729 *Weston-super-Mare*, to be duly removed later, but the rest of this batch ran nameless throughout their existence.

While the construction of this group of locomotives was in progress, the prototype, No 3312 *Bulldog*, originally classified as a variant of the 'Duke' Class, was rebuilt in March 1906 with a three-quarter coned Standard No 2 boiler, and from that time onwards the domeless-boilered 5-ft 8-in 4-4-0s became known as the 'Bulldog' Class. This was a natural replacement of

Below left *5-ft 8-in 4-4-0 No 3407* Madras *at Old Oak Common in 1931, then assimilated into the 'Bulldog' Class.* (W.J. Reynolds)

Above *One of the 1906 batch of 'Bulldogs' modernized by superheating and top-feed, No 3418* Sir Arthur Yorke *in plain green livery.* (British Railways)

Right *A Dean single, No 3079* Thunderbolt, *rebuilt with an 'Atbara'-type parallel domeless boiler.* (Loco Publishing Co)

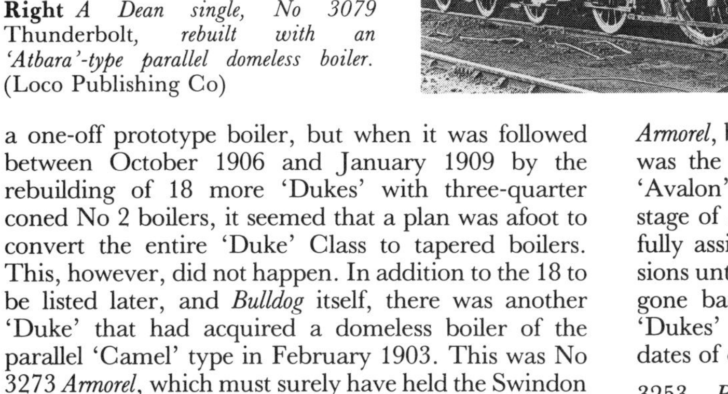

a one-off prototype boiler, but when it was followed between October 1906 and January 1909 by the rebuilding of 18 more 'Dukes' with three-quarter coned No 2 boilers, it seemed that a plan was afoot to convert the entire 'Duke' Class to tapered boilers. This, however, did not happen. In addition to the 18 to be listed later, and *Bulldog* itself, there was another 'Duke' that had acquired a domeless boiler of the parallel 'Camel' type in February 1903. This was No 3273 *Armorel*, which must surely have held the Swindon record for changes, not merely of individual boiler, but of boiler types. Although it is carrying this particular story a little ahead of our period, these changes make diverting reading:

No 3273 *Armorel* (later No 3306)

Date	**Boiler**
November 1896	Built new; domed, flush round-topped
February 1902	Parallel domeless
April 1906	Half-coned Standard No 2
October 1910	Three-quarter coned No 2
June 1912	Half-coned No 2 superheated
September 1914	Three-quarter coned No 2 superheated
June 1933	Standard No 3
January 1939	Scrapped

Armorel, by the acquisition of a domeless boiler in 1902, was the first of the 'Dukes' to join the 'Camel' or 'Avalon' Class, but, passing through the intermediate stage of a half-coned taper boiler from 1906, was not fully assimilated to the rest of the ex-'Duke' conversions until 1910, and by that time two of the others had gone back one step, to half-coned boilers. The 18 'Dukes' that were converted to 'Bulldogs', with their dates of conversion, are set out as follows:

3253	*Pendennis Castle*	February 1908
3262	*Powderham*	October 1906
3263	*Sir Lancelot*	December 1907
3264	*St Anthony*	July 1907
3268	*River Tamar*	June 1907
3269	*Tintagel*	May 1907
3279	*Exmoor*	December 1907
3280	*Falmouth*	January 1909
3282	*Maristowe*	July 1907
3286	*St Just*	September 1908
3316	*Isle of Guernsey*	February 1908
3318	*Jupiter*	February 1908
3322	*Mersey*	November 1907
3324	*Quantock*	December 1908
3325	*St Columb*	December 1908
3327	*Somerset*	May 1908
3330	*Vulcan*	December 1908
3331	*Weymouth*	July 1907

Thus by January 1909, including *Armorel* and *Bulldog* itself, the class was 141 strong, the most numerous of all Great Western passenger engines until the days of the Collett standard classes. There were three types of domeless boilers, and these began to be interchanged among a number of classes besides the 'Bulldogs'. The Dean 7-ft 8-in 4-2-2 singles got some of the parallel type, with the high-raised Belpaire firebox. Some of the 'Dukes' also acquired them, while one of the Armstrongs, No 16 *Brunel*, and five of the Badmintons—*Barrington*, *Alexander Hubbard*, *Monarch*, *Charles Mortimer* and *Samson*—had spells with these boilers before eventually getting the three-quarter coned Standard No 2. There was no significance in these changes. It was just a case of putting the first available No 2 boiler on to an engine in the Works for heavy repair. The change that was significant was that applied to the 'Badmintons'. In 1905–6 it was intended to incorporate them in the 'City' Class, and all except three received Standard No 4 boilers; later, when the time came for superheating, they were fitted with three-quarter coned Standard No 2 boilers. So far as non-superheated engines were concerned, Churchward had reached finality in the No 4 boiler put on to the 'Cities' in 1903, and in the three-quarter coned No 2 used on the 'Bulldogs' from April 1904 onwards. The cylinders, valves and valve gear remained standard throughout the entire range.

An activity that might have seemed no more than incidental, and concerned more with the maintenance of individual engines than anything else, was the amount of frame strengthening that became necessary from 1904 onwards. The reason for it might seem rather obscure. The inner and outer plates on the double-framed engines from the 'Dukes' onward were $\frac{3}{4}$ in thick, and one would imagine that the combined strength of two such plates on each side of the engine would provide a more robust framing than the single $1\frac{1}{8}$ in plates of the new standard engines. But it was desirable to tie each pair of inner and outer plates together as close as possible to the coupled wheel axleboxes, otherwise the $\frac{3}{4}$ in plates would tend to flex under the loads carried in the frames. The axles themselves had generous bearings 8 in long in the outside frame and 7 in in the inside. With the introduction of more powerful double-framed engines, and particularly those with 6-ft 8-in driving wheels, the cross-ties between the inner and outer frames could not be placed near enough to the axleboxes to counteract flexing, which eventually caused frame cracking. So one saw the rather extraordinary expedient of patching on the frames. Naturally the patches were put on the inside, but their presence could be detected by the array of rivets showing on the outer surface of the frames. As the frames got older and more susceptible to cracking, more and more patching was added.

Contemporaneously with his careful development of the No 2 standard boiler, with the change from the original half-coned to the three-quarter cone type for his small engines, there came his memorable paper read to the Institution of Mechanical Engineers in February 1906 on 'Large Locomotive Boilers'. He began thus: 'The modern locomotive problem is principally a question of boiler. The great increase in the size of boilers and in the pressures carried, which has taken place during the past few years, has necessitated the reconsideration of the principles of design which had been worked out and settled during many years' experience with comparatively small boilers carrying low pressures. The higher temperatures incidental to the higher pressures have required the provision of much more liberal water-spaces and better provision for circulation. Locomotive engineers have now apparently settled down to the use of one or two types of boiler for very large engines, the wide firebox extending over the frames and wheels, and the long narrow box sloping up over the axles behind the main drivers. In Great Britain the contracted loading-gauge prohibits the use of the wide fire-box type over wheels larger than 4 feet 6 inches diameter, so that it is not being used so generally as in America, where it has become practically universal.' It was remarkable that within almost a year from his paper to the 'Mechanicals' Churchward had his proposal for a 'super' locomotive accepted by the Board and a sum of £4,400 voted to pay for it.

In my lecturing days when talking about the Great Western I was frequently asked about *The Great Bear*, but never in such intimidating circumstances as when I was asked to talk to the Swindon Engineering Society, and I found F.W. Hawksworth in the front row of the audience. Sure enough at question time came a youthful voice from the back of the hall: 'Please, sir, tell us about *The Great Bear*'. This was it! I noticed that Hawksworth was immediately on the alert. After all, he had made the general arrangement of the engine, and the copy that I possess bears his initials. When I was giving my considered opinion of the reasons for the building of the engine I could see out of the corner of my eye that Hawksworth was at first very attentive, and as I proceeded he was smiling and apparently nodding approval. I had expressed the view that the engine was an exercise in boiler design. Such was the upward surge in traffic resulting from the enterprising new services put into operation in 1906 that Churchward foresaw the time when his four-cylinder 4-6-0s would be extended to their limit, and that still more powerful engines would be required. I had the pleasure of a private talk with Hawksworth after the meeting, and he confirmed generally that the building of *The Great Bear* was a Swindon adventure in larger boiler design.

None of the American wide-firebox boilers to which Churchward paid particular attention in his paper to

Above The Great Bear *as first built, in photographic grey.* (British Railways)

Right The Great Bear *in running colours and with top-feed on the safety valve cover, posed adjacent to the previous No 111, a 2-4-0.* (British Railways)

the 'Mechanicals' had combustion chambers extending forward into the boiler barrel, as became common in later years. But that practice involved some very intricate press-work, and flanging of the firebox front and tube plate, and at that time in the development of high-pressure boilers at Swindon it was enough to effect a firebox with a relatively simple shape. Having decided that point, and at the same time maintaining the same dimensional relations as on the 'Star' for the smokebox tube plates in relation to the cylinders, the length of the boiler barrel was determined by the wheel spacing. On *The Great Bear* the spacing between the centre and the rear pair of driving wheels was made 7 ft as between the leading pair and centre pair. But even with this slight reduction, the boiler barrel came out at 23 ft. By comparison with British 'Pacifics' of much later years this dimension could be criticized as excessive, but it was the subject of very careful consideration in the design stage, and the tube size was increased from 2 in diameter on the 'Stars' to 2½ in. In his paper of 1906 to the Institution of Mechanical Engineers, Churchward said:

> 'The ratio of diameter to length of the tube undoubtedly has a most important bearing upon the steaming qualities of the boiler and upon the efficiency of the heat absorption. This is more particularly noticeable when the boilers are being worked to the limit of their capacity. If 2 in tubes, say, are employed in barrels 11 to 12 feet long, when the boiler is being forced the length is not sufficient to absorb the heat from the amount of gases that a 2-inch tube will pass, and overheating and waste result.'

While the ratio of diameter to length of tube was less on *The Great Bear* than on the 'Stars', the reputation that the engine earned at first for being an indifferent steamer was almost certainly due to the difficulty firemen experienced in feeding a grate that was so unlike those already in use on the Great Western Railway. This has occurred time and again with new locomotive designs, when engineers from the Drawing Office have had to ride the locomotives for weeks on end, fire themselves, and find by hard experience the correct technique to use. One has known firemen almost break their hearts (and their backs!) shovelling for dear life, when a much simpler and less fatiguing method would have produced far better results. This was certainly the case on the first Stanier 'Pacifics' on the LMS, the boiler proportions of which have many points of similarity to those of *The Great Bear*. In later years the engine steamed well. I came to know some of the men who worked regularly on her, and they had nothing but praise for her general working, and beautiful riding.

Like the Gresley 'Pacifics', however, good riding was not obtained from the start. The springing of the trailing truck was subject to some modification. The engine had the characteristic short cab, though at first a

Above The Great Bear *in her full pre-war running glory.* (British Railways)

Left The Great Bear *ready to start from No 1 platform at Paddington with a 'County tank', No 2233, alongside.* (Author's collection)

move to provide more top shelter was made by extending the roof rearwards beyond the side-sheets. It is extraordinary how enginemen of the 'old school' seemed to rebel against any attempt to close them in on the footplate. On 'The Bear', a fireman unused to having a roof above the fall-plate managed to get a fire-iron so jammed between the roof and the floor that three men were needed to dislodge it. Afterwards the roof was cut back somewhat. The tender was something of a curiosity. In capacity it was no larger than the rather small six-wheeled standard type at first attached to the 'Stars', carrying 3,500 gallons of water and 6 tons of coal. It was nevertheless built as an eight-wheeler, to match more appropriately the impressive appearance of the engine. It was adapted, after construction had already begun, and to the end of its days it carried a patch covering the hole where the water scoop would have been on a six-wheeler. The bogies were of standard locomotive type but with a shorter wheelbase.

The water pick-up was in the middle, and a questionable feature was the siting of the manhole for filling in the dome covering the top end of the duct from the water-scoop. This did not last long. One day someone either forgot to fasten the manhole cover, or did not fasten it down securely, and at the first water troughs the strong upward rush of water burst it open, and surged with such force over the back of the tender as to burst open the gangway door of the leading coach, and flood that coach throughout to a depth of some 18 in!

Th engine had its first trial trip on 4 February 1908. As with many large engines of new design there were minor clearance troubles. When 'The Bear' went to Paddington for the first time the leading step, opposite the smokebox, scraped a platform, and was later removed. At the time of its construction the Civil Engineer would not accept the engine on any route except between Paddington and Bristol, because of its axle-loading. But while this would have given adequate scope for the development of the design to perfection, in the haulage of heavy loads at high speed over a level track that could be very trying in adverse weather conditions, it so happened that the engine took the road at the time of the celebrated feud between many senior officers of the GWR, led by Churchward, and the General Manager, Sir James Inglis.

How far development work would ultimateley have been carried out on the engine it is not possible to say. The 1913 modifications had scarcely begun to show their effect when war broke out, and any further experimenting with a prototype locomotive had inevitably to stop. Nevertheless, although there had never seemed to be any occasion for proving the full capacity of the engine, either on a special dynamometer car test, or in regular service, in many ways, both officially and by railway enthusiasts, it continued to be regarded as the 'flagship' of the fleet, and it occupied the principal position in published material and internal documents. In 1919, when the GWR published its shilling booklet containing the names, numbers, types and classes of its locomotives, while all other classes were illustrated by no more than a broadside official photograph. 'The Bear' had in addition a weight diagram, and she was the only engine of the entire stud for which full details of the heating surfaces, boiler and firebox dimensions, and even steam and exhaust port sizes, were quoted.

Over the years several modifications were made to *The Great Bear*. It was in shops from June to December 1913, when the Swindon No 1 superheater was replaced by the No 3 pattern. The superheating surface was reduced from 545 sq ft to 506 sq ft. This was a special form of No 3 superheater with four pairs of elements in each flue. In about 1920 the normal pattern of No 3 superheater, with three pairs of elements per flue, was fitted, making the superheating surface 399 sq ft. Each of the superheater modifications made a slight increase in the free area through the tubes, and thus made some small improvement to the steaming. At this same period a cast iron chimney, four-cone injector and a steel cab roof were fitted. Modifications were also made to the springing, and a number of adjustments were made to the weight distribution. In 1916 the total adhesive weight was given as 61 tons 6 cwt, and Ahrons quoted 61 tons 7 cwt, the distribution between axles being different in the two cases.

In her earlier days 'The Bear' had worked on the Bristol expresses, and a regular turn was the down evening dining car train, non-stop to Bath. After the war, however, still stationed at Old Oak Common, she was in a link of four engines which included the first 5-ft 8-in 2-8-0 No 4700 and two 4-6-0s. This was before the '47XX' Class had grown beyond the pioneer engine, and No 4700 was in some ways an isolated engine, as much as *The Great Bear*. It was during the years 1919 and 1923 that the engine became most familiar to travellers and to the limited number of railway enthusiasts then existing. Although working, as always, on the Paddington-Bristol route it was, however, not used on the fastest and hardest trains. There were, from the autumn of 1921, four expresses running non-stop between Paddington and Bristol in the even two hours. Three of these, the 11.45 am and 5.15 pm up and the 1.15 pm down, were Bristol turns, and were thus worked by 'Saint' Class engines. The remaining turn was the 11.15 am down worked by Old Oak and Laira sheds on alternate days as part of a double home duty between Paddington and Plymouth. *The Great Bear* worked on such unexciting duties as the 10.45 am down, and it was on this train that it became frequently photographed in those years.

After Churchward's retirement at the end of 1921, his successor resumed work on the design of a larger passenger engine, and found that by careful design a worthwhile increase in size could be attained in a 4-6-0 which met the requrements of the Civil Engineer. The introduction of this class, the 'Castle', in 1923 was the occasion for a big publicity campaign, proclaiming the 'Castle' as the most powerful passenger engine in Britain (based on a dubious criterion of tractive effort). *The Great Bear* then ceased to have any publicity value; indeed, it became an embarrassment in the presence of the 'Castles'. In 1924 it required heavy repairs, and it was therefore dismantled, work beginning on 7 January. Parts of the engine were used in the production of a 'Castle' carrying the same number but a different name. Despite the removal of the need of *The Great Bear* for publicity purposes, there is said to have been indignation in some quarters at Paddington when news was received of its decease, and Churchward is known to have been very upset.

Early in 1925 I was at Old Oak Common sheds with a party from the Institution of Mechanical Engineers and in company with a few from Darlington, who had recently been involved in the comparative trials of the Gresley and Raven 'Pacifics' with the North Eastern dynamometer car between Doncaster and King's Cross. The scrapping of *The Great Bear* was very much in their minds, and both they and I were very fortunate in having as a guide for our party an engineer at the time based at Old Oak Common who had been very much involved in the dynamometer car tests of *Caldicot Castle* which had been run about a year earlier. The North Eastern men got this engineer talking about 'Pacifics', and I have never forgotten the quiet enthusiasm with which he said: 'I liked "The Bear", and so did everyone who worked on her'.

One of the greatest unsolved queries concerning Great Western locomotive practice of the period is why Churchward continued the use of double frames on the inside-cylinder 4-4-0 engines, after Dean had definitely retired. It was not just a case of completing orders already in the shops. From midsummer of 1902 he built 125 more 4-4-0s with double frames, continuing until January 1910. The design certainly had some advantages. It made possible a total length of bearing of 15 in on each side of the engine. Then the short length of inside bearing enabled the big-end journal to be made 5 in wide, with massive crank webs 4½ in wide. The cylinders could be spaced farther apart leaving more room for the steam chest and greater space for the exhaust passages from the valves to the blastpipe. On the other hand, it made for heavier construction and higher first cost. The outside-cylinder 'Counties' were exactly the same weight as the 'Cities', although having a nominal tractive effort some 15 per cent greater. Another disadvantage of the double-framed engines was the much higher incidence of broken crank axles. The highest concentration of weight on the axle was outside the wheels, and this accentuated flange blows at the rail. A careful record at Swindon indicated that failure of crank axles, either by complete fracture, or through hairline cracks indicating fatigue flaws, were roughly three times as many on double as on single-framed engines—which merely heightens the mystery as to why Churchward kept building the type for so long.

The picturesquely named 'Flower' series of 6-ft 8$\frac{1}{2}$-in 4-4-0s of 1908 was a case in point. By that time Churchward had 30 of the new outside-cylinder 'Counties' at work, part of the main standardization plan. The 'Flowers' had deeper frames than the 'Atbaras', and consequently were heavier; in fact their adhesion weight was 35 tons 14 cwt, compared to 34 tons 6 cwt on the 'Counties'. The weight on the bogie of the latter engines was heavier. Although the 'Flowers' carried the three-quarter cone Standard No 2 boiler and the usual inside-cylinder arrangement of valves and valve gear, a certain amount of additional design work had obviously been put into these engines. That they were great favourites of Churchward himself was well known. He was an expert horticulturist, and it was generally understood that the names of these 20 came from some of the most cherished flowers in his own garden, thus:

4101	*Auricula*	4111	*Anemone*
4102	*Begonia*	4112	*Carnation*
4103	*Calceolaria*	4113	*Hyacinth*
4104	*Calendula*	4114	*Marguerite*
4105	*Camellia*	4115	*Marigold*
4106	*Campanula*	4116	*Mignonette*
4107	*Cineraria*	4117	*Narcissus*
4108	*Gardenia*	4118	*Polyanthus*
4109	*Lobelia*	4119	*Primrose*
4110	*Petunia*	4120	*Stephanotis*

In South Wales, while 4-6-0 locomotives worked as far as Cardiff, they did not then often go beyond, so when the GWR began to work up the Ocean Mail traffic via Fishguard, tempting the inward-bound Cunard liners to set down passengers and mails by tender and save a day on the journey from New York to London, compared to going via Liverpool and the LNWR, the new 4-4-0s were put on to the job. Truth to tell 4-4-0s were not ideal for the sharp gradients of the main line west of Cardiff, particularly around Swansea and west of Carmarthen, and a good deal of assisting engine mileage was necessary.

There was another important detailed change on the 'Flowers'. Not only were the frames made deeper than on the 'Atbaras', and reinforced at the back, but there was also a change in the bogie. Compounding apart, Churchward had been very impressed with certain details of the de Glehn 'Atlantics' imported from France, and one of these was the bogie. This was adapted with some ingenuity to the outside-framed type used on the inside-cylinder 4-4-0s; instead of the Dean suspension arrangment, brackets were fixed to the main frames, incorporating an inverted hemisphere. These rested in suitably shaped cups with a flat base, beneath which slid brackets, with a flat top, which were fixed to the bogie frame. The side control, by a pair of helical springs, was modified from the Dean arrangement to agree with French practice. This modified bogie arrangement, which could be recognized by the absence of the large caps and nuts beneath the bogie frame, was later applied to all the inside-cylinder 4-4-0s, and to the range of standard outside-cylinder locomotives with the bar-frame type of bogie. William Stanier also took it with him to the LMS.

Another change on the 'Flowers' was a reversion to ordinary screw reversing gear. As locomotives became larger, and the reversing mechanism tended to get heavier, there was a general feeling that something ought to be done to lessen the physical labour needed in actuating the gear, and various forms of steam reverser were introduced, notably by Dugald Drummond and James Stirling. From my own footplate experience I have noted that these were fiddling things to adjust and that it was not always easy to get the exact setting of the

Left *A 'Flower', No 4120* Stephanotis, *decorated in honour of hauling a Royal Train conveying the King of Sweden.* (British Railways)

Above right *One of the 'Bird' series of 'Bulldogs', No 3733* Chaffinch. (British Railways)

reverser that was required. Churchward and the Swindon Drawing Office produced a manually-operated screw reverse that was both easy to adjust and precise in its setting, and this proved another welcome feature in the equipment of the 'Flowers'. Another change was the use of the vacuum brake instead of steam brake on the locomotive, though this did not go to the extent of putting brakes on the bogie wheels, as on the standard 4-6-0 express locomotives. From the start the 'Flowers' had the larger 3,500-gallon tenders with a raised fender instead of the coal rails on the older type.

The last group of double-framed inside-cylinder 4-4-0s came in 1909–10, with a further series of improved 'Bulldogs' having the modified bogie, deeper frames and screw reverse. They came in two distinct batches—Nos 3731–5 in May 1909 and Nos 3736–3745 in November 1909 to January 1910. All were named after birds, and one might imagine that Churchward was supplementing his love of gardening with names of his feathered friends, except that one or two of the titles were hardly of garden visitors:

3731	*Blackbird*	3735	*Flamingo*
3732	*Bullfinch*	3736	*Goldfinch*
3733	*Chaffinch*	3737	*Jackdaw*
3734	*Cormorant*	3738	*Kingfisher*
3739	*Nightingale*	3743	*Seagull*
3740	*Peacock*	3744	*Skylark*
3741	*Pelican*	3745	*Starling*
3742	*Penguin*		

These were among the last of the GWR 4-4-0s to survive, and all of them came into national ownership in 1948. So far as individual names were concerned, it has always intrigued me to note the locomotives of a class that were chosen for painting in photographic grey for the official photograph. There is every suggestion that Churchward himself made the choices. Among the 4-6-0s, for example, there was *Butleigh Court*, the home of one of his closest personal friends, rather than the first of the 'Court' series, while the chosen engines of the 'Flower' and 'Bird' Classes were *Begonia* and *Chaffinch*, probably garden favourites.

8. Finalization of pre-war engine design

The year 1909 was a milestone in the development of Great Western locomotive practice. Until then the railways of Great Britain generally had been some of the most backward in the adoption of superheating. When J.F. Gairns wrote his classic work *Locomotive Compounding and Superheating*, information in his possession showed that in 1906 out of 287 locomotives fitted with the Schmidt superheater only one was British, the GWR two-cylinder 4-6-0 No 2901 *Lady Superior*. It has, however, been claimed equally that the first British adoption of this equipment was on an 0-6-0 goods locomotive of the Lancashire and Yorkshire Railway, by George Hughes. The tardiness of British locomotive engineers in taking up superheating was undoubtedly due to the abundance of good steam coal in this country, and the relatively short runs, which it was thought gave little time for a superheated locomotive really to warm up to its work. Churchward was, of course, ready enough to try any device that gave promise of a reduced coal consumption, though reluctant to adopt in its entirety a proprietary design, and particularly one that had certain strings attached to it, like the Schmidt superheater. In view of the remarkably swift change to superheating that began at Swindon in 1909, the steps leading to the finalization of superheater design at Swindon may be recalled.

There were two things about the Schmidt superheater that Churchward did not like. The degree of superheat attained was in his opinion too high in that heat was thrown away in the exhaust, but from a practical maintenance point of view the design was such that the upper elements could not be removed for inspection or cleaning without withdrawing the lower ones first. So as far as Churchward was concerned the Schmidt superheater was out, regardless of what so many other railways were doing. His interest in American practice then came to the fore, and in May 1907 the last of the new 'Stars' of that year, No 4010 *Western Star*, was built new with the Cole type of superheater. The attraction of this apparatus was that the elements were straight, and any one could be removed without disturbing any of the others, but the actual design of the elements was unacceptable at Swindon, and work began on a design of their own, in which the details were due to Messrs C.C. Champeney and G.H. Burrows. There were three stages in this development; the Swindon No 1 type was tried on No 4011 *Knight of the Garter* in 1908, and the No 2 on No 2922 *Saint Gabriel* later that year. The final version, the No 3, was introduced in 1909. Its first application on a passenger locomotive was on the four-cylinder 4-6-0 No 4021 *King Edward*, the first of that new series and the only one to have a superheater when new. No 4021 was completed in June, but it had been preceded by a 2-8-0, No 2808, in March of that year, with an apparatus of slightly different dimensions. So far as 4-4-0s were concerned, 'Bulldog' No 3728 (afterwards 3438) was the first to have a superheater on the No 2 boiler, in August 1909, and the first on a No 4 boiler was on No 3478 (afterwards 3825) *County of Devon*, in October 1909. The application to the three types of boiler was therefore almost simultaneous.

The increased potential of superheated steam is most clearly shown by comparision of the volumes per pound, namely 2.3 cu ft saturated, against 2.9 cu ft superheated to 550°F, an increase of 26 per cent. It was this fundamental point that led many locomotive engineers to increase the diameter of the cylinders of superheated locomotives in relation to those of similar saturated designs. With the Schmidt superheater, as it came to be used on the London and North Western Railway, with steam temperatures of about 650°F, the volume of a pound of steam was about 3.25 cu ft or 43 per cent greater than that of saturated steam. This led some engineers to reduce boiler pressures, to reduce boiler maintenance charges, as well as to increase cylinder diameters. On the Great Western Churchward did neither; he kept boiler pressure and cylinder diameter the same, and in actual performance on the road there was less apparent difference between the work of saturated and superheater locomotives than on any other British railway.

A down South Wales express near Westbourne Park hauled by No 2902 Lady of the Lake. (Loco Publishing Co)

North Star *at Laira, converted from the 4-4-2 type, with superheater and top-feed but still retaining the original number 40.* (P.J.T Reed)

Referring again to the construction of the Swindon No 3 superheater, the header itself consisted of two distinct chambers, one for saturated and one for superheated steam, and a number of passages at the back of the header connected those two chambers, thus to establish communication with the steam tubes, causing circulation of saturated steam through the superheater. At opposite ends of the header there were connections to the boiler and to the cylinders, so that steam passed from the regulator into the header, through the superheater tubes, and thence to the cylinders. Covering the portion of the superheater that projected into the smokebox was a casing provided with a damper for regulating the proportion of the furnace gases that passed through the superheater flues and the ordinary tubes respectively. This damper was closed normally, but was opened by a small cylinder fixed on the outside of the smokebox, which was in turn supplied with steam only when the regulator was opened, and when steam was therefore passing through the superheater tubes.

Associated with the development of superheating was the introduction of piston valves. Churchward began experimenting with these at an early date, and again he was much attracted to contemporary American designs. It was the semi-plug valve among these that was eventually chosen for standardization, of 10 in diameter for the standard two-cylinder classes with 18 in cylinders, as on the 'Counties'. In this design the rings were pressed outwards to the liners by steam pressure, and locked in position there by the wedge rings, so that they automatically adjusted themselves to the bore and floated in it with very little friction. It was a good production job for the Works, and required little in the way of hand fitting. Nevertheless they were an assembly rather than a fitting job, consisting of a lot of bits and pieces—rather complicated—and decidedly heavier than the simple plug type of piston valve with a series of narrow Ramsbottom rings, which in later years was found so effective by Stanier on the London, Midland and Scottish Railway. The British patent rights of the American semi-plug valve were, however, acquired by the GWR and it became a Swindon standard from 1910. In due course an 8-in diameter version was produced for the smaller locomotives and this was standardized from 1914 onwards on 'Cities', 'Flowers', 'Bulldogs' and so on.

In 1909 there appeared the third series of 'Stars', named after Kings of England. The first of the batch, No 4021 *King Edward*, has already been mentioned as the first engine to be fitted with the Swindon No 3 superheater. The remaining engines of the batch had saturated boilers with, as commonly happened in this period, slight variations in dimensions. Even these nine boilers were not identical. There was a small but significant change in the shape of the casing over the inside cylinder, the sides of which were given concave curvature. The effect was to make the casing less obtrusive, and to blend it more into the generally tapered front of the engine. This feature continued through the remainder of the 'Stars' and was also seen in the earlier 'Castles'. The names of this series were as follows:

4021	*King Edward*	4026	*King Henry*
4022	*King William*	4027	*King Richard*
4023	*King George*	4028	*King John*
4024	*King James*	4029	*King Stephen*
4025	*King Charles*	4030	*King Harold*

Whilst this batch was appearing, *The Engineer* published a series of articles on 'British Locomotive Practice of Today'. The articles invoked a long correspondence, including some letters from one correspondent which were highly critical of the GWR. It was pointed out that numerous types of ten-wheeled passenger engines had been built, which, to the writer, seemed to have made no difference to the 'revenue earning capacity of the locomotive'. The writer quoted from the half-yearly returns which railways made to the Board of Trade. These showed that on the GWR the expenditure on locomotive renewals and repairs for the half-year ending in December 1908 was £175 per locomotive, which was quite the highest of any railway. For the Lancashire and Yorkshire the figure was £100, and other railways ranged up to £157, which applied to the Great Eastern and to the North Eastern. The total figure of locomotive expenditure for the GWR had increased half-year by half-year. The appearance of one particularly critical letter in a reputable technical journal could not escape the notice of the Directors of the GWR, and Churchward was asked to explain how it was that the London and North Western could build three 4-6-0 locomotives for the cost of two of his. Churchward's reply, even though it had become slightly apocryphal in the telling, remains one of the classics, or chestnuts, of Great Western lore. It has been related many times before. 'Because one of mine,' he said, 'could pull two of their bloody things backwards.'

The outcome was the celebrated locomotive ex-

Above left *The locomotive exchange of 1910: No 4005* Polar Star *working the 10 am Anglo-Scottish express from Euston to Crewe at Bushey.* (Author's collection)

Left No 4033 Queen Victoria *with the Royal Train southbound from Shrewsbury.* (Author's collection)

Below *Engine No 4038* Queen Berengaria *at Laira shed.* (P.J.T. Reed)

change between a non-superheated 'Star' and an LNWR 'Experiment' Class 4-6-0. On the North Western working between Euston and Crewe, apart from the quietness of the exhaust beat, it cannot be said that the running of the Great Western engine made much impression with the footplate men. Her driver was evidently set on a practice of 'coal-dodging' rather than to run the trains to time. Even so for many years there was a good story at Old Oak Common that if one wanted to cause a monumental fracas in one of the pubs at Camden Town you had only to walk up to the counter and ask for 'a pint of Polar Star'! In 1910 Churchward's vindication lay not in any triumphal time-gaining performances such as those indulged in by *Caldicot Castle* and her crew 15 years later, to the discomfiture of the LNER, but in the obvious discrediting of the LNWR 4-6-0 *Worcestershire*. The odds were against her before she had turned a wheel out of Paddington. She was deficient in tractive effort, but she might have been able to slog along in the characteristic North Western style if her crew had been assured of plenty of water. On the West of England main line, however, the water troughs were few and far between, as compared with those between Euston and Crewe, and on the Great Western stops had to be made for water. The losses in time incurred by the North Western engine were all that Churchward needed to convince his Board that his engines were vastly superior, and production of the 'Star' Class continued.

The next series, named after Queens, followed indeed, no more than weeks after the conclusion of the interchange trials, and they were all fitted with the No 3 superheater. A year later one of this series, No 4039 *Queen Matilda*, was subjected to a full-dress dynamometer car trial on the 11 am two-hour express from Paddington to Bristol. I had the privilege of studying the roll taken on that run, and it seems that the Drawing Office people were intent on studying the effect of short cut-off working rather than power output because from Hanwell onwards, with a 13-coach train of 400 tons gross behind the tender, they varied the cut-off between 11 and 24 per cent, all the time with a fully opened regulator, and only when they had passed Didcot 5 minutes late did this adjustment cease. After a moderate signal check at Swindon they passed Chippenham 6 minutes late and the Bath slip portion was detached and that station passed in 111 min 55 sec from Paddington, still 5 minutes late. Bristol was reached in 124¼ minutes, two slight signal checks accounting for 2 minutes. It was evident that the testing staff from the Drawing Office were more concerned with examining the engine working than strict timekeeping on that occasion.

The introduction of superheating, and the removal of the natural lubricating qualities of saturated steam, made it necessary to give special attention to cylinder lubrication, even though the conditions were less severe with the low degree of superheat used in Great Western engines compared to the far higher steam temperatures coming into use elsewhere. While his contemporaries were using various forms of mechanical lubricator, Churchward, characteristically, set out to perfect a design of his own that embodied a lubricator of a sight feed type, in which the driver could see the drops of oil passing through.

The up 'Torquay Diner' on the Teignmouth sea wall, hauled by No 4060 Princess Eugenie. (M.W. Earley)

It was a beautifully contrived apparatus, the working of which could be observed when riding on the footplate. The principle was hydrostatic, and it was controlled from the regulator handle. It had actually been introduced before superheating, but it was readily adaptable, and supplied atomized oil into the steam pipes between the superheater header and the steam chest. Steam was fed from the steam fountain to the combining valve into which the oil entered from the lubricator. On the opening of the regulator, a quadrant was raised by a projecting pin which lifted the combining valve and allowed the steam to pick up the supply of oil, atomize it and deliver it to the steam pipes. But the arrangement also included a device which ensured that a small amount of steam with oil was fed into the cylinders when running with the regulator closed.

This system of cylinder lubrication was a highly cherished feature of Great Western locomotives, so much so that in later years, when higher degrees of superheat were introduced, and with them mechanical lubricators, the top-link express enginemen always averred that the later engines were not so free-running as those which had the hydrostatic sight feed lubricators.

After having built 40 engines of the four-cylinder 4-6-0 type, Churchward reverted late in 1911 to the two-cylinder type for new construction, and they were the first of the 'Saint' Class to be built new with the standard Swindon superheater, and with the cylinder diameter increased to 18½ in. These engines included a new noticeable external feature in the top-feed clack valves fitted on each side of the safety valve bonnet. This was the result of another long and painstaking development at Swindon, under Churchward's direction.

That it was under consideration as early as 1906 was evident from the discussion on Churchward's paper to the Institution of Mechanical Engineers on 'Large Locomotive Boilers', when one speaker had suggested that the disadvantages of introducing a cold water feed into the boiler could be mitigated by feeding the water into the steam space, well above the water line. It was a simpler way of doing it than using one of the proprietary forms of feed water heater, which would, of course, involve patent rights. Churchward assured the speaker that they were working on it, and intended to continue to do so until they had some positive results. At the time, boiler feed arrangement on the GWR varied. Some of the older engines, notably the Dean 7-ft 8-in single-wheelers, had an ornamental clack valve on the side of the boiler, while on Churchward's own earlier engines the feed was delivered at the bottom of the barrel, just behind the smokebox.

Although it was intended that the clack valves should be somewhere on the top of the boiler it was thought to be insufficient to dump the feed directly into the boiler. As with the lubricating oil feed to the cylinder, it was thought that some degree of atomizing was desirable, and the idea formed of allowing the feed water entering through the clack to pour downwards through a series of trays, through which it cascaded, getting hotter all the time, finally falling into the water in the form of a fine spray. The experiments to determine the shape and inclination of the trays were carried out on a 'hook-up' built in the open Works yard at Swindon, on which a metered supply of water was fed over a series of trays. Early in 1911 the proportions of the device had been finalized, and the arrangement began to be fitted as standard to all Churchward's locomotives.

With 40 four-cylinder 4-6-0s in service by the end of 1910, together with an equal number of two-cylinder 'Saints', the opinion of the running inspectors was setting definitely in favour of the 'Stars'. The general view of that important body of men, to whose views Churchward always paid the closest attention, was that in the heaviest express work the 'Stars' were 'one coach better' than the 'Saints'. Whether the majority of the top-link enginemen would have agreed with this is certainly open to question. At that time the 'Stars' had their original cylinder diameter of 14¼ in. It had not been increased on the 'Queen' series which were superheated from the outset, and as the earlier batches were fitted with superheaters no change was made. The nominal tractive effort of the 'Saints' and of the first 40 'Stars' was practically equal at 24,395 lbs and 25,100 lbs. Churchward, despite the views of the running inspectors and equally of his men in the Drawing Office, always kept his ears to the ground for the opinions of the footplate men, and after building the 'Queens' the very next set of top-line express passenger engines were of the 'Saint' Class, with all the latest improvements, including the top-feed apparatus.

The new engines were named after stately homes in the West Country, the first being No 2931 *Arlington Court*. One can, however, sense that the inspiration for the names of this particular series arose from Churchward's friendship with Neville Grenfell. Although an engineer to his fingertips, Churchward was very fond of country sports and was often a guest at Grenfell's home, Butleigh Court, not far from the 'cut-off' line from Castle Cary to Cogload, at Keinton Mandeville. It is perhaps significant that the official photograph of the 'Court' series of engines, in 'photographic grey', was not that of the pioneer, but of No 2934 *Butleigh Court*!

The new engines, of which there were 25 in all, were built in three batches, the first ten being completed at the end of 1911, and the second in the summer of 1912. The names and numbers of these 20 engines were:

2931	*Arlington Court*	2941	*Easton Court*
2932	*Ashton Court*	2942	*Fawley Court*
2933	*Bibury Court*	2943	*Hampton Court*
2934	*Butleigh Court*	2944	*Highnam Court*
2935	*Caynham Court*	2945	*Hillington Court*
2936	*Cefntilla Court*	2946	*Langford Court*
2937	*Clevedon Court*	2947	*Madresfield Court*
2938	*Corsham Court*	2948	*Stackpole Court*
2939	*Croome Court*	2949	*Stanford Court*
2940	*Dorney Court*	2950	*Taplow Court*

While the above included names that are well known in the West Country, perhaps the best-known of all, that used on engine No 2943, did not refer to the well-known and famous royal residence at all, but to the relatively obscure Hampton Court, the very beautiful seat of the Arkwright family near Leominster, Herefordshire. It is interesting that several of the names came from great family homes in the Welsh Border Country, such as *Caynham Court* near Ludlow, and *Madresfield Court* near Malvern. But as with the 'Castle' Class engines in more recent times, no attempt seems to have been made to link the actual duties of the engines with their names, and as will be told later, *Hampton Court* came to distinguish itself greatly in a run on the 'Cornish Riviera Express'.

I have seen it suggested that the final order for 'Court' Class engines, to be built in 1913, was for ten, but that the last five were cancelled and replaced by five

Above *No 2941* Easton Court *at Laira sheds.* (P.J.T. Reed)

Right No 2937 Clevedon Court *leaving Penzance with the 6 pm Postal Special in 1924.* (O.S. Nock)

new 'Stars'. Be that as it may, the erecting shop at Swindon was switched without intermission from one type to the other, and No 4041 followed 2955 immediately. The last five 'Courts' were: 2951 *Tawstock Court*; 2952 *Twineham Court*; 2953 *Titley Court*; 2954 *Tockenham Court*; and 2955 *Tortworth Court*. Engine No 2955 was evidently considered to be a unit of such significance as to be finished in photographic grey and posed for an official portrait, and it was this engine that represented the 'Saint' Class in the first of the list of Great Western locomotives issued officially from Paddington, in 1919. In the 4th edition of the enlarged publication, issued in 1946, the class was represented by No 2929 *Saint Helena*, which had been modernized at the front end with outside steam pipes.

Reverting to 1912, however, that year was significant in that it saw the conversion of the Churchward 'Atlantic' engines to the 4-6-0 type. Engine No 171, which was built as a 4-6-0 and temporarily altered, had been changed back again in 1907; all the rest were converted at various times during 1912, the last to be treated being No 180 *Coeur de Lion*. At the beginning of 1913, the engines built prior to 1906 were renumbered, bringing them uniformly into the 'Saint' or '2900' series. Engines Nos 171-190 became 2971 to 2990, while the two pioneers Nos 100 and 98 became 2900 and 2998. Unlike some renumbering schemes on other railways which one can only recall with a sense of frustration, the new Great Western numbers were allocated in such a way that the originals could easily be identified.

By the summer of 1913, the two-cylinder series of 4-6-0s had thus been brought into a uniform group, and all were eventually superheated. The numbering ran thus: 2900, originally No 100; 2901-10, 'Ladies'; 2911-30, 'Saints'; 2931-55, 'Courts'; 2971, originally No 171 *Albion*; 2972-90, 'Scotts' etc; and 2998, originally No 98. After the rebuildings of 1912 the only 'Atlantics' remaining on the GWR were the three French compounds Nos 102, 103 and 104, which were not renumbered. The 'Saint' or '29XX' Class, as finally constituted, thus consisted of 77 engines. They were all uniform in their equipment, except that those built prior to 1907 had lever, instead of screw, reversing gear; but more importantly, No 2900 retained the original piston valves and valve gear with which it was equipped when first built in 1902, though the valves were subsequently enlarged to $7\frac{1}{2}$ in from the original

Above *The first 'Star' to have 15-in cylinders, No 4041* Prince of Wales. (British Railways)

Right *The last Star to remain in regular service, No 4056* Princess Margaret *at Old Oak Common in the 1920s.* (W.J. Reynolds)

6½ in. Valve setting with the piston valves of 10 in diameter was always treated as a matter of prime importance at Swindon.

After completing engine No 2955 *Tortworth Court*, the erecting shop was switched immediately on to more 'Stars', but with a difference in that engine No 4041 had 15 in cylinders, bringing the nominal tractive effort up to 27,800 lbs. It was sometimes said of Swindon that the attitude towards locomotive practice was inclined to be rather parochial, indeed a self-satisfied feeling that their products were of a quality to exceed those of all others. Certainly the results of the 1910 locomotive exchange gave them that impression, whatever might be thought about it on the other side. But what Churchward might have thought about it privately was another matter; despite his homely remarks about Crewe locomotives across the Board Table at Paddington, Churchward himself was intensely aware of what was going on in the locomotive world in general, and he would have studied the dynamometer car records from Bowen Cooke's superheater 4-4-0 engines carefully. Then, when at the beginning of 1913 Crewe produced a large superheater four-cylinder 4-6-0 with a tractive effort equal to that of the 'Saints' and almost equal to that of the first 40 'Stars', it seemed that the time had come to take notice.

It is impossible to say now whether the production of the LNWR 'Claughton' Class had any influence on Churchward, but the sudden switch in 1913 from the avowed intention to build ten more of the 'Court' series, and then to stop half-way and begin building 'Stars' with larger cylinders, certainly causes one to think. Of course, to use larger cylinders was a logical development after the successful introduction of superheating; but in succeeding years, when there were many more 'Stars' with 15-in cylinders, it was interesting that at the running shed that became famed for some of the most brilliant express running, not only on the Great Western but in the whole of Great Britain, Stafford Road, Wolverhampton, many of the top-link drivers preferred the smaller-cylindered 'Stars'. Referring back to the Crewe four-cylinder 4-6-0s, I have wondered what Churchward privately thought of the trial runs of engine No 1159 *Ralph Brocklebank* made in November 1913, full details of which were released to *The Engineer* in February 1914. Certain it was that the records of horsepower handsomely surpassed anything that had been registered in the Swindon dynamometer car, at that time. I add this last proviso because in my own experience the mightiest efforts of the 'Stars', and the 'Saints', came in the 1920s. For the pre-war record, Churchward built another 15 'Stars' with 15-in cylinders, the 'Princess' series in 1914.

9. The Great Western locomotive status *in toto*

In the previous chapter, while describing the ultimate pre-war developments of the Churchward 4-6-0s, I must admit to taking more than one look over my shoulder to keep in touch with what was happening on the rest of the line. I remember vividly one day, about 1913, when I had been thrilled beyond measure to see a brand new 'Prince' Class 4-6-0 sweep through Reading station on a down West of England express and then, almost immediately afterwards, an up express drew in and stopped hauled by a Dean 4-2-2 single No 3006 *Courier*. I have noted from past records that at the beginning of 1912 there were still 44 engines of that famous series running, though 19 of them were to be scrapped in the ensuing year. Even so, it was not until December 1915 that the last two of them were withdrawn. It was interesting that these two represented both stages of boiler renewal applied to the original engines of Dean design. No 3050 *Royal Sovereign* was the last of the class to be fitted with one of the 'Camel' domeless boilers and high-raised Belpaire firebox, while No 3074 *Princess Helena* received a domed boiler and Belpaire firebox in 1913. When the new 'Princess' series of 'Stars' was built in 1914, engine No 3074 gave her name to the 4-6-0 No 4051, and for the last year of her life ran nameless.

It might have seemed from 1900 onwards that there was an intention to fit the entire class with 'Camel'-type domeless boilers, in that 15 were so treated between 1900 and 1904. Then the scheme appeared to lapse, and only one isolated engine, No 3050, was rebuilt as late as 1909. When in 1910 the introduction of new domed boilers with Belpaire fireboxes began, eight of them which had previously received 'Camel'-type boilers were rebuilt a second time, while a further 15 which had not previously been altered received the new Belpaire domed boiler. These officially had the great domes painted green while the driving wheel splashers, the valances and the underframes were naturally shorn of the crimson lake in which they were decked in the days when they made such great running with the Ocean Mails of 1904. But judging from certain contemporary photographs, some sheds cleaned the green paint off those domes and polished them up as brightly as in days of yore. There is no doubt that there was an 'official' affection for those locomotives, because when the Great Western Railway Magazine in 1919 published the first list of engine names, numbers, types and classes, for one shilling (!), among the beautifully produced illustrations, with details of weights, dimensions and so on, was one of a 7-ft 8-in single, even the last of which had been scrapped three years previously. The engine illustrated was No 3027 *Worcester*, which had been withdrawn in 1914. I remember seeing one of the survivors of 1915, No 3050 *Royal Sovereign*, when I was at Paddington with my father, but I have not the exact date now.

A single with a 'Camel'-type boiler, No 3016 Lightning *on a non-stop Worcester express near Hayes.* (Loco Publishing Co)

The last of the singles to be fitted with a 'Camel'-type boiler, No 3050 Royal Sovereign. (Author's collection)

It is difficult to imagine nowadays that even after the time that such engines as the four-cylinder 'Kings' and 'Queens' were on the road there were still some crack Great Western expresses worked by 4-2-2 singles. One such train was the 8.5 am from Worcester to Paddington, and I have tabulated two runs clocked by Mr Goodyear made by engines with most appropriate names—*Racer* and *Thunderbolt*. Both of these engines were at the time rebuilt with 'Atbara'-type boilers. This train, like the 1.40 pm and the 4.45 pm down, was worked by Stafford Road men running through from Wolverhampton to Paddington via Worcester. The two stages of the journeys detailed in the table below are disproportionately timed—64 minutes from

GWR: 8.55 am Worcester–Paddington

Run No		1		2	
Engine No		3018*		3079*	
Engine name		*Racer*		*Thunderbolt*	
Load (tons, E/F)		182/190		199/210	
Distance (miles)		**Actual (min sec)**	**Speed (mph)**	**Actual (min sec)**	**Speed (mph)**
0.0	WORCESTER	0 00	—	0 00	—
3.8	Norton Junction	5 15		5 36	—
5.7	Stoulton	7 55	58	8 19	67
7.9	Pershore	9 54	69	10 18	70
10.7	Fladbury	12 15	68½	12 40	66½
13.8	EVESHAM	15 20	—	15 27	67
—		sig stop	—	—	—
16.1	Littleton	20 58	44	17 38	64
18.7	Honeybourne	23 57	50½	20 10	58
20.6	Campden	31 19	33	27 18	33
25.6	Blockley	33 49	57	29 39	60
28.7	MORETON-IN-MARSH	37 35	51½	33 04	—
35.8	KINGHAM	44 17	66½	39 25	—
38.8	Shipton	46 57	67	41 55	73½
43.8	Charlbury	51 16	70½	46 08	70½
50.0	Handborough	56 32	74	51 16	73
53.2	Yarnton	59 15	66½	53 56	72
—		—	—	sigs	—
57.0	OXFORD	63 52	—	58 58	—
0.0		0 00	—	0 00	—
5.1	Radley	7 30	56	7 26	61
7.3	Culham	9 49	59	9 36	66½
10.6	Didcot East Junction	13 09	52	12 46	50
14.9	Cholsey	17 54	60	17 15	65
18.6	Goring	21 40	62	20 30	69
21.8	Pangbourne	24 50	63	23 18	68½
27.4	READING	29 48	67½	28 12	55
—		—	—	sig stop	
32.4	Twyford	34 15	70½	38 15	—
—		—	—	sigs	—
44.9	SLOUGH	45 05	68	54 26	60
—		sigs	—	—	64
54.3	Southall	53 39	—	63 36	63
62.1	Westbourne Park	62 38	—	71 10	—
63.4	PADDINGTON	65 36	—	73 32	—
	Net times (min)	59¼ + 65		58½ + 63½	

* Engines rebuilt with domeless boiler and Belpaire firebox

Worcester to Oxford and 70 minutes from Oxford to Paddington. The average speeds involved, of 53.5 and 54.3 mph, are nearly equal: but Oxford stands higher above ordnance datum than Worcester, and up expresses have to climb the Honeybourne bank, with its 4½ miles of continuous 1 in 100. To Honeybourne the tendency is rising, though with moderate favourable and adverse gradients intermediately.

On the first of the two runs tabulated, *Racer* got away well, with speeds round 70 mph on the level between Pershore and Fladbury; but the signal stop at Evesham, though no more than momentary, gave an added interest to the run, since the engine had attained no more than 53 mph before tackling the Honeybourne bank. I should add that there is nearly a mile of 1 in 126 before Honeybourne station in addition to the bank itself. The 4-2-2 engine did very well. At Honeybourne speed was 50½ mph and it fell rapidly at first to 40 mph half-way up the bank; then the fall was more gradual, and after the last 1½ miles through Campden tunnel the speed was practically sustained at 33 to 33½ mph. With some good speed to Yarnton, the effect of the Evesham stop was wiped out, and Oxford was reached on time.

Thunderbolt had a clear road until the immediate approach to Oxford, where there was a slight signal check. The start out of Worcester was not so fast as that of *Racer*, but with a clear run through Evesham at 67 mph she drew ahead to the extent of 4 minutes on passing Campden, and with an average of 72 mph for the 14 miles down the Evenlode valley, Oxford was reached just over 5 minutes early, despite the signal check. Both engines ran well between Oxford and Paddington, reaching speeds of 69 to 70 mph on level road with their trains of some 200 tons weight. It was unfortunate that *Thunderbolt* should have been so severely checked between Reading and Maidenhead, but in recovering from this the driver made what was almost an 'Ocean Mail' approach to Paddington, with his time of 2 min 22 sec in from Westbourne Park.

Racer, again clocked by Mr Goodyear, made an excellent run on the sharply timed 4.45 pm from Paddington, non-stop to Worcester, and carrying a two-coach slip portion to be detached at Moreton-in-Marsh. It is interesting to find from contemporary notes that in the days of single-wheelers no use ever seemed to be made of the racing descent from the Cotswold escarpment to the Severn valley, where one of the 'Castles' reached 100 mph just before the Second World War. The finest part of this run was the average of over 60 mph up the gradual ascent of the Evenlode valley, which took the train through Moreton-in-Marsh in just over 95 minutes from Paddington; this permitted a mere dawdle down the Honeybourne bank, and even suffering a signal stop, an arrival in Worcester 2½ minutes early. *Racer* was scrapped in 1913 and *Thunderbolt* in 1911.

GWR: 4.45 pm Paddington–Worcester
Load (tons E/F) to Moreton, 184/195; to Worcester, 132/140
Engine 4-4-2 No 3018 *Racer*

Distance (miles)		Actual (m s)	Average speed (mph)
0.0	Paddington	0 00	—
5.7	Ealing	8 40	39.5
9.1	Southall	12 16	57.0
18.5	Slough	21 15	63.0
24.2	Maidenhead	26 54	60.0
31.0	Twyford	33 34	61.1
36.0	Reading	38 25	61.9
—		sigs	
44.8	Goring	48 16	54.5
48.5	Cholsey	51 57	60.8
52.8	Didcot East Junction	56 24	57.3
56.1	Culham	59 44	59.2
63.4	Oxford	67 00	60.3
76.6	Charlbury	80 21	59.8
84.6	Kingham	88 10	61.2
91.7	Moreton-in-Marsh	95 07	61.4
101.7	Honeybourne	105 10	59.8
		sig stop	—
106.6	Evesham	112 40	—
112.5	Pershore	119 08	55.6
120.4	Worcester	127 25	—
	Net time	123½ minutes	

A Birmingham district suburban train leaving Acocks Green hauled by 2-4-2 tank engine No 3608. (O.S. Nock)

Another pre-standard locomotive class for which I have a certain affection were the '3600' series 2-4-2 tanks. They dated from the Dean-Churchward transition period, and the prototype was built in 1900. They had originally the 'Camel' type non-taper domeless boiler, but when I knew them they had been superheated and had Standard No 2 taper boilers. The cylinders were 17 in by 24 in and the coupled wheels of 5-ft 2-in diameter. My own associations with them were twofold. When I was still a schoolboy, and visiting some relations in Birmingham in 1921, not having seen any Great Western trains since my parents left Reading five years earlier, I went out to Acock's Green one Saturday afternoon taking my newly acquired folding Brownie camera with me. I had not yet got the knack of treating fast-moving trains with that apparatus, and the expresses I shot were not much good; but in between times a down suburban train hauled by a '36' Class 2-4-2 tank stopped at the station and the photograph I took of it starting away was reproduced in *The Railway Magazine* in February 1923. As will be understood, engine No 3608 and my first appearance in the technical press were cherished memories. The only other personal contact with engines of that class, which were mostly in the Birmingham district, came about ten years later in my commuting days at Ealing Broadway. My regular morning train, as noticed in an earlier chapter in this book, was the through service to the Metropolitan line which used to change from steam to electric traction at Bishops Road. My run behind No 3601 came otherwise.

Although with generous photographic permits and a relation then resident in Reading I was 'out and about' on the Great Western a good deal in the later 1920s, I cannot recall having seen a '36' anywhere until this particular one arrived to take me up to Paddington. The usual engines were the '22' Class 4-4-2 tanks. The stranger, however, did me proud, with a not inconsiderable load for an engine of such modest dimensions. At that time, with superheating, the boiler pressure was 195 psi. The log of the journey is given in the accompanying table.

GWR: Ealing Broadway–Paddington

Engine 2-4-2 tank No 3601
Load 216 tons tare, 225 tons full

Distance (Miles)		Time (min sec)	Speed (mph)
0.0	Ealing	0 00	—
0.5	Post $5\frac{1}{4}$	1 30	—
1.0	Post $4\frac{3}{4}$	2 20	36.0
1.5	Acton ($4\frac{1}{4}$)	3 02	42.9
2.0	Post $3\frac{3}{4}$	3 40	48.7
2.5	Post $3\frac{1}{4}$	4 15	51.6
3.0	Post $2\frac{3}{4}$	4 48	54.0
4.5	Westbourne Park	6 35	—
5.75	Paddington	9 10	—

These outer-suburban and longer-distance residential trains in the London area were mostly hauled by the so-called 'County tanks', the 6-ft $8\frac{1}{2}$-in 4-4-2s of the '2221' Class. They were high-stepping fast engines as I knew from my prep-school days, because one of them used to haul the train that took me from Mortimer into Reading each morning. It originated at Basingstoke, and after calling at the intermediate stations on the 'Hants' section of the Berks and Hants line ran fast up to Paddington. In 1912 the stud of 'County tanks' was increased by a further batch of ten, their numbers running from 2241 to 2250. These were built with all the latest Churchward improvements, medium-degree superheat, top-feed, and the No 2 standard taper boiler. This brought the stock of these handsome engines up to 30, and like all Churchward's standard types in pre-war days they were finished and beautifully maintained in the full passenger livery. In later years, although I photographed them on various occasions, I never seemed to get a run behind one of them.

I now come to one of the most useful engines the Great Western ever had. My good friend the late Harry Holcroft, when he was at Swindon in the Locomotive Drawing Office, was told that Churchward did not wish to perpetuate the double-framed

Left *A 'County tank', 4-4-2 No 2227, in 1914.* (W.J. Reynolds)

Right *A standard 'Mogul', No 4331, in photographic grey showing the full passenger engine livery.* (British Railways)

One of the first batch of the '4300' Class 'Moguls', No 4302, with short cab and frames. (British Railways)

eight-wheeled tender engines for secondary work, but to replace them with inside-framed inside-cylinder engines, with 10-in diameter long-travel valves on top of the cylinders. The proposal was not working out at all well, and Churchward, as was his wont, came into the Drawing Office to have the difficulties explained to him personally. He went away without much comment. About two years previously Holcroft had been one of a party of young engineers visiting Canada and the USA to study current practice, and on his return to Swindon he was asked to furnish a report. He made emphasis as to the use of the 2-6-0 freight engine with coupled wheels of about 5-ft diameter as a general-purpose locomotive on secondary services and country branch lines. Whether Churchward had read this report, or had the substance of it told to him by the Chief Draughtsman, cannot now be said, but a few days later when he again came to Holcroft's drawing board he said: 'Very well then; get me out a 2-6-0 with 5-ft 8-in wheels, outside cylinders, and No 4 boiler and bring in all the standard details you can'. And, so far as Churchward was concerned, that was that!

The resulting engine, the celebrated '43' class, was to all intents and purposes a tank-engine version of the well established '31' Class 2-6-2 tank, with the same leading dimensions. To reduce the length over buffers, the 'Saint' Class cab was used, which was the shortest, to secure the maximum of availability on lines where short turntables might limit the use; but after the first 20 had gone into service, the running department found that the layout of the injector gear was somewhat cramped. They would rather lose a little availability to have the trailing end lengthened and have more room for injectors. After the first 20 the cab was lengthened 9 in at the footplate by using the 'County' Class cab instead of that of the 'Saints'. While the very first of the 'Moguls', No 4301, had its portrait taken in all the finery of the passenger livery, Churchward also sent a portrait of the modified version, represented by No 4331, to *The Locomotive* magazine, and the reproduction in January 1914, compared to that of No 4301, clearly shows the difference.

Before the later and final version of the '43' class was on the road, the first stages of what had been called an 'epidemic' of 'Mogul' building had started on British railways. The first example was on the Great Northern, in 1912, when Gresley built the first of his '1600' Class, with outside cylinders and Walschaerts valve gear. Then came L. Billinton's 'K' fast goods class in 1914, while two Scottish lines, the Caledonian and the Glasgow and South Western, both introduced inside-cylinder 2-6-0s for the same class of work. The last-mentioned designed by Peter Drummond was about the most generally useful large engine the G & SWR had in its later years. On the Great Western itself, the '43' Class were universally acclaimed, and construction of many more batches continued throughout the war years. In keeping with the austerity trends of the times, the ornate livery of all Great Western locomotives, passenger and goods alike, was changed

A standard 'Mogul', No 4375, in plain green, though with polished chimney cap. (W.J. Reynolds)

to a plain green, devoid of any lining and with the brass and copper work covered by the same plain green. In its issue of July 1918, *The Railway Magazine* signalized this era in Great Western locomotive history by publishing a fine 'F. Moore' colour plate of No 4331. By that time, however, the running numbers of these engines had extended almost to the 200 mark.

Before then a batch of them, Nos 5319–26 and 5328–30, was engaged in a very different kind of service from that originally foreseen when Churchward laid down the initial specification. These 21 engines, as soon as each had been run in, were loaned in 1917 to the Railway Operating Division of the British Army on the Continent, and based at the ROD headquarters at Audruicq, on the line between Calais and St Omer. They were put on to hauling the very heavy and vital supply trains for the British Second Army, which was holding the critical sector of the Allied front line around the Ypres Salient. The task of the Great Western '53' Class 2-6-0s lay in hauling loads of roughly 1,000 tons—1,000 tons!—between the concentration yards outside Calais, at Les Fontinettes, and the military supplies railheads east of Hazebrouck. They won golden opinions from all who had to use them, and those included many railwaymen who had not been particularly partial to Great Western locomotive practice in pre-war years.

When I came to London for my engineering training in 1921, I received the privilege of walking passes on certain Great Western lines in the London area, but I must admit I was principally interested photographically in the big engines, and when plans were made for a family holiday in Cornwall in the late summer of 1924, and when the GWR issued me with a walking pass between St Austell and Penzance, my thoughts were directed to the 'big stuff' again. It was therefore a disappointment photographically to find that at that time practically everything west of Plymouth, passenger and goods alike, was worked by the 'Moguls'. There was one exception, which I discovered on my first visit to Penzance shed. The friendly shedmaster was taking me round when I saw at the back of the shed a smartly groomed '29', No 2917 *Saint Bernard*. It transpired that this was then a regular working for the West of England postal special. It was worked by an Exeter 4-6-0, on a double-home basis, and while the men slept during the day their engine languished at the back of Penzance shed, completely occult from public gaze until the return working at 6 pm. On this the engine went right through to Paddington via Bristol, being remanned at Exeter, also on the double-home basis.

Through the kindly interest of that shedmaster I was initiated into the more intimate details of 'Mogul' working, including a sight of the coal sheets; and it was explained to me that these engines were very economical. Of course the duties on which they were engaged were not heavy, but after many years of footplate journeys on them the Great Western footplate tradition remained to ensure the minimum of coal consumption no matter how light the load, by regulating the firing to avoid 'blowing off' at all costs. On those visits I saw and photographed engines numbered between 4341 and 5383, and when we travelled home on the up 'Cornish Riviera Express' our engine, as far as Truro, was one of the latest to be built, No 6350. But with no more than 195 tons to St Erth, and 235 tons to Truro, the engine was not at all pressed. The usual load of the 'Limited' in Cornwall was then five coaches, including a restaurant car for Penzance and one through carriage each for Falmouth and St Ives. There were no through carriages for Newquay carried on the 'Limited' at that time and the train ran non-stop between Plymouth and Truro. On the down journey one

A standard 'Mogul', No 4371, with a built-up chimney, being prepared for an express passenger train working: note the headlamps. (W.J. Reynolds)

'Mogul' was relieved by another at Truro.

Referring to train loads, I have often wondered what speeds were attained by the 1,000-ton trains worked by the Great Western '53' Class 'Moguls' under ROD management, in view of one of my own experiences between Shrewsbury and Leamington with engine No 5346 in May 1929. I was travelling by the 3.12 pm from Chester to Paddington just after a Bank Holiday and the 'Mogul' took over haulage of the train at Shrewsbury, with a normally loaded train, for this service, of about 380 tons. It included a through portion for the old route to London, and with the Salop-based engine continuing through to Oxford it was only at Leamington that the Old Oak engine took over the fast portion via Bicester. The 'Mogul' kept exact time to Wolverhampton, climbing the 1 in 132 to Hollinswood Tunnel at 33 mph and not exceeding 64 mph down the Shifnal bank, 19.6 miles from Wellington in 28 minutes. But when we got to Wolverhampton, such a crowd of passengers was waiting that two more coaches were backed on to the rear of the train making our tare load up to 404 tons, and the gross load with people standing in the corridors at least 440 tons. The continuing 12.6 miles on to Birmingham were not sharply timed, but I had already begun to wonder what would follow. This train, the 6 pm out of Snow Hill, was booked right up to the 'two-hour Birmingham' standard. As if this were not enough, Snow Hill had yet another coach to be attached in rear.

So the little mixed traffic engine went out of Birmingham with a load of 434 tons tare, and fully 470 tons full. What happened can be seen from the accompanying log. As far as Solihull the line is on a gradual rise, but it becomes level after that and the speed had reached 60 mph before Knowle. On the descent to Lapworth water troughs acceleration continued rapidly to 69 mph, and the sharp rise to Hatton was taken without falling below 60 mph. Then the engine must have been taken down the Hatton Bank with no change in the working conditions, because the speed worked up to a full 75 mph passing Warwick, and the last 2 miles into Leamington took no more than 2 min 10 sec! Thus we kept, but for a trifling loss of 25 seconds, the time then allowed to the up Birmingham two-hour trains. I must admit that after this I found the continuation to Paddington, with *Restormel Castle* and a reduced load of 350 tons, somewhat of an anti-climax, although we three times reached maximum speeds of well over 80 mph!

Returning to the year 1911, after recalling some of my earlier experiences of the working of the celebrated 'Mogul' engines, it is necessary to back-step a stage in

GWR: 6 pm Birmingham–Leamington

Engine 2-6-0 No 5346
Load 434 tons tare, 470 tons full

Distance (miles)		Schedule (min)	Actual (m s)	Speed* (mph)
0.0	Birmingham (Snow Hill)	0	0 00	—
1.1	Bordesley		3 15	—
3.2	Tyseley		6 06	51
7.0	Solihull		10 35	48
8.5	Widney Manor		12 20	56½
10.4	Knowle		14 15	60½
12.9	Lapworth		16 40	69
17.1	Hatton	19	20 35	60
21.3	Warwick		24 15	75
23.3	Leamington	26	26 25	—

* Max and min by stop-watch

One of the 2-8-0 standard heavy freight tank engines introduced for use in South Wales, No 5217. (British Railways)

the chronology of new engine building at Swindon, because at the end of the year 1910 the last new standard type without the top-feed arrangement on the boiler was introduced, the very powerful 2-8-0 tank of the '42' Class. It was a standard type in having $18\frac{1}{2}$ in by 30 in cylinders, the Standard No 4 superheated boiler, and the same coupled wheels as the '28' Class 2-8-0 heavy mineral engine. It was designed for short-distance work in South Wales where the loads offered were getting a little beyond the capacity of the 'Aberdares'. The '42' Class tank engines had a tractive effort of 33,300 lb. Only the first two or three of the class were minus the top-feed apparatus, because it had been perfected and standardized before the first batch of 20 was completed. The coupled wheelbase of these engines was 20 ft but this was eased by providing the trailing pair of wheels with sliding axle-boxes which allowed considerable side play, and the coupling rods were fitted with spherical joints to secure the same end. The new engines, despite the work-a-day nature of their duties in the South Wales mining districts, were originally finished in all the pre-war brilliance of the passenger livery.

Early in 1911 work started on increasing the stud of main-line heavy goods and mineral locomotives. In view of the volume of traffic originating in South Wales it is remarkable that this step should have taken so long to materialise. There is no doubt that express passenger traffic, not excluding the calls of the ocean liners at Fishguard, occupied high, perhaps the highest, priority in the managerial strategy of the Great Western Railway in the years before the First World War; how else could the building of more than 80 4-6-0s of first line tractive power by the end of 1910 be justified, against no more than 30 2-8-0s for the heaviest goods traffic by that same time. But while the '42' Class 2-8-0 tanks were being built, the shops were busy with more '28s', numbered from 2831 onwards, including the Swindon superheater and the latest arrangement of top-feed apparatus. They, of course, carried the same boiler as fitted on the 4-6-0 express passenger engines and, working at 225 psi, the nominal tractive effort was 35,380 lbs. They, also, were at first finished in the full passenger livery.

Early in 1912 the last batch of 'County' Class 4-4-0s was built. They were originally intended for the West to North route, via the Severn Tunnel, and eight of the ten engines in this batch were divided between the sheds at Bristol and Coleham (Shrewsbury). It cannot be said if the original track restrictions on locomotive weight over the joint line between Hereford and Shrewsbury still prevailed; certain it is that for some years 4-6-0s did not run between Bristol and Shrewsbury. The new engines, superheated and with the standard top-feed to the boiler, were soon doing fine work, especially when war conditions sent the train loads up, sometimes to around 400 tons. The names and numbers of the new engines were:

3821	*County of Bedford*	3826	*County of Flint*
3822	*County of Brecon*	3827	*County of Gloucester*
3823	*County of Carnarvon*	3828	*County of Hereford*
3824	*County of Cornwall*	3829	*County of Merioneth*
3825	*County of Denbigh*	3830	*County of Oxford*

Knowing that these additions brought the total strength of the class up to 40, a reader might query the numbers; but the first batch was numbered from 3473 to 3482,and these still existed when Nos 3821–3830 were built. When the general renumbering of many of the older engines took place, the original 3474–3482 became 3831–3839, and the class leader, *County of Middlesex*, became No 3800.

Even before this new allocation, and certainly for many years after it, Bristol became the principal concentration centre of the 'County' Class. It was so indeed in my early Westinghouse days when I was attached to the Works at Chippenham for some time in 1926. 'Counties' were the regular power on the 5.30 am from Paddington, and they worked many other trains. At that time they had been displaced from the West to North route via the Severn Tunnel, but they

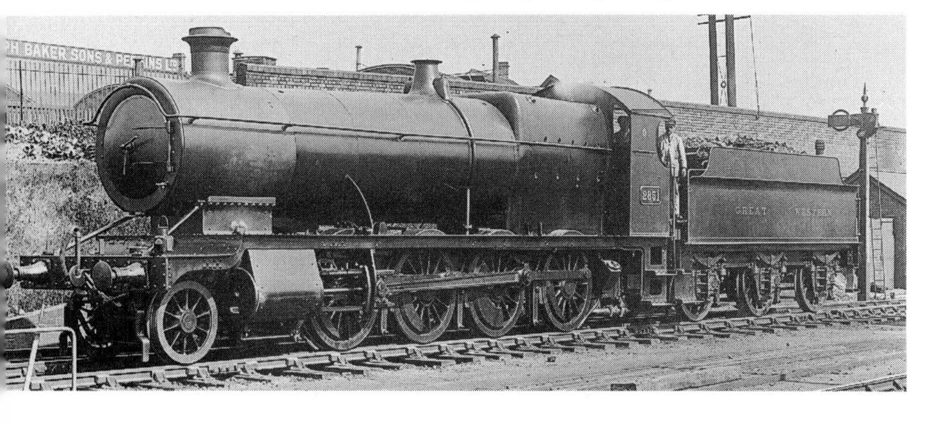

Left *2-8-0 standard heavy freight and mineral engine No 2851.* (W.J. Reynolds)

Above right *One of the '2800' Class, No 2861, in BR days working a train of empty mineral wagons eastbound along the sea wall between Teignmouth and Dawlish.* (E.D. Bruton)

Right *First of the final batch of 'Counties' built in 1912, No 3821* County of Bedford *in photographic grey.* (British Railways)

were the mainstay of the Bristol-Birmingham route via Cheltenham and Stratford-on-Avon, part of which was Midland over which the Great Western had running powers, and over which the Midland steadfastly refused to have 4-6-0 engines running. Reverting to the use of 'Counties' over the Bristol–Shrewsbury line, it is a little odd that the two finest runs in my collection between Hereford and Shrewsbury were made not by any of the engines newly allocated in 1912, but by units of the very first batch built in 1905, but by the time of these runs superheated and renumbered in the '38' series.

The pre-war timing of the principal expresses from Hereford to Shrewsbury was 64 minutes. This would not seem very enterprising with an average speed of only $47\frac{3}{4}$ mph compared to the schedules regularly maintained on the West of England line, but for 28 miles out of Hereford the ascent is gradual and continuous, although there is a pronounced dip in the grading through Woofferton Junction, of which drivers usually took advantage to pile on some speed in readiness for a stiff $1\frac{1}{4}$ miles at 1 in 112–131 approaching Ludlow. Then, after what could in certain conditions be a testing half-hour of running, came the main pull up to Church Stretton on gradients averaging 1 in 197 between mileposts 22 and $13\frac{3}{4}$, with 5 miles at 1 in 103 to 112 between Craven Arms and the summit. The descent from Church Stretton into Shrewsbury, although well aligned for the most part, was timed very slowly, with no less than 17 minutes for the concluding steeply downhill $12\frac{3}{4}$ miles. Generally one found drivers ran without steam for most of the way.

GWR: Hereford–Shrewsbury

Engine No			3834	3832
Engine Name			*County of Somerset*	*County of Wilts*
Load			330	410
Distance (miles)		**Schedule (min)**	**Actual (min sec)**	**Actual (min sec)**
0.0	Hereford	0	0 00	0 00
7.5	Dinmore	—	10 29	11 25
12.6	Leominster	16	16 00	16 43
18.9	Woofferton Jc	23½	22 44	23 00
23.5	Ludlow	28	27 48	27 05
28.1	Onibury	—	33 22	—
31.1	Craven Arms	37	36 56	36 26
35.6	Marsh Brook	—	42 28	—
38.2	Church Stretton	47	46 00	47 18
44.6	Dorrington	—	51 58	53 10
—		—	—	sigs
51.0	Shrewsbury	64	61 37	63 30

The 'County' Class engines, the work of which is tabulated herewith, ran admirably, keeping the uphill scheduled times with very heavy loads for Great Western 4-4-0 engines. *County of Somerset* made a very rapid start from Hereford, but was overtaken by the more heavily loaded *County of Wilts* after Woofferton which was making some very hard running, including an exceptionally fine uphill average of 61.3 mph from Dinmore to Ludlow. Then after this engine had taken the lead as far as Craven Arms, there came the astonishing final effort of *County of Somerset*, in averaging no less than 44.2 mph over the last 2.6 miles from Marsh Brook up to Church Stretton, which put her substantially in the lead once again. The heavily loaded *County of Wilts* fell to a minimum of 34 mph at Church Stretton, even though keeping sectional time. This again was a very fine run.

10. The war years: a time for reflection

In August 1914 the outbreak of the First World War closely coincided with the completion of the last batch of 'Star' Class four-cylinder 4-6-0s, the 15 named after Princesses, and having 15-in diameter cylinders. Then Churchward had incomparably the largest, the most powerful, and most thermo-dynamically efficient stud of big locomotives in Great Britain; for in addition to the 61 'Stars', recently reinforced by the 15 'Princesses', there was the solid block of two-cylinder 4-6-0s, lately augmented by the conversion of the 'Scott' series of 'Atlantics' to the 4-6-0 type. After this operation was completed, the Great Western had only the three French compounds remaining as 'Atlantics', and these were in due course modified by the fitting of Standard No 1 boilers, the Swindon superheater and the standard top-feed apparatus. All three engines were eventually stationed at Oxford. The two larger-cylindered ones, *President* and *Alliance*, had a tractive effort not far short of that of the 15-in 'Stars', 26,935 lbs against 27,800 lbs, but I know of no instances of their doing remotely comparable work in their later state.

So far as power output was concerned, Swindon, and particularly those members of the Drawing Office staff concerned with dynamometer car testing, had received, as has already been mentioned, a severe jolt when the full results of the tests of the London and North Western 'Claughton' Class 4-6-0 *Ralph Brocklebank* were published in *The Engineer* early in 1914. But despite the comprehensive nature of the data published, the Great Western men, and many others also, regarded it as a 'one-off' job, not to be repeated on any ordinary occasion. Travellers on the West Coast Route in the halcyon days of Bowen Cooke's management of the locomotive department knew that this was far from being the case, and I myself have published data elsewhere in substantiation. On the other hand, the test results published in *The Engineer* concerning *Ralph Brocklebank* of November 1913 included no references at all to coal consumption, and from results published in LMS days one could infer that the earlier ones involved considerably higher consumptions than were then customary with 'Stars' or 'Saints' even when these engines were being well extended. From the historical point of view, I am always sorry that the need never seemed to have arisen for one of these engines to be put on a maximum output trial, as one of the 'Castles' was in Collett's time. The only trial of a superheated 'Star', that of *Queen Matilda*, between Paddington and Bristol in November 1911 was as much of an exercise for the testing staff as anything else, and in the end they did not even keep *net* time, let alone arrive punctually in Bristol!

Quite apart from designing and building excellent locomotives for all classes of service, in the 12 years from his succeeding Dean to the outbreak of the war Churchward had proved himself a team leader of rare distinction. He was no remote figurehead whose name appeared on the publicity bestowed on all his new locomotives and carriages. He was the vital commander-in-chief who was always out and about in the Drawing Office, in all the workshops, in running sheds, on the footplate; and while he could be at times a bit 'up stage' in his comments, the men in whatever grade knew they could be sure of a sympathetic hearing. One of the major results of his administration, which lasted as long as the Great Western Railway itself, was the harmony and whole-hearted co-operation between the Drawing Office and the footplate staff. The running inspectors became the eyes and ears of the indoor staff, not only of the individual draughtsmen, but also of section leaders and many times of Churchward himself. His homely words to Inspector Flewellyn at the start of the Ocean Mail race from the West in 1904 will be recalled with many a chuckle! The liaison between the running inspectors and the Drawing Office paid off in many ways. Unlike their counterparts in many places elsewhere on the British railways, these men were always regarded as the friends and advisers of the footplate men, with the result that the equipment was used as it was designed to be used. The men appreciated their engines, and always got the best out of them. I cannot recollect ever having heard of a fitting that the men disliked.

One of the de Glehn compound 'Atlantics', No 104 Alliance, *as rebuilt with a standard GWR taper boiler superheater.* (Real Photos Co Ltd)

Above *A 'Knight' in pre-war splendour: No 4016* Knight of the Golden Fleece. (British Railways)

Left *No 4023* King George *on an up Birmingham and Wolverhampton express near Solihull.* (H.W. Burman)

Below left *A down Bristol express near Kensal Green, hauled by engine No 4026* King Richard. (Loco Publishing Co Ltd)

In later years I had the privilege of riding many thousands of miles on Great Western engines, from 0-4-2 tanks and 'Dukedogs' to 'Castles' and 'Kings', and one of my most lasting impressions is of the consistent precision of the firing. It did not seem to matter whether it was with a 'King' going hammer and tongs all the way with a 500-ton load on the up 'Dutchman', or on a 'Mogul' with four coaches working an all-stations 'stopper' from Ruabon to Barmouth. The firing was superbly regulated, so that not only was the pressure up to 'sizzling' point the whole way, but there was no blowing off. This, as anyone who has tried firing a locomotive will know, is not the easiest thing to do on a free-steaming engine working a light train when the demands for steam are intermittent, to say the least of it. I know comparisons can be odious, but I cannot help constrasting one immaculately managed run of 1½ hours on a Great Western engine with one I experienced about a fortnight later on another part of British Railways on a large modern express locomotive hauling a not immoderately heavy train on no more than a brisk schedule. But the firing was done in such a slap-happy fashion, with prolonged spells of blowing off, that not only did we have to 'drink deeply' at the two successive sets of water troughs on our route, but the waiting time at the next intermediate station had to be prolonged while the fireman topped up the tender tank once again, although the next set of water troughs were less than 40 miles ahead. And there was an inspector on the footplate too!

When war came in August 1914, there were at first very few persons who thought it would last long, or who had the remotest idea of what it would involve before the enemy was finally overthrown. But apart from the brief spell of intense troop train movements in connection with the despatch of the British Expeditionary Force, it was a case of 'railway business as usual' in England. An article under that very title appeared in *The Railway Magazine* for October 1914, and during the first winter of the war express train services in Great Britain were practically unchanged from normal. On the Great Western, indeed, the majority of the crack schedules were maintained for a further two years, although the special summer facilities in 1915 and 1916 were on a much reduced scale. But the demand for travel was unchanged, and the result was exceedingly heavy loading on the more popular expresses. Fortunately for the Great Western, the capacity of Churchward's engines to tackle these heavy loads had already been amply demonstrated, and the traffic department could pile on the coaches with confidence.

The story of Great Western operating during the war years did, in its own way, reflect the mood of the nation as a whole. The spirit of high endeavour that followed the declaration of war, the acute anxiety of the days after Mons, and the renewed optimism that came with the spring of 1915 gradually gave place to sterner thoughts as the ghastly completeness of the stalemate on the Western Front was realized. And when the full weight of our new armies launched against the enemy in the prolonged battles of July and August 1916 produced relatively small results at the price of fearful casualties, it became clear that nothing short of an all-out effort of the whole nation would ensure survival, let alone victory. From 1 January 1917, the Great Western cancelled the running of all restaurant cars. All the crack trains were so decelerated as to be almost unrecognizable, and still further easing out of running times took place in the ensuing two years.

My somewhat derogatory remarks about the timekeeping of the 11 am Bristol express on the dynamometer car test run with *Queen Matilda* in 1911 were, I feel, prompted by knowledge of the splendid running put up by other engines of the 'Star' Class on less formal occasions. It has puzzled me why this train, in pre-war days, should have been named the 'Bath Spa Express', when it did not even deign to stop, and usually detached no more than a one-coach slip portion in passing through! Names apart, in 1916 the train made a very splendid run with a load almost equal to that worked by *Queen Matilda* in 1911. The engine, too, was a celebrity, none other than the 'Star' the quiet going of which in 1910 astonished the men of the London and North Western Railway, *Polar Star*. Her log on the 'Bath Spa Express' is tabulated alongside that of *Queen Matilda*, and the contrast is striking. The signal check at the start did not cost more than a minute, and then *Polar Star* went ahead to make an immaculate run, displaying for 50 miles on end the '2-ton pull at 70

GWR: the 'Bath Spa Express'

Date			1911*	1916
Engine No			4039	4005
Engine name			*Queen Matilda*	*Polar Star*
Load To Bath, tons full			400	380
To Bristol, tons full			370	350

Distance (miles)		**Schedule (min)**	**Actual (m s)**	**Actual (m s)**
0.0	Paddington	0	0 00	0 00
—			sigs	sigs
9.1	Southall	11	14 42	13 30
18.5	Slough	20	24 24	22 24
24.2	Maidenhead		30 16	27 34
31.0	Twyford		37 05	33 40
36.0	Reading	37	41 58	38 10
44.8	Goring		50 30	45 43
53.1	Didcot	53½	58 56	53 00
60.4	Wantage Rd		66 15	59 38
66.5	Uffington		72 32	65 22
71.6	Shrivenham		77 36	70 06
—			sigs	—
77.3	Swindon	77	83 40	75 30
82.9	Wootton Bassett		89 53	80 46
87.7	Dauntsey		94 07	84 45
94.0	Chippenham	93½	99 24	89 41
98.3	Corsham		103 50	93 41
101.9	Box		107 07	97 04
104.6	Bathampton		109 17	99 29
106.9	Bath	107	111 55	101 53
113.8	Keynsham		118 56	easy
118.4	Bristol (Temple Meads)	120	124 15	116 35

* Dynamometer car test run

mph' standard of performance that Churchward aimed at. The average speed over the 51.3 miles from Maidenhead to Swindon was 66.5 mph, and for 10 miles west of Reading on almost level track the average was exactly 70 mph. The minimum speed up the gradual ascent through the Vale of the White Horse was 63 mph near Uffington and the maximum at Dauntsey 82 mph. With Chippenham passed nearly $3\frac{1}{2}$ minutes early, the rest was easy.

Exactly 20 years after the northward foray that surprised the pundits of Euston and Crewe, I encountered *Polar Star* in my own personal travelling; and although the experience is right out of the period of this chapter, the similarity in performance is so striking as to make a reference to it very appropriate. At that time, family business in Reading was taking me there periodically, usually at weekends, and I usually travelled by the 1.45 pm Worcester express, which always carried a load of well over 400 tons and provided a good test of locomotive capacity to keep the 40-minute start-to-stop timing from Paddington. But on this particular occasion I made for the 3.15 pm and at the head of a train of 370 tons gross was *Polar Star*. There were no checks on that day, and after a brilliantly smart start we averaged 67 mph over the $27\frac{3}{4}$ miles from West Drayton to Twyford, then easing down to avoid being 3 minutes early at Reading. Between Slough and Twyford the time of 11 min 7 sec was faster than on the tabulated run of the 'Bath Spa Express', and the maximum was 71 mph at Slough. Sadly enough, the engine which had thus shown such tremendous form, then stationed at Gloucester, was withdrawn for scrapping only four years later.

In my journeys to Reading in 1930 I several times travelled behind the Worcester-based 'Star' No 4017, and it is something of a coincidence that one of the finest ever runs in the pre-deceleration days of 1917 should have been made by this engine, also on the 'Bath Spa Express'. It was made in July 1914 when the engine still carried the resounding title *Knight of the Black Eagle*. In view of the events of the following month its name was changed to *Knight of Liege* more discreetly than those of the North Western express engines named *Germanic* and *Teutonic*, which had the names scored through for everyone to see and the substitute names added on a subsidiary plate. Engine No 4017 had an enormous 59-axle train packed to its utmost capacity

Above Polar Star *as she was when running on the LNWR between Euston and Crewe in 1910.* (P.J.T Reed)

Above left *The name that became unacceptable in 1914:* Knight of the Black Eagle, *later changed to* Knight of Liege. (Real Photos Co Ltd)

Left *No 4017* Knight of Liege *on an up Worcester express in Sonning Cutting.* (M.W. Earley)

Great Locomotives of the GWR in colour

Right *Replica of the broad gauge 8-ft 4-2-2* Iron Duke. (R.C. Riley)

Below *The preserved 4-4-0 No 3440* City of Truro *and 'Dukedog' Class 4-4-0 No 3217* Earl of Berkeley *at Didcot, 4 June 1989.* (R.C. Riley)

EARL of BERKELEY
3217
MCH

Left *The preserved 'Dukedog' Class 4-4-0 No 9017 on the Bluebell line at Sheffield Park in April 1962.* (R.C. Riley)

Below left *Preserved 4-4-0 No 3217* Earl of Berkeley *at Didcot in May 1985.* (R.C. Riley)

Right *4-6-0 No 4092* Dunraven Castle *and an unnamed 'Bulldog' Class 4-4-0 climbing Hemerdon Bank with the up 'Cornish Riviera Express' in 1926.* (From a water colour painting by O.S. Nock)

Below *Churchward 'Atlantic' 4-4-2 No 182* Lalla Rookh *at Laira sheds in 1905.* (From an oil painting by Paul Gribble)

Left *'Saint' Class 4-6-0 No 2910* Lady of Shalott *leaving Penzance with the 6 pm Up Postal Special in 1924.* (From a water colour painting by O.S. Nock)

Below *'Saint' Class 4-6-0 No 2934* Butleigh Court, *in BR lined black livery, at Swindon in June 1950.* (T.B. Owen)

Right *2-6-0 No 6378 on an up goods train near Cowley Bridge Junction, Exeter, in July 1961.* (R.C. Riley)

Below right *The preserved 2-6-0 No 5322, in GWR livery, at Didcot in September 1974.* (R.C. Riley)

GREAT WESTERN

Above *'4500' Class 2-6-2 tank engine No 4552 at Penzance in April 1960.* (R.C. Riley)

Left *The preserved '61' 2-6-2 tank No 6106 at Didcot in June 1989.* (R.C. Riley)

Above right *2-6-2 No 6165 on a train of empty stock at Royal Oak in October 1963.* (R.C. Riley)

Right *Four-cylinder 4-6-0 No 4056* Princess Margaret *at Old Oak Common, September 1959.* (R.C. Riley)

ROYAL OAK
6165

4056
PRINCESS MARGARET

Left *One of the 5 ft 8 in express goods 2-8-0s, No 4705 at Laira shed in September 1960.* (R.C. Riley)

Below *No 3813, one of the later engines of the '2800' Class of 2-8-0s with a modern cab, at Worcester in August 1962.* (R.C. Riley)

Right *4-6-0 No 6028* King George VI *at Old Oak Common in May 1956.* (R.C. Riley)

Below right *4-6-0 No 6003* King George IV *(with double chimney) at Ranelagh Bridge yard in June 1962.* (R.C. Riley)

6028

F46

SAINT MARTIN
4900

7903

Above left *The rebuilt 'Saint' Class 4-6-0* Saint Martin, *after being renumbered 4900 and becoming the Class leader of the 'Hall' Class, at Old Oak Common in September 1956.* (R.C. Riley)

Left *The now preserved 'Modified Hall' Class engine No 7903* Foremarke Hall *at Old Oak Common in May 1956.* (R.C. Riley)

Above *4-6-0 No 5034* Corfe Castle *at Bristol Bath Road shed in July 1959.* (R.C. Riley)

Right *The preserved 4-6-0 No 5051* Drysllwyn Castle *at Didcot in May 1985.* (R.C. Riley)

7037
SWINDON

Above left *4-6-0 No 5055* Earl of Eldon *with the up 'Devonian' on Teignmouth sea-wall in July 1959.* (R.C. Riley)

Left *The last 'Castle' Class 4-6-0 to be built, No 7037* Swindon, *at Old Oak Common in March 1961.* (R.C. Riley)

Above *0-4-2 tank No 1451 at Uffculme on the Culm Valley line to Hemyock, June 1962.* (R.C. Riley)

Right *The preserved 0-4-2 tank No 1466 at Didcot in September 1974.* (R.C. Riley)

Above *4-6-0 No 6800* Arlington Grange *at Penzance in April 1961.* (R.C. Riley)

Left *4-6-0 No 7823* Hook Norton Manor *at Laira shed in July 1956.* (R.C. Riley)

Above right *0-6-0 pannier tank No 9710 with condensing apparatus, at Old Oak Common in March 1961, with the GWR monogram of 1934 still showing faintly on the tank side.* (R.C. Riley)

Right *2-8-2T No 7228 on an up freight train at Wednesbury Central in May 1960.* (R.C. Riley)

9710

Left *The first Hawksworth 'County' Class engine, No 1000* County of Middlesex, *in BR green livery at Old Oak Common in May 1956.* (R.C. Riley)

Below *4-6-0 No 1018* County of Leicester, *with later type double chimney, at Penzance in April 1960.* (R.C. Riley)

with passengers and luggage, and weighing 505 tons gross behind the tender. Naturally one could not expect so rapid a start as with *Polar Star* on my own run on the 3.15 pm down, and 2½ minutes were lost on the rather optimistic initial timing out to Southall. But from there onwards the work was magnificent, with speed averaging 60.9 mph between Slough and Reading, 61.4 mph between there and Didcot and, most notable of all, 61 mph between Didcot and Swindon. So the 77.3 miles from Paddington to Swindon were covered in 80¾ minutes, and far from being short of steam after this long gradual uphill effort, the engine was driven downhill in such style that the Bath slip coach was detached and at rest in the station in 107¾ minutes from Paddington, a start-to-stop average of 59 mph.

A study of this performance and an estimate of the extent to which the engine had been pushed to its limit was inevitable, in view of the details of another maximum load run published at that time in *The Railway Magazine*. The result, however, was very different. The engine *King John* had an even heavier load, 530 tons, and almost kept pace with *Knight of the Black Eagle* to Slough; but after that there was a steady falling off. It took 84 min 55 sec to pass Swindon and after that there was a general collapse, and it took 115 min to reach Bath. Reverting to the work of engine No 4017, the average speed of 61 mph from Didcot to Swindon was made against gradients averaging 1 in 800, which would have involved a continuous drawbar pull of 0.63 tons. For the coaching stock of that period, the train resistance at 60 mph was evaluated at 11.5 lbs per ton, or 2.6 tons, which indicated that between Didcot and Swindon the engine was exerting a continuous pull of 3.2 tons on the drawbar, a horsepower of 1,160. This figure should be borne in mind when some post-war GWR engine performances are reviewed.

The 11 am from Paddington may have been officially known as the 'Bath Spa Express', though as we have seen it did not stop there, but in the height of the holiday season a high proportion of its passengers would be bound for stations on the Somersetshire coast, particularly Weston-super-Mare. On the other hand, the 'Star' Class engines and their crews were on a double-home turn to Plymouth and back. In the down direction the engine that had worked down from London coupled off at Bristol and went forward on one of the North to West trains. The remarkable capacity of the 'Star' Class engines, shown particularly in the work of No 4017, could I think be traced to the enginemen having improved their techniques of handling the engines. Firemen perfected the 'Haycock' fire, with a deep bed of coal on the horizontal section at the rear of the grate. Welsh coal gave excellent results with this method of firing, and there developed a tradition of rock-steady steaming, with the needle of the pressure gauge apparently fixed just below the blowing-off

The down 'Cornish Riviera Express' leaving Paddington before the First World War behind No 4042 Prince Albert. (Loco Publishing Co)

point. On other lines some engines might run for long periods with the boiler pressure well below the blowing-off point, full pressure being used only for hill climbing or other extra efforts, but on the GWR a feather of steam from the safety valves became a sign that the engine was steaming normally. If the pressure fell by 20 psi below the blowing-off point, the engine was considered to be steaming badly.

An important feature that assisted in the maintenance of these rock-steady steaming conditions was the continued use of Ramsbottom-type safety valves; the 'pop' type of valve was never used on GWR engines. With Ramsbottom valves the pressure could be kept at 'sizzling point' without full blowing-off. There was no 'in between' stage with 'pop' valves, and full blowing-off usually resulted in a drop of 5 to 10 psi before the valves closed.

The ability to hold pressure near to the blowing-off point for long periods depended not only on skilful firing but also upon the driver maintaining a fairly constant steam rate to the cylinders. On the long, gentle gradients of the Brunel routes this was easy, but on routes with rapidly changing gradients, frequent adjustments of the reverser were required. Over the years drivers developed the habit of making the necessary adjustments to keep the steam rate as near as possible steady, and intermediate passing times were regularly disobeyed because they made uneven demands upon the boiler. In later years, when the testing of engines at constant steaming rates was perfected, it was shown that the most important contribution to working an engine economically was a steam rate which remained as nearly constant as the gradients and speed restrictions allowed. Many GWR drivers had by their own instinct and experience long since arrived at very nearly the ideal conditions. The haycock fire was developed to suit the properties of Welsh coal, which burns most effectively on a thick and very hot firebed; but variations of the technique proved equally effective with the hard coals from Staffordshire and North Wales which were supplied to the northern sheds of the GWR.

The growth of the West of England traffic was due largely to the popularity of the holiday resorts, and exceptional peaks of traffic at holiday periods were therefore inevitable. From about 1910 onwards, train-loads of 500 tons were found at these periods. In the early years of the First World War no further increases were made in train services, but the traffic continued to grow, and very heavy trains became more common. There were no general decelerations until January 1917, and the 'Stars' proved their ability to work the heaviest trains to pre-war schedules. Not all the heavy trains kept time, but sufficient records exist to show that the engines could reach Exeter in 3 hours with trains of up to 470 tons, although some of the in-

GWR: Down 'Cornish Riviera Express'

Run No			1			2		
Date			Summer 1914			1916		
Engine No			4045			4018		
Engine Name			*Prince John*			*Knight of the Grand Cross*		
Load cars, tons tare/full								
To Westbury			13, 441/470			14, 457/490		
To Taunton			13, 441/470			11, 373/400		
To Exeter			13, 441/470			9, 301/320		
Distance (miles)		**Schedule (min)**	**Actual (min**	**sec)**	**Speed (mph)**	**Actual (min**	**sec)**	**Speed (mph)**
0.0	PADDINGTON	0	0	00		0	00	
9.1	SOUTHALL		13	39		12	49	
16.2	Langley					19	53	64
						severe sig		
18.5	SLOUGH	20	22	38	67 max	22	41	
24.2	Maidenhead					30	32	
31.0	Twyford					37	24	64
35.0	Milepost 35		37	35				
36.0	READING	37	38	40		42	17	
44.8	Aldermaston					52	29	58
53.1	NEWBURY	56	57	41		61	21	
61.5	Hungerford					70	28	53/58
70.1	Savernake	73½	76	23	42½	80	20	44
81.1	Patney					90	38	71/66
82.0	Milepost 82		87	05				
91.4	Edington					98	42	83
94.0	Milepost 94		96	30	80½ max			
95.6	WESTBURY	97½	98	17	slack	102	39	slack
101.3	FROME				slack	110	32	slack
106.6	Witham					117	26	
108.5	Milepost 122¾		116	23	39½			
115.3	CASTLE CARY	120	122	17	79½	125	42	80 max
125.7	Somerton					134	17	
137.9	*Cogload Junction*	144	141	10		144	29	78 max
142.9	TAUNTON	149	145	38	63.4†	149	14	
150.0	Wellington		153	03	51.0†			
150.8	Milepost 171		154	01	51.0†	157	33	
151.8	Milepost 172		155	26	42.5†	158	50	46.7†
152.8	Milepost 173		157	15	32.8†	160	19	40.5†
153.8	*Whiteball box*		159	31	26.5†	161	54	37
158.8	Tiverton Junction					166	33	76 max
166.5	Silverton					172	52	
173.7	EXETER	179*	177	41		179	29	slip arrival

* 180 minutes on run No 2
† Average over full mile

Net time 175¼ min

termediate times would not be observed with such a load. Five years earlier it seemed that 400 tons was the limit for timekeeping on these services.

The accompanying table shows two examples of heavy loads on the down 'Cornish Riviera Express'. Run No 1 was unusual in that the full load of 470 tons was taken through to Exeter, and it is probably the finest down run recorded in the pre-war period. In the early days of the three-hour bookings to Exeter, the passing times allowed for cautious running over the Somerton cut-off line where the earthworks were still consolidating. Subsequent alterations to the timetable never made the demands upon the locomotive even throughout the journey from Paddington to Exeter, and drivers could normally count on recovering some lost time between Castle Cary and Taunton. The driver of *Prince John* was thus able to drop nearly 3 minutes in the first 70 miles to Savernake, in which there is little respite other than the Reading slack, and after passing milepost $122\frac{3}{4}$ $2\frac{1}{4}$ minutes late, to be nearly $3\frac{1}{2}$ minutes early at Taunton, without attaining any unusually high speeds. The allowance of 24 minutes for the 22.6 miles from Castle Cary to Cogload Junction was cut to 18 min 53 sec, an average of 71.8 mph. Speed was well maintained on the approaches to Wellington, suggesting that cut-off was being advanced progressively, and the train thus had sufficient momentum to cover the final mile from milepost 173 to Whiteball box at an average of 26.5 mph without excessive demands upon the engine. Time was dropped on the climb, but the driver had judged his running well, and he was through Exeter in $\frac{1}{4}$ minute less than the allowance of 179 minutes.

On the second run in the table, made in 1916, coaches were slipped at Westbury and Taunton, as was normal for the 'Limited'. For a train of 490 tons, the start was vigorous, with a time of 12 min 49 sec to Southall. Speed rose to 64 mph at Langley, but there was a bad signal check at Dolphin Junction, Slough. This cost at least 4 minutes, but the driver was not discouraged, and on the gentle rise to Twyford he worked up to 64 mph again. The train was $5\frac{1}{4}$ minutes late through Reading, and a further $1\frac{1}{2}$ minutes were dropped to Savernake, despite a fine climb from Bedwyn with a minimum of 44 mph. On the falling gradients to Westbury, time was soon recovered; a maximum of 83 mph was reached near Lavington, and the Westbury slip was detached less than 5 minutes late. Even with the load reduced to 400 tons, the allowance of $22\frac{1}{2}$ minutes for the 19.7 miles from Westbury to Castle Cary was not easy, including as it did the recovery from the slacks to 30 mph at Westbury and Frome, and the climb to milepost $122\frac{3}{4}$. On this stretch, $\frac{1}{2}$ minute was dropped, but the recorder did not note the details of the climb. Between Castle Cary and Taunton the remaining lateness was wiped out. With the load reduced to 320 tons, there was no difficulty in reaching Exeter on time. For the passenger travelling to Exeter or beyond this was an excellently judged performance, but against this it must be noted that the Westbury passengers reached their destination 5 minutes late, due nevertheless mainly to the signal check near Slough.

Many excellent runs must have escaped the attention of recorders, and the only record of them was in the guard's journal. Fortunately, on the publicity-minded GWR the details from the guards' journals of a number of notable runs were published from time to time, and the run tabulated overleaf was revealed in this way. On 10 June 1916 the down 'Limited' loaded to 15 coaches from Paddington, and as the train was crammed with passengers the gross load must have been at least 535 tons. This was reduced by slipping at Westbury, Taunton and Exeter to about 435, 340 and 265 tons. Even if a variation of a minute either way is allowed in the guard's passing times, the performance remains outstanding. Four minutes were dropped to Reading, and a permanent way slack between there and Newbury contributed to a further loss of $3\frac{1}{2}$

A stalwart of Laira around 1913–16: No 4018 Knight of the Grand Cross. (P.J.T. Reed)

GWR: Down 'Cornish Riviera Express', 10 June 1916

Engine No 4018 *Knight of the Grand Cross*
Load, cars, tons, tare/full
To Westbury 15, 494/535
To Taunton 12, 402/435
To Exeter 9, 314/340
To Plymouth 7, 244/265

Distance (miles)		Schedule (min)	Actual (min)	Average speed (mph)
0.0	PADDINGTON	0	0	
18.5	SLOUGH	20	23½	47.3
36.0	READING	37	41	60.0
			pws	
53.1	NEWBURY	56	62	48.8
70.1	Savernake	73½	81	53.7
95.6	WESTBURY	97½	104	66.6
115.3	CASTLE CARY	120	127	51.4
137.9	*Cogload Junction*	144	146½	69.5
142.9	TAUNTON	149	151	66.7
153.8	*Whiteball box*	161½	162½	56.9
173.7	EXETER	180	180	68.3
193.9	NEWTON ABBOT	203	202½	53.8
202.5	Totnes	215½	214½	43.0
209.4	Brent	225	227½	31.9
225.7	PLYMOUTH	247	246	52.9

minutes to Savernake; the Westbury slip was detached 6½ minutes later. The running from Castle Cary to Taunton was slower than on the two previous runs described, but time recovery continued right to Exeter, a minute being recovered between Taunton and Whiteball and another minute by Exeter. The train was finally recorded as 1 minute early at Plymouth.

At this stage a pause can be made to reflect upon the results achieved so far, in the great development work on the four-cylinder simple engines of Swindon design, pioneered by Churchward. The close of the year 1916 rang down the curtain upon the first phase of high-speed express running. The development of the design had taken seven years, in moving from the 'Atlantic' No 40 to the first of the 15-in engines, No 4041. Runs like those of *Prince John* and *Knight of the Grand Cross* on the down 'Limited' showed clearly the potentialities of these engines; but the loadings were exceptional, and everyday demands were not so severe. No 'Star' had yet produced a dynamometer car record of power output to equal, let along surpass, the maximum achieved up to that time in Crewe. But the quality was there, and what was more, the design was capable of very considerable enlargement. Four lean years were nevertheless to follow before the 'Stars' began really to sparkle once again.

The first 5-ft 8-in 2-8-0 No 4700 after being fitted with a large boiler. (W.J. Reynolds)

When the war was over, Churchward at first sought to increase the steaming capacity of his larger tender engines by fitting larger boilers to the 'Saints', 'Stars' and '28XX' Class 2-8-0s. This proposal was coupled with the design of the '47XX' 2-8-0. A drawing dated May 1919 showed the estimated weights for these types fitted with a larger boiler; but the Civil Engineer could not accept the increase in axle-load of the 4-6-0s. In the event, the '47XX' was the only one of these types to receive the larger boiler, and the first of that type ran for some time with a No 1 boiler.

This engine, the last of the Churchward standard types, was developed as a result of the success of *The Great Bear* in working the Bristol to London fast vacuum-fitted freight train known as 'The Cocoa Train' and to overcome the route restrictions imposed on the 'Pacific'. It appeared very soon after the termination of the First World War (April 1919), and as far as the engine was concerned was developed from standard parts, but as it required a new boiler with a 10-ft firebox for which new flanging blocks were necessary, the first engine, No 4700, was built with a Standard No 1 boiler, a lengthened smokebox making up the difference between the Standard No 1 and the larger boiler for which it was designed. Eight further engines were built with cylinders increased to 19 in by 30 in and incorporating the Standard No 7 boiler which had a 10-ft firebox, 30.28 sq ft of grate area, a heating surface of 2,556 sq ft, boiler pressure of 225 psi and a tractive effort of 30,460 lbs. These engines were built with outside steam pipes from the smokebox to the cylinders and, as soon as a new boiler was available, No 4700 was brought up to date. This class ran very successfully an extended service of fast vacuum-fitted freight trains, generally at night, with loads up to 70 vehicles, and for this service they were eminently suitable on account of their high tractive effort and steam reserve.

11. Churchward's retirement: the new team, and engine tests

After the war it was evident that labour relations were changing, even in so close-knit an organization as the Locomotive Department of the GWR. It was not only relations with the workforce, as Churchward's rebuff from the Civil Engineer over larger boilers demonstrated, and rather than resume the all-out attack of 1909, he accepted the decision of 1919. Then, at a meeting of the Institution of Locomotive Engineers many years later, Sir William Stanier told this story:

'After the First World War a deputation had visited Churchward to tell him of their wishes. Churchward had rather an autocratic way and used to tell his people what to do. The leader of the deputation, the district organizer, said "You know, the time has come when we wish to be asked to do a thing and not ordered to do it". Like a flash came the reply, "D— it all, it is time the 'old man' retired".' But the situation was more serious for Churchward than an occasional brush with the trade unions. It lay in the recent changes in the 'high command' at Paddington, for in July 1921 Felix J.C. Pole was appointed General Manager.

The new man, only 44 years of age, had been a protégé of Sir James Inglis and there is little doubt that he had heard of the deadly feud that developed between Inglis and Churchward over the plan to bring all the chief officers under the General Manager, instead of reporting to specific members of the Board. Pole extracted the Inglis plan from the innermost recesses of the General Manager's safe, and took an early opportunity of speaking to Churchward. He suggested very tactfully and very courteously that there was really no need for him to make the journey to London specially for Board meetings, but Churchward replied, not very tactfully or courteously, that he would stay away only when the Chairman told him to do so! This incident, however, told him the way the wind was blowing, and at the end of the year, although not 65 years of age, he retired. In other circumstances, being still in good health, one felt he would have liked to continue for several more years; after all, his successor continued as Chief Mechanical Engineer until he was 70. Churchward was a man of wide interests, apart from railway engineering. He was a Justice of the Peace, he was a skilled horticulturist, and he enjoyed country pursuits such as fishing and shooting; this is not to say that he lost interest in the work of his former command and how his young men were progressing.

Churchward's successor, C.B. Collett, was essentially a workshop man rather than an all-round railway locomotive engineer. Stanier, who had previously been Locomotive Works Manager, was promoted to be Principal Assistant to the Chief Mechanical Engineer. On other railways that post would have carried the title Deputy CME, because that was the job that Stanier carried very successfully for the next ten years. In his retirement when I was writing his biography, Stanier told me that he had words with Collett over the appointment of his successor as Locomotive Works Manager. They both agreed that F.W. Hawksworth was one of the coming men in this department. He had already had a long spell in the Drawing Office and was firmly regarded as the 'power behind the throne', while G.H. Burrows continued as Chief Draughtsman and in view of future developments Stanier felt that Hawksworth should have a further spell in top management in the works. Collett would have none of it, arguing that he could not spare him from the Drawing Office, and appointed R.A.G. Hannington as Locomotive Works Manager, an admirable choice, none the less. Hawksworth succeeded Burrows as Chief Locomotive Draughtsman in 1925.

Unlike some of the major railways of Great Britain, the Great Western had added no new express passenger locomotives to its stock during practically the entire period of the First World War. The 'Princess' series of four-cylinder 4-6-0s was completed shortly after the outbreak of war. This was in itself a tribute to the reliability and general usefulness of the 'Star' and 'Saint' Classes; but to meet the needs of expanding traffics in the early 1920s more engines were needed, and as there had been no opportunity since Collett became Chief Mechanical Engineer for a new design to be worked out, an order was given for 12 more 'Stars'. These engines, Nos 4061–4072 were named after Abbeys. They were turned out at midsummer 1922 in the plain green livery of wartime, and with cast iron chimneys unadorned by any of the pre-war finery. That was to come back later. The 'Abbeys' included one significant change from former practice in that they had hollow crank axles. This arose primarily from an improvement in manufacturing technique. At Swindon they were then starting to heat-treat the axles, which greatly improved the outside, but did not at first penetrate to the centre. But in boring out the axle, the coolant affected the structure of the metal at the heart of the axle, and gave an excellent uniformity throughout. It also had the advantage of reducing dead weight. However, while every consideration had to be given to means of saving dead weight, this was not the primary cause of the change in design. As Stanier put it to me, 'The reduction in dead weight was a bonus'. Nevertheless, in view of the heavier and more powerful

Left *Fourteen-coach 500-ton trains did not wait for the introduction of the 'Castles': No 4064* Reading Abbey *on a down 'Cornish Riviera Express' of caravan length at Twyford.* (Author's collection)

Below and bottom *Two views of* Caerphilly Castle *in photographic grey as posed for the camera in August 1923.* (British Railways)

locomotives then in contemplation the use of hollow crank axles on the 'Abbeys' can be regarded as an interesting try-out of a practice that Stanier was to carry to all the axles of his own 'Duchess' Class 'Pacifics' on the LMS.

Details apart, the 'Abbeys' were splendid engines. However, one can quite imagine that their relatively sombre appearance and lack of enhanced tractive effort did not please the fire-eating General Manager when a month or so previously the Great Northern had introduced the first two of the Gresley 'Pacifics' with a tractive effort considerably greater than that of the 'Abbeys'. It was all very well for the recently retired Churchward to poke fun at the new Great Northern 'Pacific' exclaiming, 'What did that young man want to build it for, when we would have sold him ours!' The honour of possessing the most powerful express engines had passed from the Great Western, and Pole told Collett he must do something about it. Churchward's own scheme for fitting larger boilers to the 'Saints' and 'Stars' having been vetoed by the Civil Engineer, Collett set the Drawing Office to work out a compromise by making the greatest increase in boiler size which was possible consistent with retaining the full 'Red' route classification. This resulted in a boiler which was significantly better than the No 1 boiler, but was lighter than the No 7 boiler proposed in 1919.

In basic dimensions, the 'Castles' showed remarkably little difference from the 'Stars' other than in the boiler. The wheelbase of the engine was the same, but 1 ft was added to the rear of the frame. This helped to accommodate a longer firebox, but it also allowed the fitting of a larger cab. By reducing tyres and clearances, it was found possible to increase the cylinder diameter to 16 in. As the same size of valve was used as in the 'Stars', the valve and port size in relation to cylinder diameter was less favourable than in the latter. However, the design of the cylinders was so similar to that of the 'Stars' that the initial drawing for issue to the works was made by altering in red certain dimensions on a copy of a 'Star' cylinder drawing. The pattern for the inside cylinders had a loose section which provided the smokebox saddle, and could be changed to allow the manufacture of cylinders for both 'Star' and 'Castle' boilers. There was a minor change in the valve setting in that the lead was $\frac{3}{16}$ in in place of $\frac{1}{8}$ in on the 'Stars'. The layout of the motion and chassis was almost identical with the 'Stars', and again changes in the dimensions of the motion parts were made, where necessary, by alterations to a 'Star' drawing.

In the boiler, the main increase was an addition of 1 ft to the length of the firebox, making it 10 ft. To give a further increase to the grate area, the water space above the foundation ring was reduced below the normal Churchward figure of $3\frac{1}{2}$ to 3 in. The grate area was thus 30.3 sq ft. This was an increase of 12 per cent on the 'Stars', which closely matched the increase of 14 per cent in the nominal tractive effort. The barrel was 3 in greater in diameter throughout than in the No 1 boiler, but 3 in less than in the No 7. The back of the firebox was sloped slightly outwards, so that the increase in length was less at the top than at the bottom; the back of the firebox in the No 1 boiler was vertical. The general proportions of the boiler followed normal Churchward lines, except for the reduction in the water space.

Outwardly the changes in the locomotive were more spectacular than the internal changes. The outside steam pipes were an innovation for a GWR 4-6-0, though their introduction on the 5-ft 8-in 2-8-0s of the '4700' Class reminds me of an amusing Drawing Office incident told me by W.N. Pellow who was Locomotive Running Superintendent during the last years of the GWR. On all the standard two-cylinder engines, the cylinders and valve chests were contained in a pair of iron castings which included the steam and exhaust passages and also included the saddle carrying the smokebox. While the exhaust passages were fairly direct, the steam passages, consisting of pipes inside the smokebox and through the composite iron casting to the valve chests, were rather tortuous.

Pellow, as a young draughtsman, had the job of laying out the proposed new arrangement, and one day Churchward came along to see how things were progressing. From the many stories I have heard at Swindon, it seems that 'The Old Man' liked nothing better than to settle down at a drawing board and listen to all the 'pros and cons' of any new proposal that was being

Above *No 4078* Pembroke Castle. (W.J. Reynolds)

Top *No 4081* Warwick Castle *at Old Oak Common sheds.* (W.J. Reynolds)

investigated, and on this occasion he sat down at Pellow's board. The Chief Draughtsman, G.H. Burrows, began to explain what they were trying to do. But Churchward cut him short with: 'You shunt up, Burrows. Let the young man tell me himself.' Pellow then explained how they were trying to get a straight and direct passage from the regulator to the steam chest, and Churchward remarked, 'Oh yes, I know; this is one of Stanier's novel ideas. Go on.' And the 'novel idea' was accepted and afterwards became standard practice on all the future outside-cylindered Great Western locomotives of both two- and four-cylinder types, though in the case of 'Castles' and 'Kings', the outside steam pipe could not be straight because of the disposition of the outside cylinders in relation to the smokebox saddle.

This change brought several benefits. The joints of the steam pipes for the outside cylinder were removed from an inaccessible position at the rear of the smokebox to the outside. The 'Star' steam pipes emerged from the bottom of the rear of the smokebox, and then turned through two right angles to reach the cylinders. Their removal from this position not only made a useful clearance in the congested space between the frames, but also removed an obstruction from the lower smoke tubes, access to which had previously been difficult. The new pattern of steam pipe was more flexible than the old one, and was therefore less affected by those movements of the cylinders on the frames, and the flexing of the frames themselves, which were euphemistically described as 'breathing'.

The appearance of the 'Castle', with its higher boiler, larger cab and outside steam pipes, was automatically more impressive than that of the 'Star', but the effect was clinched by the restoration of the embellishments which had characterized Swindon engines in pre-war days—copper-capped chimney, brass beading on the splashers, and fully-lined livery. The only weakness in the effect was the continuation of the small 3,500-gallon tender. The increase of 12-14 per cent in potential output was achieved for an increase of 6 per cent in the weight. This permitted a total increase of 5 tons 9 cwt on the coupled wheels. For this small increase in weight, a significant improvement was made in the most outstanding British type of the pre-war period; adherence to existing standards made manufacture simple and cheap, and the engine was able to go straight into main-line service.

The names of the first ten of these engines were:

4073 *Caerphilly Castle*
4074 *Caldicot Castle*
4075 *Cardiff Castle*
4076 *Carmarthen Castle*
4077 *Chepstow Castle*
4078 *Pembroke Castle*
4079 *Pendennis Castle*
4080 *Powderham Castle*
4081 *Warwick Castle*
4082 *Windsor Castle*

No 4073 *Caerphilly Castle* appeared in August 1923, and was followed, between December 1923 and April 1924, by nine more. The first six were named after Welsh castles, but the series ended with *Windsor Castle*. The publicity which had attended the introduction of the class was further developed with this last engine. On 28 April 1924, Their Majesties King George V and Queen Mary visited Swindon Works. The Royal Train was worked by *Windsor Castle*; at the end of the visit, on the return journey from the works yard to the station, the King and Queen rode on the engine, and the King drove. Brass plates were later fitted to the cab sides bearing the following remarkable inscription, and from that time, for many years, *Windsor Castle* became the recognized GWR Royal engine.

G R
This engine
No 4082 'Windsor Castle' was built at
Swindon in April 1924
and was driven from the works to the
station by
His Majesty King George V
accompanied by Queen Mary
on the occasion of the visit by their
Majesties
to the Great Western Railway Works at
Swindon on April 28th 1924
With Their Majesties on the footplate
were

Viscount Churchill	*Chairman*
Sir Felix Pole	*General Manager*
Mr C.B. Collett	*Chief Mechanical Engineer*
Locomotive Inspector	*G.H. Flewellyn*
Engine driver	*E.R.B. Rowe*
Fireman	*A.W. Cook*

Then amid all the euphoria and the publicity engendered by the book *Caerphilly Castle*, issued officially by the GWR at Paddington and sold in tens of thousands in the first months, Collett dropped his bombshell into the headquarters—he scrapped *The Great Bear*! The technical reasons for this have been referred to in an earlier chapter of this book, but the impact at Paddington, particularly in the highest echelons of management, was stunning. Despite all the recent 'ballyhoo' surrounding the introduction of the 'Castles'—the most powerful passenger train engine in the Kingdom—to many Great Western men *The Great Bear* was still the flagship of the fleet. As recently as January 1920, *The Railway Magazine* included as frontispiece a beautiful colour plate in the finest 'F. Moore' style of the great engine as it was in the wartime livery, and accompanied the plate with some extended references to it in some fully authoritative 'Pertinent Paragraphs' including a dimensional diagram. One gathers that Collett was summoned to Paddington to face an exceedingly irate General Manager to be asked, in as many words', 'What the h— was he doing?' Of course all the familiar reasons were quoted, like limited route availability and so on, and some amends were afterwards made by naming the rejuvenated engine No 111, in its 'Castle' guise, *Viscount Churchill*. But the references to route availability gave Sir Felix Pole food for thought. With the retirement of W.W. Grierson from the post of Chief Civil Engineer at the end of 1923, the last of the chief officers of the Company who reported direct to the Board were gone, and Pole, as he afterwards expressed it, became the first true General Manager of the Great Western Railway.

In 1924 there was held in London the First World Power Conference. Collett himself read a paper on 'Testing of Locomotives on the Great Western

Above left Caerphilly Castle *in running colours with a bowler-hatted inspector on the footplate at Old Oak Common.* (W.J. Reynolds)

Left *No 4076* Carmarthen Castle *at Old Oak Common.* (W.J. Reynolds)

Above The Great Bear *in her last days at Old Oak Common shed in plain green.* (Real Photos Co Ltd)

Right The Great Bear *rebuilt as a 'Castle', retaining the old number 111 and the original tender but named* Viscount Churchill. (British Railways)

Railway'. The paper gave an account, a most detailed account indeed, of that part of Swindon's work which had then been published, but also were included the results of the full-dress trials carried out on the new 4-6-0 engine *Caldicot Castle* in March of that year. Although naturally Collett presented the paper himself on so important an occasion, the draft had been prepared by the senior draughtsman in charge of engine testing at that time, C.K. Dumas. No more than abridged versions appeared in the technical press of that year; but in 1926 the full script was published in *The Railway Magazine* under Dumas's own name, but not including the details of the *Caldicot Castle* test runs. As enthusiasts of the present generation are probably unfamilar with the equipment and procedure of dynamometer car testing and the duties required of the staff involved, some excerpts from Dumas's article may prove helpful.

* * *

Taking first the dynamometer car itself, it included apparatus for recording the following items:

1 The pull of the drawbar
2 The speed of the train
3 Time
4 Passing of mileposts, stations and so on.
5 Points at which indicator cards are taken
6 The working of the engine
7 The work done at the drawbar

All these items are recorded on a roll of paper which is passed over a table at a speed proportional to that of the train, the travel of the paper usually being from 6 in to 1 ft per mile run. The actuating gear is driven from one of the axles of the car or, in some cases, from an extra wheel which can be lowered into contact with the rail when required.

The drawbar pull may be recorded by attaching the drawbar of the car to a spring which will, of course, be deflected by an extent depending on the pull. A bracket is also connected to the drawbar, or to a suitable portion of the spring gear, and this bracket is mounted over the table across which the paper travels in such a way as to move with the deflection of the spring, in a direction at right angles to the motion of the paper. A stylographic pen is attached to this bracket which draws a line on the paper in the same way as the line drawn by a recording barometer. The distance between this line at any instant and that which the pen would have drawn had there been no deflection on the spring is, of course, a measure of the drawbar pull at that instant. The latter line is drawn by means of a fixed pen suitably attached to the table.

The speed of the train may be recorded in various ways. Usually it is combined with the record of time in the following manner. A pen, which is mounted over the paper on which the records are made, is attached to an electromagnet in such a way that when the magnet is energized the pen is deflected and a serration is made in the line it is drawing. In the car is a clock arranged to make electrical contact, and so energize the magnet at regular intervals, usually of a few seconds. It will readily be seen that the faster the train, and consequently the paper, is travelling, the greater will be the distance between the serrations, and by measuring this distance with a suitably graded scale the speed can be read at any point.

The passing of mileposts, stations and so on is recorded by means of another electromagnetic pen

Below *Two views of the interior of Churchward's dynamometer car as modernized for tests carried out in 1955.* (British Railways)

similar to that used for recording time. In this case contact is made by means of an ordinary bell-push in the car by an observer riding therein, whose duty it is to watch the road and press the button at the moment of passing any object, such as a station, which it is desired to record. He will, at the same time, call out the name of the station, which is written down against the mark made by the pen by an operator at the table.

The points at which indicator cards are taken is similarly recorded, the button in this case being in the shelter attached to the front of the engine. Another button on the engine footplate enables the observer riding there to record changes in the boiler pressure, and cut-off. In this case notes must be made, and the observer's notebook subsequently compared with the record made in the dynamometer car; the changes in the working of the engine can then be written down against the serrations in the line on the record.

The work done at the drawbar is measured and recorded by means of an instrument known as an 'integrator'. In its most usual form this consists of a horizontal revolving disc, which is driven from one of the car axles or from the extra wheel referred to above. Its speed of revolution will consequently be proportional to that of the train. A small vertical roller rests on this disc, the frictional contact with which causes it to revolve. This roller is connected to the drawbar pull recording gear in such a way that the greater the pull the further is the roller from the centre of the disc and consequently the faster it will revolve for any given speed of the train. The revolutions of the roller will thus be a measure of the work done and they can be indicated by means of a counter and also recorded on the paper by an electromagnetic pen.

The steam pressure is read at intervals by an observer riding on the footplate, and from his readings the average pressure throughout the trip is obtained. The degree of superheat is determined by measuring the temperature of the superheated steam by means of a pyrometer. The temperature of the saturated steam can be determined from its pressure by reference to what is known as a 'steam table', and when this temperature is known a simple subtraction sum will give the degree of superheat.

The distribution of steam in the cylinders and the mean effective pressure on the pistons are both ascertained by means of an instrument known as an 'indicator'. This information is extremely useful and the application of the instrument, commonly called 'indicating' the engine, is frequently carried out alone apart from any other experimental work. There are various makes of indicator, differing in details, but they all work on the same principle. A small cylinder of about $\frac{5}{8}$ in bore is connected, at its bottom end, to one of the cylinders of the engine. In this small cylinder is a piston, the upward motion of which is resisted by a spring. A pencil is connected to the rod of the piston through the medium of a lever by means of which the motion of the pencil represents, on an enlarged scale, the motion of the piston. It will readily be seen that the greater the pressure of steam in the engine cylinder at any instant, the higher will be the position of the indicator piston, and consequently of the pencil, at that instant. That is to say, the position of the pencil at any time will be a measure of the steam pressure in the cylinder at that time.

Attached to the indicator cylinder is a drum around the base of which a cord is wound. By pulling the cord the drum can be rotated, the rotation being resisted by a spring. When the cord is released the drum will, of course, rotate in the opposite direction. A lever is connected at its long end to the crosshead of the engine and the short end consequently repeats the motion of the piston but on a reduced scale.

To obtain a record, a piece of paper is coiled around the drum and clipped to it. The cord on the drum is then attached to the short end of the lever and the motion of the drum will then repeat that of the piston, but on a smaller scale. Between the engine cylinder and that of the indicator is a cock, so arranged that in one position the lower end of the indicator cylinder is open to the atmosphere and in another is in connection with the engine cylinder. With the cock in the former position the pencil is pressed against the drum and as the latter reciprocates a straight line will be drawn on the paper. This is known as the 'atmospheric' line. The cock is then turned to the other position and the pencil again pressed against the drum. This time a curved line will be drawn the height of which from the atmospheric line at any part of the travel of the drum will be a measure of the pressure of steam on the engine piston at the corresponding part of its stroke. The record thus obtained is known as an 'indicator card' or 'indicator diagram'.

By taking such indicator cards from each end of the engine cylinder, the distribution of steam throughout the stroke can be seen at a glance and the 'mean effective pressure', ie the average steam pressure on each stroke less the average back pressure on the return stroke, readily calculated. It is usual to indicate one side of the engine only, that is to say one cylinder in the case of a two-cylinder engine or one inside cylinder in the case of a four-cylinder engine. As both sides of the engine are actuated by similar valve gear, cards from each side would be identical.

Indicator cards are taken at intervals which must be sufficiently short to enable the average performance of the engine throughout the trip to be determined with reasonable accuracy. From the mean effective pressure, speed, dimensions of cylinders and diameter of driving wheels, the horsepower developed in the cylinders can be calculated. The horsepower so obtain-

Right *No 4074* Caldicot Castle *with the Swindon dynamometer car and test train ready for the historic trials between Swindon and Plymouth in 1924.* (British Railways)

Below right *A view looking forward into the indicator shelter on the left-hand side of the engine.* (British Railways)

ed is termed the 'indicated' horsepower, and is often referred to as the 'IHP'.

To obtain a true record it is essential that the pipes connecting the indicators to the engine cylinders should be short. These instruments will thus be situated close to the cylinders, and the men operating them must therefore ride there. A shelter is necessary to protect them (and anyone else who may be riding on the front of the engine for the purpose of reading smokebox vacuum, etc) from the wind and weather and to prevent them from falling off.

* * *

In March 1924, No 4074 *Caldicot Castle* was given a thorough series of tests between Swindon and Plymouth. The test trains were made up to the maximum tonnage allowed to an unassisted engine over each section of the line, as follows:

Down line:	Swindon to Taunton	485 tons
	Taunton to Newton Abbot	390 tons
	Newton Abbot to Plymouth	288 tons
Up line:	Plymouth to Newton Abbot	
	Newton Abbot to Swindon	485 tons

The logs of the three down journeys, as between Swindon and Taunton, are tabulated opposite. Weather conditions varied between the runs, the effect of west winds being very apparent on the exposed stretch of line over the marshes south of Bridgwater. Before Badminton, the passing times were fairly uniform, and a further table, on page 122, shows the variations in cut-off which contributed to this uniformity.

No high speeds were attempted down to Stoke Gifford, and it was beyond Pylle Hill Junction that the running became energetic again. On each run 25 per cent cut-off was used as far as the summit at Flax Bourton, and on the first run this cut-off was maintained to Uphill. On the dead level between Yatton and Puxton, speed was between 73½ and 75 mph, with a drawbar pull of 2.3 to 2.4 tons and full boiler pressure. At Uphill, cut-off was reduced to 22 per cent, and speed fell away gradually to 62 mph south of Bridgwater.

On the second run, cut-off was reduced to 21 per cent at Flax Bourton, and speed fell to 62½ mph at Uphill, but it then varied by no more than 2 mph over the next 18 miles. On the third run conditions were more favourable, and a cut-off of 20 per cent from Flax Bourton gave a steady speed of 68 mph for 14 miles from Brent Knoll. The effect of the wind was also marked on the return trips; on 15 March a drawbar pull of 2.25 tons sufficed for a speed of 64 on the level, but on 20 March 2.75 tons was needed for 56 mph. The handling of the engine on the climb to Whiteball was interesting. Cut-off was fixed at 30 per cent once the train was under way from Taunton, and was left in this position to the summit. By this date it was more usual for cut-off to be advanced progressively on a climb such as this.

By 1923 there were few British locomotives off the GWR which could better 4 lb of coal per drawbar horsepower hour, and many famous types were using 4½ to 6 lb. The figure for No 4074 was 2.83 lb. To make this figure a true basis for comparing engines burning different grades of coal, allowance must be made for the heat content, or calorific value, of the coal. For Northern hard coals, the figure equivalent to this would be about 3.0 lb, but no allowance for calorific value could make this other than a remarkable result. More than one engineer came to the conclusion that it just could not be true; E.S. Cox has told how this opinion was reached at Horwich after a detailed comparison had been made between the 'Castle' and the Hughes 4-6-0 to see if any difference in design could be found which would account for the difference between the 2.83 lb of the 'Castle' and the 5 lb of the Lancashire & Yorkshire engine.

GWR: Dynamometer car trials, March 1924

Engine 4074 *Caldicot Castle*
Load 14 cars + dynamometer car, 484 tons tare

Run No		1		2		3	
Date		14 March		19 March		25 March	
Distance (miles)		**Actual (m s)**	**Speed (mph)**	**Actual (m s)**	**Speed (mph)**	**Actual (m s)**	**Speed (mph)**
0.0	Milepost 78	0 00		0 00		0 00	
2.0	Milepost 80	5 55		5 06		4 55	
		check		check			
4.9	Wootton Bassett	9 43		9 20		8 36	
9.0	Milepost 87	15 12		13 53		12 56	
11.0	Milepost 89	17 07	63½	15 47	65	14 43	69
16.0	Milepost 94	22 15	52	20 57	53	19 37	53
18.0	Milepost 96	24 34	51½	23 16	50½	21 54	52
20.0	Milepost 98	26 55	51½	25 36	51½	24 14	50½
21.0	Milepost 99	28 07	50	26 46	51½	25 24	51½
22.0	Badminton	29 19	50	27 56	51½	26 36	50
		check		check		check	
26.6	Chipping Sodbury	34 12		33 00		31 24	
31.9	Winterbourne	40 51	65	39 19	66	37 48	66
34.8	Filton Junction	44 46		43 18		41 35	
38.0	Stapleton Road	50 26		49 06		47 08	
				sigs			
40.3	*Pylle Hill Junction*	55 14		55 43		52 49	
41.6	Milepost 120	58 11		57 43		54 53	
44.6	Milepost 123	62 18	45	61 51	44	58 51	45
45.9	Flax Bourton	63 51		63 26		60 09	
50.6	Milepost 129	68 00	75	67 44	71	64 37	73
55.2	Puxton	72 05	73½	72 04	68	68 47	72
59.6	Milepost 138	75 23		75 37		72 12	
60.2	Uphill	75 57	70½	76 14	66½	72 48	69
64.1	Brent Knoll	79 23	65½	79 47	66½	76 13	68
66.9	HIGHBRIDGE	81 57	63	82 17	64½	78 39	68
70.7	Dunball	85 35	62	85 49	65½	82 02	68
73.2	BRIDGWATER	87 55	63	88 03	65½	84 12	68
77.6	Milepost 156	92 05	62	92 04	65½	88 05	68
						sigs	
79.6	Milepost 158	94 12	55½	93 59	61	90 03	
81.6	Milepost 160	96 14	60	95 53	64½	sigs	
83.6	Milepost 162	98 15		97 46		sig	
84.7	TAUNTON	100 30		100 15		stop	
	Average speeds:						
	Milepost 129 to 138	73.2		68.5		71.3	
	Mileposts 138 to 156	64.7		65.7		68.0	

Location	Actual (m	s)	Average speed (mph)	Cut-off (per cent)	Regulator opening
Milepost 163¼ (Taunton yard)	0	00		45	Full
Milepost 163¾				35	Full
Milepost 164	1	57		35	Full
Milepost 164½				30	Full
Milepost 165	3	23	41.9	30	Full
Milepost 166	4	34	50.6	30	Full
Milepost 167	5	42	52.9	30	Full
Milepost 168	6	51	52.2	30	Full
Milepost 169	7	59	52.9	30	Full
Milepost 170	9	08	52.2	30	Full
Milepost 171	10	15	53.7	30	Full
Milepost 172	11	29	48.6	30	Full
Milepost 173	13	00	39.6	30	Full
Milepost 174 (Whiteball)	14	48	33.3	18	⅛
Milepost 177	18	03	55.4	18	⅛
Milepost 179 (Tiverton Junction)	19	42	72.7	18	⅛
Milepost 180	20	34	69.2	18	⅛
Milepost 182	22	13	72.7	18	⅛
Milepost 185	24	45	71.0	18	⅛
Milepost 187	26	27	70.6	18	Full
Milepost 189	28	03	75.0	18	Full
Milepost 191	29	40	74.3	18	⅛
Milepost 192	31	29	73.5	18	Shut
Milepost 193½	32	08	54.6	18	Shut
EXETER (193.9 miles)	32	50		25	Full
Milepost 194 PASS	32	59	35.3	25	Full

In fairness it should be said that, although this figure came from the average of several trials, in later years, when the standard of testing at Swindon had been raised still higher, more confirmation of figures between road and plant tests would have been demanded before a published claim was made. At this time the testing plant at Swindon could not absorb the power of a large locomotive, so road tests were the only means of obtaining the information.

12. The 'Castle' storm centre

The coal consumption figure of 2.83 lb per drawbar horsepower hour claimed for *Caldicot Castle* on one of her three return trips from Swindon to Plymouth and back in March 1924 not only took the British locomotive world completely by surprise but it caused a good deal of controversy and disbelief for many years afterwards. Naturally Swindon was anxious to establish the new engines as something to beat all others that had gone before, but I have thought that the publication of a chart in Collett's paper showing comparative figures for coal consumption of 'Star' and 'Castle' Class engines at that early date in the history of the latter class was stretching things a little too far. The figure related to the first four months of 1924. Doubtless the 'Castle' figures covered all the ten engines of the class then running, all stationed at Old Oak Common, but there were then 73 engines of the 'Star' class, and one would be curious to know if any selection had been made, or whether Collett's chart covered the working of the entire stud, barring those stopped for repair or general overhaul. The figures included on the charts were:

Months (1924)	**Jan**	**Feb**	**March**	**April**
Coal (lbs/mile)				
'Star'	45.7	46.7	46.5	46.2
'Castle'	44.7	41.3	42.8	43.0

To a locomotive enthusiast like myself, the introduction of the 'Castles' was of course a major event, and in my College days and living in South Kensington I had many opportunities for observing the working at Paddington. In those early months I formed the impression that apart from the down 'Limited' and its balancing turn, the up 'Dutchman', the 'Castles' were not being used on the heaviest trains, as for example those to and from South Wales. A day's photography on the lineside in early May confirmed that impression, that the only trains 'Castle'-hauled were the down and up 'Limited' and the up 'Dutchman'. A further visit to Twyford, when I met the veteran photographer H. Gordon Tidey at the lineside, brought even more negative results to Tidey's great annoyance; not a single 'Castle' all day!

Before the time of these lineside visits there had been the Empire Exhibition at Wembley, the greatest exhibition seen in Britain. In the Palace of Engineering were displayed, end to end, No 4073 *Caerphilly Castle* and London and North Eastern No 4472 *Flying Scotsman*. Both engines glistened in the highest finish which their respective Works could achieve, the brass beading and copper chimney cap of the 'Castle' being matched by the fittings of the 'Pacific' which were made from an alloy devised at Doncaster to look more like gold than normal brass. To the casual observer there can have been little doubt about the capacities of the engines. With its extra wheels, higher boiler and vast firebox, the 'Pacific' almost dwarfed the 'Castle', and the comparision was accentuated by the eight-wheeled tender of the former. What then of the board displayed before the 'Castle' proclaiming it to be the most powerful passenger engine in Britain?

Fortunately for later LNER locomotive history, the idea of putting the claim to the test occurred to other people than the exhibition visitors and the amateur railway fraternity. The suggestion for an exchange of locomotives seems to have been made by Sir Felix Pole to his opposite number on the LNER; when asked about this at a later date, Pole was reticent, but this may have been because he regretted the ill-feeling which was later caused by the exchange. Gresley is said to have been unenthusiastic, as he was not yet fully satisfied with the performance of his 'Pacifics', but to those close to him he gave the impression of welcoming an opportunity for an interchange of technical information.

A mighty haul without a 'Castle': Neath Abbey *on the 'Torbay Limited'.* (Author's collection)

Left *Visitor to the East Coast main line in 1925: No 4079* Pendennis Castle *at Old Oak Common.* (W.J. Reynolds)

Below and bottom *The protagonists at King's Cross Top Shed;* Pendennis Castle *and* Flying Fox. (W.J. Reynolds)

The proposal was accepted by the Boards and managements of the two companies, and it was arranged that a 'Castle' should work on the LNER for a week, and a Gresley 'Pacific' on the GWR. Coal and water consumptions would be measured but, unfortunately, although both railways had dynamometer cars they were not used.

In the very week when I was writing this chapter, news came through that *Flying Scotsman* was being shipped to Australia to take part in that country's bicentennial celebrations. One could take with the proverbial 'pinch of salt' the same newspaper's statement that plans are being made for a Sydney-Perth race against an Australian locomotive, although one of the preserved New South Wales 'Pacifics' of Class 'C38' would doubtless provide an interesting contrast in appearance to the British locomotive. But while *Flying Scotsman* is in Australia, why could not his great rival of 1925 meet him again, none other than *Pendennis Castle*? One can be sure that there are still LNER men living who recall the thunderous and surefooted way in which *Pendennis Castle* took the test trains of 1925 out of King's Cross, making faster times up the Holloway bank and on over the Northern Heights than ever the Gresley 'Pacifics' managed before their valve gear was improved. I know that *Pendennis Castle* is now ensconced on the Hammersley Iron Railway, in the far north-west of Australia, with no railway connection to the rest of he Commonwealth systems. But having shipped *Flying Scotsman* half-way round the world, could not *Pendennis Castle* be moved down to Perth?

Now reverting to the actual week of the Interchange Trials, 27 April to 2 May 1925, there could be no doubt that Gresley was very disappointed by the performance of his 'Pacifics' on the LNER main line, the chosen King's Cross engine failing and being taken off its train on the first day, and the substitute proving to be a poor choice. On the Great Western, engine No 4074 and her crew did some excellent work keeping the exacting sectional times of the down 'Limited' with maximum loads on the very first day. The 'Cornish Riviera Express' between Paddington and Plymouth was without much doubt the most severe task then set to a British express locomotive, and to keep time at all, not only on the very first day, was a remarkable feat for a strange engine and crew. But this is a book about Great Western locomotives, and I have already referred briefly to the impression created by the brilliant work of *Pendennis Castle* between King's Cross and Doncaster. As for *Caldicot Castle*, whether by official instigation or by the sheer *joie de vivre* of her crew, her maximum effort in their apparent disregard of the timetable caused consternation on all sides, delight to the GWR supporters, and annoyance to their rivals, which aroused serious repercussions later.

Caldicot Castle and her crew began the week by bringing the up 'Limited' into Paddington exactly 15 minutes early. The gain in time, as shown in the accompanying log, was from Exeter, where the train had made its usual passenger stop and attached an extra coach on this particular Monday. The 'Castle' carried a heavier load than the LNER 'Pacific' on all the latter's up journeys from the West of England. More than this, there was a permanent way speed restriction on the upper part of the 1 in 222 bank between Lavington and Patney which cost *Caldicot Castle* about 2 minutes in running. Fortunately for the LNER engine the track work had been completed on the Tuesday, and the visitor could steam at full speed up the Patney bank. But despite this hindrance, and the extra load, *Caldicot Castle* averaged 63.5 mph from Exeter to Paddington, and the running average over the 168.9 miles from Stoke Canon to Westbourne Park was 65.2 mph or 66.2 mph net. The average speeds from point to point are shown in the last column of the log, while of the principal uphill speeds the minimum at milepost 122¾ was 46½ mph. After Westbury speed was worked up to 68 mph on the level before Lavington, and 4 miles of the 1 in 222 bank had been mounted without falling below 61 mph when the permanent way check came.

After regaining speed and breasting the rest of the climb to Savernake there came the brilliant finish which brought the train into Paddington just a quarter of an hour early. Spectacular as this was, however, the time

GWR: Up 'Cornish Riviera Express', 27 April 1925

Engine 4074 *Caldicot Castle*
Load 358 tons tare, 380 tons full

Distance (miles)		Schedule (min)	Actual (m s)	Average speed* (mph)
0.0	Exeter	0	0 00	—
3.5	Stoke Canon		6 14	33.7
12.6	Cullompton		15 33	58.3
14.9	Tiverton Junction		18 07	54.5
19.9	Whiteball box		23 31	55.3
23.7	Wellington		26 54	67.2
30.8	Taunton	33	32 15	78.8
35.8	Cogload Junction	38	36 30	70.5
58.4	Castle Cary	61	56 10	69.7
61.8	Bruton		59 11	67.6
65.2	Milepost 122¾		63 09	51.5
72.4	Frome		70 00	62.1
78.1	Westbury	83	76 14	55.5
82.3	Edington		81 00	53.5
87.3	Lavington		85 21	68.9
—			pws	
92.6	Patney		92 10	46.7
98.4	Pewsey		98 00	59.7
103.6	Savernake		102 57	63.1
120.6	Newbury	124	117 19	71.0
135.9	Southcote Junction		129 59	72.5
137.7	Reading	142	132 10	48.6
142.7	Twyford	147	136 58	62.4
155.2	Slough	159	147 09	72.7
164.6	Southall	168	155 01	71.4
172.4	Westbourne Park		161 27	72.5
173.7	Paddington	179	164 01	—

Net time 162 minutes

* Average speeds from point to point

Above *Laira-based No 4086* Builth Castle *on the 14-coach down 'Limited' at Twyford.* (M.W. Earley)

Left *Another Laira-based engine, No 4085* Berkeley Castle, *on a down stopping train near Twyford.* (M.W. Earley)

of 66 min 1 sec over the 75.3 miles from Pewsey to Paddington was not such a record as might at first appear. Less than eight months before the Interchange Trials I was travelling by the up 'Cornish Riviera Express' and recovering some of the time lost by delays further west, we ran the concluding stretch from Pewsey to Paddington in 66 min 40 sec. This was with engine No 4066 *Malvern Abbey* and an eight-coach train of 315 tons full. But even better was the run reported in *The Railway Magazine* of December 1924, on which engine No 4008 *Royal Star* practically equalled the time of my own run, 66 min 32 sec, but with a ten-coach train, of 370 tons full. The circumstances on each of the 'Star' runs were that there was time to be made up, whereas on the first day of the 1925 trials *Caldicot Castle* was already running nearly 7 minutes ahead of time when she passed Pewsey. Her running afterwards was an almost exact copy of those of *Malvern Abbey* and *Royal Star* with a 380-ton load.

While the working of the up 'Limited', even with a load of nearly 400 tons, could be regarded as something of a 'romp' with a 'Castle' and a clear road, the westbound train with its maximum winter loading was without much doubt the most severe task set to any British locomotive at that time. Indeed, some of the regular drivers who were a little less punctilious over their sectional timekeeping used to lose 2 and 3 minutes on the severe initial allowance of 97½ minutes for the 95.6 miles from Paddington, detach their slip coaches there a little behind time, and knowing that all being well they could easily regain those lost minutes between Castle Cary and Cogload Junction. But on the last day of the Interchange running, *Caldicot Castle* was worked hard from the very start and passed Westbury nearly 3 minutes early, in the fastest time I have ever seen with a 'Castle' and such a load as 530 tons. It is noteworthy that the downhill speeds from Savernake were not exceptionally high. The intermediate booking of 22½ minutes from Westbury to Castle Cary was severe, and it was not until the latter junction had been passed that really substantial gains on schedule time began to be made. In comparison with many noteworthy 'King' runs on the down 'Limited' made since the by-pass lines were constructed, the effect of the speed restrictions through Westbury and Frome stations, essential at the time of the Interchange trials and for some years

GWR: Down 'Cornish Riviera Express', 2 May 1925

Engine 4074 *Caldicot Castle*
Load cars, tons, E/F
To Westbury: 14, 498/530
To Taunton: 12, 426/455
To Exeter: 10, 363/385
To Plymouth: 8, 292/310

Distance (miles)		Schedule (min)	Actual (m	s)	Average speed (mph)
0.0	Paddington	0	0	00	—
1.3	Westbourne Park		3	15	24.0
5.7	Ealing		9	08	43.9
9.1	Southall	11	12	42	56.9
13.2	West Drayton		16	41	61.8
18.5	Slough	20	21	26	67.0
24.2	Maidenhead	25½	26	36	66.2
31.0	Twyford	31½	32	49	65.7
34.1	Sonning box		35	38	65.2
36.0	Reading	37	37	25	62.8
37.8	Southcote Junction		39	31	51.3
41.2	Theale		42	57	59.1
44.8	Aldermaston		46	20	63.7
49.6	Thatcham		51	06	61.8
53.1	Newbury	56	54	38	59.2
58.5	Kintbury		60	05	59.5
61.5	Hungerford		63	12	59.0
66.4	Bedwyn	69½	68	17	58.0
70.1	Savernake		72	25	53.6
75.3	Pewsey		77	25	62.6
81.1	Patney		82	16	72.6
86.9	Lavington		87	00	73.3
91.1	Edington		90	38	69.3
95.6	Westbury	97½	94	40	67.2
101.3	Frome		101	40	48.9
106.6	Witham		108	03	49.8
108.5	Milepost 122¾		110	24	56.0
111.9	Bruton		113	25	67.7
115.2	Castle Cary	120	116	18	69.0
120.2	Keinton Mandeville		120	26	72.6
122.4	Charlton Mackrell		122	30	65.0
125.7	Somerton		125	28	66.6
129.9	Langport		129	16	66.5
134.9	Athelney		133	30	70.7
137.9	Cogload Junction	143	136	06	69.9
142.9	Taunton	148	140	30	72.5
144.9	Norton Fitzwarren		142	22	63.5
150.0	Wellington		147	17	62.4
151.7	Milepost 172		149	19	50.4
152.7	Milepost 173		150	42	43.4
153.8	Whiteball box		152	12	43.9
158.8	Tiverton Junction		156	46	66.0
161.1	Cullompton		158	38	72.7
165.3	Hele		161	58	77.4
170.2	Stoke Canon		166	00	73.1

Distance (miles)		Schedule (min)	Actual (m s)		Average speed (mph)
172.4	Cowley Bridge Junction		167	50	72.0
173.7	Exeter	179	169	10	58.2
174.5	St Thomas's		170	40	31.9
178.4	Exminster		174	40	58.5
182.2	Starcross		178	00	62.2
185.9	Dawlish		181	50	57.8
188.7	Teignmouth		184	54	54.7
193.9	Newton Abbot	203	190	25	56.9
—			pws		
195.0	Aller Junction		192	25	33.0
197.7	Dainton box	209½	197	40	30.8
202.5	Totnes	215½	203	00	53.9
205.3	Tigley box		206	55	42.9
207.1	Rattery box	223	210	25	30.9
209.4	Brent	225	213	28	45.1
211.6	Wrangaton		215	40	60.0
214.9	Ivybridge		219	10	56.6
219.0	Hemerdon box	237	223	10	61.3
221.7	Plympton		225	41	64.1
—			pws		
223.8	Laira Junction		228	30	44.5
225.4	Mutley		231	10	36.1
225.7	Plymouth North Road	247	231	58	—

thereafter, was to increase the running time between Edington and Witham by about 5 minutes.

Although the gain on time over the Langport cut-off was more than 3 minutes, the running there was not exceptionally fast and there is little doubt that the crew were conserving their efforts for what proved to be an all-out attack on Whiteball. This began immediately after Cogload Junction, and the mile-a-minute rate was sustained almost to Wellington. The minimum speed on the 1 in 80 part of the bank just at the tunnel entrance was a shade over 40 mph, but in the tunnel itself, where the gradient eases to 1 in 127, there was an acceleration, and by the time Whiteball signal box was passed, just over the summit, there was a notable quickening. With some fine speed down the valley, though not reaching 80 mph anywhere, Exeter was passed in the record time of 169 min 10 sec from Paddington. Detaching the slip portion there involved yet another speed restriction because at that time the train was routed through the down platform line, involving a reduction to 25 mph. Three years later after the 'Kings' had been introduced, and the London-Plymouth non-stop time had been cut to the even 4 hours, arrangements were made to detach the Exeter slip portion clear of the station to enable the main train to take the centre road and pass at 70 mph. The slowing enjoined in 1925 involved a time of 6 min 50 sec over the 6 miles between Cowley Bridge and Exminster with *Caldicot Castle*, as compared to 4 min 50 sec on a run with *King James I* in 1928, but by running at the maximum permissible speeds over the coastal section *Caldicot Castle* was able to gain nearly another 3½ minutes to Newton Abbot, and to pass there 13½ minutes early.

But there was little further time to be gained in the last exceedingly difficult 31.8 miles. The fastest time of which I have any knowledge from Newton Abbot to Plympton in Great Western days was made by the now-preserved *Lode Star*, 33 min 40 sec, with a load of 260 tons. *Caldicot Castle*, hampered by a permanent way check between Newton Abbot and Aller Junction, took 35 min 15 sec and so slipped back to 12½ minutes ahead of time at Totnes. The hill climbing was first class, however, but brilliantly as they had mounted the Rattery incline they slipped back a minute between Rattery box and Brent. No—the schedule time of 225 minutes is not a misprint; it is one of the jokes of the GWR working timetables of those days, in booking the down 'Limited' to cover the 2.3 miles from Rattery box to Brent in 2 minutes, an average speed of 69 mph! On 2 May 1925 *Caldicot Castle* and her crew did well to cover the distance in 3 min 3 sec, accelerating from the 30 mph at Rattery summit to a little over 60 mph at Brent. But the curving lengths of the South Devon line are not the place for speeding, and it was only down the Hemerdon bank that a maximum of just over 70 mph was briefly exceeded. At the very finish another permanent way cost them a minute but did not prevent them from clocking in to Plymouth a quarter of an hour early.

The two permanent way checks, at Newton Abbot and Laira Junction, cost about 2 minutes, leaving the net time for the complete run as 230 minutes, or 17 minutes inside schedule; but if account is taken of the speed restrictions which were later removed from the working of the 'Cornish Riviera Express', at Westbury, Frome and Exeter, 7 minutes in all, the equivalent net time comes down to the remarkable figure of 223 minutes, an average of 60.7 mph for the run from Paddington. One hazard that used to affect the running of the train in its approach to North Road station at Plymouth, but which was of no account on that occasion, was the timing of the Southern Railway stopping train from the Friary terminus to Exeter, which took the GWR main line at Lipson Junction and was booked to arrive at North Road only 3 minutes ahead of the down 'Limited'. There was no conflict with Southern local trains on that memorable second of May.

Partisanship among locomotive enthusiasts ran high in the months that followed the Interchange trials, though studying all that was written, now more than 60 years later, I am amazed that so little was made of the magnificent performance of *Caldicot Castle* and her crew on the last day. Of course, certain commentators felt that this was not sporting, to show how much the GWR had in reserve on a competitive occasion like that, especially as it had become common knowledge by the end of the week that the LNER had not been too fortunate in the choice of 'Pacifics' to represent them on their own line. But what really 'set the heather alight' were two short broadcasts, innocuous in themselves but lethal in the construction subsequently put upon them. At that time Cecil J. Allen was doing a good deal of broadcasting, and it was natural that he, as a 'railway expert', should be asked to give talks on the topic that had just recently been all but front page news. He gave two, one in the Children's Hour and one in the evening programme, on his impressions of the Interchange Trials. As Allen himself admitted in replying to some voluminous correspondence in *The Railway Magazine*, his articles and his broadcasts resolved themselves into a defence of the Gresley 'Pacifics'. The latter utterances did not go down at all well at Paddington, and when someone told Sir Felix Pole that Allen was an LNER employee, the fat was really in the fire!

Less than a month after the conclusion of the trials, the Great Western Railway Magazine included a long statement of the results and the *coal consumptions*, and details were issued to many publications in the popular and technical press. Of course the LNER were furious and a strong letter was sent to Sir Felix Pole by Sir Ralph Wedgwood, Chief General Manager. Sir Felix put the blame firmly upon Cecil J. Allen, explaining that as one of their staff had broadcast the LNER version it was necessary to put their views. The subsequent press release from King's Cross had several innuendos that even today make one smile:

> 'The recent friendly exchange of locomotives between the London and North Eastern Railway Company and the Great Western Railway was held by mutual arrangement for the purpose of securing valuable data which would be useful to both railways, but details of these results were not intended for publication. A report having appeared in the Press, the following facts will be of interest:
>
> 'The tests between the London and North Eastern "Pacific" engine and the Great Western "Castle" engine were carried out with loads of from 345 tons to 500 tons, but the London and North Eastern "Pacific" was designed for working up to 600 tons, which it has done successfully.
>
> 'The coal consumption of the "Castle" engine was lower than the "Pacific". This amounted to about 7 lb of coal per thousand ton-miles, and the lower coal consumption was obtained by the increased boiler pressure carried by the Great Western engine. The saving, however, in cost of coal is discounted by the increased cost of maintaining a boiler having 45 lb per sq in higher pressure.
>
> 'The "Pacific" engine on the Great Western was not able to run on the falling gradients at as high a speed as on the L & N E main line. It was found that with the extra weight, and with the larger boiler necessarily placed higher from the rails, the weak spots in the GWR permanent way set up considerable oscillation. Consequently, in order to maintain punctuality, a higher speed than scheduled was necessary and attained on the rising gradients, and naturally this involved greater coal consumption. As an instance, from Westbury to Savernake the London and North Eastern Railway "Pacific" with a load of 345 tons passed over the top of this gradient at 64 miles per hour, having run the whole 25½ miles in 26 minutes, a feat never yet recorded by the Great Western engine with a similar load.
>
> 'The Great Western road to Plymouth is very hilly, and has many severe curves with speed restrictions, whereas the East Coast main line is practically free from both. An intimate knowledge of the road was not attainable in the short period of the tests and placed the "Pacific" enginemen at a considerable disadvantage. The actual figures relating to coal consumption show that this was so, as the "Pacific" performance improved as the trials proceeded.'

The outcome was that the Great Western, certainly as far as the high management was concerned, was for some time outside the comity of the British railways. This was a pity because the LNER men, engineer and footplate men alike, made many friends particularly in Plymouth, and I like to recall the rousing farewell chorus of engine whistles that cheered the 'Pacific' and its men as they passed Laira shed on their last up run with the 'Cornish Riviera Express'. On the other hand, when the British Empire Exhibition was re-opened that year it would have seemed that the official attitude of abrasive action was continued in that the Great Western exhibit at Wembley, still adjacent to the LNER stand, was not *Caerphilly Castle*, but *Pendennis Castle*, which had proved such a thorn in the side of the Gresley 'Pacific' earlier that year.

Another ten 'Castles' were built at Swindon that summer. It was evidently intended that there should be many more of them, because the names selected only went to the letter 'D'; they were:

4083	*Abbotsbury Castle*	4088	*Dartmouth Castle*
4084	*Aberystwyth Castle*	4089	*Donnington Castle*
4085	*Berkeley Castle*	4090	*Dorchester Castle*
4086	*Builth Castle*	4091	*Dudley Castle*
4087	*Cardigan Castle*	4092	*Dunraven Castle*

Engines 4085 and 4086 went new to Laira shed. I saw them frequently when I was in South Devon that summer and the former gave me my first run ever behind a 'Castle' on the 5.8 pm from Newton Abbot to Paddington. I was not impressed because although we had a fairly heavy load from Taunton we lost time all the way to Maidenhead, and then picked up a little on the final stage. My view of the performance was undoubtedly jaundiced by the magnificent run on the same train I had clocked ten days earlier with a 'Star' and a load of 550 tons from Taunton, on which we had lost but a single minute. *Berkeley Castle* with 465 tons from Taunton lost 3½ minutes. I shall have a good deal more to say about *King Richard*'s epic run in a later chapter of this book.

I did not have any more runs behind 'Castles' until 1926 when for a time I was based at the Westinghouse works at Chippenham, and when the prolonged coal strike of that year, and the consequent foreign coal, was affecting all engines, 'Castles' and otherwise. I had another run behind *Berkeley Castle*, but although her driver did well on the rising gradients these efforts left him short of steam and he could not run as of old to regain time. But another event of 1926 other than the coal strike came to affect the locomotive department of the GWR most seriously. At the beginning of August at Eastleigh Works there was completed the first of the Southern Railway's four-cylinder 4-6-0s No 850 *Lord Nelson*, and the fact that its nominal tractive effort of 33,500 lb exceeded that of the 'Castles' at 31,625 lb gave everyone at Swindon, and at Paddington too, cause furiously to think! The Great Western Railway could no longer claim to have the most powerful express passenger locomotive in Great Britain. Then, not only the Southern but also the affairs of the London, Midland and Scottish came to affect the Great Western. Sir Guy Granet, their Chairman, had become increasingly concerned in the deep division of opinion between his Chief Mechanical Engineer and the Operating Department as to the most suitable form of locomotive for the heaviest express passenger duties; Sir Henry Fowler and his senior staff favoured a large compound 'Pacific' on the French de Glehn system, but the Chief Operating Manager would have nothing of it.

Meeting quite informally, Sir Guy told his friend Sir Felix Pole of the difficult position he was in, and how in view of the vehemence of the opposition he had to instruct Fowler to stop work on the two 'Pacifics' already authorized, even though the frames were already cut. In the meantime designs had been prepared at Crewe for larger boilers for the former London and North Western four-cylinder 4-6-0s of the 'Claughton' Class, which the operating people approved of, but while this proposal would provide a welcome increase in tractive power, Granet did not think it was really enough. Then it can well be imagined that Sir Felix Pole, ever ready to wave the Great Western flag, said, 'Well, try one of ours'. Whether or not the deal was settled in this way cannot be said for certain, but one of the latest 'Castles' of the batch built new in that same year was loaned to the LMS at the beginning of October, and at first worked from Crewe North shed on expresses running non-stop between Crewe and Euston. The driver who had done so well with *Pendennis Castle*, W. Young, was chosen to do the job, and he and his fireman worked on a double-home basis, up from Crewe one day and down the next. Their engine was No 5000 *Launceston Castle*. During the first two weeks on the 10.50 am from Crewe and down on the 10.30 am from Euston it was entirely an Operating Department job. Young had one of the regular drivers with him as road pilot, and the GWR Chief Running Inspector G.H. Flewellyn also rode on the footplate; but the CME of the LMS was not represented. Both trains worked were booked to cover the 158.1 miles in 175 minutes, an average speed of 54.2 mph, and in the first week with the normal load of that train, about 400 tons, it was a simple job for a 'Castle'. In the second week, when Cecil J. Allen was a passenger, the southbound train was made up to 489 tons tare, 505 tons full, and no difficulty was experienced; in fact, the net time after allowing for the signal and permanent way checks experienced *en route* was no more than 166½ minutes.

In the third week of the trials *Launceston Castle* and her crew worked between Crewe and Carlisle taking the morning Euston-Glasgow express with its normal winter loading, about 300 tons, while Driver Young was learning the road. The booked time of the down train, 165 minutes non-stop from Crewe to Carlisle, had not been accelerated to its pre-war level, but it provided a good introduction to the route before the more serious trials that were to follow. In the following week the Horwich dynamometer car and the testing team

from CME headquarters at Derby were added to the scene, and *Launceston Castle* went north on the 1.10 pm Scotch express from Crewe with a load of 415 tons. As was to be expected no difficulty was experienced, and Carnforth, 78.2 miles, was passed in 83 min 40 sec, nearly 6 minutes early, despite a severe check for relaying near Warrington. Care was taken to keep the uphill sectional times between Carnforth and Shap Summit although the GWR engine did not surpass all contemporary LMS work in the way one writer, reflectively, credits the engine and crew. No more than a year previously, in dynamometer trials between Preston and Carlisle, a 'Claughton', No 30 *Thalaba*, handsomely surpassed *Launceston Castle*'s climb to Shap, with a near identical load.

But climbing to Shap or elsewhere the 'Castle' made a profound impression everywhere she went and it is significant that J.E. Anderson, the Motive Power Superintendent, who from the time of Grouping had never been known to praise any but Midland Railway engines, admitted that he would like to have 50 'Castles' for the next season's summer traffic, but added this proviso, that he did not know what state they would be in after six months in Western Division sheds! Certainly the Great Western Railway was asked if they could build 50 'Castles' in time for the 1927 summer traffic. Of course Swindon could not do this for legal reasons, and when this was pointed out a second approach was made to purchase a complete set of working drawings. This request also having been refused, the LMS Chief Mechanical Engineer's department went instead to Waterloo, where the new *Lord Nelson* 4-6-0 was also a near approach dimensionally to what Derby thought would be necessary to work the new Anglo-Scottish expresses proposed for 1927. What eventuated from this latter approach is no part of the Great Western story, except to add a tailpiece, which when it became known caused a certain amount of merriment at Paddington and Swindon. In all the earlier LMS documentation concerning the new express passenger 4-6-0s, then being built at top speed by the North British Locomotive Company, they were referred to as 'Improved Castles'!

Top left *The 'Castle' trials in 1926: No 5000* Launceston Castle *entering Crewe with the 10.30 am Euston to Liverpool and Manchester express. An unidentified LNWR 'Jumbo' 2-4-0 stands on the left.* (Courtesy E.S. Cox)

Above left Launceston Castle *was one of the first engines to have the larger tender. Engine No 5010* Restormel Castle, *seen here, although numbered in the 5000s had the smaller one.* (W.J. Reynolds)

Left Launceston Castle *at Durran Hill (ex-Midland) sheds at Carlisle, prior to the southbound dynamometer test run to Crewe.* (Courtesy E.S. Cox)

13. New smaller engines

When the Grouping took effect in January 1923, the enlarged Great Western system included six of the former independent Welsh railways as 'constituent companies' of the new Group. These were the Barry, the Cambrian, the Cardiff, the Rhymney, the Taff Vale and the Alexandra (Newport and South Wales) Docks and Railways. The subsidiary companies included the Brecon and Merthyr, the Neath and Brecon, and, outside Wales, the Midland and South Western Junction. In his fascinating book *Swindon Steam*, Kenneth J. Cook has written:

> 'During the war, with the Works heavily engaged on direct munition work, great arrears of maintenance of rolling stock accrued and a large arrears of maintenance fund accumulated. Now, with the pressing demand for motive power, there was a complete embargo on condemnation and scrapping, which was unfortunate and definitely uneconomical in a number of cases, without really assisting the locomotive position. Once in a position of heavy arrears of maintenance on such a stud of some four thousand locomotives, it is like a millstone round one's neck and it is a terrific struggle for months and months. Actually it went on for years as there were further complications when the daylight at the end of the tunnel was appearing, but in the end it was overcome. Total locomotive stock was rather in a state of flux at that time. Dean Standard Goods and 43XX class were coming back into stock from service with the army overseas; all the Absorbed engines came into GW stock and it was some time before the Authorised Stock became established and static.
>
> 'Just over 800 locomotives came into stock by virtue of the Grouping Act, of which 148 were in Swindon Works within a few weeks. There were some sizeable classes on the bigger lines such as the Taff Vale, Barry, Rhymney, Brecon and Merthyr, Cambrian and the Midland and South Western Junction Railway, but on the remainder, lines like the Llanelly and Mynydd Mawr, Swansea Harbour Trust, Cardiff and the Alexandra Docks and Railway Co, they were mostly ones and twos. The only line whose locomotives were hardly seen at Swindon was the Rhymney; its locos and boilers had been well maintained.
>
> 'All these locomotives were investigated by the Drawing Office to ascertain what standard GW boilers would suit them, and where this was possible, a number of engines might be cleared by one set of drawings, but although a standard might suit, there was generally a good deal of subsidiary work required to smokeboxes, cabs, boiler carrying and holding down brackets and saddle plates from the cylinders to accept the drumhead type of smokeboxes. More were covered by designing three modified standard boilers, but using standard flanged plates and altering length of firebox or barrel. For instance, the standard No 10 boiler, which was a standard 2 with a different length of firebox, was suitable for the Taff Vale A Class, some of the B and M, and Rhymney engines and ten of the M and SWJR. The standard 9 was developed from 2301 class with a lengthened firebox and sloping grate and suited many of the Barry and some of the Cambrian.'

The 0-6-2 tank locomotive, prevalent on practically all the constituent and absorbed railways in South Wales, was something new for Swindon, and to meet the locomotive shortage of the immediate post-Grouping period it was considered necessary to design and build a powerful engine of this type for general use in South Wales. A.W.J. Dymond was the draughtsman concerned, he who afterwards became personal assistant to the CME, and at a still later date Mayor of Swindon. While in 1924 Burrows was still Chief Draughtsman, Hawksworth was in charge of new design work, and Dymond told me how the latter came to his drawing board to outline the project, and how he emphasized that it was to be a quantity production job right from the outset. Hawksworth ended his briefing of Dymond thus: 'Don't forget, we're in for fifty!' The design of these engines was pressed forward at the same time as that of the 'Castles', though the first of the 0-6-2s of the '5600' Class did not appear until the end of 1924. They had 18 in by 26 in cylinders, coupled wheels of 4 ft 7½ in diameter and with a working pressure of 200 psi the nominal tractive effort was 25,800 lbs.

Restricted clearances and curves precluded the use of large outside cylinders, as the GWR would have liked to use, but the trailing pair of carrying wheels enabled a large bunker to be provided, and long mileages to be worked without the need for refuelling. The trailing radial wheels were of 3 ft 6 in diameter. To provide support for the Standard No 2 boiler, which could not be accommodated without alteration on the indigenous 0-6-2 tank engines of the South Wales railways, the wheelbase of the '5600' Class had to be made longer, 7 ft 3 in between the leading intermediate pair and 8 ft 0 in between the intermediate pair and the trailers. The coupled wheels were independently sprung. These engines had a new design of three-bar motion crossheads, one large bar at the top and two smaller ones at the side a little lower with the gudgeon pin suspended below. Space above the leading coupled axle of such engines in which to support the slide-bars is restricted, and the former general arrangement of four bars was not very satisfactory, but the new design was a great improvement. A smaller version of this crosshead was used a few years later on new small standard tank engines.

These engines worked up and down the Welsh valleys, chiefly between collieries and ports with shipment coal, working chimney-first up the valleys, and when running down bunker-first, the guiding wheels in front increasing their stability at the higher speeds. This was particularly noted when they were working passenger trains. In general it was a very successful engine, and eventually a total of 200 was built, partly at Swindon and partly by contractors. An unusual feature occurred on some engines in that they became out in their beats and had to have their valves reset. They had 8-in piston valves above the cylinders pitched somewhat high, and it appeared that on these particular engines there were some residual stresses in the cylinder castings which on their early working and heating up expanded the castings upward to release the stresses. After resetting the valves they remained correct. GW locomotives had extreme regularity in their exhaust beats and certainly could not permit of anything like two beats and a wuffle which was noticeable on some other railways.

Although I may be criticized for 'telling tales out of school', I cannot help referring to an experience with one of these engines in the bad old days of 1947. It was one of the ironies of the time that our one great source of natural wealth in Great Britain, coal, was proving exceedingly difficult and intransigent to exploit. Locomotives in the South Wales mining valleys, above all places (!), were being fired with coal imported from the USA, and from all parts of the country one heard of trains in difficulty. Well, one day in that summer after concluding some business in Merthyr, I joined the late afternoon train which made a convenient connection with the last express to Paddington. I noted that the engine was a '5600' Class 0-6-2 tank but not much more till we stopped in mid-section. I was busy and did not take any more notice until we stopped a second time and, looking out, I saw the fireman walking the length of the train pulling the cords on the release valves of the brake cylinders. We were so short of steam that the brakes could not be released. This agonizing process continued, with me all the time worrying about my connection in Cardiff. But when we eventually reached Pontypridd a Taff Vale 0-6-2 tank was waiting to couple on and assist, and steaming freely she took the '56' and the train into Cardiff in good style.

Now reverting to the early 'twenties the '43' Class 2-6-0s were providing such generally useful engines that they were sometimes put on to duties that were really beyond their capacity, having regard to their having the cylinder power of a 'Saint', but with the boiler power of a 'County'. One such job was a new fast express goods train that originated at Southall. At first the load consisted of vans loaded with margarine, and with them the train ran eastwards, after Hanwell taking the Perivale loop to the north main line, and picking up a large consignment of Lyons' tea at Greenford. Then, with a maximum load of 50 covered vans, vacuum fitted throughout, it made a non-stop run to Oxley Sidings, north of Wolverhampton, where haulage was transferred to the LMS. This train was guaranteed to be in Scotland in 14 hours, and it was not long before there were complaints of poor steaming by the '43' Class engines allocated to the job. Such complaints about engines supplied with first class Welsh coal were not to be treated lightly at Swindon, and in his book Cook tells how he was instructed to ride on the footplate of the engines concerned. He rode on No 4358, and another one brand new from Robert Stephenson and Co at Darlington, No 6395. He made several trips on

Below *An ex-Brecon and Merthyr 0-6-2 tank No 11, rebuilt with a standard Great Western boiler.* (British Railways)

Bottom *The standard GWR 0-6-2 tank built for South Wales services, No 5600.* (British Railways)

both engines in maximum load conditions.

The trouble was that this train had been timed to considerably higher speeds than those normally provided for in the standard hitherto expected in the working timetables. Cook's experience was that if the load was light or, if up to maximum, they did not get a clear road, all was well, because the pauses when they were slowed for signals gave the fireman a chance to build up pressure again. With a full load, however, and no signal checks, the boiler could not meet the continuous demand for steam at the higher scheduled speed. It was not a case of 'poor steaming' but of an under-powered engine being put on the job. Cook estimated that at times the firing rate was rising above 100 lbs per sq ft of grate area per hour, which apart from being uneconomic was pretty rough on the fireman! Eventually the Running Department allocated high-mileage 'Saints' or 'Stars' to the job. This was, however, more than an interim measure for while the 4-6-0s coped with the steam requirements of these fast goods, no footplate man likes to have a run-down engine, however well it will steam, on a long reasonably fast run. I shall not forget the experience of riding a rough, very-run-down 'King Arthur' on a fast night express goods non-stop from Salisbury to Nine Elms!

Cook naturally took the problem back to the Drawing Office, where of course Churchward's famous scheme of 1901 provided for a 4-6-0 carrying the Standard No 1 boiler with 5-ft 8-in coupled wheels. On reflection, however, it was felt that a 4-6-0 with 6-ft wheels would meet the case posed by the Southall-Oxley night express goods better, and the decision was taken to rebuild one of the 'Saint' Class 4–6–0s as an experiment with 6-ft wheels. Engine No 2925 *Saint Martin* was the chosen 'victim' of the change, and the rebuilding was done in 1925.

The rebuilt engine was quoted as having a weight, in working order, of 72 tons 10 cwt, which was half a ton *heavier* than the original. One is a little curious to know where the extra weight was incurred, because the six new driving wheels would have weighed less. The only other difference was the cab, and that could hardly have accounted for an extra half-ton, plus the difference between 6-ft 8½-in driving wheels. One can recall the design considerations at the time the Northern Railway of France was working out the Bréville 'Super Pacific' in the early 1920s, and adopted 6-ft instead of 6-ft 9-in wheels, to save weight! Nevertheless, the weight quoted on the diagram of the 'Saint' in later years, 72 tons 10 cwt, was the same as that ascribed to the 'Courts' when they were new in 1911. At the time of its rebuilding, *Saint Martin* was fitted with automatic train control apparatus, including the massive contact shoe and plunger. This of course would add to the weight. That any of the standard 'Saints' which were fitted with the automatic train control gear would have had a similar increase in weight had not been taken into account when the weight diagram was last issued in 1945.

The rebuilt *Saint Martin* remained an isolated engine for three years. That she was being watched and reported on constantly I have no doubt; but one can infer that Collett's plan for the routine replacement of older locomotives had been somewhat disrupted by Sir Felix Pole's intervention and the subsequent 'crash' programme of building the 'Kings'. How Collett would have proceeded if left to himself must remain anyone's guess. At the time *Saint Martin* was rebuilt, *The Railway Magazine* published a report that nine more 'Saints' were to be rebuilt with 6-ft diameter wheels, though this proved incorrect. In the meantime *Saint Martin* was proving a useful and versatile engine, and when the 'Kings' were launched into traffic and the worry of derailed bogies surmounted, Swindon was ready to go ahead

Left *One of the '43XX' 2-6-0s in BR days at Swindon, No 6385, painted in passenger green and fully lined out.* (K.H. Leech)

Below left *A '43' No 6316, on the 1.12 pm Barmouth to Ruabon train at Llandderfel, when the author was riding on the footplate.* (O.S. Nock)

Right *Prototype of the 'Hall' Class: engine No 2925* Saint Martin *rebuilt with 6-ft 0-in diameter coupled wheels.* (Loco Publishing Co)

Below *One of the first batch of 'Halls', No 4931* Hanbury Hall *at Old Oak Common in 1930.* (W.J. Reynolds)

with quantity production of the 6-ft 4-6-0s.

The naming of the new engines after 'stately homes' was a development of the 'Court' theme, which, as has already been mentioned, originated, I believe, from Churchward's great personal friendship with Neville Grenfell, the owner of Butleigh Court, near Castle Cary. It was one thing, however, to find names of 25 Courts, but quite another when it came to a first consignment of 80 Halls, with the prospect of many more to follow. The long-term replacement programme envisaged the steady building of 'Halls' throughout the 1930s. A list was prepared, in alphabetical order from Adderley to Wrottesley, and then the search began for more. In this connection there is a story that became, privately, one of the classics of old Swindon. Apparently the Drawing Office was asked for contributions to the list, a request that I regret to add was not taken very seriously. The best they could do was *Albert Hall*, *Henry Hall*, *Fred Hall* and *B— 'All*! Henry Hall was, of course the popular radio purveyor of dance music, while Fred Hall was the genial Locomotive Running Superintendent, who afterwards became Principal Assistant to the CME. The search for Halls eventually became nationwide, gathering in names from the Lake District and the Yorkshire Dales as well as such incongruous titles as *Caxton Hall*, *Colton Hall* and *Marble Hall*.

Enough of names for the moment, however, for I must take a jump forward to 1936 so that the performance characteristics of the new engines may be considered together with those of their 5-ft 8-in counterparts, the 'Grange' Class. By that time the 'scrap and build' programme was under way with a vengeance. 'Saints' and 'Stars' were being cut up, and the time had also come for the earliest of the '43XX' Class 'Moguls'. It was not that these were considered an obsolete type, but that with heavier mixed traffic duties something more powerful was needed. At the beginning of 1936 it was announced that a number of these

Top *An up Weymouth express at Reading West hauled by No 5971* Merevale Hall. (M.W. Earley)

Above *Up Gloucester and Cheltenham express leaving Reading, hauled by No 5960* Saint Edmund Hall. (M.W. Earley)

2-6-0s were to be rebuilt with leading bogies and larger boilers, in two separate series, one with a smaller boiler than the Standard No 1. The announcement went so far as to publish the names that had been chosen for what were described as the 'Manor' and 'Grange' series, but the 'Manors' did not materialize until January 1938. Although the 'Granges' were stated to have 'new cylinders of an improved design', there was nothing basically different in them from the 'Halls', except the wheel diameter, and the boiler centre-line being lowered to 8 ft 4 in. The 'Halls' were finished in the full passenger livery, but the 'Granges', although provided with copper-capped chimneys, polished brass safety valve bonnets and brass beading over the splashers, were unlined.

It is now time to take a more critical look at the three classes of two-cylinder 4-6-0 having the Standard No 1 boiler. Because of the reduction in wheel diameter, the respective nominal tractive efforts were 24,395 lbs on the 'Saints', 27,275 lbs on the 'Halls' and 28,875 lbs on the 'Granges'. These reflected the work they were designed to do. The Standard No 1 boiler provided for a balanced output of power in express passenger service on a 'Saint' hauling, for example 450 tons at 70 mph on level track. It is true that the same boiler was used on the 'Stars', which had a higher nominal tractive effort of 27,800 lbs; but the Walschaerts valve gear on these latter engines enabled a greater power output to be sustained at express speed, and one recalls the consensus of opinion among the running inspectors, conveyed to Churchward around 1910 or 1911, that the four-cylinder engines were 'one coach better' than the two-cylinder on similar express work. When one of the 'Halls' was put through a gruelling series of tests on the stationary plant at Swindon after Nationalization, one could see that this was so. Thus, although the 'Hall', with a tractive effort of 27,275 lbs, was nearly equal to the 'Star', one could hardly expect them to do equal work. In one very important respect, however, these two-cylinder engines had the edge on the 'Stars', and this was the justification of retaining the Stephenson link motion as the standard valve gear for decades after it had been superseded elsewhere.

If one looks at the respective proportions of the 'Saints', 'Halls' and 'Granges', when each class is running at the same revolutions per minute and thus taking an equal amount of steam from the boiler, the corresponding road speeds to a sustained 70 mph by a 'Saint' are 63 mph with a 'Hall' and $59\frac{1}{2}$ mph with a 'Grange'. Both the latter classes of engine could run a great deal faster if needed, just as a maximum speed of 90 mph was recorded with a 'Saint' in ordinary service by Cecil J. Allen. At the same number of revolutions per minute, the speeds would be 81 mph with a 'Hall' and $76\frac{1}{4}$ mph with a 'Grange'. Although they were fitted with long-lap, long-travel valve gear, all the Great Western two-cylinder engines were generally worked with a cut-off of not less than 20 per cent and a partly opened regulator. I have seen a 'Saint' worked in 18 per cent very successfully, but this was exceptional. In tests carried out on the stationary plant at Swindon, it was shown that a 'Hall' could be linked up as short as 10 per cent, but the working was much more comfortable and free from vibration at 22 per cent or longer. Vibration does not occur of itself. It needs energy to cause it, and that energy is being wasted instead of being put to good use in hauling the train. It was the opinion of the testing staff at Swindon that the 'Halls' were as economical when working in 22 per cent cut-off with a partly opened regulator as when a full regulator opening was maintained and the cut-off shortened accordingly.

The valve travel in full gear was 6$\frac{7}{8}$ in , the steam lap was 1$\frac{3}{4}$ in and the exhaust clearance nil. The lead was negative in full gear, nominally $\frac{1}{8}$ in; it became nil at about 55 per cent-off, and then increased to about $\frac{1}{8}$ in at 30 per cent, and very gradually thereafter to about $\frac{5}{32}$ in at 15 to 20 per cent. Although the instinct and experienced enginemanship of drivers, as well as their own comfort, led them to stay at 22 to 25 per cent rather than link up farther and use a partly opened regulator, tests on the stationary plant at Swindon showed that the earliest cut-offs were not necessarily the most economical so far as power developed at the drawbar were concerned. It was true in the case of the 'Halls' that the earliest cut-offs were the most economical in relation to power developed in the cylinders; and on certain occasions indicator diagrams were taken at '60 mph' on the test plant at 9 per cent cut-offs with the regulator full open. Nevertheless, in such light working conditions, only 730 ihp, a high proportion of that power is used for moving the engine itself. When the coal used was related not to the total power developed in the cylinders, but only to that part that was available for hauling the train, then the relationship altered, and the most economical cut-off from the latter point of view was found usually to be neither very early, nor very late, but somewhere in between. Good drivers with a sure understanding of the 'feel' of an engine had found this out for themselves.

It is interesting to observe from the results of scientific testing at Swindon how the performance varied over the normal range of working speeds, because this gave an important measure of the effectiveness of Churchward's setting of the valve gear. At a constant steam rate of 20,000 lbs per hour, the drawbar horsepower varied as follows:

Speed (mph)	20	30	50	60	70
Dhp	990	1,070	1,060	750	686
Cut-off with full regulator	47	36	28	18	10

These, of course, were ideal characteristics for a mixed traffic engine, showing its maximum potentiality at 30 to 40 mph. From what I have written earlier it may be assumed that similar drawbar horsepower figures would have been obtained had the cut-off been kept at 23 per cent above 50 mph and some closing of the regulator made to avoid exceeding the steam rate.

So far as economy in working is concerned, it is important to differentiate between overall figures of coal consumption on a run with a service train, with all the incidentals of traffic intervening, and those on a clear undisturbed spell at a constant steaming rate on the stationary testing plant. On the latter, working the equivalent of a 400-ton passenger train on level track, the coal consumption per drawbar horsepower hour was between 2$\frac{1}{2}$ and 3 lbs; but on a service run it could be as much as 4 lbs due to acceleration from intermediate stops, signal checks, and spells of easy steaming when light firing was still necessary, but when hardly any work was being done on the drawbar. Even in testing plant conditions, the effect of light working was strikingly demonstrated. With an equivalent load of a 300-ton passenger train on the level, the basic consumption went up to 3 or 3$\frac{1}{2}$ lbs per dhp hour, and with 200 tons, to nearly 4 lbs. Apart from such detailed considerations, the 'Hall-Grange' family were excellent and economical motive power units, as might have been expected from their direct descent from such celebrated engines as the 'Saints'.

The 11.20 am (Sunday) Penzance-Wolverhampton express turning off from the main line for the Weston-super-Mare loop at Uphill Junction behind No 4905 Barton Hall. (W.S. Lockett)

By the mid-1930s, the 'Halls' were coming into general use all over the line. In Cornwall, apart from the 'Cornish Riviera Express' itself, they had practically taken complete occupation of the main line. They were doing much valuable work on fast fitted goods services, and a particularly welcome development was their introduction on the Wolverhampton-West of England express services over the North Warwickshire line. For many years this had been a stronghold of the 'County' Class 4-4-0s, because they were the largest Great Western locomotives that the LMS would permit over the section between Standish Junction and Yate. This arose from mistaken impressions that persisted in many areas of the effect of locomotives on track

Engine No 5915 Trentham Hall *at Truro.* (O.S. Nock)

and underline structures, which were not corrected until after the report of the Bridge Stress Committee that was published in 1929. The 'County' had a static weight distribution very similar to, though slightly lighter than, that of the Midland compounds—21 tons 4 cwt + 19 tons 8 cwt + 18 tons 4 cwt, against 22 tons 10 cwt + 19 tons 15 cwt + 19 tons 9 cwt—and therefore was acceptable. The heavier Great Western 4-6-0s, although having lighter maximum axle loads, were not permitted on account of the greater concentration of weight. When the unwarranted veto on their use was withdrawn, the 'Saints' were permitted to run, but for such a road the 'Halls' were ideal.

They were seen at their best climbing the long bank from Milepost 16 (from Tyseley) up to Earlswood Lakes, and with the Penzance-Wolverhampton express were frequently developing more than 1,000 dhp at the summit of the bank. One run in particular made by an engine of one of the earliest batches of the class deserves special mention, because a careful study of its details suggests that the engine was briefly being steamed up to the very limit of the boiler. The engine in question was No 4928 *Gatacre Hall* with a load of 332 tons tare and 350 tons full. On the 3 miles of slightly falling gradient past the Bearley junctions, speed was worked up to 58 mph, after which, on the 7 miles of 1 in 150 past Henley-in-Arden, speed fell off to 48 mph. But then, on the final 2 miles of slightly easier gradient, 1 in 181, to Earlswood Lakes, there was a pronounced quickening to 51½ mph. Here I estimate that the equivalent drawbar horsepower was 1,155, which according to the Swindon test figures would require a cut-off of between 27 and 30 per cent if full regulator was being used. This was not quite up to the boiler limit if good Welsh coal was being used; but in all probability, being an engine stationed at Wolverhampton, it was being fired with Staffordshire coal. In any event, however, it was a mighty good effort. On another occasion the same engine made excellent time with a heavier train of 410 tons, not falling below 4½ mph on the 1 in 150 section of the bank, and registering an estimated 1,050 dph in the process. In later years, however, this train became part of a double-home working between Wolverhampton and Newton Abbot, and was worked by 'Castle' Class engines.

Although designated 'mixed traffic' engines, the 'Halls' had a remarkable turn of speed as I noted several times in my journeys to and from Reading. Joining an intermediate express at Ealing Broadway one day in 1933, I logged a start-to-stop run at almost 60 mph with a 320-ton train. The accompanying log shows the excellent performance of *Colston Hall* and its equally vigorous continuation to Didcot on that occasion. But for sheer speed, that run pales utterly compared to the exploits of *Trematon Hall* on the 2.50 pm from Reading, when we covered the first 24½ miles from the dead start in 23½ minutes, and it was only a bad signal check at Hayes that prevented us from making a 35-minute run from Reading to Paddington. As will be seen from the log, *Trematon Hall* ran freely at 74–75 mph on level track.

One of my most interesting experiences on the footplate was with No 5915 *Trentham Hall* on the up 'Cornish Riviera Express' between Penzance and Plymouth, because it showed most strikingly the advantage a skilled driver had with the Stephenson link motion over a four-cylinder 4-6-0 with Walschaerts gear. The Cornish main line includes plenty of really

GWR: Ealing Broadway–Didcot

Engine 4-6-0 No 5923 *Colston Hall*
Load 304 tons tare, 320 tons full

Distance (miles)		Actual (m s)	Speed (mph)
0.0	Ealing Broadway	0 00	—
1.7	Hanwell	3 37	45½
3.4	Southall	5 46	52
7.5	West Drayton	10 01	66
10.5	Langley	12 43	68
12.8	Slough	14 39	71½
15.3	Burnham	16 47	70½
18.5	Maidenhead	19 33	68½
25.3	Twyford	25 29	68
28.4	Sonning box	28 23	62
30.3	Reading	30 30	—
2.6	Tilehurst	5 13	48½
5.5	Pangbourne	8 22	58
8.7	Goring	11 27	64½
12.5	Cholsey	14 55	68
17.1	Didcot	19 30	—

No 5914 Ripon Hall *in the post-war style of painting.* (British Railways)

GWR: Reading–Paddington

Engine 4-6-0 No 5949 *Trematon Hall*
Load 219 tons tare, 235 tons full

Distance (miles)		Actual (m s)		Speed (mph)
0.0	Reading	0	00	—
2.0	Milepost 34	3	57	47
5.0	Twyford	7	10	65
11.8	Maidenhead	13	01	73
15.0	Burnham	15	39	74
17.5	Slough	17	39	75
19.8	Langley	19	31	72
22.8	West Drayton	22	02	71
24.5	Milepost 11½	23	29	71
—		severe sig		20
26.9	Southall	28	06	53
28.6	Hanwell	29	59	58
30.3	Ealing Broadway	31	36	62½
32.7	Old Oak West Junc	33	53	67
34.7	Westbourne Park	35	48	—
36.0	Paddington	38	20	

Net time 35 minutes

steep climbing on gradients between 1 in 60 and 1 in 70, and, with a load of 350 tons, cut-offs up to 45 per cent with full regulator were needed; with this working, the 'lead' of the valves was practically nil at speeds of about 30 mph and the power developed in the cylinders proportionately large. Some of the most impressive work was done in climbing the 5¾ miles from Bodmin Road to Doublebois, where I had a striking comparison between 'Castle' and 'Hall' with identical loads, both on the 'Cornish Riviera Express'. From the footplate I could see how both engines were being worked; and as the weather conditions were the same and favourable in both cases, and the steaming consistently free, one could see the two performances alongside each other with certainty. The speeds through Bodmin Road were 40 mph in each case, and the subsequent 5.8 miles up to Doublebois took 11 min 38 sec by the 'Castle', and 11 min 13 sec by the 'Hall'. The minimum speeds on the curving length of 1 in 70 leading to Largin signal box were 22½ and 25 mph. The cut-offs were 40 and 45 per cent respectively on locomotives having a nominal tractive effort of 31,625 and 27,275 lbs. The advantage in this severe hill-climbing seemed definitely to lie with the 'Hall', despite the lower tractive effort.

14. 'Saints' and 'Stars': The Golden Years

My footplate work on locomotives of the Great Western Railway, and subsequently those of British Railways Western Region, did not begin until 1944, but I felt that my experience on *Trentham Hall* was so appropriate to the theme of the previous chapter that I inserted it out of context, as it were. Despite all the developments at Swindon, despite the advent of the 'Castles' and the still greater things to come, I have always felt that the mid 1920s was one of the Golden Ages of engine performance on the GWR and of its star performers, Churchward's original masterpieces of the 'Saint' and 'Star' Classes. As far as the 'Saints' were concerned, I must admit that my principal information is second-hand. But in my earlier membership of the Institution of Mechanical Engineers I made acquaintance and later close friendship with a great enthusiast

GWR: Newport–Paddington

Run No			1	2	3
Engine No			2901	2972	2928
Engine Name			*Lady Superior*	*The Abbot*	*Saint Sebastian*
Load (tons E/F)			355/385	365/390	390/420
Distance (miles)		**Schedule (min)**	**Actual (min sec)**	**Actual (min sec)**	**Actual (min sec)**
0.0	NEWPORT	0	0 00	0 00	0 00
3.8	Llanwern	—	6 35	6 25	6 20
9.8	SEVERN TUNNEL JUNCTION	12	13 10	13 00	13 00
—		—	—	pws	—
15.3	Severn Tunnel East	—	19 25	24 35	19 30
20.3	Patchway	30	29 05	36 15	29 10
21.9	Stoke Gifford East	32	31 40	39 05	31 55
24.9	Coalpit Heath	—	35 25	43 10	35 55
28.8	Chipping Sodbury	—	40 00	48 00	40 45
33.4	Badminton	47	45 50	53 40	46 15
39.2	Hullavington	—	52 10	59 20	51 50
43.7	Little Somerford	—	55 55	62 50	55 35
50.5	Wootton Bassett	63	62 40	69 00	61 55
56.1	SWINDON	69	69 00	74 30	67 50
61.8	Shrivenham	—	74 35	79 35	73 30
66.9	Uffington	—	79 10	83 50	78 20
—		—	—	pws	—
73.0	Wantage Road	—	84 35	92 20	83 55
80.3	DIDCOT	95	90 50	98 55	90 25
84.9	Cholsey	—	95 10	102 55	94 50
91.9	Pangbourne	—	102 05	109 05	101 35
97.4	READING	112	107 20	113 50	107 10
—		—	—	—	pws
102.4	Twyford	—	112 10	118 20	114 00
109.2	Maidenhead	124	118 30	124 05	120 20
114.9	SLOUGH	130	124 00	129 00	125 30
124.3	Southall	139	133 15	137 15	134 30
127.6	Ealing	—	136 25	140 15	137 45
—		—	pws	—	sigs
133.4	PADDINGTON	150	147 05	147 10	147 05
	Net times		143½	136½	142½

who had been a pupil of Sir Henry Fowler on the Midland Railway at Derby, and who, after taking his University degree and completing his pupilship, joined the technical staff of the Institution of Mechanical Engineers, E.L. Diamond by name. He was one of those enthusiasts who despite his scholastic attainments and having achieved no mean status in the world of professional locomotive engineering, never lost his love of observing the details of train running from a seat in an ordinary express train.

As a result of frequent travelling as a passenger between London and his parents' home in Cardiff, he was able to amass a 'bank' of running data, principally on the 10.15 am express from Cardiff to Paddington, that was invaluable for setting on record the ordinary daily work of the 'Saint' Class locomotives, because when he was travelling, in the 1920s, the power for that train was always provided by 'Saints' stationed at Landore and working through to Paddington. The train was booked non-stop from Newport to Paddington, 133.4 miles in 150 minutes, an average of 53.4 mph; the gross load was never less than 375 tons, and at peak periods it rose to 520 tons. On such occasions a stop had to be made at Severn Tunnel Junction for a bank engine, because with such a load assistance would certainly have been needed for climbing the severe gradients out of the Severn Tunnel, and particularly the steep single-track bore of Patchway Tunnel in which slipping frequently occurred. I have tabulated three of Mr Diamond's runs that were made without any assistance, with loads rising from 385 to 425 tons.

The first of the three, which was undelayed until the immediate approach to London, passed Southall 5¾ minutes early, whereas on the second permanent way checks caused Stoke Gifford East box to be passed 7 minutes late. On that occasion magnificent running, despite the hindrance of another permanent way check, brought the train into Paddington nearly 3 minutes early. The third run also included some splendid running and the absence of delays in the early stages saw the train passing Reading all but 5 minutes before time. On the first run *Lady Superior* made a fast passage through the Tunnel, slacking to 33 at the Junction and reaching 71½ at the foot of the decline. Minima at Pilning and Patchway were 33½ and 23½ respectively. Then followed a wonderful acceleration up the 1 in 300, speed reaching 50 mph as early as Winterbourne, and actually rising to 56 between Coalpit Heath and Sodbury—with 385 tons. The engine was eased through Sodbury, but reached 74 mph at Somerford, passed Wootton Bassett at 50 and attained 70 at Wantage Road and from Didcot to Cholsey. Speed subsequently lay between 60½ and 66½ mph, but sufficient time was in hand to meet the concluding delays.

On the second run, again with a 390-ton train, engine No 2972 *The Abbot* was delayed by a long permanent way check right in the depths of the Severn Tunnel, and the driver had some anxious moments getting his big load properly on the move again on slippery rails. He must have been glad of the surefootedness of a 'Saint', rather than those unmentionable modern developments that were foisted on to a certain South Wales shed in BR days! Even so, *The Abbot* was nearly 7 minutes late on passing Badminton. A magnificent and successful effort was then made to recover the loss. Diamond himself told the tale vividly:

> 'The engine was not spared on the ensuing descent, and mile after mile was covered at a sustained 79 mph. Seven succeeding adverse miles at 1 in 300 did not bring us below 57, but as we swung over the junction at Wootton Bassett the exhaust from the engine sharpened into an audible roar, significant indeed from a Great Western 4-6-0. In the next 5½ miles to Swindon, despite a faintly rising grade, we accelerated to 65 mph. At Shrivenham the rate was 71 mph and at Uffington no less than 74 and it was still rising when we

Below *No 2905* Lady Macbeth *before superheating.* (P.J.T. Reed)

Bottom *A West to North express leaving Teignmouth behind No 2947* Madresfield Court. (Loco Publishing Co)

were suddenly brought to a crawl over a culvert under repair at Challow. But by a marvellous acceleration this heavy train was worked up to the mile-a-minute in less than 4 miles and at Didcot we had regained a speed of 72 mph. At Pangbourne the rate had dropped to 66; 3 miles further on it again reached 70 and remained at this rate through Reading. Then after a brief fall to 68 in Sonning Cutting there came the culminating effort to 69 at Twyford, 72 at Taplow, and 73 at Slough, while after a fall to 67 a final burst to 69 through Acton and a fast finish into the terminus rounded off a very wonderful performance.

'On run No 3 the load had increased to 420 tons—14 vehicles well filled. Yet the running of *Saint Sebastian*, especially in the early stages, seemed unaffected by the heavier train. Indeed, right through to Reading, aided by an absence of checks, the times are in advance of any in the table, while the first stage to Stoke Gifford was clearly the fastest. Splendid starts were made both from Cardiff and Newport, speeds being 59 mph at Marshfield and 58 at Magor. In the tunnel 66 was the maximum rate, but an excellent climb followed, speed being 31 at Pilning, actually recovering to 40½ on the short level, and falling finally, after some slipping in Patchway tunnel, to 24 mph. We accelerated up the 1 in 300 with characteristic vigour, reaching 52 at Chipping Sodbury and passing Badminton at 49. The maximum at Somerford was 75 mph and the minimum at Wootton Bassett again 57. Speed then rose gradually to 69 at Steventon, but was eased to 61 by Pangbourne. From the check at Reading we made a further fine recovery to 70 mph at Maidenhead and 71 at Taplow, after which the rate fell to 62 at Southall, as time was well in hand.'

On yet another run on the 10.15 am up from Cardiff, engine No 2902 *Lady of the Lake* had the somewhat staggering load of 16 coaches, 449 tons tare and at least 485 tons full. With such a load assistance was needed through the Severn Tunnel and over the steep gradients beyond, and a pilot in the form of a 2-6-2 tank engine was taken from Severn Tunnel Junction

through to Swindon, where a stop was made on the centre road to detach. At this point a locomotive inspector joined the engine crew. The running from Swindon to Reading was really superlative. The mile-a-minute rate was attained before passing Shrivenham, the first station out of Swindon; at Uffington the speed was 66 mph, at Challow 68, at Wantage 69, at Steventon 72 and at Cholsey 73, at that time a record speed on a level track for any unaided engine of comparable dimensions with so tremendous a load. At Pangbourne the rate was 68 mph, at Tilehurst 70, and on passing Reading, 41.3 miles from the start, in 39 min 45 sec, 25 miles had been covered at an average rate of 70 mph. Mr Diamond thought that the 75-minute booking to Paddington might possibly have been kept with a continuance of the same effort, but the driver now eased his engine. The rate fell to 62½ in Sonning Cutting, recovered to 67 at Maidenhead, gradually dropped to 60½ at Southall, and rose finally to 65 at Acton, and the train stopped in Paddington station exactly 76 minutes after leaving Swindon. Fifty consecutive miles were covered on this occasion with our load of 485 tons at an average speed of 67½ mph. This was a very splendid effort by *Lady of the Lake* and her crew.

In the westbound service from London to South Wales, the 8.55 am and 7.55 pm departures from Paddington, after calling at Reading, made non-stop runs to Newport, slipping portions for Bristol at Stoke Gifford; there was of course no station at Parkway at that time. I used the 8.55 am on one or two occasions when I was bent on a long day's lineside photography in the Reading area, and one day in June 1925 I caught one of the colossal loads sometimes experienced by E.L. Diamond on his journeying to and from Cardiff, in my case 471 tons tare, and at least 505 tons full. The engine was No 2940 *Dorney Court*, and although it took some little time to get that immense train really going, we passed Slough in 22¾ minutes at 64½ mph. But then I should imagine the boiler pressure was falling, because the speed fell away to 56 mph at Maidenhead and had not recovered above 58 mph at Twyford. We reached Reading in exactly 42 minutes instead of the 40 minutes scheduled. On another heavy load run, this time on the 7.55 pm, which carried roof boards lettered 'Irish Mail via Fishguard', my friend thought the crew of No 2942 *Fawley Court* had done remarkably well to get a 485-ton train to Reading in 40 min 50 sec, and the continuation of the run is tabulated herewith. On this journey, the slip portion for Bristol was so heavy, 124 tons tare, that it was deemed advisable to stop and detach it at Stoke Gifford, and the tabulated log ends there, because delays seriously affected the continuation to Newport.

Fawley Court got away from Reading in grand style with speed up to 60 mph in 5½ miles of level track with the 485-ton load, and after attaining a maximum of 66½

Top *Another austerity finish: No 4001* Dog Star *at Old Oak Common.* (W.J. Reynolds)

Above *The 'Abbeys' smartened up. These engines were turned out in plain green; this is No 4067* Tintern Abbey *in full glory.* (W.J. Reynolds)

Left *No 2936* Cefntilla Court *at Old Oak Common in 1919 in wartime plain green.* (W.J. Reynolds)

GWR: Reading–Stoke Gifford (The Irish Mail via Fishguard)

Engine No 2942 *Fawley Court*
Load 459 tons tare, 485 tons full

Distance (miles)		Schedule (min)	Actual (m s)	Speed* (mph)
0.0	Reading	0	0 00	—
2.7	Tilehurst		5 05	31.9
5.5	Pangbourne		8 10	54.5
12.5	Cholsey		14 40	64.5
17.1	Didcot	19	19 05	62.5
20.5	Steventon	22½	22 20	62.7
24.4	Wantage Road		26 10	61.2
30.5	Uffington		32 05	61.7
35.5	Shrivenham		37 00	61.0
—			pws	
41.3	Swindon	43½	44 15	47.0
46.9	Wootton Bassett	49½	50 10	56.9
53.7	Little Somerford		56 40	64.0
58.2	Hullavington		61 30	56.0
64.0	Badminton	67½	67 45	55.7
68.8	Chipping Sodbury		71 55	66.1
73.9	Winterbourne		76 25	70.5
75.5	Stoke Gifford East box	78 *pass*	*79 20* +	—

* averages from point to point
\+ stop to detach slip portion

mph beyond Goring averaged over 60 mph all the way up the gradual rise to Shrivenham and would have passed on time but for an intervening permanent way check. But it was after getting on to the Badminton line that *Fawley Court* and her crew really excelled themselves. At that time a definite speed restriction was required over the facing junction at Wootton Bassett, and after recovery from this the speed had not exceeded 64 mph in the Somerford 'dip'; but then the 10-mile rise to Badminton was taken at a sustained minimum speed of 55 mph, and Badminton was passed within 15 seconds of scheduled time. This extraordinary effort was equivalent to a drawbar pull of at least 3½ tons on level track, and apparently the engine (and the boiler!) was game for any amount of further hard work, because the speed quickly reached 74 mph on the ensuing descent. Even after detaching the Bristol section of the train, there was still a load of 355 tons to be taken into Wales, and at Stoke Gifford, working through to Swansea, the crew still had another 80 miles to go. The start-to-stop run of 79¼ minutes from Reading to Stoke Gifford, with its net average speed of 58.3 mph with 485 tons, was a magnificent performance.

When the short route to Birmingham via Bicester was opened in 1910, while the traffic was light many of the fastest trains consisted of no more than six coaches, some indeed had only four, and the 'Saint' Class were mostly used. After the war it was very different, with 400-ton loads and 'Stars' in general use. But in the summer service of 1927 the 'Shakespeare Express' was put on leaving Paddington at 9.25 am and connecting at Leamington with a road motor tour of the Shakespeare country, including Warwick, Kenilworth and Stratford-upon-Avon, arriving back in Leamington to connect with the departure of the up 'Shakespeare Express' which left on a non-stop run to Paddington at 6 pm. It was interesting travelling through my own native Warwickshire with a party of which I was the only Englishman, except for the courier. I still chuckle at how he explained what 'being 'ad up' meant to the Americans, referring to how

Shakespeare himself got hauled up in front of Sir Thomas Lucy for poaching deer in Charlecote Park! So at the end of a delightful day we came back to Leamington and to the 'Shakespeare Express', which I was pleased to see in this direction headed by *Saint Catherine*. I was congratulating myself on finding an empty compartment near the front end of the train when at the very last minute in dashed six American ladies whom I noticed had been on the motor tour but to whom I had not spoken all day.

Alas for some quiet logging of the run! To them the day had been gloriously fine; the sights they had seen were terrific and to one and all life was simply just great. But I noticed that amid the torrent of joyous conversation there were numerous sidelong glances at my stop-watch and I began to fear the worst. The blow fell just after we had passed Haddenham and were beginning what I judged to be an exceptionally fast climb of the bank through Princes Risborough to Saunderton. Then the youngest, and certainly not the least attractive of my travelling companions, leaned across the compartment. 'Excuse me,' she said, 'but what are you doing with that watch?' It was useless to explain that I was measuring the speed. The whole party joined in, and bombarded me with questions. 'How did I do it?' 'Where were the mileposts?' The stop-watch was passed from one to another. They crowded round the window. Amid shrieks of delight they started and stopped the watch. 'Say, Eleanor, you try; I can't see any mileposts at arl.' Then, at me: 'How do you see the mileposts at night?' Little by little, the intricacies of rail-joint timing had to be explained, and we were nearing the outer suburbs of London before their questions ceased. Then the youngest, and I repeat not the least attractive of them, aptly summed up the situation, 'Well, you sure have been caancentratin'!'

Concentration or not, opposite is the log I recorded. It was a very fine run, made notable by the fast uphill work rather than the carefree dashes down the banks which characterized some of the 'Castle' running at that period. Not many weeks after this run I had one with *Restormel Castle* on which successive maximum speeds of 84, 84 and 82 mph were attained working the regular 6 pm up from Birmingham from Leamington onwards with much lower uphill speeds than those attained by *Saint Catherine*. On the up 'Shakespeare Express' we started off in great style, sustaining 57 mph up the 1 in 187 of the Southam Road bank, but this performance was surpassed, just as I was getting entangled by my American lady companions(!), by the same speed up the 1 in 167 stretch of the up line between Princes Risborough and Saunderton summit. I calculate that *Saint Catherine* was putting forth an equivalent drawbar pull of 2.73 tons on the ascent, equal to a drawbar horsepower of 905. Recalling Churchward's famous target of performance for his 4-6-0 express locomotives of a 2-ton drawbar pull at 70 mph, 2.73 tons at 57 mph seems a worthy counterpart, 20 years after the engine was built.

E.L. Diamond, writing to Cecil J. Allen concerning one of his runs on the South Wales service on which gargantuan loads were hauled by 'Saint' Class 4-6-0s, exclaimed: 'Why on earth a tired old "Saint" to haul

Above left Reading Abbey *climbing Filton bank with the 11.45 am two-hour express from Bristol to Paddington in 1935.* (G.H. Soole)

Left *A West to North express near Patchway, with an inspection car next to the engine, No 4043* Prince Henry. (G.H. Soole)

GWR: Leamington–Paddington, 6.0 pm up 'Shakespeare Express'

Engine No 2918 *Saint Catherine*
Load 184 tons tare, 200 tons full

Distance (miles)		Schedule (min)	Actual (min	sec)	Speed (mph)
0.0	Leamington	0	0	00	
3.7	Fosse Road box		5	35	56.9
6.1	Southam Road		8	05	56.9
11.1	Fenny Compton		12	50	65.2
					58.4
16.2	Cropredy		17	50	75
19.8	Banbury	23½	21	05	69.2
23.3	Kings Sutton		24	05	64.3
24.9	Aynho Junction	28½	25	45	64.3
30.1	Ardley		31	00	56.9
33.9	Bicester		34	25	71.5
36.9	Blackthorn		36	55	75
39.9	Brill		39	30	63.4
43.1	Ashendon Junction	45	42	50	65
					54.2
					63.4
47.2	Haddenham		45	55	60
52.6	Princes Risborough	54	52	15	67.1
					60
55.8	Saunderton		55	25	56.9
58.5	West Wycombe		57	45	75
60.8	High Wycombe	63	60	10	50 (slack)
					56.9
65.6	Beaconsfield		65	30	56.2
69.9	Gerrards Cross		69	30	70.3
72.5	Denham		71	50	67.1
75.2	Ruislip		74	15	69.2
77.0	Northolt Junction	79	75	50	69.2
79.5	Greenford	81	78	00	72.6
82.7	Park Royal		81	05	—
83.8	Old Oak West Junction	86	82	50	—
			pwr		
86.0	Westbourne Park		86	25	—
		sig stop 2 minutes, Westbourne Bridge			
87.3	Paddington	92	92	15	

Net time 87½ minutes

such a load as this?', to which question Allen admitted that he had no answer. At that time, 1929, Kenneth H. Cook's important book *Swindon Steam* had not been published; indeed, Cook himself, as assistant to the Locomotive Works Manager, was actually engaged in developing some of the important shop practices that enabled the Churchward locomotives to remain evergreen over so many years. In that same spring, travelling north for the Easter holiday weekend, I experienced my best ever run with a 'Saint'—until after the Second World War, that is. This may seem a rather extraordinary statement, particularly in view of Diamond's remarks about 'tired old "Saints" '; but in the concluding chapters of this book I have some startling tales to tell. However, back to Easter 1929 when on Maundy Thursday I went to Paddington to catch the 2.10 pm to Shrewsbury. As I expected, the train was running in two portions, the main one, very heavy, headed by *Princess Augusta* and the relief leaving 5 minutes earlier, only 295 tons tare it is true, hauled by *Lady of Lynn*, which I had photographed several times at Penzance when she had been hauling the up West of

England Postal Special. As might be expected, I joined the relief and not the main train. At that time the 2.10 pm was one of the very few 2-hour Birmingham expresses that ran non-stop from Paddington to Snow Hill, and this first portion carried no slip carriages.

All the 2-hour trains had a very sharp timing to High Wycombe, 30 minutes for the 26.5 miles from Paddington. With the heavier trains, even in the days of 'Castles' and 'Kings', it was hardly ever kept, though in the case of trains stopping at Leamington the drivers seemed to make it a point of honour to arrive at that first passenger stop on or before time, whatever the load. However, the driver of *Lady of Lynn*, once over the Old Oak junctions, went flat out for High Wycombe. He sustained 62½ mph up the 1 in 264 rise from Greenford to Northolt Junction, passed Ruislip at 68 and reached 72½ mph at the viaducts before Denham. Then, having cleared the 1 in 176 bank to Gerrards Cross at 63½ mph, the engine was *accelerated* to 64½ mph on the continuation 1 in 264 to Beaconsfield. A maximum of 74 mph at Tylers Green put the finishing touch on a remarkable piece of running, which took the train through High Wycombe in 28 min 35 sec from Paddington. The sustained 64½ mph on the 1 in 264 gradient from Gerrards Cross to the summit just before Beaconsfield represented, as near as I can calculate, a drawbar pull of 3.45 tons—a terrific effort, representing a drawbar horsepower of about 1,350.

After this initial effort the driver ran closely to the easier times booked to the 2.10 pm, and as the log shows he passed Aynho Junction almost exactly on time. But a slower train from the Oxford direction had immediately preceded us over the junction and it blocked the way to Birmingham where we were 10½ minutes late. I did not see what the offending train was, but we were given the road ahead of it from Snow Hill and our driver immediately regained 2 minutes on the awkward length to Wolverhampton. Here the load was reduced to 256 tons tare, but *Lady of Lynn* still continued to head the train, and sure enough I clocked up some more record times. Crowds of passengers had joined at Birmingham and Wolverhampton and we left the latter station with many standing in the corridors, a gross load so far as I could judge of 280 tons. The gradients are undulating as far as milepost 148, 6 miles from the start, and our speed varied between 56 and 61 mph; then came the descent to the valley of the River Worf, a tributary of the Severn, and speed increased quickly to 75 mph. From the foot of this grade to Hollinswood Siding there is a bank of 5½ miles, inclined at 1 in 150 at first, and then for 3½ miles above Shifnal station continuously at 1 in 100. Incidentally, the draughtsmen who prepared the original gradient profiles for *The Railway Magazine* many years ago made an error here by specifying this gradient as 1 in 150. It was not until I received the official profile some years later that I appreciated that on the Eastertide day of 1929 *Lady of Lynn* had given me another piece of outstanding hill climbing.

I cannot be sure from my old notes that the minimum speed approaching Hollinswood summit was absolutely sustained, but certainly the drop in speed over the last three-quarters of a mile was minimal, and my horsepower calculation is based on a speed of 46 mph. This, with a trailing load of 280 tons and an engine of 112 tons, yields an equivalent drawbar pull of a fraction over 5 tons, and at 46 mph gives almost exactly the same drawbar horsepower as between Gerrards Cross and Beaconsfield, 1,340. After this effort, *Lady of Lynn* was taken down the steep gradient to Wellington without exceeding 66 mph and after a slight check for permanent way works touched 70 mph at the Severn crossing at Upton Magna. Apart from a bad signal check at the conclusion we should

A Plymouth express, via Bristol, at Rattery summit, South Devon, with engine No 4070 Neath Abbey. (O.S. Nock)

GWR: 2.10 pm Paddington–Shrewsbury, first portion

Engine No 2906 *Lady of Lynn*
Load To Wolverhampton: 295 tons tare, 320 tons full
To Shrewsbury: 256 tons tare, 280 tons full

Distance (miles)		Schedule (min)	Actual (m s)	Speed* (mph)
0.0	Paddington	0	0 00	—
3.5	Old Oak West Junction	6	6 05	—
7.8	Greenford	11	11 15	62½
10.3	Northolt Junction	13½	13 40	62½
12.1	Ruislip		15 20	68
14.8	Denham		17 40	72½
17.4	Gerrards Cross		20 00	63½
21.7	Beaconsfield		24 00	64½
24.1	Tylers Green box		26 05	74
26.5	High Wycombe	30	28 35	40 (slack)
31.5	Saunderton		36 10	39
34.7	Princes Risborough	40	40 15	easy
44.2	Ashendon Junction	50	49 35	—
50.4	Blackthorn		56 10	69
53.4	Bicester		59 05	easy
62.4	Aynho Junction	69	69 10	—
67.5	Banbury	74	sigs	
—			75 20	
			sigs	
87.3	Leamington	94	99 25	
—			sigs	
100.2	Knowle		119 40	
107.4	Tyseley		126 55	69
110.6	Birmingham Snow Hill	120	130 50	
2.6	Handsworth		5 00	
5.9	Swan Village		9 30	63
7.4	Wednesbury		11 15	slack
10.9	Priestfield		15 20	54
12.6	Wolverhampton	20	18 00	
1.0	Dunstall Park		2 15	
4.8	Codsall		6 30	61/56
7.7	Albrighton		9 30	68
—		—	—	75
12.5	Shifnal		13 40	62½
14.5	Madeley Junction		15 50	49
15.4	Hollinswood box		17 00	46½
16.6	Oakengates		18 20	61
—			—	66
19.6	Wellington (Salop)		21 00	50 (slack)
—			pws	50
23.5	Walcot		25 30	64½
26.0	Upton Magna		27 50	70½
—			sigs	—
29.9	Shrewsbury	40	33 55	—

* Max and min by stop-watch

GWR: Paddington–Exeter, 12 noon 'Torbay Limited'

Engine No 4042 *Prince Albert*
Load 13 70-footers, 469 tons tare, 500 tons full

Distance (miles)		Schedule (min)	Actual (m s)	Speed* (mph)
0.0	Paddington	0	6 00	—
3.5	Old Oak West Junction		6 15	—
5.7	Ealing Broadway		9 20	50
9.1	Southall	11	13 10	55
13.2	West Drayton		17 30	60
18.5	Slough	20	22 25	65
24.2	Maidenhead	25½	27 45	63½
31.0	Twyford	31½	34 15	61½
36.0	Reading	37	39 05	45
37.8	Southcote Junction		41 40	—
41.2	Theale		45 20	58½
44.8	Aldermaston		49 00	59
49.6	Thatcham		54 00	56
53.1	Newbury	56	57 50	53
—			pws	—
61.5	Hungerford		69 00	—
			sig stop	—
—			70 05	—
66.4	Bedwyn	69½	79 15	48
70.1	Savernake		84 15	41
75.3	Pewsey		89 45	69
78.8	Woodborough		92 55	64½
81.1	Patney		94 55	68
86.9	Lavington		99 40	80½
91.4	Edington		103 10	74
95.6	Westbury	97½	107 00	slack
—	Westbury troughs		—	55
100.0	Milepost 114¼		112 20	41
101.3	Frome		114 00	slack
106.6	Witham		120 50	50½
108.5	Brewham box		123 15	44½
111.9	Bruton		126 35	75
115.3	Castle Cary	120	129 25	69
117.2	Alford		130 50	72½
—			pws	—
120.2	Keinton Mandeville		134 05	—
122.4	Charlton Mackrell		136 55	57
125.7	Somerton		140 30	56
131.0	Curry Rivel Junction		145 30	72½
134.9	Athelney		149 05	64½
137.9	Cogload Junction	144	151 55	60
140.5	Creech Junction		154 30	62½
142.9	Taunton	149	156 50	55½
144.9	Norton Fitzwarren		159 00	57½
150.0	Wellington		164 55	47½
151.7	Milepost 172		167 25	40
152.7	Milepost 173		169 20	30½
153.8	Whiteball box		171 45	25½
155.8	Tiverton Junction		176 55	74

Distance (miles)		Schedule (min)	Actual (m s)	Speed* (mph)
161.1	Cullompton		178 45	75
165.3	Hele		182 05	76½
166.5	Silverton		183 05	75/70½
170.2	Stoke Canon		186 05	75
172.4	Cowley Bridge Junction		188 05	—
173.7	Exeter	180	190 10	—

* Max and min by stop-watch

have reached Shrewsbury in 31½ minutes from Wolverhampton, a gain of 8½ minutes on schedule.

While the runs of *Saint Catherine* and *Lady of Lynn* showed bursts of remarkable energy intermediately and as required, my outstanding runs with the 'Stars', both made within the same fortnight in 1925, involved well-nigh all-out efforts sustained without a break for distances of 170 and 140 miles. The down run on the 'Torbay Limited', as it was then named, probably represents the highest level of achievement reached by the 'Stars' on the 3-hour schedule to Exeter, and was made on the last Friday before the introduction of the summer service in 1925. At that period in Great Western history, the 11 am West of England service from Paddington did not run during the winter months, and the 'Torbay' carried a through portion for Penzance which was detached at Exeter. Thirteen 70-ft coaches was by no means an exceptional load to be worked from Paddington to Westbury, but it was a very different matter to take such a load right through to Exeter. In Chapter 4 of this book details are given of a run on the 'Limited' on which 470 tons were taken through in grand style, but in view of the difficulties that developed on this run of mine I would place the level of engine performance as even higher. After the immediate start from Paddington, which was extremely vigorous, no running of exceptional note followed until the Kintbury slack for relaying was succeeded by a dead stand for signals at Hungerford. From the restart, the 112.2 miles on to Exeter were covered in a few seconds over the even 2 hours, despite one further check for permanent way work on the cut-off line near Keinton Mandeville. The net time of 117½ minutes from start to stop, with its average speed of 57 mph, was an outstanding effort—even for the GWR in those great years of resurgence.

The very start from Hungerford is severe, up a gradient of 1 in 114 at once, with a short length of 1 in 220 to follow, and the collar work continuous in easier inclinations, till the final stiff pull up to Savernake is reached. To attain 48 mph beyond Bedwyn and to clear Savernake summit, 8.6 miles, in 14 min 10 sec was a measure of the determination put into the job by the crew. It was no less significant, however, of the kind of engine they had at their command. I was travelling at the front of the train, and could hear that No 4042 was being worked hard. But in writing of this run nearly 65 years afterwards, and with the mind fresh with the memories of many more recent journeys, one cannot fail to be impressed by the tremendous advantage conferred upon later generations of enginemen by the elimination of the Westbury and Frome service slacks. In addition to giving a useful margin for recovery, the coal those by-pass lines saved must have been prodigious. Some years ago, Col H. Rudgard, in his Presidential Address to the Institution of Locomotive Engineers, displayed a nomogram indicating the additional coal used in recovering from slacks. From this diagram certain figures may be quoted. In slowing from 60 mph down to 30, and then accelerating up to 60 mph again, with a 425-ton train, the additional coal was 141 lbs, while with a similar slack from 70 mph the cost in coal was 208 lbs. Although such figures cannot be taken as anything more than a rough guide, they do indicate the order of things, and one might say that the Westbury and Frome slacks together cost, in round figures, some 300 lb of coal per journey. With seven non-stopping trains a day in the winter service of 1924–5, this would mean roughly a ton of coal every day.

But in 1925 the by-pass lines did not exist, and so round the curves we went. I have many times remarked upon the difficulty of the point-to-point booking between Westbury and Castle Cary, and to keep this time while carefully observing the speed restrictions was one of the finest features of this very fine run. Note especially the rapid acceleration to 55 mph at Fairwood troughs, in no more than 1¾ miles from Westbury station; the summit at milepost 113¼, near the site of Clink Road Junction box, was cleared at 41 mph, and following the Frome slack came the fine uphill speeds of 50½ mph near Witham and 44 over Brewham summit. Later expresses using the cut-off lines and making no more than ordinarily good progress could cut at least 3 minutes from the time of 20 min 5 sec that we made over the 17.1 miles from Edington to milepost 122¾, while on one occasion I saw the time cut to 15 min 51 sec. The slack near Keinton Mandeville spoiled what might have been a fast run over the Somerton cut-off line, and it was not until Langport that we really got going again and touched 72½ mph.

But by this time Whiteball was looming ahead. With such a load our driver would have been fully justified in stopping at Taunton for assistance, or at least to take a rear-end bank engine from Wellington. The taking of such assistance for a relatively short incline almost invariably resulted in loss of time, though the chances of stalling on the grade were obviated. To go up without assistance usually saved time in the end, even though the point-to-point bookings may not have been kept; but on a bank of the severity of Whiteball, only a driver who had supreme confidence in his engine would have attempted the climb unassisted with such a load as 469 tons tare. Although the running over the approach grades from Taunton was not especially fast, No 4042 was handled most ably on the Whiteball bank itself, and to the accompaniment of a truly thunderous exhaust we did the last quarter-mile to the tunnel entrance at 30 mph. In the last mile, speed fell off further to 25½ mph, but the time of 14 min 55 sec from Taunton to Whiteball box speaks for itself. If any further testimony were needed that the engine was on top form it is to be seen in the high-speed descent to Exeter, following this uphill effort.

As if this were not enough, when I returned from that particular holiday, just over a fortnight later, I was treated to the Herculean performance detailed herewith. It was one of those railway occasions on which the interest works up by degrees. I was travelling from Paignton, and after the Kingswear and Cornish sections of the train had been combined at Newton Abbot the running was at first of no special consequence;

The 11.45 am non-stop Bristol-Paddington express nearing Stoke Gifford junction, engine No 4015 Knights of St Patrick. (G.H. Soole)

GWR: 6.28 pm Taunton–Paddington

Engine No 4026 *King Richard*
Driver W. Springthorpe (Old Oak Common)
Load To Newbury: 16 coaches, 514 tons tare, 550 tons full
To Paddington: 15 coaches, 480 tons tare, 515 tons full

Distance (miles)		Schedule (min)	Actual (m s)	Speed (mph)
0.0	TAUNTON	0	0 00	—
—		—	sig stop	—
2.4	Creech Junction	—	7 40	—
5.0	Cogload Junction	6	11 00	50
8.0	Athelney	—	14 15	58½
11.9	Curry Rivel Junction	—	18 15	61
15.0	Long Sutton	—	21 40	50
17.2	Somerton	—	24 15	48
—		—	—	58½
20.5	Charlton Mackrell	—	27 45	55
22.7	Keinton Mandeville	—	30 05	60
25.5	Alford Halt		32 45	64½
27.6	CASTLE CARY	30	34 45	58½
31.1	Bruton	—	38 35	45
34.4	Milepost 122¾	—	44 40	24
36.3	Witham	—	47 05	66
41.6	FROME	—	52 30	slack
—	Fairwood troughs	—	—	62½
47.3	WESTBURY	53	59 40	slack
51.5	Edington	—	65 00	53
56.0	Lavington	—	69 35	61½
—	Milepost 82	—	—	48
61.8	Patney	—	76 20	—
67.6	Pewsey	—	82 35	60
72.8	Savernake	—	88 10	53
76.5	Bedwyn	82	91 50	66
81.4	Hungerford	—	96 00	72½
84.4	Kintbury	—	98 30	75
89.8	NEWBURY (slip coach)	94	102 55	74
93.3	Thatcham	—	105 50	72½
96.2	Midgham	—	108 15	72
98.1	Aldermaston	—	109 50	72
101.7	Theale	—	112 50	72
105.0	Southcote Junction	—	115 55	—
106.9	READING	112	118 20	40
108.8	Sonning box	—	120 45	50
111.9	Twyford	117	124 15	57
118.7	Maidenhead	124	130 45	65
121.9	Burnham Beeches	—	133 40	68
124.4	SLOUGH	130	135 50	69½
126.7	Langley	—	137 50	68
129.7	West Drayton	—	140 30	69½
133.8	SOUTHALL	140	144 25	68
137.2	Ealing	—	147 35	67
138.6	Acton	—	148 55	62½
—		—	sig check	—
141.6	Westbourne Park	—	154 40	—
—		—	sigs	—
142.9	PADDINGTON	152	158 00	—

Net time 152 minutes

with a 450-ton load we ran from Newton to Exeter without exceeding 59 mph, and the time from Exeter to Taunton was 52½ minutes due to a lengthy signal stop at Tiverton Junction. But at Taunton three more coaches were added to the train, and I remember the disgust with which the guard came up and said: 'Here's a nice load: 16 and no bank engine!'

'Who is your driver?' I asked.

'Oh, I think we shall be all right,' he replied. 'It's Walter Springthorpe, the finest fellow on the road.'

What happened east of Taunton is shown in the table. At the time, to me, in all the burning enthusiasm of youth, it was indeed a phenomenal effort. But I had not long previously collected an engineering degree, and in the course of my studies had learned, among other things, to regard with suspicion any test results, or calculations, that gave sensational, or even unusual, results. And so on arrival at Paddington I walked the length of that huge train twice to make sure that my computation of the tare load was correct. As to the increment to be added for passengers and luggage I need only say that the run was made toward the end of July, and the day was a Saturday. No further comment is necessary! Connoisseurs of Great Western locomotive performance will no doubt study the log in very great detail, but in commenting upon it, 65 years after the event, I am going to take the very last stage first, since this last stage now seems to hold the key to the whole run. If comparison is made with the dynamometer car test journey with *Knight of St Patrick* in Chapter 3, it will be seen that the times over the 15.1 miles from Maidenhead to Southall were 13 min 33 sec by No

Above *The up 'Cornish Riviera Express' passing Kennet Bridge box, east of Reading, hauled by No 4034* Queen Adelaide. (M.W. Earley)

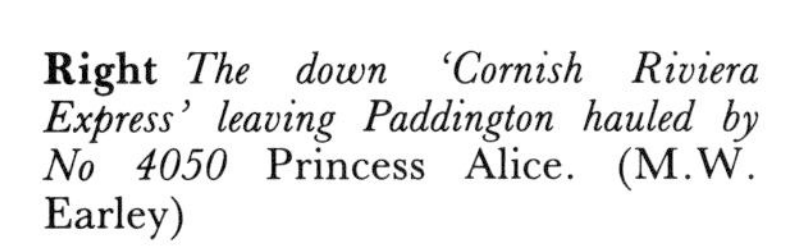

Right *The down 'Cornish Riviera Express' leaving Paddington hauled by No 4050* Princess Alice. (M.W. Earley)

Heavy traffic in June 1926: the second and third sections of the 'Cornish Riviera Express' ready to leave Paddington. On the left is No 4078 Pembroke Castle *with the third portion, on the right No 4018* Knight of the Grand Cross *with the second part.* (F.R. Hebron, Rail Archive Stephenson)

4013 and 13 min 40 sec by No 4026—near enough the same. And yet *King Richard* had 515 tons behind the tender, against 390 with *Knight of St Patrick*. On this basis of comparison it would seem that the recorded drawbar pull of 2.2 tons at 69 mph on the 1908 test would be increased, by simple proportion, to 2.9 tons on my own run of 1925; in various earlier references to this run, indeed, I have quoted a figure of roughly 3 tons. Unfortunately, comparison cannot truly be made on so simple a basis. The 'Torquay Diner' of 1908, on which No 4013 was tested, was made up of 12 coaches having a tare weight of 335 tons, an average of 28 tons apiece. In addition there was the dynamometer car. On the other hand, the 6.28 pm from Taunton on the day of my run had 16 vehicles, each having an average weight of 32.2 tons—in fact, nearly all of them were of the 70-ft stock.

It so happens that in 1924 the new express engine No 4074 *Caldicot Castle* had been tested with the dynamometer car between Swindon and Plymouth; the tare load of the special test train, 483½ tons, was almost exactly the same as the 6.28 pm from Taunton to Paddington, east of Newbury, and while running that test train at speeds varying between 65 and 70 mph on the level track between Bristol and Taunton, on three separate days, the drawbar pulls registered were between 2.2 and 2.4 tons. This is little more than the 'drag' of the 390-ton test train hauled by *Knight of St Patrick* in 1908, when it is evident from details of the make-up that many clerestory coaches were included in the rake. In the absence of a dynamometer car record one cannot say precisely how the 515-ton train hauled by No 4026 was pulling, but on the basis of *Caldicot Castle*'s work on the 1924 tests I would be inclined to doubt if the drawbar pull east of Maidenhead exceeded 2.5 tons. Having drawn the veil of moderation over some of my earlier eulogies on this run, it still remains as something of a phenomenon. Whatever the train resistance at 70 mph may have been, it was the dead weight of those 16 coaches that mattered between Langport and Somerton, between Lavington and Savernake, and above all on the Bruton bank. The average speed over the 21.3 miles from Edington to Savernake ws 55.2 mph, and here the average inclination is 1 in 430; taking a train resistance figure based upon the contemporary *Caldicot Castle* tests, the drawbar horsepower, corrected for gradient, works out at about 1,170, with a corresponding drawbar pull of 3.5 tons. But whatever the precise horsepowers involved, I don't think I have ever had a more thrilling journey in all the 70 years during which I have been clocking locomotive running.

15. Design and introduction of the 'Kings'

The researches of the Bridge Stress Committee, set up by the Government in 1919 to review the methods of calculating the stresses in bridges, with particular reference to the allowance to be made for impact loading, sent a flutter of disbelief through the locomotive departments of even some of the most august administrations of this country. The question centred upon the methods used to balance the reciprocating parts. While methods of doing this had been well established in many drawing offices, and locomotives which were smooth-running and comfortable for the crews to ride upon were in service on all the British railways, the investigations of the Bridge Stress Committee revealed that many of the most revered types of express locomotives were having a severe effect on the track and the underline bridges. Not least of those that came under censure in this respect were the Great Western 'Stars'. Until that time it was the practice at Swindon to balance a proportion of the reciprocating parts separately for the inside and outside cylinders, in the leading and middle pairs of coupled wheels respectively. Although the balance applied to the leading coupled axle was opposed to that of the middle one, and the total engine hammer-blow was relatively small, the hammer-blow from each of the individual axles actually exceeded that of the two-cylinder 'Saint' Class! During the course of the Bridge Stress Committee's work the method of balancing was revised, and the relative figures for the 'Saints', 'Star' and 'Castle' Classes were then as follows:

Engine Class	Max Axle Load (tons)	Speed at 6 rps (mph)	Hammer-blow at 6 rps (tons)		Max Combined load at 6 rps (tons)
			Whole engine	Axle	
'Saint'	18.4	86	17.9	6.9	25.3
'Star'	18.6	86	3.7	3.7	21.5
'Castle'	19.7	86	3.5	3.5	23.1

Until the work of the Bridge Stress Committee, civil engineers had not made any concession in the maximum axle load limits imposed; the limits had been based on dead weight.

Then, in 1926 had come the construction of the Southern Railway's 'Lord Nelson' Class 4-6-0 with a nominal tractive effort of 33,500 lbs. The publicity folks at Waterloo immediately proclaimed, by poster and other means, that their new engine was the most powerful in Great Britain—which it was on the basis of nominal tractive effort—and the Great Western, which had taken immense pride in possessing that distinction up to that time, in the 'Castle', had cause for much concern. The deliberations of the Locomotive Committee of the Directors under the enthusiastic and well-informed chairmanship of Sir Aubrey Brocklebank made a strong plea for the relaxation of the 20-ton axle loading and, as the strength of bridges imposed the limitation on axle load, the Civil Engineer should prepare diagrams to show what each bridge could carry. The Civil Engineer, J.C. Lloyd, was called in, and he agreed to produce the information. He was also asked what axle load was now provided for in new bridges, and he replied that for 22 years all new bridges had been designed for a nominal axle load of 22 tons. Because of the hammer-blow in GWR two-cylinder engines, the static axle load had been limited to 19½ tons; but in the light of the Bridge Stress Committee's work he could now agree to a static axle load of 22 tons for four-cylinder engines on bridges which had been rebuilt to these standards.

This increase in bridge strength had been agreed before the opening of the shortened route to the West of England in 1906 and no doubt the bridges on the new cut-off lines, Stert to Westbury and Castle Cary to Langport, had been built to the improved standard. But as the two-cylinder 'Saint' Class 4-6-0s were still in general use on many of the fastest trains, one can well understand why Inglis, while Chief Engineer, did not tell Churchward about the 22-ton limit for the new bridges. In the 1926 discussions Lloyd was asked if he could allow a further concession to 22½ tons on four-cylinder engines, and to this he agreed. Pole then instructed Collett to prepare the design of a locomotive with a 22½-ton axle load, and to have the first engine ready for the summer traffic of 1927. The Civil Engineer was instructed to have the Paddington-Plymouth route ready for the increased axle loading, and it was found that only four bridges remained to be strengthened. In commissioning this new design, Pole was as much concerned with prestige as with meeting traffic requirements. As the Southern had seen fit to equate tractive effort with power in its publicity, the only answer which the GWR could make to this claim was the introduction of an engine with a still higher tractive effort. The 1926 exchange had shown that a larger passenger engine could be expected on the LMS, and Collett was therefore instructed to get the tractive effort up to 40,000 lbs, a figure which was unlikely to be exceeded on other railways for some time.

The dimensional factors contributing to the tractive effort formula were settled as follows:

Dimension	**Castle**	**'Super-Castle'**	**Increases in nominal tractive effort (lbs)**
Cylinders diameter (in)	16	16¼	990
Cylinders stroke (in)	26	28	2,560
Boiler pressure (psi)	225	250	3,980
Coupled wheel diameter (ft in)	6 8½	6 6	1,145

Of these, on the engines as first built the increase in cylinder diameter was no more than nominal, and only the first six engines were built new with 16¼ in cylinders. The rest were bored to 16 in, but of course they would be increased with successive reborings on overhaul, and the dimension of 16¼ in was regarded as the official figure for purposes of calculating the nominal tractive effort. The two major factors contributing to the enhancement of power were the increase in cylinder volume, and the raising of the boiler pressure. One gathers that Collett would have been satisfied to use the standard diameter of coupled wheels, and avoid the cost of making new patterns and the subsequent design changes that were occasioned at the front end. With 6-ft 8½-in wheels the nominal tractive effort of the new engine would have been 39,100 lbs. But Sir Felix Pole was most anxious to have at least 40,000 lbs and so 6-ft 6-in coupled wheels were adopted, with the attendant problems they introduced.

The design detail of the new engine was the work of F.W. Hawksworth, who was then Chief Draughtsman, and a remarkable piece of design work it was, to build a locomotive of such tractive capacity with an overall weight of no more than 89 tons. The boiler was to be longer than that of the 'Castles' and this, together with the greater weight, called for an increase in wheelbase. The spacing of the coupled wheels was increased by 1 ft 6 in and the bogie wheelbase by 8 in, the distance from the rear bogie wheels to the leading coupled wheels remaining unchanged. Except for changes resulting from these increases in length, the motion remained unchanged from the previous four-cylinder locomotives. Adhering to Churchward's insistence on horizontal inside cylinders meant that the use of smaller driving wheels reduced the clearance under the cylinders. This could have been met by adopting Churchward's early practice of having the cylinder centre line offset from the centre of the driving axle, but in fact the wheel diameter of the bogie was reduced from the previous standard figure of 3 ft 2 in to 3 ft and the bogie was redesigned.

The standard Swindon bar-framed bogie was an adaptation of an earlier design to include certain features of the French de Glehn compounds which gave greatly superior riding and which had been adopted on the GWR from the introduction of the 'Knight' series of four-cylinder 4-6-0s in 1908. At the time that the first steps towards the design of the 'Super-Castles' was under way there were a number of failures of Churchward bogies through rivets breaking and for the new engines Hawksworth felt that a plate-framed bogie would be stronger. The draughtsman concerned was A.W.J. Dymond and he soon found that it was very difficult to fit inside plate frames under the inside cylinders, consistent with making the frame of adequate depth. He therefore arrived at a design in which the frame abreast of the leading bogie axle was outside the wheels, and the rear part of the frame inside the wheels. This curious arrangement was submitted to Collett who, to the designer's surprise, immediately accepted it.

Later investigation showed that the weakness of the Churchward bogie lay not in the strength of its frames, but in the inadequacy of diagonal bracing. A proposal to fit plate-framed bogies to the 'Halls' was therefore abandoned in favour of inserting additional diagonal bracing in the standard bogie. Had this decision been reached a little earlier, the 'Kings' would probably have had a standard Churchward bogie. The equalizing bar arrangement was abandoned, and the new bogie had individually sprung axles. At first the only springing for the axleboxes was short laminated springs with rigid hangers. To mitigate the effects of the longer engine wheelbase, the trailing coupled axleboxes were given one inch of lateral play under the control of inclined slides, like the Cartazzi slides of the standard GWR pony truck. The trailing section of the coupling rods had spherical bushes to accommodate the translation of the trailing axle.

Apart from the bogie, which in its original form gave Swindon many a headache, the new engines were a logical enlargement of the 'Stars' far more so than the 'Castles', the design of which had been restricted by the weight limits imposed on the Locomotive Department at the time. Even so, the increase of 27 per cent in the nominal tractive was not fully matched by the increase in boiler capacity. The maximum diameter was 6 ft as in the No 7 boiler, and the firebox length 11 ft 6 in. The barrel length was 16 ft, an increase of 1 ft 2 in on the No 1 boiler. The grate area was 34.2 sq ft, an increase of $16\frac{1}{2}$ per cent on the 'Castle'. This was balanced by an increase of 18 per cent in the firebox heating surface, and of 19 per cent in the superheating surface. To distribute the weight of the boiler evenly over the rear section of the engine frame, flat leaf springs about 8 in long were fitted in grooves in the boiler-carrying brackets beneath the firebox.

The class was initially referred to as the 'Super-Castles' and it was thought that the engines were to be named after cathedrals. The plan to send the first engine to America led to the choice of a more striking name, and the decision to name them after Kings of England was taken before the first engine had been completed. Unlike the 4021–30 series of 'Stars', which omitted the numbers of individual monarchs, the 'Kings' were named after individual Kings of England, starting with King George V and running in reverse order to King Stephen. Whether this arrangement was of greater assistance to railway enthusiasts in teaching them the order of the English Kings, or in helping them to remember the numbers of the 'King' Class engines, is not recorded.

The striking appearance of the 'Kings' came from a combination of their generally massive size and specific details of the design. The chimney was shorter and of larger diameter than that of the 'Castles'; the outside bearings of the bogie and the conspicuous front stretchers of the bogie frame implied solidity, and the straight diagonal top line of the main frames adjoining the inside cylinders, together with the box-like steam chest cover, gave a more thrusting appearance ahead of the smoke-box than in the 'Stars' and 'Castles'.

In the meantime, over in the USA, Daniel Willard, President of the Baltimore & Ohio Railroad, was already considering how his Company would celebrate its centenary in 1927. He therefore commissioned an eminent railway enthusiast, Edward Hungerford, to attend the centenary celebrations of the Stockton & Darlington Railway, and to report his observations. During his stay in England, Hungerford met Pole, and from their conversation emerged the idea that an English engine (that is, for Pole, a GWR engine) should take part in the celebrations. When the decision to build the new engine was taken, it was clear that this was the engine which must go to America, though at first this was not appreciated in Swindon Works. K.J. Cook, then Assistant Locomotive Works Manager, has told how the general outline of the new class was known, but that very few drawings had yet reached them. Then one day he was called into his chief's office; Stanier was there, and Cook began to explain how he was planning to have the first engine of the new class completed by the end of September. But Stanier cut him short by saying, 'Young man, she's got to be in the USA by August!' The task was achieved with sufficient margin for the engine both to complete the necessary trial trips and to be exhibited at a number of stations in aid of the GWR 'Helping Hand' fund, which aided members of the staff in time of need. At Paddington, on 1 July, nearly 3,000 people inspected the engine, and many were turned away disappointed. On 20 July the engine worked the down 'Limited' for the first time, and made an excellent run.

King George V *ready for the USA with a Westinghouse brake fitted.* (W.J. Reynolds)

The expedition to the USA was in the personal charge of Mr W.A. Stanier, as he was then, in his capacity of Principal Assistant to the Chief Mechanical Engineer. The engine arrived at Roath Dock, Cardiff,

King George V *at the Baltimore & Ohio Cententary Pageant, with Miss Lilian Schuler as 'Britannia'.* (British Railways)

on 2 August 1927, and was loaded on the SS *Chicago City* on the following day. It was accompanied by the replica Broad Gauge engine *North Star*. The boiler was loaded separately from the chassis on the deck of the ship, no crane capable of lifting the locomotive in one piece being available. It reached Locust Point, Baltimore, on 21 August, and was taken thence to the Mount Clare shops of the Baltimore & Ohio. The fineness of its detailed work compared with contemporary American locomotives immediately attracted attention.

The exhibition was open from 24 September to 15 October, and was visited by a quarter of a million people. No 6000, handled by Driver W. Young and Fireman Pearce of Old Oak Common, led the procession each day, and attracted great interest. An oval track had been laid in the exhibition grounds, and a procession of locomotives paraded round the track past the viewing stands. There was a gentle slope approaching the grandstand, and Young allowed No 6000 to coast down it. The engine moved past the stand in complete silence, whereas the American engines, even new ones, groaned, squeaked and clanked. Never was the excellence of Swindon workmanship shown up more strikingly. Amongst the visitors who were allowed to ride on the engine was Henry Ford I, who took many photographs and announced his intention of making a model of the engine.

In addition to engine No 6000, five more 'Kings' had been completed at Swindon in July 1927, and these were put into express traffic at once. Soon after, however, reports were received of rough riding, and as wear developed in the axle-boxes the engines developed alarming motions, nosing at the front and lurching from side to side at the rear. On 10 August 1927, the bogie of No 6003 was partially derailed whilst travelling at speed near Midgham on straight track. Fortunately the derailment did not spread to the train, and the results were not serious. They were, however, alarming, not only because there was no obvious reason why this derailment should have occurred on good track, but also because No 6000 was about to be tested in America, where the track might be well below GWR standards.

There is a story, possibly apocryphal, that Collett visited the scene of the derailment and, poking his umbrella into several sleepers, found that the metal tip penetrated. He therefore blamed the Civil Engineer for the derailment on the grounds that the track was defective. Nevertheless, an immediate investigation was made into the riding of the 'Kings' and, as suspicion fell on the bogie springs, a section was cut from the head of a rail on the weighbridge at Swindon. This allowed one wheel to drop, and it was found that a drop of $1\frac{1}{2}$ in relieved the wheel of all load. There was thus little margin for defects in the track consistent with the wheel loads remaining sufficiently great to ensure adequate flange control. Coil springs were therefore introduced into the spring hangers to soften the springing. Plates were also inserted in the trailing axle-boxes to reduce the lateral clearance to $\frac{1}{16}$ in in place of 1 in and the inclined slides were later removed. From the seventh engine onwards the slides were omitted, but the spherical bushes were fitted to all the engines of the class. It was not until the mid-1950s that it was realized that these were no longer required, and they were then replaced by cylindrical bushes.

These changes eliminated the rolling of the engines, but fracturing of bogie springs continued, and after some months the trailing coupled wheel springs were redesigned to make them softer (33 plates at 1.8 in, and one in $\frac{1}{2}$ in, in place of 21 at $\frac{7}{16}$ in and at one at $\frac{1}{2}$ in). This cured the trouble and the 'Kings' then gained the reputation of being amongst the best-riding engines in Britain. After the Midgham derailment, Stanier received a cable from Collett telling him that No 6000

Left *No 6003* King George IV *on the 1.30 pm ex-Paddington passing Sonning signal box. A week later this engine, while working the down 'Cornish Riviera Express', suffered the derailment of its bogie while running at 60 mph near Midgham.* (M.W. Earley)

Right *After its return from the USA with the bell mounted on the buffer beam,* King George V *poses at Old Oak Common alongside two earlier generations of Great Western four-cylinder 4-6-0s, No 5010* Restormel Castle *and No 4004* Morning Star. (W.J. Reynolds)

was not to be run on a main line until permission was received from Swindon. When the modifications to the bogie springing had been agreed, details were sent to Stanier, and he was able to arrange with the Baltimore & Ohio Company for the necessary work to be done in their shops.

Two days after the close of the exhibition, on 17 October, No 6000 was given a test run on the Baltimore & Ohio railroad. Starting from Baltimore, the engine ran to Washington (36 miles) and then made a trip to Philadelphia ($132\frac{1}{2}$ miles); finally it returned to Baltimore. The load comprised a dynamometer car and six coaches which, in the heavyweight American stock of the day weighed 544 tons tare. The task set for Driver Young and Fireman Pearce was thus formidable. The load was as great as that handled on the West of England trains, but instead of the progressive shedding of load by the 'Limited' on its 4-hour journey, this load was to be hauled over 272 miles, with a total running time for the day of 7 hours. Instead of the familiar soft Welsh coal, the engine was burning hard gas coal, which formed large quantities of clinker, and was better suited to grates of twice the size of that of *King George V*. Added to this was the Westinghouse brake, a strange road, the different feel of the roadbed, the need for additional vigilance on a railway without fencing, and the general unfamiliarity of all the lineside equipment. And to crown it all, the work of the engine was being studied in the dynamometer car by senior officers of three American railroads.

A 'Star' and two 'Castles' had previously maintained the honour of the Great Western when tested on two 'foreign' lines in England. Now, under much more severe conditions, *King George V* and its crew ably maintained the honour not only of Swindon but of British locomotive engineering generally. Pearce's contribution was notable; despite the difficult fuel, pressure was never below 205 psi, and on the last leg of the test was maintained at 235–245 psi. There was an almost complete absence of black smoke from the chimney, in contrast to the American engines both at the exhibition and in ordinary service. At the request of the railroad officials speed did not exceed 74 mph and for much of the test was limited to 65, but the general running was up to the standards maintained on the home railway. The gradients varied down to 1 in 79. Amongst notable figures recorded was a drawbar pull of 5 tons sustained at 48 mph on a gradient of 1 in 115; the equivalent drawbar horsepower was nearly 1,700.

Although the Baltimore & Ohio had water troughs, the water level was lower than on the GWR and No 6000's scoop was ineffective. Two stops were thus needed for water, one at Camden station, Baltimore, and the other at Elks Mills. The start from Elks Mills was on a 1 in 115 gradient, and it was here that the drawbar pull of 5 tons at 48 mph was recorded. The American officials were very impressed with the riding of the engine, but, as was recorded earlier, it might well have given a different impression. No 6000 was fitted with a bell for its trial run, and retained this for the remainder of its life. It bears the inscription: 'Presented to the locomotive *King George V* by the Baltimore and Ohio Railroad in commemoration of its centenary celebrations, September 24–October 15, 1927'. Two medals were also fixed to the cab sides. The clean lines of the engine created a great impression in the United States, and a number of express engines on the Baltimore & Ohio and other railroads appeared with cleaner external lines and, in some cases, with copper-capped chimneys.

The potential of the 'Kings' was exploited quickly; in the winter timetable of 1927, 7 minutes were cut from the schedule of the down 'Limited'. But despite the publicity that accompanied the introduction of the 'Kings', and the magnificent appearance of the new engines, there was definitely something about them

Above *No 6004* King George III *on the down 'Cornish Riviera Express' near Twyford — a 14-coach train.* (M.W. Earley)

Left King George V *on a 15-coach down West of England express near Somerton.* (Author's collection)

Below *The down 'Cornish Riviera Express' between Reading West and Southcote Junction with engine No 6015* King Richard III. (M.W. Earley)

that left the more thoughtful of outside observers slightly unimpressed. By the year 1927 the slight recession in Great Western locomotive performance that had followed the Coal Strike in 1926 had largely disappeared, and both 'Stars' and 'Castles'—not to mention the trusty old 'Saints'—were back on top form. And when vast new locomotives were introduced to do work that the older engines had done so brilliantly, when conditions were favourable, the need for so great an advance was questioned. The publicity was inclined to be regarded purely as publicity. After all, it was argued, if *Knight of the Grand Cross* could take 530 tons out of Paddington on the down 'Limited', and with appropriate reductions of load at Westbury, Taunton and Exeter, bring the train into North Road 3 minutes early, was there really a need for locomotives of 40,300 lbs tractive effort, in order to cut a mere 7 minutes off the schedule? In any case, the Interchange Trial of 1925 had shown that a 'Castle' could cut 15 minutes off the schedule!

The inaugural runs of engines Nos 6000 and 6001 on the 'Cornish Riviera Express' included nothing that was really significant in the way of performance. If the 'Stars' had taken 288 tons over the South Devon line, on the proportions of tractive effort to load the 'Kings' ought to have had 410 tons, not 360. It only needed news of the derailment at Midgham to give a slightly jaundiced view of the new locomotives. Neither was the first detailed account of their working any more reassuring. Following his very successful footplate run from Paddington to Plymouth on a 'Castle' in the autumn of 1924, Cecil J. Allen was accorded a similar privilege on a 'King' in October 1927, with results that led to a good deal of controversy in the columns of *The Railway Magazine*! All the arguments that had centred around the differences in boiler design between Swindon and Doncaster practice were revived, and the instances of bad steaming of GWR engines during the period of the 1926 Coal Strike were recalled.

The engine was No 6005, and the loads on the four successive stages of the journey were much the same as on Allen's footplate run with *Pendennis Castle* three years earlier, namely 525, 450, 380 and 270 tons gross behind the tender. The tender had been loaded with indifferent coal, however, and although having a nominal tractive effort vastly greater than that of a 'Castle', the engine was never master of the schedule until the load was reduced to seven coaches at Exeter. By Slough, 1 min 40 sec had been dropped, and speed was only 62½ mph. A permanent way slack to 40 mph caused further delay, and the lateness rose to 3½ minutes. There was a further permanent way slack at Aldermaston, and speed did not rise above 57½ mph until Savernake had been passed 6 minutes late. There was a gradual recovery, and by Taunton lateness was under 2 minutes, but with only 380 tons a further minute was lost by Exeter. However, there was no difficulty in recovering this loss after Exeter, and Plymouth was reached in 237 min 50 sec, or 233½ minutes net. Much work with the pricker had been needed, and the interest of the run lay in the fireman's efforts to combat difficulties which at that time were not frequent on the GWR. The publication of this run, in very extended detail, caused something of a sensation among students of locomotive performance, and there were some, with no particular partisan feelings, who were inclined to the view that Swindon design practice, in enlarging the 'Star' to the proportions of the 'King', had overreached itself, and that for locomotives of 40,000 lbs tractive effort the large boiler and wide firebox favoured by Doncaster was preferable.

16. 'A machine of precision'

When Kenneth J. Cook became President of the Institution of Locomotive Engineers in 1955 he gave his Presidential Address the title 'A Machine of Precision'. At that time he had been away from Swindon for some years, and was then Chief Mechanical Engineer of the Eastern and North Eastern Regions of British Railways, with his headquarters at Doncaster. But the theme of his address was centred mainly on the work in which he was deeply involved when he was Assistant Locomotive Works Manager at Swindon, when Collett was Chief Mechancial Engineer. His time as Assistant covered a period when there were big changes in personnel on the Great Western Railway, but Cook was fortunate in having the rock-like steadfastness of Collett at the head of the Mechanical Engineering department of the Company. First of all, at midsummer 1929, came the resignation of Sir Felix Pole, having been tempted by an offer of very high authority in the electrical industry, which one may add he carried exceedingly well. On the GWR his deputy James Milne stepped up into his place and carried the General Managership with quiet distinction for the remainder of the life of the Company, until December 1947.

Milne was an engineering graduate, trained in the

Above *The last 'King' to be built, engine No 6029* King Stephen *renamed* King Edward VIII *in 1936.* (British Railways)

Left *No 4000* North Star, *rebuilt as a 'Castle', on a down West of England express near Reading West.* (M.W. Earley)

Above right *The 'Cornish Riviera Express' in Sonning Cutting in 1935; No 6020* King Henry IV *and a train of 'Centenary' stock.* (M.W. Earley)

Locomotive Department at Swindon, but his was an altogether quieter temperament than that of Sir Felix Pole, and he left Collett to carry on in his own way, without the constant urgings to keep the GWR in the fore in locomotive development. One of the last of Pole's acts in this direction was the acceleration of the 'Cheltenham Flyer', to a start-to-stop run of 70 minutes for the 77.3 miles from Swindon to Paddington in July 1929, making it then undisputably the 'World's Fastest Train'; with 'Castles' to haul it and a load usually of not more than 250 tons it was a relatively easy task. Indeed, in the first year of its running some very fine runs were made by 'Star' Class engines, notably *Knight of Liege* and *Tresco Abbey*. My own first trip on it in the early autumn of 1929 produced some magnificent running after what appeared to me at the time a somewhat indifferent start. Then I was not aware of the special signalling arrangements adopted by the Great Western Railway to provide additional

security for this train, and also for the 'Bristolian', when it was introduced in 1935. For these high-speed trains the line was divided into sections covering a

GWR: 'Cheltenham Flyer'

Date			19 October 1929			15 December 1934		
Engine No			5003			5025		
Engine Name			*Lulworth Castle*			*Chirk Castle*		
Load (tons, E/F)			254/270			248/265		
Distance (miles)		**Schedule (min)**	**Actual (min**	**sec)**	**Speed (mph)**	**Actual (min**	**sec)**	**Speed (mph)**
0.0	Swindon	0	0	00	—	0	00	—
5.7	Shrivenham		7	40	68	7	02	75
—			sigs					
10.8	Uffington		11	55	74	11	01	80½
13.4	Challow		14	00	79½	12	57	81
16.9	Wantage Road		16	35	81	15	31	83½
20.8	Steventon		19	25	83½	18	18	85
24.2	Didcot	22/21	21	50	86½	20	44	83½
28.8	Cholsey		25	05	85	24	04	82½
32.6	Goring		27	45	85	26	48	82½
35.8	Pangbourne		30	00	83½	29	11	79½
38.7	Tilehurst		32	05	86½	31	20	82½
41.3	Reading	36½/34	34	00	77½	33	17	80½
43.2	Sonning box		35	30	75	34	42	80½
46.3	Twyford		37	55	78	37	00	82½
53.1	Maidenhead		43	10	76½	41	50	86½
56.3	Burnham Beeches		45	40	78	44	04	85½
58.8	Slough	51/47	47	35	75	45	50	85½
61.1	Langley		49	30	69	47	27	82½
64.1	West Drayton		52	05	69	49	41	81
68.2	Southall	59/54½	55	35	72½	52	43	82
69.9	Hanwell		57	00	74	53	57	82½
71.6	Ealing Broadway		58	20	75	55	13	79
73.0	Acton		59	50	—	56	19	75
76.0	Westbourne Park		63	15	—	59	19	—
—			sigs		—	—		—
77.3	Paddington	70/65	67	15		62	15	

number of ordinary block sections, and these would form one block section. At the entrance, 'Line Clear' would not be given until all the intervening sections were clear. On this run of mine, restrained speed was maintained until after Shrivenham had been passed, the speed at milepost 70 being only 66½ mph, whereas on a later run with the train it was nearing 80 mph.

From Uffington onwards, however, we went like the wind, averaging no less than 84½ mph between Steventon and Reading. The log of this exciting journey is tabulated herewith, and it will be seen that we were half a minute down at Steventon because of our slightly delayed start, but were 2½ minutes early at Reading, and progressively earlier still afterwards. Our maximum speed of 86½ mph, at Didcot and again at Tilehurst, was attained on level track. When the train was further accelerated, first to 67 minutes and then in 1933 to 65 minutes, the working time to passing Reading was 34 minutes, and although on my run with *Lulworth Castle* we eased down considerably after Reading we were still running approximately to the later schedule. Although it represents a somewhat later stage in the 'Castle' saga, covering a development in constructional practice referred to later in the present chapter, I have tabulated alongside the run with *Lulworth Castle* what I consider my finest on the 'Cheltenham Flyer', made on a wintry day in December 1934. I was travelling from Gloucester on this occasion and before the train arrived from Cheltenham I was interested to see that the engine to take us on was one of the very latest 'Castles' built that same year. But the weather conditions were very far from being propitious, a strong east wind bringing sleet and snow at times. The train arrived late at Gloucester, with one coach over the normal, but the driver made a magnificent and unchecked run from Swindon to Paddington. Blizzard or not, the effort was sustained as far as Acton, when visibility compelled an easier pace into the terminus. I have several times clocked finishes on the 'Cheltenham Flyer' a full minute less from Acton, and but for the weather we might have clipped a further minute from the excellent time set out in the table.

In between the dates of these two runs the Great Western Railway staged the World Record Run of the train on 6 June 1932 when, with engine No 5006 *Tregenna Castle*, the 77.3 miles from Swindon to Paddington were covered in 56 min 47 sec. It was a memorable occasion for British railways in general, but the engine performance though spectacular was slightly discounted by the lightness of the load. On all my own runs on the 'Cheltenham Flyer' in normal working conditions, the load had never been less than seven coaches, about 220 tons tare, whereas on the World Record trip it was only six, 186 tons tare. I compare below the relative efforts involved with my own run of 15 December 1934.

With *Tregenna Castle*, the official engine working involved the use of 17 per cent cut-off from Shrivenham

	6 June 1932	**15 December 1934**
Engine No	5006	5025
Engine Name	*Tregenna Castle*	*Chirk Castle*
Load Coaches	6	8
Tons (E/F)	186/195	248/265
Average speed, Shrivenham-Acton	88.7	83.2
Estimated train resistance (lb/ton)	19.2	17.57
Haulage effort	375	465

The 'Cheltenham Flyer' near Steventon hauled by an unidentified 'Castle' Class engine. (Real Photos Co Ltd)

to Goring, 18 per cent thence to Maidenhead, 17 per cent to Southall and 18 per cent to milepost 2, all with a fully opened regulator throughout. On my run I had the pleasure of a short talk with the driver when we got to Paddington and he told me he had used 20 per cent cut-off with full regulator throughout to Acton, where he had very much eased up. I repeat, a magnificent run by *Chirk Castle* and her crew.

The next event that was eventually to cause a stir in the Locomotive Department at Swindon was the side-stepping of Sir Henry Fowler, Chief Mechanical Engineer of the LMS, to be an assistant to one of the Vice-Presidents. For although there was a very able engineer and administrator to take the job of the CME, he was in fact no more than a caretaker charged with the tasks of finding a successor, before he moved on to still higher planes of office. How Stanier was chosen for the job, and the successive stages in which he was interviewed by the LMS people, has been told elsewhere, but when the 'beatings about the bush' were completed and Sir Harold Hartley definitely made him the offer, he had of course to tell Collett. Therein lay certain difficulties. Not many years previously Collett's wife had died, and it was said by those who were nearest to him in Swindon that the shock very nearly killed him. He had barely recovered from this blow when there came the thought of losing Stanier as well, and with something of a heavy heart he went to London to put the situation before Milne.

Collett was then coming up to 62 years of age, and one can read between the lines that he had some thoughts of early retirement. Any ideas in that direction were quashed at once by the top management of the GWR, because Lord Churchill was also present at his talk with Milne, and he said at once that they wanted Collett to go his full course as CME, and that there was no chance of Stanier becoming Chief Mechanical Engineer for many years ahead.

Actually Collett did not retire until ten years after that momentous interview, when he himself had turned 71 years of age. So Stanier went to the LMS with the good wishes of everyone on the staff of the GWR Chief Mechanical Engineer. To replace him John Auld was appointed Principal Assistant, and this was another very popular move. Before the amalgamations of 1923, Auld had been Mechanical Engineer of the Barry Railway, and in the enlarged Great Western he had been appointed Docks Assistant to the Chief Mechanical Engineer. He had been a tower of strength to the management in the difficult years following the prolonged Coal Strike of 1926, and continued as 'number 2' at Swindon almost to the time of Collett's retirement.

Barely two years after Stanier had gone to the LMS there occurred the tragic death of he to whose vision and skill the whole edifice and development of twentieth-century Great Western mechanical engineering had been founded, George Jackson Churchward. While increasing age was bringing on some deficiences of sight and hearing, living as he did alongside the railway they did not prevent him from taking a lively interest in all that was going on. Unlike his successor he was an all-round railwayman, and when he began to hear the characteristic noise of a 'hanging' rail joint not far from his house he got on the phone to the Divisional Engineer, Bristol, urging him to do something about it. Days passed and nothing was done, and with the noise getting worse one foggy December morning he told his housekeeper he was going out 'to find where that damned joint is'. Those were the last words he spoke, because on the line searching for that faulty rail joint in the muffled air of that foggy morning he did not hear the approach of the 8.55 am from Paddington to South Wales, and was knocked down and killed. The engine concerned was not one of his very own, but a near enough relation, No 4085 *Berkeley Castle*.

With Churchward's passing and Sir Felix Pole having gone to other activities, it is interesting to speculate as to how these two great men of former Great Western days would have reacted to the tremendous upsurge in speed and enterprising locomotive development pursued by the north-going railways in the 1930s, which were eventually to push the Great Western 'off the front page', as it were. But Collett, and Milne for that matter, were men of a different kind of stamp, and the greatness of the Great Western gradually partook of a more subtle form which the engineers of the other railways came to experience in full measure under the harsh glare of nationalization. Collett was above all a scientist, who sought improvement in the intrinsic quality of locomotive and other machinery under his care, rather than the more spectacular achievements of ever faster running with passenger trains. After all, under his supervision the Great Western had by far the most powerful express passenger locomotives in the country and he could afford to sit back, as it were, and concentrate on the detail technical features which continued to put them ahead of all rivals.

When he was Locomotive Works Manager he had already taken some steps to bring precision into boiler manufacture, though he caused serious resentment among the boilermakers by appointing a fitter as Chief Boiler Foreman. As with all Collett's acts, however, there was sound judgement in the appointment, and in the 25 years that his nominee had the job, as Collett hoped at the outset, he greatly improved the equipment of the shop with its heavy flanging and plate-forming appliances, and the tools generally. In Churchward's time, before the First World War, a great amount of design work and shop experimenting had been conducted at Swindon to finalize the design of the taper boiler and its firebox to the stage of excellence it had

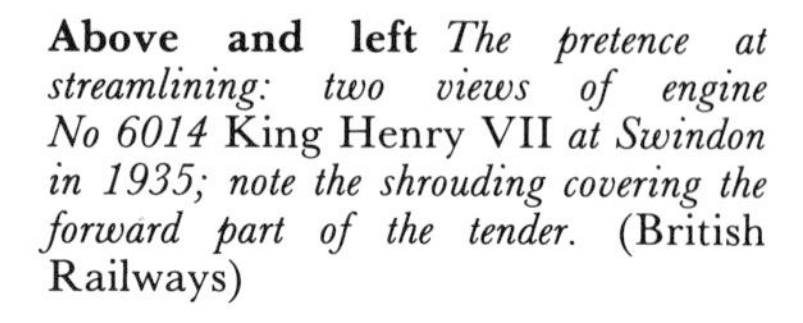

Above and left *The pretence at streamlining: two views of engine No 6014* King Henry VII *at Swindon in 1935; note the shrouding covering the forward part of the tender.* (British Railways)

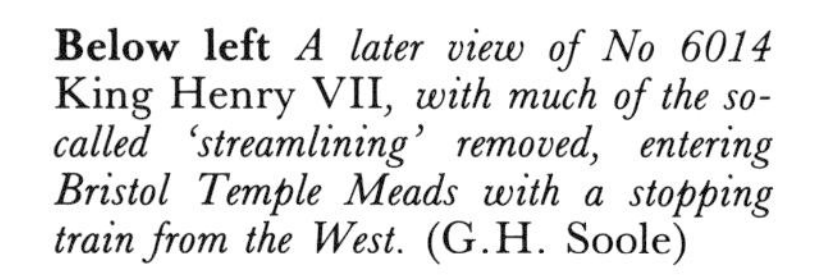

Below left *A later view of No 6014* King Henry VII, *with much of the so-called 'streamlining' removed, entering Bristol Temple Meads with a stopping train from the West.* (G.H. Soole)

Below *The partially streamlined 'Castle', No 5005* Manorbier Castle, *similarly modified, hauling a West to North express through Patchway.* (G.H. Soole)

Below right *The up 'Torbay Limited', a 15-coach train near Norton Fitzwarren hauled by No 6018* King Henry VI *in 1928.* (F.R. Hebron, Rail Archive Stephenson)

then obtained. But it was not a simple design, particularly in the specialized shaping of the firebox in the different sizes of boiler, and there was much justification in the way Churchward's contemporaries eschewed the taper barrel and the highly specialized form of Belpaire firebox that went with it, on the grounds of high initial cost and high maintenance charges afterwards. Under Collett, not only was the first cost of the rather 'fancy' Swindon boiler much reduced, but also the repair procedures were so improved that the eventual life of the standard boilers was increased more than *100 per cent*. In his book *Swindon Steam*, Cook writes:

> A few years earlier, 400,000 miles was regarded as about the life of a boiler and the number of boilers at or above this mileage influenced our requests to the CME for orders for new boilers. Now this mileage was being reached in some cases before the boiler had been taken off the frames for its first heavy repair and we began to talk in terms of a million miles. Our monthly tabulation of the condition of our spare boiler stock now showed the number of boilers above 800,000, 900,000 and a million miles in order to anticipate what might be condemned next time in shops.'

No dissertation about 'machines of precision' would be appropriate without some reference to lubrication, and after the 'Kings' had been in service for two years or so, some signs of heating on the large end bearings of the connecting rods appeared. As power of locomotives was increased there was a tendency to encroach upon the maximum loads per square inch of bearing surface, and as there were stringent limits to overall width permitted by the loading gauge, no relief could be obtained by lengthening the outside crank pins. On the inside connecting rod bearings there was a conflict between the lengths available for the axle-box bearings. the crank pins and the width of seating for the webs of the built-up crank axles plus the eccentric sheaves. There were no cases of serious failure, but during periodical examinations suspicions were aroused. Whilst investigating this, a number of the brasses of inside connecting rods and bushes of the outside rods were examined on locomotives being dismantled for repair of the 'Castle', 'Star' and 'Saint' Classes. It was noticed that some of these were showing signs of fretting and were not really happy, so that brought them back to fundamentals.

The standard method of lubrication of these bearings was by plug worsted trimming in an oilbox machined out of the solid connecting rods, the motion of which splashed oil on the top of the trimmings which fed drops to a groove across the top of the bearings. There was no question of the oil not reaching the bearings, but it did not spread evenly over the bearing surface, appearing instead to work downwards and outwards leaving a portion in the centre of the bearing which did not receive its full share and which tended to blacken from fretting. Various devices to direct the oil to the centre of the bearing were tried, such as cutting a shallow circular groove to deflect the oil back to the centre, but without much effect.

It was recalled that on one or two machine tool spindles, lubrication was applied by a felt pad, and this suggested a method of spreading the oil over the whole width of the bearing. Actually, an extremely small quantity of oil was necessary provided that it was spread over the whole surface of the pin and bearing to maintain continuity of a film of oil. Felt pad lubrication introduced a completely different method of oil feed and required the elimination of the worsted trimming, a portion of the routine working of locomotives deeply engrained with enginemen. The felt pad had two functions to perform; to regulate the flow of oil from the oilbox so that the pad remained saturated but the oil was not allowed to be dispensed too freely, and to spread oil over the whole width of the crank and maintain an oil film.

Consultation with the felt manufacturers revealed

that felt could be made of any thickness and of any density, so they were able, by trial, to establish the density to meet the conditions and then to produce a spring-loaded gauge by which this density could be tested. Subsequently every large sheet of felt purchased was tested by the gauge before acceptance and cutting into pads. Thickness of the sheets of felt was approximately 1 in. The felt pad had to regulate the flow of oil and, above all, prevent any leakage from the oilbox which had always previously been controlled by the worsted trimming. The oilboxes were relatively small, but the supply had to last for a non-stop run from Paddington to Plymouth; it was necessary to ensure that it had not leaked away by, say, Westbury. The pressure of the pad on the bottom of the oil holes was therefore important. It was at first deemed necessary to cut pads to fit into a tin tray container which was itself kept in position in a machined slot in the brasses or bush and thus exert pressure by the pad on the oil hole. From the point of view of lubrication and the full continuous maintenance of an oil film in the bearing, this was extremely successful.

Some time later it was found that on the bushes they could dispense with the tin tray and insert a plain pad, end on to the grain of the felt, pressing it in by hand to a slot machined in the bush. This was a great step forward as it enabled them to do the final machining of the bush after it had been pressed into the coupling or connecting rod and thus avoid any distortion of the surface. A two-spindle vertical grinding machine, with micrometer adjustment for the positioning of the spindles, was modified to take a wide cutting tool for the final cut of a few thou, which produced an extremely good plane surface. This killed two birds with one stone, as it produced the bearing surface they had been wanting, a plane smooth bore one thou per inch of diameter larger than the crank pin which was virtually a fit, and also good accuracy in the lengths between the centres of the bushes in coupled rods.

The felt pad lubrication was the answer to a number of problems which had faced them in earlier years, particularly on the inside big ends of the connecting rods on the 'Kings' and 'Castles'. From time to time there had been complaints against the Works of bad fitting when cases had arisen at sheds of slackness and some peculiar cases of hammering between the brasses and the containing steel backplate. Actually, the causes were primarily in the oil film lubrication, and once this occurred fretting between the metals started, and this of course gave rise to wear and slackness which became progressive.

Slackness in the working parts of a steam locomotive were by no means confined to the machinery as such. The mechanical basis of the machine in itself was unique in that its power was developed through two, three or more axes which should be parallel to each other, but at the same time there was relative movement. On a locomotive framing and its housing for the axles, which may have been over a total length of 20 ft, it was not an easy matter to measure or to check that the setting was correct. It required equipment which would ensure axes being at right angles to the cylinder lines, parallel to each other and at correct distances apart. Within the 20 ft or so there were other smaller lengths to be catered for on different locomotive classes. Upon the accuracy of the setting of the axles would depend the closeness of the fits of coupling rod bushes on the crank pins with the consequent effects upon wear, slackness and noise. The smaller the initial tolerance which could be provided, the less rapidly would wear develop.

It was on the 1934 batch of 'Castles', commencing with No 5023 *Brecon Castle*, that a very important improvement in constructional methods was introduced. The performance of a locomotive, and its general reliability in service, depended to a large extent upon the accuracy with which it was built, and particularly the alignment of the frames, axle-box guides and cylinders. At Swindon, as nearly everywhere else, the traditional method of alignment with wires, centre-pop and trammels had hitherto been used. In the 1930s the German State Railways were making use of Zeiss precision optical gear for lining up locomotive frames, and the experience of that administration was that the time of lining up was cut to between one-quarter and one-third of that previously taken. Furthermore, a locomotive so treated would run a greater mileage between repairs than previously. This method was studied by the engineers of the Great Western Railway, and after modification of the Zeiss apparatus to suit production methods at Swindon, it was adopted as standard practice for all new and repaired locomotives.

The basis of the apparatus was a telescope mounted within a tube, arranged so it could be pivoted in vertical or horizontal planes by two dials. When these two dials were both set at zero, the telescope was in exact central alignment with its external tube, which was set with a self-centring spider in the front bellmouth of one cylinder, and by an adaptor in the stuffing box at the back of the cylinder. A spirit-level ensured that the vertical and horizontal axes were correct, and a measuring surface set level with the front cylinder face by a straight edge provided zero for distance. The overall width across each pair of horns was measured by a vernier, after which a sighting scale, was clamped to each in turn and the scale read through the telescope. The sighting scale was similar to a surveyor's staff and the reading gave the distance of the cylinder axis to the outside edge of the horn. The distance plus half the width over that pair of horns gave the distance to the theoretical centre-line of the engine. If that sum did not amount to the same total at each horn, the cylinder axis was not parallel with the centre-line of the engine. A certain tolerance could be allowed there and the telescope pivoted horizontally until its centre was parallel with the engine centre-line; but if the correction would have been beyond the allowed limit it would have been necessary to cut down some stiffeners or cross-stays and reset the frames.

Assuming that the telescope was set parallel with the theoretical centre-line of the engine, the sighting scale was removed and a collimator, clamped to a tube in such a way that it was dead at right angles to the axis of the tube, was supported at the driving horn, the tube being right across the frame between both driving horns. The tube was held in a stand, the top of which could be moved vertically or horizontally to or from the cylinder, and through an angle horizontally. The collimator was an optical apparatus carrying two sets of cross scales illuminated by an electric lamp, and had the property of accepting at zero on its infinite scale only rays parallel with the telescope. If on sighting from the telescope the telescope cross-lines cut the horizontal and vertical lines of the infinite scale of the collimator at zero, then the telescope and collimator were truly parallel, though not necessarily at the same place. How much they were out of place could be read by focusing the telescope on the infinite scale of the collimator and reading the graduations. The horizontal, vertical and angular adjustments provided for in the collimator stand allowed the latter to be brought easily into alignment with the telescope. As the collimator was then parallel with the telescope and was fixed accurately at right angles to the collimator cross-tube, it followed that the cross-tube was then between the driving horns at right-angles to the cylinder axis.

A dial indicator was used to obtain the distance of each horn cheek from the collimator cross-tube, and the latter was traversed longitudinally until it was central between the driving horns. A length gauge with dial indicator from locating points on the telescope tubes and the collimator tube gave a direct reading of the distance from the cylinder face to the centre of the driving horn, and from the collimator cross-tube, a locating stud on each frame was set at a definite distance from the horn centre. Length gauges enabled further locating studs to be set at each of the other horns, ie 'leading', 'intermediate' and 'trailing', and from those similar measurements could be made to each of the corresponding horn checks. By means of the accurate rods and the dial indicator, all those measurements could be easily read to within a thousandth of an inch, although the total length between the leading and trailing horn centres might have been as much as 20 ft.

Thus a very accurate survey of the salient points of a locomotive frame could be made expeditiously, and from this decisions taken as to the amount of corrections to be made. I have dwelt on the process at some length because it proved the very cornerstone of Swindon constructional practice. It enabled valve gear parts to be made with precision, with an absolute minimum of clearance when new, so that newly out-shopped locomotives ran with the quietness of sewing machines. Such was the tightening up of clearance possible as a result that the situation became one that was vividly described by one ex-Great Western man, after nationalization when the differing practices of other famous locomotive manufactories came under review. This engineer said: 'We scrap at the amount of clearance they start with.' Dimensions previously maintained to within an accuracy of plus or minus 0.010 in were henceforth made to within an accuracy of plus or minus 0.002 in. This apparatus was used on older engines as they went through the works, and it is not without significance that the 20 engines of the 'Castle' Class numbered between 5023 and 5042 quickly gained the reputation of being the best yet of the whole class. No 5030 *Shirburn Castle* achieved the remarkable record of running 420,000 miles before the removal of the boiler from the frames, although it had,

An up Ocean Special in Sonning Cutting hauled by engine No 4094 Dynevor Castle. (M.W. Earley)

of course, received intermediate repairs.

What the new 'Castles' could do has already been shown earlier in this chapter by the splendid performance of No 5025 *Chirk Castle* on the 'Cheltenham Flyer' on a stormy December evening, but the very utmost of 'Castle' running with this train must surely have been reached when No 5023 *Brecon Castle*, the first of the new batch, was faced with hauling a load of 401 tons tare on the 65-minute schedule, and in the hands of a very expert engine crew they very nearly did it. The observer was himself an expert, Mr H.F. Maybank, and I have added the point-to-point average speeds to the timings included in his log herewith. Speed never quite reached 80 mph. The maximum was 79 mph, sustained on the faint descent between Steventon and Didcot; but a speed of 77.5 mph on the dead level approaching Reading indicated the remarkable drawbar horsepower of 1,070, and the fact that speed had averaged 76.8 mph from Uffington to Maidenhead shows clearly that this was no mere flash in the pan, achieved by mortgaging the boiler. It was a most splendid example of sustained steaming at a very high rate of evaporation. It was very unfortunate that so magnificent an effort, the product solely of a keen and resolute engine crew and a first-class engine, should have been marred by signal checks. From a careful examination of all the figures I am doubtful if strict time would have been kept. I think they would have been a minute out on arrival, but what is a mere minute against such a display as this! Of course there was a pair of real sportsmen on the footplate. Driver Street had as fireman C.E.Brown, who in Western Region days was a top-link driver of rare calibre, too, and gave me some fine runs.

GWR: 'Cheltenham Flyer'

Engine No 5023 *Brecon Castle*
Load 13 coaches, 401 tons tare, 435 tons full
Driver F.W. Street
Fireman C.E. Brown

Distance (miles)		Schedule (min)	Actual (m	s)	Average speed (mph)
0.0	Swindon	0	0	00	—
5.7	Shrivenham		8	00	42.7
10.8	Uffington		12	17	72.2
16.9	Wantage Road		17	07	75.7
24.2	Didcot	21	22	40	78.2
32.6	Goring		29	10	77.5
35.8	Pangbourne		31	46	73.8
41.3	Reading	34	36	06	76.7
46.3	Twyford		40	03	76.0
53.1	Maidenhead		45	20	77.2
—			sigs		
58.8	Slough	47½	52	20	48.9
64.1	West Drayton		57	19	63.8
68.2	Southall	54½	60	68	67.1
71.6	Ealing Broadway		63	48	71.3
—			sigs		
76.0	Westbourne Park	61	68	35	
77.3	Paddington	65	71	41	

17. Engine testing: new advanced practices

While the Works was engaged in markedly improving the constructional practices in building locomotives, as in the Zeiss system of lining up frames and so on, the Drawing Office was simultaneously involved in some important investigations into the finer points of express train running, an investigation that ultimately led to far-reaching results when the Great Western Railway had been merged into the National railway network after 1948. Despite the worldwide trade depression of the early 'thirties, there still seemed some lingerings of the spirit of Sir Felix Pole in the corridors of Paddington, in yearning for a more accelerated service of express passenger trains, particularly as there were certain moves in this direction, slump or no slump, in the Southern Area of the London and North Eastern Railway. On the other hand there was the increasing need for economy in every spending department of the Great Western Railway, and any thoughts of accelerated services were damped down by the Chief Civil Engineer in insisting that any acceleration of service must not involve higher maximum speed—80 mph was the limit. Those of us who had made a practice of logging express train running, not only Cecil J. Allen but also older exponents of the craft such as A.V. Goodyear and R.E. Charlewood, felt that the Chief Civil Engineer's department had really no idea of the speeds that were run on occasions, particularly on the Birmingham 2-hour trains, and these veteran practitioners came to the conclusion that *The Railway Magazine* was not read in the CCE's department at Paddington!

It was far otherwise in the Locomotive Drawing Office at Swindon. In the dynamometer car section, the legendary C.K. Dumas had retired, and a brilliant young engineer who was to rise very high in the British railway world, Charles Roberts, had succeeded him. For some time it had been felt at Swindon that the times sacrosanct in the working timetables, particularly on the West of England main line, were not really representative of the speeds actually run when a keen driver was making up time, and Roberts was authorized to make some dynamometer car trials to record what was actually taking place. These were not full dress occasions with the taking of indicator diagrams, as with *Caldicot Castle* in 1924, but a friendly get-together in which the traditional *camaraderie* between Drawing Office, running inspectors and the engine men was fully manifested. After making a number of runs on the West of England service on which all the drivers were allowed to carry on in the way they usually did, after studying the results of these runs Roberts and his immediate colleagues in the Drawing Office were drawn to the conclusion that the variations between booked time and actual times were the results of drivers working their engines at an approximately constant steam rate and thus making a constant demand on the boiler.

Hitherto all scientific testing, whether in Europe, the USA and, to a very limited extent, at Swindon itself, had been conducted on the basis of constant speed, apart of course from road trials with service trains. On the GWR it was well known that H.N. Gresley of the LNER had long been a strong advocate of a National Locomotive Laboratory, such as that at Vitry in France, where all the tests were naturally on a constant speed basis. But as a result of their dynamometer car runs on the West of England trains, Roberts and his associates were coming to the conclusion that tests to have any practical value should be made at constant steaming rates on the open road. Then true thermodynamic comparison could be made with constant speed tests on the stationary plant. The only trouble with the Swindon plant was that it had a maximum capacity of only about 500 horsepower. When Churchward installed it its primary object seems to have been to obviate the need for new engines to make their trial runs out on the line. It is interesting to read some impressions in the technical press at the time. One observer wrote that a four-coupled engine running at 70 mph and not moving an inch as a sight not easily forgotten. 'And what would happen,' he added, 'if the drawbar broke which is holding back the roaring locomotive as if it were a raging lion?'

The correspondent of *The Engineer* was naturally reassuring. He wrote:

> 'As the drawbar pull of something over one ton is considered good duty at 70 miles an hour, representing as it does nearly 500 horsepower net, there is not much danger. When we have become a little reconciled to the deafening roar of the wheels, and made up our mind that nothing is going to fly to pieces, we can begin to learn things. In the first place, we see that the bearing-springs of the engine have no movement; this is because the locomotive is virtually running on a perfectly smooth and rigid road; there is no rolling or pitching. We have, in fact, nothing but the internal disturbing forces to act. They assert themselves by a tendency to fore-and-aft oscillations, not at all marked at 40 miles an hour, not even at 50 or 60, but becoming violent at 70. At these enormous velocities of heavy moving parts the whole machine seems to be alive, and we can very well understand that no one cares to run an engine being tested up to 80 miles an hour, while 60 is considered sufficient for all useful purpose.'

In Swindon Works the plant got the nickname of the 'home trainer' from the devices then current by which racing cyclists could practice at home; but when Churchward's development of the early 1900s had been completed, the plant had been rarely used. In the early 'thirties Roberts's work came under the surveillance of Hawksworth, who would naturally convey the substance of it to Collett. The importance of the theme Roberts had embarked upon tended to highlight the need for a more powerful form of the 'home trainer', and at that very time Collett became aware that with Stanier gone to the LMS and engaged upon a major locomotive development of his own, his former assistant could well provide substantial backing for Gresley's long-cherished hope of a National Locomotive Laboratory. Stanier himself knew of the limitations of the Swindon plant and was ready enough to back Gresley up to the hilt. The need for it was emphasized in the most public manner possible by Gresley's getting authority from the LNER Board to send his new 2-8-2 express locomotive *Cock o' the North* to France for trials on the Vitry plant and for subsequent confirmatory road tests on the Paris–Orleans main line. Bulleid was still on the LNER at the time, and he went with the engine.

Ever since the unpleasantness following the Interchange Trials of 1925, and more so since his own sad bereavement, Collett had taken little or no part in inter-railway discussions, but all the time he took care to keep himself well informed. While he was in deadly opposition to the Institution of Locomotive Engineers (which he once described as 'a lot of b— commercial travellers'!), the London Divisional Locomotive Superintendent was always under his instructions regularly to attend all their meetings and to report what was going on. So this particular grapevine told him that Gresley and Stanier were getting together on the subject of a National Locomotive Testing station and that in due course Swindon would be invited to join in, and would undoubtedly be asked to contribute to the cost. Then, what one of his assistants once called the 'diabolical cunning' of C.B. Collett came into play, and in all secrecy, so far as the LNER and LMS were concerned, and very much so with the Institution of Locomotive Engineers, he set A.W.J. Dymond the task of completely modernizing the 'home trainer', and of making it capable of absorbing the maximum output of the largest engines.

I am not certain of the date when the curtain was drawn aside to reveal the new set-up, but sure enough there came jointly from Gresley and Stanier tentative proposals to Collett for a joint participation in a new British locomotive testing station. His reply was to invite representatives of the LNER and LMS to Swindon; and when they arrived there they were taken to see the testing plant in action, and a 'Saint', No 2931

No 6001 King Edward VII, *with improved draughting, at 75 mph on the test plant.* (British Railways)

Arlington Court, going all-out at 70 mph. Indicator diagrams were being taken, and far from being able to absorb only 500 horsepower, here was a 'Saint' developing nearly 1,200! But the visitors were told this was a relatively old engine. The plant as modernized could take 2,000 horsepower or even more. Obviously Swindon had no need to participate in any new project. Stepping some ten years ahead to my own detailed association with Great Western locomotive affairs, I can tell how I first saw an engine of the 'King' Class working under heavy express speed conditions. I wrote at the time:

> 'The engine is securely anchored at the cab end, and each of the coupled wheels rests on a carrier wheel, in the same way as the exhibitional model locomotives seen at Paddington and elsewhere are mounted. When the driver of the locomotive under test puts on steam, the movement of the coupled wheels causes the carrier wheels to revolve; hand brakes are applied, hydraulically, to drums on the axles of these carrier wheels, and the brake force is so regulated that the power needed to revolve the wheels is equivalent to that involved in the haulage of various loaded trains on the road. By careful adjustment the speed can be held steady for an hour or more at a stretch, and thus under truly constant conditions a scientific test can be conducted. On the Swindon plant each run, at steady speed, lasts for two hours, and all data secured relates to the average performance obtaining during that period.'

At the time of my visit, engine No 6022 *King Edward III* was on trial, and the test conditions called for the use of 20 per cent cut-off, regulator full open, and a speed of 60 mph. Now, on a footplate journey with *King Henry III* it needed no more than 16 per cent with only the first valve of the regulator to do 60 mph on the level with a 14-coach train, so I anticipated a very thrilling spectacle when *King Edward III* was worked up to speed on the stationary test plant under considerably heavier steaming. I was not disappointed. After a short spell of easy running to warm up, the engine was opened out; the man at the controls applied more and more brake force, and so the test conditions were gradually worked up until the prescribed figures were attained, and the great engine was indeed in full cry. The sight of it alone was impressive beyond words, and for a moment one just watched, fascinated. There was plenty of noise, of course, with the wheels revolving at 258 revolutions per minute, but one quickly became acclimatized and ready to note the details of the performance.

The most immediate impression was of the extraordinary quietness of the exhaust beat; the bulk of the noise was coming from the brake wheels rather than from the locomotive. I was able to walk along the gallery, within a few inches of the moving cranks and rods, and to look through the opening in the frames ahead of the outside cylinders and see the valve motion oscillating. It was much the same kind of view that one used to obtain in the engine room of a steamship fitted with reciprocating engines, though on this locomotive the movement of the valve gear was very much more rapid. Indicator diagrams were being taken off the right-hand outside cylinder; the shape of this diagram revealed an excellent cylinder performance, and the horsepower developed was about the same as if the engine had been hauling 20 corridor coaches at 60 mph on a level stretch of line. Up in the cab the atmosphere was just the same as on an express locomotive at speed, except that the fireman was digging the coal from a special bunker. The regular Swindon passenger enginemen took their turns in working on the test plant, though it was not often that in actual road service they had the opportunity to open engines out to the same extent as was required on these stationary 'runs'.

In the past, thermodynamic analysis had been confined to constant speed testing. Stationary testing plants, including the one at Swindon, had been designed and run with the maintenance of constant speed as a prime consideration, so much so that in the minds of most testing engineers constant speed was regarded as a necessary condition in testing analysis rather than a means to an end. On the other hand, the sole business of railways is the running of trains, and that they should run efficiently is the job of the locomotive engineer. While Dymond was modernizing the testing plant, Roberts and his assistants were working on means of freeing the practice of road testing from the artificiality of constant speed. Their exploratory trials with the dynamometer car in the early 1930s, and the manner in which they observed the locomotives to be habitually driven, had one overriding and vitally important result, that it could be applied immediately to demonstrative road testing.

Engine No 7916 Mobberley Hall *at speed on the Swindon test plant.* (British Railways)

The special apparatus involved was of the simplest kind. With a dynamometer car raised to the status of a complete testing unit, the system, under the name of the Controlled Road Testing System, met with immediate success and, for the first time, in moving a normal train, the instant-by-instant values of the efficiency of the locomotive as a power plant, and of the efficiency with which fuel was being utilized in doing work on the train, of the coal per ton mile and of the coal per mile, were demonstrated and recorded.

At Swindon, where it was developed, it was known as the Summations of Increments Method from the way in which the steam and coal rates were recorded and measured. In practice, tolerance of no more than + $\frac{1}{8}$ in was allowed on the boiler water level. The fireman took coal from a "scuttle"; as the last piece of coal was removed, another increment was tipped in. The increments of coal were always of equal weight and were put in bags; the size of the increment was so chosen that it took 5 minutes or so for its consumption. Because of the effect of fine coal on the boiler efficiency, each bag contained a certain percentage of half-inch-to-dust screenings in order to keep the size analysis uniform when friable or 'soft' coals such as the Welsh were used.

The Controlled Road Testing System did not come into its full maturity until after the Second World War, when Roberts had moved to posts of higher responsibility; he eventually became Chief Mechanical and Electrical Engineer of the Scottish Region of British Railways. The mantle of Testing Engineer at Swindon devolved upon one of his most brilliant assistants, S.O. Ell, with whom, in post-war years, I enjoyed many instructive trips in the dynamometer car and on the test plant at Swindon. With a control over the rates of evaporation and firing which was independent of speed, by apparatus and methods which were easily ap-

Above and left *No 6005* King George II *fitted with front-end shelters, indicators and other equipment for a full dress dynamometer trial.* (British Railways)

Below left *The right-hand cylinder of No 6005, showing the special fittings for the indicator trials.* (British Railways)

Below right *A 'Saint' in its prime, No 2939* Croome Court. (R.D. Stephen, National Railway Museum)

plied to road testing, the Controlled Road Testing System came into being as a logical development of the work carried out on the stationary plant. The load was made up of ordinary stock with a normal dynamometer car as the leading vehicle. The air injection apparatus of the flowmeter was carried in the car. Connected into the air line were at least two manometers, one in the driver's cab with just an adjustable pointer, and the other, complete with pressure scale, in the car for setting and supervisory purposes. A steel plate was fixed across the shovel plate of the tender to form a temporary 'scuttle' as on the stationary plant. Weighed coal in bags was carried on the tender and a bagful or increment was tipped into the scuttle as soon as the last of the previous increment had been taken by the fireman. Water injected and overflow were metered when a bell signal was received from the footplate signifying the end of each coal increment. Thus, the summations of increment of coal and water were plotted against elapsed time in the dynamometer car in order to establish the actual rates. Of the results with different classes of locomotive much will be said in Chapter 22.

Reverting to the Testing Plant itself, on reflection one may wonder a little at the choice of locomotive for the demonstration on behalf of the representatives of the LMS and the LNER when they came to see it in action. One would have thought it would have been at least a 'Castle', if not a 'King', if Swindon wanted to show off the maximum capacity of their rejuvenated plant. But instead they put on 'a tired old "Saint" ', to use again E.L. Diamond's expression when writing to Cecil J. Allen about South Wales performance some ten years previously. *Arlington Court* was certainly one of the later engines of the class, being the first of the batch built new in 1911, with superheaters, top-feed and all the eventual refinements of the design. But it seems as if no particular preference was exercised in the choice of the locomotive for display. If the visitors had but known it, the 'tired old "Saints" ', or one of them in particular, were basking in an expected burst of glory at that very time. When I was observing the comings and goings of the Exeter engines on the West of England Postal train in Cornwall in 1924, one of the 'Saints' thus engaged was No 2937 *Clevedon Court*; some ten years later she had been transferred to Reading, and was frequently doing no more energetic task than acting as main-line standing pilot. Then, three times in a very short period in 1936 her days of glory came.

The first instance took place on 7 April when the 3.30 pm West of England express from Paddington was observed arriving at Plymouth (North Road) only about 5 minutes late behind *Clevedon Court*. This train had stops at Taunton, Exeter and Newton Abbot, with an allowance of only 5 minutes over the level 3 hours from Paddington to Exeter. The initial load would be much less west of Newton Abbot by the detaching of the Torquay line portion, but it was evident that some excellent work had been done after *Clevedon Court* had been substituted for the regular engine. The next occasion came only a fortnight later, and was reported in more detail by a correspondent of *The Railway Magazine* who was travelling from Paddington to Taunton.

At the time of the centenary of the Great Western Railway, the train service to the West of England was augmented by a second morning express leaving Paddington 5 minutes after the 'Cornish Riviera'. The latter express carried through portions for none save Cornish destinations, while the 10.35 am served stations and routes previously covered by slip portions off the 'Cornish Riviera Express'. The 10.35 slipped a portion for Weymouth at Heywood Road Junction, but stopped at Taunton to detach its through carriages for Ilfracombe and Minehead, and at Newton Abbot to detach its Kingsbridge through carriage.

The Railway Magazine correspondent was first of all surprised that when approaching Reading his train was drastically slowed down, and then put through the relief line platform, before crossing over to take the Berks and Hants line and to continue normally. But while passing through Reading station he was astonished to see that the 'King' Class engine on the 'Cornish Riviera' had coupled off, and was in the process of being replaced—yes—by *Clevedon Court*! The 'Castle' working his own train recovered the time lost by the diversion through the relief line platform at Reading, and reached Taunton at 12.57 pm on time in 142 minutes from Paddington (142.7 miles). Having detached the Ilfracombe and Minehead portions, it left again at 1 pm. Not being in any hurry to leave the station, he waited. Very soon afterwards the down main line signals were pulled off, and at 1.05 pm the 'Limited' stormed through with *Clevedon Court* going flat-out, as that correspondent put it.

Unfortunately, no one thought to ask the traffic department for copies of the guard's journals on what must have been two notable examples of 'Saint' performance, but *Clevedon Court*'s hour of glory was not yet finished, and on the third occasion there was fortunately a very experienced recorder travelling passenger on the train. Having come to the rescue of the 3.30 pm from Paddington, and then the 'Cornish Riviera', it was next the turn of the 'Bristolian', of all trains, then regularly worked by a 'King'.

With engine No 6015 *King Richard III* the London driver had made an exceptionally vigorous start; too vigorous perhaps, because by Maidenhead the engine was running hot, and had to be eased down. One could imagine the driver echoing the cry of the engine's namesake, 450 years earlier: 'A horse! a horse! my kingdom for a horse!' Certainly his distress signal was very promptly and efficiently answered, for when he stopped at Reading, *Clevedon Court* was ready; the changing of engines took, to be precise, no more than 6 min 57 sec, and the London driver and fireman took over the Reading pilot. The rare quality of the 'Saint' Class locomotives was never displayed better than on this occasion, for although a top-link Old Oak engineman would have been familiar enough with the running characteristics of these famous engines, Reading shed cannot have had much more than 5 minutes notice that their standing pilot was needed, and to get her ready for what was involved.

In earlier chapters of this book I have detailed various fast-running exploits of the 'Saint' Class engines when they were new, or sharing the top-link honours with the 'Stars', but rarely can they have been called upon for such an effort as this. The schedule of the down 'Bristolian' allowed no more than 72 minutes for the $82\frac{1}{4}$ miles from passing Reading at full speed to arriving at Temple Meads, an average speed of 68.5 mph, and this included the regular speed restriction to about 30 mph through Bath. No such assignment was ever given to the 'Saints' in their main-line heyday, and in 1936 with what would officially have been considered a totally unsuitable engine for the job, no blame would have been laid upon the driver and fireman if they had lost time. In that halcyon year, however, the

A North to West express including many LNWR coaches just after leaving Shrewsbury, hauled by No 2941 Easton Court. (P.W. Pilcher, National Railway Museum)

reputation of *Clevedon Court* as a substitute would probably not have been entirely unknown among the top-link Old Oak drivers following her twice having taken over the haulage of crack West of England expresses, and worked through to Plymouth. So, on this third occasion, the driver set about the continuation of the run to Bristol as though he had a 'Star' engine—which indeed it was soon proved he had!

In presenting the accompanying log of the journey it should be explained that the meticulously accurate recorder of the times and speeds, the late R.E. Charlewood, always timed to mileposts at or near the stations, instead of using the easier but less precise method of timing to the centre of the station, and using a distance to the first place of decimals of a mile approximating to the exact chainage quoted in the working timetable. Thus at Didcot, for example, Mr Charlewood timed to milepost 53¼, at Wootton Bassett to milepost 83, and so on. But his methods only serve to underline the authenticity of the outstanding performance he recorded.

At the very start there was none of the 'warming up' that one might have expected on a locomotive requisitioned at little more than a moment's notice. They got away from Reading with electrifying vigour, and on level track were doing 78 mph in 9 minutes from the dead start. There were slight signal checks on either side of Steventon, which cost about 1¼ minutes, but then the driver took the engine into a magnificent piece of running up through the Vale of the White Horse. In studying the speeds set out in the table it should be appreciated that except for a single mile of level track, before Shrivenham, the line is rising throughout. The gradient is nowhere steeper than 1 in 660, but even on a rise of 1 in 834, about 200 horsepower is needed to overcome the force of gravity upon an engine and train totalling 340 tons at 83½ mph. The train resistance

GWR: 'Bristolian', Reading–Bristol Temple Meads, 1936

Engine No 2937 *Clevedon Court*
Load 7 coaches, 216 tons tare, 225 tons full

Distance* (miles)		Schedule (min)	Actual (m s)	Speed (mph)
0	READING	0	0 00	—
5½	Pangbourne		6 32	—
8¾	Goring		9 15	78
12½	Cholsey		12 09	77½
17¼	DIDCOT	13½	15 53	76
—			sigs	60
20½	Steventon	16½	18 35	—
—			sigs	55
24½	Wantage Road		22 32	—
28	Challow		25 34	75
30½	Uffington		27 34	76½
35½	Shrivenham		31 21	82
39½	Milepost 75½		34 16	83½
41¼	SWINDON	33½	35 34	78
47	Wootton Bassett		39 57	80
51¾	Dauntsey		43 19	90
56	Milepost 92		46 18	83½
—			sigs	—
58	CHIPPENHAM	47	48 18	46½
62¼	Corsham		52 15	72½
65	Milepost 101		54 28	76½
70	Milepost 106		58 28	—
70⅞	BATH	58½	59 29	34
75¼	Saltford		63 55	72
77¾	Keynsham		65 55	76½
—			psw	—
80¾	St Annes Park		68 50	40
—			sigs	—
82¼	BRISTOL	72	72 28	—

Net time 69 min

* to exact mileposts

would require about 700 horsepower, thus leaving the remarkable equivalent drawbar horsepower of 900 at 83½ mph.

During the exhaustive stationary plant and dynamometer trials of one of the 'King' Class engines in 1952, the maximum equivalent drawbar horsepower at 83 mph was 1,000, this with the boiler steamed up to the maximum rate that could be sustained continuously, and by comparison it might at first seem unbelievable that a 'Saint', with a considerably smaller boiler, should be able to approach so closely to the 'King' maximum. It is fairly certain, however, that on Clevedon Court some mortgaging of boiler capacity must have taken place after Challow.

The speed was eased a little through Swindon and on the falling gradient of 1 in 660 to Wootton Bassett the speed did not at first exceed 80 mph, and the equivalent drawbar horsepower represented by this would not have been more than 400, a very big difference from the 900 between Shrivenham and milepost 75½. Not that there was any slackening of the effort in terms of speed, and at the foot of the Dauntsey bank the thrilling maximum of 90 mph was sustained for a full mile. The signal check at Chippenham cost about a minute, and speed was restrained to no more than 76½ mph descending through Box Tunnel, and in the outer approaches to Bath. A minute had been dropped on the sectional time of 58½ minutes from Reading to Bath, but the checks between them had cost 2¼ minutes and the net time from Didcot was only 41¼ minutes, against the 45 minutes scheduled.

The flying average over the 64½ miles from Pangbourne to milepost 106 (covered in 51 min 56 sec) was 74.5 mph, all checks included, or no less than 77.8 mph net, and on the final length, where the booked point-to-point time gives a little margin for recovery, a little time was gained, despite checks from Keynsham inwards. Charlewood estimated the net time from start to stop as 69 minutes, but at the normal speed of the 'Bristolian' passing Reading, the 8¾ miles to Goring would have taken about 6¾ minutes instead of the actual 9¼ minutes from a dead start, so in comparison with the 'Bristolian' schedule the running of *Clevedon Court* was equivalent to a net time of 66½ minutes from Reading to Bristol, a remarkable gain of 5½ minutes on schedule, and a pass-to-stop average speed of 74 mph—an astonishing performance.

In the later 1930s, 'Saints' were not only involved with the 'Cornish Riviera' and the 'Bristolian', but also took at least one turn on the 'Cheltenham Flyer'. Fortunately on one occasion in 1937 there was an experienced recorder travelling by the train. The 'Castle' rostered for the job had failed on the shed at Gloucester at the last minute, and *Tockenham Court* was a hastily requisitioned substitute. Unlike *Clevedon Court* at Reading, she was not on stand-by duty and her tender was coaled with inferior fuel. The driver and fireman, however, were a pair of real sportsmen and they took the train down to Swindon with every intention of making a 65-minute run onwards to Paddington, even though the engine was not steaming freely on the poor coal. When they got to Swindon, however, they found that two more coaches were to be added to the train, making a tare load of no less than 316 tons, and a gross load behind the tender of 340 tons. The resulting run, as tabulated herewith, was magnificent on any account, but having regard to the poor coal it was almost heroic! On arrival at Paddington the driver said that they never had more than 200 psi 'on the clock', and it was often down to 170. In such circumstances *Tockenham Court* and her crew ran the 65.9 miles from Shrivenham to Ealing Broadway in 55 min 48 sec, an average of 70.8 mph.

GWR: 'Cheltenham Flyer', 1937

Engine No 2954 *Tockenham Court*
Load 316 tons tare, 340 tons full

Distance (miles)		Schedule (min)	Actual (m s)	Speed (mph)
0.0	Swindon	0	0 00	—
5.7	Shrivenham		7 24	67
10.8	Uffington		11 43	72
13.4	Challow		13 49	73½
16.9	Wantage Road		16 30	75
20.8	Steventon	18½	19 47	74½
24.2	Didcot	21	22 34	73
28.8	Cholsey		26 19	72
32.6	Goring		29 32	69½
35.8	Pangbourne		32 15	72
38.7	Tilehurst		34 41	73½
41.3	Reading	34	36 51	72
46.3	Twyford		41 12	70½
53.1	Maidenhead		46 53	72
58.8	Slough	47	51 47	69½
64.1	West Drayton		56 28	65½
68.2	Southall	54½	60 11	65
71.6	Ealing Broadway		63 12	70
76.0	Westbourne Park		67 08	—
77.3	Paddington	65	69 26	—

A 'Saint' in its last years: a dingy and unidentified engine going hard near Twyford with an up Weymouth express. (J.F. Russell-Smith, National Railway Museum)

18. Maximum performance in the later 'thirties

The Centenary of the Great Western Railway in 1935 was marked by the introduction of a new high-speed train, the 'Bristolian', running between Paddington and Bristol in 1¾ hours. Departure time was 10 am and the return train left Temple Meads at 4.30 pm. The load was strictly limited to seven coaches including a buffet car, and at first 'King' Class engines were always used although not without the occasional mishap, as related in the previous chapter! But reference to the 'Bristolian' in the present context leads on immediately to the agitation that developed in 1936 for similar high-speed services to Birmingham. Ever since the short route via Bicester had been opened in 1910, the Great Western had made the most of their improved track facilities by running many fast trains in competition with those of the London and North Western, and in the recovery years after the First World War 2-hour expresses from Paddington to Birmingham were scheduled at 9.10 and 11.10 am, and 2.10, 4.10, 6.10 and 7.10 pm. The service, which was closely paralleled in the up direction, was therefore very much more lavish than provided between London and Bristol, and all the Birmingham trains were very well patronized. Why then should Bristol get a high-speed train?

This very justified plea from the Midlands fell, however, on stony ground at Paddington. It seemed as if the top management of the GWR did not want to know about acceleration to Birmingham. Correspondence in *The Railway Gazette* in the autumn of 1937 had a curious result. The Editor, J.A. Kay, was privately a very ardent Great Western fan and was in the confidence of many of the most senior officers, and

Left *Engine No 6028,* King Richard I *leaving Bristol for the West with a light train.* (G.H. Soole)

Below *A memory of a distinguished class: No 3827* County of Gloucester *working a heavy rake of Great Central stock on the Newcastle-Bournemouth express near Tilehurst. GWR engines worked between Leicester and Basingstoke.* (Loco Publishing Co)

not a few of the directors also, and between them they persuaded him to publish an article in February 1938 which in veiled terms was an apologia for doing nothing about it. Worse still, they got Collett to get the train timing section of the Swindon Drawing Office to prepare charts showing the speeds that would be necessary to maintain a 1¾-hour non-stop timing from Paddington to Birmingham with 'King' Class engines and a 300-ton train. By that time there were many locomotive enthusiasts with an expert knowledge of train running conditions on the Birmingham route of the GWR and those diagrams appeared to them as a mere travesty of everyday actuality. Some of those enthusiasts were not long in expressing their opinions in the correspondence columns of *The Railway Gazette* while others, some of those with the longest experience of speed recording over the route, 'opened their hearts' to Cecil J. Allen. At the time, however, he was greatly exercised in extolling the high speeds of the 'Silver Jubilee' on his own line, the LNER, and took no more than a passing interest in the fracas over the Birmingham service.

By the time the controversy was at its height, the expert and veteran train-timers in the West Midlands, headed by A.V. Goodyear, had been reinforced by one who ultimately amassed a bank of knowledge on the running of the 2-hour Birmingham trains that was completely unsurpassed, G.P. Antrobus. In the Civil Service he was one of the elite Corps that were called 'The King's Foreign Service Messengers' and held the badge of the Silver Greyhound, not that his professional duties gave him much chance of normal railway observing or train timing. He was a member, and eventually head, of the Communications Department of the Foreign Office, and about 1935 he left London to reside in Leamington Spa. Before his untimely death in 1940 he had written a fascinating book on his experiences, *King's Messenger, 1918–1940*, in which there is a brief glimpse of his other interests thus:

> 'Another of the joys of living in the country and working in town is the opportunity of travelling by train. All sane men love railways, and the longer their daily journeys, so much the more are they contented. I do not mean such journeys as the King's Messengers take across Europe; there is no opportunity to extract the local railway-colour in these trips; you have too much to think about, too much responsibility, too little time for anything except the discharge of your duties. You cannot chat with drivers and pointsmen and wheeltappers without neglecting your bags—the unforgivable sin. But in going to and from your daily work you can do well these things, and in finding them you create for yourself a new world in which you can forget the cares and anxieties of that to which you properly belong. Blessed is he that hath an interest in his job, but thrice-blessed he that hath an interest in someone else's as well.'

No 6005 King George II *on a Birkenhead-Paddington express emerging from Harbury Tunnel.* (H. Weston)

Interest indeed! Before the 2-hour Birmingham service was suspended on the outbreak of the Second World War, Antrobus had logged in meticulous detail no fewer than 1,412 runs on the 6.10 pm from Paddington to Leamington, on which he returned home from the Foreign Office each day, and to substantiate my assertion that the 'official' speed charts gave not the slightest idea of what the 'King' locomotives with their regular crews from Stafford Road shed, Wolverhampton, were actually doing, I have tabulated the speeds shown on

Below *No 6013* King Henry VIII *at Old Oak Common.* (W.J. Reynolds)

Bottom *No 4032* Queen Alexandra, *rebuilt as a 'Castle', at Ponsondane sheds, Penzance.* (O.S. Nock)

the charts. When the service had been suspended, Antrobus prepared a summary of typical runs which were in due course published in *The Railway Magazine*; but in correspondence with A.V. Goodyear subsequently, I learned that the published runs were no more than typical of his best, and that they were equalled many times over in his log books. Antrobus himself was killed in an air raid, which practically destroyed his home in the night Blitz of 1940; with him went the records of his runs between Paddington and Leamington. When Goodyear in his advancing years bequeathed to me his log book from 1935 onwards, it included some correspondence with Antrobus which shows how regular and not exceptional was the running on the 6.10 pm. Of course he got to know all the drivers, and they told him the cut-offs they were using on the most severe

GWR: 6.10 pm Paddington–Leamington Spa

Run No			1		2		3		4	
Engine No			6017		5008		6017		6017	
Engine Name			*King Edward IV*		*Raglan Castle*		*King Edward IV*		*King Edward IV*	
Load To Bicester (tons (E/F)			373/395		397/420		403/425		415/445	
To Banbury			337/357		367/388		367/388		380/407	
To Leamington			273/290		297/315		298/315		314/335	
Distance (miles)		**Schedule (min)**	**Actual (m s)**	**Speed (mph)**	**Actual (m s)**	**Speed (mph)**	**Actual (m s)**	**Speed (mph)**	**Actual (m s)**	**Speed (mph)**
0.0	Paddington	0	0 00		0 00		0 00		0 00	
—			sigs		sigs		sigs		sigs	
1.3	Westbourne Park		3 55		4 01		3 13		3 06	
									sigs	
3.3	Old Oak West Junction	7	8 06		7 49		6 54		7 31	
—			pws	10			pws	20	pws	15
7.8	Greenford	13	15 23	61	12 52	63½	13 42	59	16 02	
									pws	25
10.3	Northolt Junction	15½	17 49	62½	15 13	62	16 15	60	20 40	
									pws	10
14.8	Denham		21 47	72	19 21	71	20 21	72	27 57	56
17.4	Gerrards Cross		24 07	65½	21 53	60½	22 46	64½	30 55	52
21.7	Beaconsfield		28 05	64½	26 20	60	26 43	66	35 36	56
					pws	50				
24.2	Tylers Green box		30 14	69	28 39	68	28 52	73	37 49	74
26.5	High Wycombe	32	32 47	—	31 15		31 12		40 04	
28.8	West Wycombe		35 29	55½	34 10	49	34 02	56½	42 45	53
31.5	Saunderton		38 27	58½	37 34	50	36 56	61	45 56	54½
			42 25							
34.7	Princes Risborough	42	43 05		41 00		39 56		49 10	
37.4	Ilmer Halt		47 22	78	43 09	86½	42 08	82	51 10	91½
40.1	Haddenham		49 31		45 06		44 11		53 00	
44.0	Ashendon Junction	49½	52 43		48 21		47 49		55 57	
47.4	Brill		55 46		51 40	60	51 32	54	59 08	62
50.4	Blackthorn		58 07	81½	54 14	75	54 13	74	61 34	80
53.4	Bicester	58½	60 29	—	56 47		56 57		63 59	
57.2	Ardley		63 54	65½	60 28	60½	60 51	59	67 32	63
62.4	Aynho Junction	67	68 29		65 30		65 43		72 00	
67.5	Banbury	72	73 00	73	70 15	70	70 40	66	76 44	72
71.1	Cropredy		76 05	68	73 29	—	74 14	63	79 52	69
					pws	35				
76.2	Fenny Compton		80 23	85	79 05	81	78 58	72	84 15	88
81.2	Southam Road		84 02	75	83 00	74	83 16	68	87 46	84
					sigs					
83.5	Fosse Road box		85 48	84	85 21	—	85 12	80	89 23	91
							pws			
87.3	Leamington Spa	90½	89 21		90 00		89 27		92 59	
	Net times		81½		86½		87		83	

banks. These details make it quite clear that they were beyond the range of what Swindon expected to be used on the 'Kings' in normal running.

I have prepared a table showing extended detail of ten outstanding runs on the 6.10 pm from Paddington, eight with 'Kings' and two with 'Castles'. One of the latter was a personal experience of my own, which though dating back some 60 years is still a vivid memory. Mr Goodyear clocked one of the 'King' runs, otherwise the collection comes from Mr Antrobus. Before referring in any detail to the work on individual runs, it is interesting to note that against the sustained speeds of 65 to 67 mph up the Gerrards Cross bank with a 300-ton load shown in the Swindon chart, Mr Antrobus recorded speeds of 65 mph with 395 tons, 66 with 420, 60 with 460, and 58½ mph with 505 tons.

5		6		7		8		9		10	
6017		4088		6008		6006		6008		6017	
King Edward IV		*Dartmouth Castle*		*King James II*		*King George I*		*King James II*		*King Edward IV*	
424/460		440/475		457/490		469/495		472/505		483/515	
424/460		440/475		457/490		432/455		436/465		417/445	
424/460		440/475		405/435		328/345		366/390		351/375	
Actual (m s)	**Speed (mph)**	**Actual (m s)**	**Speed (mph)**	**Actual (m s)**	**Speed (mph)**	**Actual (m s)**	**Speed (mph)**	**Actual (m s)**	**Speed (mph)**	**Actual (m s)**	**Speed (mph)**
0 00		0 00		0 00		0 00		0 00		0 00	
		sigs						sigs		sigs	
3 02		3 35		4 02		3 02		3 49		3 29	
		sigs									
5 57		7 20		7 33		6 33		7 40		7 00	
								pws	30	pws	15
11 09	62	12 55	57½	13 03	58	12 02	58	14 16		13 48	
13 40	60	15 35	54½	15 37	58	14 44	55	17 36	47	18 18	46
17 56	69	20 05	63½	20 05	63	19 19	64	22 15	65	23 20	61½
20 30	61	22 55	52½	22 45	54½	22 05	54	24 53	58½	26 12	53
24 50	60	27 50	51	27 27	59	26 53	54	29 21	58½	31 02	54
26 59	75	30 05	70½	—	69	29 10	71	31 36	72	33 21	72
29 15		32 15	50	31 50	42	31 33		34 04		35 49	
32 18	53½	35 05	47	34 45	—	34 11	53	36 41	54	38 54	49½
35 28	58	38 45	41½	37 58	50	37 28	51	39 53	53½	42 16	52
38 33		42 30	70½	41 18	70	40 55	—	43 18	—	45 43	
40 41	83½	44 40	83½	—	83½	43 05	87	45 27	87½	47 53	85
42 46		46 40		45 27	—	45 01	—	47 25	—	49 51	—
46 37		49 40	64	48 36	52	48 10	—	50 53	—	53 03	—
50 24	53	52 55	58	52 02	—	51 20	62	54 03	62	56 21	60
53 03	75	55 35	70½	54 30	75	53 50	78	56 31	78	58 53	76
55 40		58 15		56 55	67½	56 21		58 59	—	61 23	—
59 35	58	62 15	52½	60 32	59½	60 06	60	62 45	60	65 11	58½
64 27		67 15	69	65 20	68	64 46	70	67 33		70 11	
			64	sig stop							
69 19	68	71 55	67	77 00		69 16	70	72 11	70	75 01	68
72 52	62	75 15	57½	6 20	51	72 34	62	75 24	66	78 24	84
77 47	75	80 15	76½	11 35	73½	77 19	80	79 53	82	83 06	81
81 57	68	84 15	74	15 40	73	81 20	64	83 40	77	87 01	72
83 54	77	86 10	78	17 30	81	83 32	64	85 26	87	88 53	81
								sigs			
87 58		89 50		21 28		87 58		90 45		92 43	
88		89¼		87¾		88		86		88¼	

Similarly, up the 1 in 164 of Saunderton bank, against 58 mph with 300 tons there are actual records of 61 mph with 420 tons, 58½ mph with 460 tons and 53 mph with 505 tons. Although Mr Antrobus was never riding on the footplate, his acquaintanceship with the various drivers gave him engine working details, and it is clear that these fine uphill performances, particularly before the load was reduced by the detaching of slip portions at Bicester and Banbury, were being achieved by the use of far longer cut-offs than those habitually employed on the West of England main line with maximum loads.

GWR 'King' Class 4-6-0s—'official' speeds: max and min

Location	300-ton load (mph)	400-ton load (mph)
Northolt Junction	67	58
Denham	73	63
Gerrards Cross	65	54
Beaconsfield	67	56
High Wycombe	35 (slack)	35 (slack)
Saunderton	58	50
Haddenham	80	80
Ashendon Junction	50 (slack)	50 (slack)
Brill	70	65
Blackthorn	80	73
Bicester	75	68
Ardley	65	60
Aynho Junction (before)	80	72
Aynho Junction (over)	55 (slack)	55 (slack)
Banbury	70	68
Claydon Crossing	64	60
Southam Road	80/70	70
Fosse Road box	80	70
Leamington Spa	40 (slack)	stop

On the down 'Cornish Riviera Express' with a load of 530 tons, cut-offs of around 18 per cent with full regulator were used to work speed up to 70 mph at least on the level at Slough. Yet on the 6.10 pm from Paddington, the Stafford Road men were frequently using 26–27 per cent up the Gerrards Cross bank, at speeds of 65–66 mph, and sometimes up to 30 per cent to Saunderton. It would seem that these were very much transitory efforts as the boiler could not be expected to steam at such a rate for very long. This would explain the more modest level of performance represented in the Swindon graphs which probably reflected, in the uphill running, a steam rate which could be maintained for an hour or more continuously. In achieving the magnificent performance included in the table, the Stafford Road drivers and their firemen were probably mortgaging their boiler capacity on the adverse sections, knowing that they could 'pay it back' on the succeeding descents. Of course such a technique requires consummate skill and experience both sides of the footplate. It is one of my great regrets that when the time came for me to have the privilege of riding on the footplate with the Stafford Road drivers and firemen on 'King' Class locomotives after the Second World War, the train schedules had not been accelerated much above those of the war years, and a timing such as that of 109 minutes non-stop over the 87.3 miles from Leamington to Paddington, even with a 515-ton load, required cut-offs of not more than 15 to 18 per cent even on the most severe gradients.

Coming to the tabulated runs, No 1 was badly delayed by permanent way work in the early stages and then the driver made a brilliant ascent of Gerrards Cross bank, and equally of Saunderton, and but for a fatality on the line necessitating a stop at Princes Risborough, the train would have passed that station on time. The stop caused Ashendon Junction to be passed 3 minutes late, but by some very fast running onwards, aided by an unusually moderate load for the 6.10 pm, the arrival in Leamington was 1 minute early. Brilliant indeed was the running over the final stages from Banbury, whereby 2 minutes were gained on schedule time. On the next run, *Raglan Castle* and her crew did magnificently. With no initial delays a tremendous dash was made at the Gerrards Cross bank with a top speed of 71 mph at Denham, and a sustained 60 mph up the 1 in 254 to Beaconsfield summit—with 420 tons. What price the Swindon diagrams with a *'Castle'* doing such work! Despite a slight permanent way check, High Wycombe was passed nearly 1 minute early. Good climbing up the Saunderton bank was followed by a maximum of 86½ mph before Haddenham, and the Bicester slip coach was detached 2 minutes early. Plenty of time was in hand to offset the delays north of Banbury and the arrival at Leamington was 30 seconds early.

With the same load *King Edward IV* lost nearly a minute by permanent way checks, and then made a really spectacular ascent of the bank, from an initial 72 mph past Denham. Speed fell to 64½ mph at Gerrards Cross, but recovered on the continuous 1 in 254 to 66 mph. The time of 6 min 22 sec was not quite the record noted by Mr Antrobus, but very nearly. It was, incidentally, matched by my own 6 min 20 sec with *Lady of Lynn*, hauling 320 tons on the first portion of the 2.10 pm from Paddington as related in Chapter 14. But Driver Lewis and Fireman Skutt, on *King Edward IV*, went on to top even this achievement by accelerating from West Wycombe on the 1 in 164 towards Saunderton to no less than 61 mph. Mr Antrobus wrote to Cecil J. Allen on one occasion that he thought that the 'Kings' were capable of developing fully 2,500 indicated horsepower, and this feat of No 6017 and her crew bore this out. But I shall be discussing power output later in this chapter in the light of tests on the Swindon plant in post-war days. On No 3 run in the table, passing Princes Risborough 2 minutes early the crew could afford to take things easily thereafter, for this route at any rate. The same driver and fireman had the luxury of a completely clear road from start to finish on No 5 run, also with *King Edward IV* and an unchanged load. Because of heavy traffic the slip coaches for Bicester and Banbury were conveyed on a second portion of the train.

Conditions were very different on the fourth run in the table, with a succession of such severe permanent way checks from the start as to cause the train to be 8 minutes late through High Wycombe. Afterwards speed was worked up to 54½ mph on the Saunderton climb, with a 445-ton load, and then *King Edward IV* was taken along like the wind. Speed reached 91½ mph before Haddenham, 80 mph in the dip between Brill and Bicester, and a terrific finish from Banbury, with no lower speed than 69 mph on the rise past Cropredy to Clayton Crossing, 88 below Fenny Compton, nothing less than 84 mph at Southam tunnel and a final 91 mph down the Fosse Road bank. With a fast finish into Leamington, the train was only 2½ minutes late. The net time of 83 minutes made this a most exhilarating run to record. *King Edward IV* was certainly a favourite on this train when Mr Antrobus was travelling regularly, but when the 'Kings' were first introduced, as far as I can recall only one of them, No 6019 *King Henry V*, was stationed at Stafford Road. Of course the Old Oak engines came down on the 9.10 am from Paddington and returned on the 3 pm from Birmingham, but engine No 6019 was then regularly requisitioned for the 6.10 pm down. I had one or two runs myself but the results were rather disappointing after what I had logged with 'Saints' and 'Stars' previously, and I put it down to lack of experience with the new engine.

On my commuter journeys between Ealing Broadway and King's Cross, on the homeward run I frequently saw the 6.10 pm ready to start from Paddington, and in the late spring of 1930 I noticed day after day that the engine was not a 'King' at all, but invariably No 4088 *Dartmouth Castle*. The Whitsun holiday was approaching, and I decided once again to go north by the 6.10 pm as far as Shrewsbury and then make my way by night trains to join, eventually, the Furness 4.45 am mail from Carnforth. As I hoped *Dartmouth Castle* was still on the job from Paddington, and she and her crew gave me the magnificent run included in column 6 of the table. No slips were carried and the full 475-ton load was taken through to Wolverhampton. I did not speak to the driver at all, his name, A. Taylor, I learned from the very pleasant travelling ticket examiner who rode with the train every day. The signal checks out to Old Oak Common were no more than slight in consequence of taking the Relief Line out of Paddington, as on most other runs on the 6.10 pm following in the stream of outgoing suburban trains at that hour. But from Old Oak we got a completely clear road to Leamington. It must be admitted that the speed restrictions at High Wycombe, Ashendon and Aynho Junctions were taken rather liberally, doubtless to gain impetus for the succeeding uphill work; but the coach in which I was travelling rode with complete smoothness throughout, and had I not known what the actual limits laid down in the working book were I should have passed those locations without any comment.

As the tabulated details show *Dartmouth Castle* and her men were no more than seconds outside the working

Below *No 5035* Coity Castle *on the 2.10 pm Paddington-Birkenhead express near West Wycombe.* (C.R.L. Coles)

Bottom *The 2.10 pm Paddington to Birkenhead express near Saunderton, hauled by engine No 6005* King George II. (M.W. Earley)

times at High Wycombe and Princes Risborough, and on time or slightly ahead thereafter. The uphill speeds at Beaconsfield, Saunderton and Ardley were excellent with such a load as 475 tons, while 83½ mph before Haddenham and 70½ mph at Blackthorn showed fine acceleration from the previous minima. At the time that run was made, the working arrival time at Leamington was 91 minutes, and there we were three-quarters of a minute early. The continuing timing of 26 minutes for the 23.3 miles to Birmingham was reckoned for a load of only 300 tons after the usual slip portions had been detached, and for haulage by a 'King', in the ordinary way. With Hatton bank to be climbed it was inevitable that time would be lost on this section, and indeed they did lose 3½ minutes. But the crew were still game and they regained 1¾ minutes on the schedule of 20 minutes for the awkward slack-infested 12.6 miles from Birmingham to Wolverhampton. *Queen Boadicea* took over and made some fast running with a much reduced load of 325 tons.

The seventh run in the table was clocked by Mr Goodyear on the 2.10 pm from Paddington, which at that time detached a slip portion only at Banbury. Runs 6 and 7 dead-heated to passing Denham, and then of course the 'King'-hauled train began to go ahead. The acceleration between Gerrards Cross and Beaconsfield from 54½ to 59 mph was remarkable with a 490-ton train, while the driver of *King James II* was very careful in his speed reductions at High Wycombe and Ashendon Junction. A signal stop at the approach to Banbury made it necessary to stop a second time to detach the slip portion, after which, with the reduced load of 435 tons, a smart run was made onwards to Leamington. The eighth run, with engine *King George I*, was undelayed, and was noteworthy in clocking into Leamington in exactly the same time as No 5. It was a very fine run, passing Bicester 2 minutes early, and thereafter taking things more easily, particularly in the leisurely descent of the Fosse Road bank. In the early stages of this run the speeds, with 495 tons, approximated to those included in the Swindon diagram for a 400-ton train, whereas what could be done with 505 tons, if need be, was shown in Column 7.

On this run the permanent way check was severe and the speed at Northolt Junction had reached no more than 47 mph, but from this point Driver A. Smith and his fireman got some tremendous work out of engine No 6008. Speed reached 65 mph at Denham and the Gerrards Cross bank was mounted at a sustained 58½ mph. A careful slowing was made at High Wycombe, and then after Saunderton bank there came a perfect riot of speed, with 87½ before Haddenham, 78 at Blackthorn and a thrilling finish from Banbury with a minimum speed of 66 mph on the Cropredy rise and 87 mph down the Fosse Road bank, although even then the load was nearly 400 tons after Banbury. Little inferior in speed was the final run, with a still heavier load as far as Bicester. The initial checks, however, were more severe, and the train was three-quarters of a minute late passing High Wycombe. With this load, and bad weather conditions, there was not much opportunity for any substantial time regaining and the train was still 2¼ minutes late into Leamington; but the net time was not more than 88¼ minutes, another very fine run with this load.

The physical features of this route and the existence of the High Wycombe speed restriction before the Saunderton bank enabled trustworthy estimates of drawbar horsepower to be made on many of the runs, and it is interesting to compare these with the maximum efforts of the 'Kings' on the post-war trials under British Railways auspices. The differences between many of the 6.10 pm Birmingham runs and the Swindon test results emphasize the extent to which the Stafford Road men were mortgaging the resources of their boilers on many of Mr Antrobus's runs. The following details are taken from one of the test runs with engine No 6001 in July 1953 when a train of 781 tons (23 coaches) was being accelerated to full speed after a permanent way check to 15 mph on level track between Didcot and Reading. The mean coal rate was 415 lbs per hour, or 121 lbs per square foot of grate area per hour. Two firemen were being employed.

Speed (mph)	**Cut-off (per cent)**	**Drawbar horsepower**	**Indicated horsepower**
50	32	1,350	2,000
55	28	1,310	2,000
60	26	1,300	2,000
65	25	1,270	2,000
68	25	1,240	2,000

I have prepared estimates of the drawbar horsepower sustained on five of the most notable of the runs in the accompanying table. Those of the Gerrard's Cross bank showing outputs of between 1,215 and 1,351 horsepower bear a striking resemblance to the maximum output sustained on the Controlled Road Tests with engine No 6001 *King Edward VII* in 1953 when the effort was sustained and two firemen were at work. Actually the cut-off values Mr Antrobus obtained from the drivers concerned on certain of his runs correspond very closely with those of the 1953 tests, generally about 26 or 27 per cent on Gerrards Cross bank. Going up to Saunderton, however, on runs 1, 3, 5 and 9 it seems that the engine, and the boiler, must have been pressed to a rate that could not have been sustained for very long. I should explain that all the horsepowers estimated are the equivalent values related to running on level track, and as customary in such calculations, in assessing the 'gravity factor', the weight of the engine and tender is included in the total weight of the train.

Left *An up West of England express on Fairwood troughs with engine No 6002* King William IV. (G.H. Soole)

Below left *Neck and neck in Sonning Cutting: on the left, an up West of England train with a postal stowage van behind engine No 6011* King James I, *overtaking No 4085* Berkeley Castle *with a stopping train.* (M.W. Earley)

'King' Class 4-6-0s—estimates of equivalent drawbar horsepower

Gerrards Cross bank: 1 in 254

Run No	Engine No	Speed (mph)	Train load (tons)	Estimated EDHP
9	6008	$58\frac{1}{2}$	505	1,351
7	6008	59	490	1,335
5	6017	60	460	1,215
1	6017	$64\frac{1}{2}$	395	1,295
3	6017	66	425	1,338

Saunderton bank: 1 in 164

Run No	Engine No	Speed (mph)	Train load (tons)	Estimated EDHP
9	6008	54	505	1,785
1	6017	$58\frac{1}{2}$	395	1,725
5	6017	$58\frac{1}{2}$	460	2,000
3	6017	61	425	1,930

Mr Antrobus thought that on runs 3 and 5 up Saunderton bank the engines must have been producing some 2,500 indicated horsepower, although the results of the 1953 tests showed that the IHP was some 700 more than the DHP at maximum sustained output, and it seems reasonable to suppose that No 6017 was putting forth at least 2,700 IHP and probably more for those heroic minutes on Saunderton bank.

And what of the 'Kings' on the West of England line? Reverting to the days before the Westbury and Frome by-pass lines were constructed, Mr G.N. Martin sent me details of a run on the down 'Cornish Riviera Express' in 1929 during the summer service when only one slip portion was carried, and the heavy load of 405 tons was taken through to Plymouth without the assistance of a bank engine. Then there is a run on the same train in 1932 when Mr Goodyear had a footplate pass. At that time the train stopped at Exeter, and he did not continue to Plymouth, though in the process of the run down from Paddington he secured some very significant details of the engine working. Finally there are timings of a very striking run when, to compensate for some serious delays for permanent way work further west, the down 'Limited' passed Westbury $4\frac{1}{2}$ minutes early with the usual 14-coach train. Unfortunately the friend who clocked this run was travelling in the Taunton slip portion, and there is no record of how this very enterprising engine crew continued over the South Devon line. All the same, with the detaching of the Taunton and Exeter portions they would have had a considerably easier task load-wise than the men on *King George V* on Mr Martin's run. The three runs are tabulated overleaf.

It will be convenient to refer first to the second run during which Mr Goodyear was on the footplate. The immediate start out of Paddington was very smart, and yet by Westbourne Park cut-off had been reduced to 25 per cent. The regulator was then full open, and further linking up took place, to 20 per cent at Old Oak Common and to 16 per cent just beyond Hanwell. No further change in the working was made until steam was shut off for Reading, and from a study of the log it will be seen that the use of 16 per cent cut-off was enough to produce 68 to 70 mph on level road with this train of 530 tons. On the Berks and Hants line 17 per cent cut-off was used from Southcote Junction to Newbury, 16 per cent onwards to Bedwyn, 17 per cent to within half a mile of Savernake summit, and finally 18 per cent over the top.

GWR: 'Cornish Riviera Express'

	6000	6024	6020
Engine No	6000	6024	6020
Engine Name	*King George V*	*King Edward I*	*King Henry IV*
Load To Westbury (tons, E/F)	479/510	498/530	473/505
To Taunton (tons, E/F)	378/405	434/460	399/430
To Exeter (tons, E/F)	378/405	372/395	—
To Plymouth (tons, E/F)	378/405	—	—

Distance (miles)		**Schedule (min)**	**Actual (m s)**	**Speed (mph)**	**Actual (m s)**	**Speed (mph)**	**Actual (m s)**	**Speed (mph)**
0.0	Paddington	0	0 00	—	0 00		0 00	
1.3	Westbourne		2 55	—	3 00	—	2 37	
5.7	Ealing Broadway		—		8 45	57	8 13	
9.1	Southall	11	12 00	60	12 05	62½	11 36	63
18.5	Slough	20	20 20	73	20 40	70½	19 42	76½
24.2	Maidenhead	25	25 00	72	25 47	67	24 28	71½
31.0	Twyford		30 50	69	31 52	66½	30 03	74
36.0	Reading	36	35 15	—	36 20	—	34 15	45 (slack)
37.8	Southcote Junction		37 20	56	38 30	—	—	
53.1	Newbury	54	51 35	62	53 32	60/62	50 58	68/62½
66.4	Bedwyn	67	64 05	64	66 48	59	63 31	61/65
70.1	Savernake		68 00	52	70 48	51¾	67 19	53
75.3	Pewsey		72 55	75	75 45	72	72 03	77½
—			pws	15	—	—	—	—
81.1	Patney		80 05	55	80 22	—	76 42	70½
86.9	Lavington		—	—	84 46	82½	81 13	79
91.4	Edington		89 00	82	88 20	76½	—	—
95.6	Westbury	94	92 40	(slack)	92 05	(slack)	89 24	(slack)
101.3	Frome		99 30	(slack)	99 00	(slack)	pws	
108.5	Milepost 122¾		108 45	50	107 29	54/51½	108 26	51/49
—			—	82	sigs	35	—	82
115.2	Castle Cary	116	114 35	60	114 54	—	114 29	60
125.7	Somerton		124 00	72	123 55	—	123 54	—
—			sigs		—	76	—	77½
137.9	Cogload Junction	137	134 45	55	134 55	55	134 41	70½
—			sigs		pws		—	
142.9	Taunton	141½	139 57	57	140 12		140 57	slip arrival
144.9	Norton Fitzwarren		—	—	142 30	57		
150.0	Wellington		147 25	54	148 08	54½		
151.8	Milepost 172		—	—	150 15	47		
152.8	Milepost 173		—	—	151 37	44		
153.8	Whiteball box		153 20	26	153 10	39½		
—			—	—	pws	—		
158.8	Tiverton Junction		158 25	72	161 30	—		
170.2	Stoke Canon		167 30	81	173 20	72		
173.7	Exeter	171½	170 20	60	177 12			
178.4	Exminster	174	174 45	68				
188.7	Teignmouth		185 30	47				
193.9	Newton Abbot	195½	191 20	(slack)				
195.7	Milepost 216		194 10	45				
196.7	Milepost 217		195 55	32				
197.8	Dainton box		198 25	20				
202.5	Totnes		204 40	52				
205.3	Tigley box		210 20	25				

Distance (miles)		Schedule (min)	6000 *King George V* Actual (m s)		Speed (mph)
207.1	Rattery box		214	05	32
209.4	Brent	218	217	35	45
219.0	Hemerdon box	230	228	30	60
223.8	Laira Junction		233	20	68
225.7	Plymouth	240	237	00	

Adjustments of the reverser by 1 per cent at a time might well seem pedantic rather than practical; but details published of the 1953 tests on a 'King' Class engine show clearly what those changes mean. At 60 mph with full regulator, the indicated horsepowers are:

Cut-off	15	16	17	18	19	20
IHP	1,150	1,260	1,360	1,450	1,530	1,600

In a letter to me, Mr Goodyear refers to the extraordinary steadiness of the steaming; but for a slight drop to 245 psi when approaching Whiteball tunnel, the needle might have been fixed at the 250 mark. The work had been appreciably faster than that which needed cut-offs of 25 to 30 per cent on 'Castles', and with some engine types such working on shorter cut-offs could well have signified more economical working. But the Great Western four-cylinder 4-6-0 designs maintain their optimum efficiency up to the limit of the boiler to produce steam.

After passing Westbury 2 minutes early, some delays occurred between there and Taunton, but even so the latter station was still passed ahead of time. With the load reduced then to 395 tons, a fine ascent was made to Whiteball, and it would have been easily possible to arrive at Exeter in the time then scheduled, 175 minutes, but for serious delays from permanent way working before Tiverton Junction. The interesting feature of this run, however, was the use of cut-offs as short as 16 per cent with full regulator to produce sustained speeds of 68 to 70 mph on level track with a load of 530 tons. From the details of other footplate journeys over the original main line out of Paddington, one can gather that this was the usual method of working the 'Kings' with 500-ton trains.

On the first tabulated run, *King George V* drew away from Mr Goodyear's footplate journey until it was 3 minutes ahead of schedule on passing Bedwyn. But the permanent way check after Pewsey was a severe one, and the second run had overtaken the first on passing Edington. It is notable that on the winding descents of the West of England line, maximum speeds rarely exceeded much over 80 mph, in contrast to those frequently attained on the Birmingham line. *King George V* was comfortably ahead of time at Taunton and her driver could afford to take things relatively easily on the climb to Whiteball Tunnel, and with a brisk descent thereafter to pass Exeter, at 60 mph, just over a minute early. On the third run the driver evidently anticipated the effect of the serious delays that would occur beyond Westbury, and his initial running was magnificent with such a time as 67 min 19 sec over Savernake summit and 89 min 24 sec through Westbury. It seemed as though this driver had judged things well, for after the delays he was more or less abreast of the other two runs on passing Castle Cary, and the Taunton slip coach in which my correspondent was travelling arrived in a few seconds under 141 minutes from Paddington.

On the first of the three runs, the only one of which there is a record of the running beyond Exeter, the coastal section was taken briskly, with a time of only 21 minutes for the 20.2 miles from Exeter to Newton Abbot, the ample point-to-point allowance for this stretch being clipped by 3 minutes. Everything was thus in excellent form for the all-out attack on the South Devon banks. In the year 1935 I myself clocked a run with the down 'Limited' in very similar conditions, during

King George V *hauling the 15-coach down 'Cornish Riviera Express' near Aldermaston.* (M.W. Earley)

'Maximum performance in the late '30s': a Worcester-based engine that attained 100 mph down the Honeybourne bank on 31 July 1939. No 4086 Builth Castle *is seen here on the 2 pm up Worcester express near Campden.* (F.J. Arthur)

which engine No 6016 *King Edward V* took a load of 376 tons unassisted from Newton Abbot. Except that the downhill piece from Dainton Tunnel to Totnes was taken a little faster on my run, the two performances were identical. Although my own experience took place nearly 30 years ago I can still recall the thrilling sound of the exhaust as No 6016 was opened out in readiness for Dainton bank, and of the positive cannonade that developed as we climbed past Stoneycombe sidings and wound our way round the S-curve that leads to the tunnel. It would have been the same on Mr Martin's run with No 6000.

Prior to this *King George V* had put in considerably the harder work; for on my run we had conveyed no more than 440 tons from Paddington, and moreover had a station stop at Exeter. Although one could argue that an intermediate stop increases coal consumption and wear and tear on the machinery, it can be an unmitigated blessing to the enginemen. It gives them just that brief respite from the continuous work and vigilance, and opportunity was always taken to have two young lads from Exeter shed ready to climb aboard and help the fireman to get the coal forward. On the Plymouth non-stop run the fireman was 'on his own', so to speak, from the moment of leaving Paddington. Mention of getting coal forward at Exeter reminds me of an amusing occasion when I was riding on the up 'Limited', on No 6022, the first of the 'Kings' to have high-degree superheat. My friends on the footplate were very anxious to show me how well the engine would climb to Whiteball, and when we got the right away the driver instantly opened up. The moment we moved there was a scuffling sound behind us, and down amidst the coal leapt the two young heroes who had been shovelling away while we stood, and whom we had completely forgotten.

To revert to the exploits of No 6000 in July 1929, it will be seen from the log that Dainton lowered the speed to 20 mph, but on the longer ascent from Totnes to Rattery magnificent work was done. In the 2.8 miles between Totnes station and Tigley box, the gradient is nowhere easier than 1 in 71, and for nearly 2 miles it is continuously at 1 in 46 to 57. These are inclinations more associated with the West Highlands of Scotland than with the 'longest non-stop run in the world'—the honour held by the 'Limited' for so many years. In connection with Rattery I shall always remember an occasion when I was privileged to ride in the dynamometer car, in the spring of 1955, when preparations were being made for the restoration of the 4-hour schedule to Plymouth. We had come down from London in famous style behind No 6013; but with a load of 390 tons tare assistance was taken from Newton. As we listened to the 'Castle' and the 'King' together thundering up past Tigley, and watched the dial indicating the drawbar pull, R.A. Smeddle, then Chief Mechanical and Electrical Engineer of the Western, remarked to those of us sitting near him in the car: 'This is a hell of a bank!'.

On that test run we had about 415 tons gross behind the tender of the second engine; yet in 1929 No 6000, having come down non-stop from Paddington, took 405 tons up unassisted. The speed did not fall below 25 mph at Tigley, and recovered quite smartly to 32 by Rattery. Although the gradient eases considerably between these two signal boxes, one could not by any stretch of the imagination call the upper part of the bank 'easy'. The inclinations are successively 1 in 90, 1 in 95 and 1 in 65. The point-to-point timing between Totnes and Brent is exceedingly severe, demanding an average speed of 39.4 mph. Somewhat naturally time was lost here, and Brent was passed only just inside schedule time. But there is a recovery margin on the last stage, and with a clear road the 'Limited' came into Plymouth exactly 3 minutes early. The net time was about 232½ minutes, representing a very fine average speed of 58½ mph.

19. Mixed traffic units, large and small

At the time of Churchward's retirement, before the Grouping which brought in the stock of the Welsh companies, the Great Western had 3,188 locomotives, of which a little over one-third, what Cecil J. Allen once referred to as 'the amazing total of 1,100', were, believe it or not, 0-6-0 tank engines. When the first post-war booklet on GWR Locomotives was published in 1946, the relevant figures out of a total of 3,858 steam locomotives were 1,269 0-6-0 tank engines; indeed, the stock of this type had increased by 146 since 1938. When Churchward inherited the swarm of 0-6-0 tank engines from the Armstrong and Dean days, they were mostly of the saddle tank type, and appreciating there was much useful work to be done all over the line by such a type, he began modernizing them by fitting tanks of the pannier type to both the smaller variety having 16-in by 24-in cylinders, and the larger with 17½-in cylinders. At one time I believe it was the intention to superheat the latter, as was being done with the celebrated Dean Goods engines of the '2301' Class. Indeed, one authority writing in *The Railway Magazine* of 60 years ago definitely states that the '2700' Class, as the pannier rebuildings of the older 0-6-0s were classed, *were* superheated, but this was not so. The hundred engines of this class, numbered 2700–2799, were the actual forerunners of the '5700' Class, introduced in 1929, having the same basic dimensions, but an improved valve gear, the same as that used on the superheated members of the '2301' 0-6-0 tender engines.

When Churchward modernized the older 0-6-0 tanks from 1910 they were still turned out in the full passenger livery with copper-topped chimneys, polished brass safety valve bonnets and the full words 'Great Western' on their pannier tanks with the gartered crest of the Company in between. The smaller engines with 16-in cylinders were similarly adorned, and the first of them to be stationed at Old Oak Common shed and working empty stock trains into and out of Paddington aroused considerable interest by her smart appearance. The working of the pannier tanks

Top right *Precursor of the famous pannier tanks — saddle tank No 1736 smartly turned out in the early 1900s.* (Author's collection)

Above right *Pannier tank No 9701, equipped for condensing to run on the Metropolitan line to Smithfield Market.* (British Railways)

Right *A pannier tank, No 3705, on a Yealmpton branch train at Plymouth Friary.* (H.C. Casserley)

Left *The first of the taper-boilered pannier tanks, No 9400.* (British Railways)

Right *The first of the smart little 0-4-2 tanks of the '4800' Class.* (British Railways)

Below right *One of the '4800' Class, renumbered 1466, on an auto-train working.* (Author's collection)

into Paddington, of course, became a commonplace when the '5700s' were so numerous, and perhaps I can tell 'out of school' a story that I heard at Swindon concerning the domeless panier tanks introduced just before nationalization. Apparently certain directors had been impressed in the wrong way by the large number of 'antiquated' engines with large steam domes working in and around Paddington, and could not the Chief Mechanical Engineer design something more modern? Recalling the days when Churchward himself attended Board Meetings and his reactions to even the slightest attempt to interfere or criticize what he was doing, one can well imagine the explosion that such a suggestion would have brought forth! But in the much changed days of 1946, Hawksworth was told to design a pannier tank with a domeless taper boiler.

The '5700' Class proper were splendid engines. They were more than their official designation, 'Light goods and shunting engines', and by 1946 there were no fewer than 800 of them in service. Their leading dimensions were: cylinders, 17½-in diameter by 24-in stroke; wheels, 4-ft 7-in diameter; total heating surface, 1,178 sq ft; grate area, 15.3 sq ft; boiler pressure, 200 psi; tractive effort, 22,515 lbs. Their weight in working order was 49 tons. Certainly they were ideal for hauling the very heavy long-distance trains from the carriage sidings at Old Oak Common over the flyover across the main running lines to the empty carriage line on the south side, but they were universally popular all over the system. I shall always remember the comment of a driver at one of the sheds in the Welsh valleys which was using them regularly on not-so-light passenger trains. He said, 'They are dynamic'! Then there was the morning when the regular engine working the 7.45 am express from Bristol to Paddington failed at Bath, and the only immediate replacement was a 'Bulldog' Class 4-4-0 in poor condition, and a pannier tank. The roar of the latter as she pulled the train, and seemingly the 'Bulldog' as well, was a rousing start to a morning at Chippenham—dynamic indeed!

In the second chapter of this book I extolled the merits of the little 'Metro' 2-4-0 tanks. Now it is the turn of the 0-4-2s, of which there were no fewer than 155 running at the end of 1919. Dean's '517' Class of 1887, a splendid little design with 16-in by 24-in cylinders, 5-ft 2-in coupled wheels, and having a grate area of 14.7 sq ft, had been modernized to the extent of having boilers with Belpaire fireboxes, but they still had open-backed cabs, and when I saw them in the mid-1920s they still had copper-topped chimneys and polished brass safety valve covers. They were then carrying a boiler pressure of 150 psi. By the 1930s, however, the life-span of these smart engines was over, and to replace them 100 new engines of the same general design, with various 'mod cons', were built at Swindon, beginning in 1932. The '4800' Class had the same basic proportions as the Dean '517' Class, as modernized in Churchward's time, but the boilers carried a pressure of 165 psi and the boilers were smaller, having a total heating surface of 953 sq ft instead of 988, and the grate area was 12.8 sq ft instead of 14.7. The cabs were enclosed, with large windows and sliding cab-side extensions. The engines numbered 4800 to 4874 were fitted with auto-gear for working with trailer cars, while those numbered 5800 to 5819 were not so equipped.

They were sprightly little engines, as I found when I rode on the footplate of one of them from Fishguard Harbour to Clarbeston Road one morning to connect with the 11.25 am from Milford Haven to Paddington. We had only an auto-train load, but we fairly sailed up 1 in 50 bank from 'Fishguard and Goodwick' on the single-line section up to Manorowen signal box. I was glad that the train was marshalled with the engine leading in the up direction, for a 'footplate' ride, no matter how brisk the speed, is not interesting from the trailer end of the train. We had to make five intermediate stops in the 15½ miles from Fishguard Harbour to Clarbeston Road within an overall time of 38 minutes, but our stopping times were no more than brief, three of the stops being at no more than halts, Jordanston, Welsh Hook and Wolfs Castle. From the last-mentioned we had a 6-mile run to Clarbeston Road, and although much of the distance is on a steeply rising gradient, we covered this in nearly 2 minutes inside the scheduled 11 minutes.

In mid-Victorian times for the standard gauge sections of the GWR Joseph Armstrong built several hundred 0-6-0 main-line goods engines with 5-ft diameter wheels and 17-in by 24-in cylinders. They had double frames and were devoid of cabs. Some 20 years later, when brother George was the power in the land at Wolverhampton, they were rebuilt, fitted with cabs, and one of the class, No 700, became the subject of one of the earliest and most charmingly executed oil paintings in the 'F. Moore' style, and it graced H. Holcroft's book on *The Armstrongs of the Great Western*, published by *Railway World* in 1953. In Churchward's time many of these engines were rebuilt a second time, with larger boilers and large Dean-style domes; but in 1930 the time had come to replace some at any rate of these engines, the chassis of which were upwards of 60 years old, and under Collett's supervision an entirely new design of 0-6-0 was prepared, the so-called '2251' Class.

The wheels, wheelbase and machinery of the new engines were the same as the Dean Goods, though the fitting of a taper boiler and a modern closed-in type of cab necessitated the lengthening of the frames both at front and rear, while the boiler carrying a higher-working pressure than the Dean Goods further increased the overall weight. The frame dimensions as compared with the older engines were 6 ft 6 in + 7 ft 3 in +

Below *One of the '2200' class standard 0-6-0 goods, No 2211 at Swindon.* (British Railways)

8 ft 3 in + 4 ft 9 in, as against 4 ft 9 in + 7ft 3 in + 8 ft 3 in + 4 ft 0 in.

The relative dimensions of the two classes were:

Class	'2301'	'2251'
Cylinders		
diameter × stroke (in)	$17\frac{1}{2} \times 24$	$17\frac{1}{2} \times 24$
Wheels, diameter (ft in)	5 2	5 2
Heating surface (sq ft)		
Tubes	960.8	1,069.42
Firebox	106.45	102.40
Superheater	75.3	74.0
Total	1,142.6	1,245.0
Grate area (sq ft)	15.45	17.40
Working pressure (psi)	180	200
Weight of engine (tons)	36.8	43.4
Tractive effort (lbs)	18,140	20,155

The later engines were built after the war, and when the number had filled up the '2200' century a further series was begun numbered '3200' onwards. I saw these latter on rather humdrum duties, and they did not aspire to the brief hour of glory enjoyed, rather surreptitiously, by their famous predecessors of the '2301' Class not long after nationalization. Not long previously the Derby Drawing Office of the LMS had produced some little 2-6-0s of Class '2P' capacity, and these were being introduced on to some of the less important branch lines to replace ageing LNWR and Midland six-wheelers. I went up to Penrith to do some footplating on these new engines on the Cockermouth, Keswick and Penrith line, also hoping to catch some of the old LNWR 18-in goods, the 'Cauliflowers'. I rode some of these latter and some of the new '2P' 2-6-0s, and while I could appreciate the 'mod cons' of the new footplates compared to the spartan conditions of the old 'Cauliflowers', I was not very impressed by the pulling power. However, I let that pass.

A few years later, when a batch of LMS-type '2P' 2-6-0s was allocated to the Western Region, the balloon truly went up! The locomotive inspectors, who by tradition had the ears of the Swindon Drawing Office, complained that the new engines would not take the loads allocated to them, which believe it or not were the same as those worked by the Dean '2301' class 0-6-0 goods. From my increasingly friendly contacts with men of varying estate at Swindon, from Mr Hawksworth himself downwards, I had formed the impression that among the slightly lower echelons of responsibility in the locomotive department there was a feeling of unholy joy at the showing up of any shortcomings of locomotive designs other than of Great Western origin, and from all accounts the LMS '2P' 2-6-0 was swooped upon with relish. The locomotive testing section of the Drawing Office was called in; comparative tests were run, some I believe on the stationary testing plant in Swindon, with both the LMS '2P', and then the Dean Goods going all-out. I have not seen any of the results, but I gathered from some of those engaged in the trials that the Dean Goods absolutely 'walked away' with it. Whether or not the '2P' had her draughting arrangements altered, or was otherwise amended design-wise to try to step up her output, I cannot say. But the affair was a resounding triumph for the Dean Goods.

Reverting now to the early 1930s, the Operating Department in South Wales had asked for more of the standard 2-8-0 tank engines of the '4200' Class for the longer-haul coal runs, but after construction of 30 of these engines had been authorized and building commenced at Swindon, the decline in the Welsh coal trade had set in, and the need for additional 2-8-0 tank engines receded. Only 20 of them were completed and these were stored as new in the Stock Shed near the Swindon Running Shed. In 1934, however, these were modified by extending the frames to provide increased coal and water capacity, adding a trailing wheel to support, making them into heavy main-line freight

Left *One of the celebrated 'Dean Goods' 0-6-0s, No 2430, newly overhauled at Swindon.* (M.D. England, National Railway Museum)

Above right *One of the '7200' Class 2-8-2 tanks, No 7214, traversing the 'Old Incline' to the Southern Railway at Reading with a through freight train.* (M.W. Earley)

Right *An impressive broadside view of 2-8-2 tank engine No 7210 at Chippenham.* (K.H. Leech)

engines. Eventually, with the conversion of 34 additional engines of the '5200' series, there were 54 of these excellent 2-8-2 tanks, numbered 7200–7253. They were used far from South Wales; indeed, one of Maurice Earley's fine photographs reproduced herewith shows one of them traversing the 'Old Incline' eastwards from Reading to the South Eastern and Chatham line.

The next rebuilding project came in 1936. Many of the earlier engines of the '4300' Class were nearing the end of their useful lives, and the plan was formed for rebuilding them as 4-6-0s, with a Standard No 1 boiler working at 225 psi as shown on Churchward's historic diagram of 1901. The new engines were to a certain extent rebuilds, and K.J. Cook in his book *Swindon Steam* tells how about 50 per cent of components of the original 2-6-0s were used in the 5-ft 8-in 4-6-0s. However, he added, 'In this case it paid us to renew the main frames which were simple straight frames, and so avoid a considerable amount of stopping up and redrilling.' The 2-6-0s had Churchward's standard two-cylinder front end layout and in using this on the 4-6-0s the fore ends of the frames would have to be jointed as on the other standard 4-6-0s of the 'Saint' and 'Hall' Classes. On the rebuilt 4-6-0s, by virtue of combining 225 psi working pressure with 5-ft 8-in coupled wheels, the nominal tractive was 28,875 lbs as compared to 27,275 lbs on the 'Halls' and 24,395 lbs on the 'Saints'. In their overall finish, named after 'Granges', the new engines were a half-way house between the splendour of the express passenger classes and the goods and tank engine categories, having copper-topped chimneys, polished safety valve bonnets but no lining out. The tenders were those of the 2-6-0 engines they replaced.

I am sorry I cannot be more enthusiastic over the policy of naming the mixed traffic members of the GWR fleet, and in this I would also include the 'Hall' Class, as well as the smaller-boilered 4-6-0s of the 'Manor' series introduced in 1938. Some 70 years ago, in *The Railway Magazine*, E.L. Ahrons in his famous series of articles dealing with 'Locomotive and Train Working in the latter part of the Nineteenth Century' had some great fun in poking the finger of ridicule at some results of the practice of the Brighton Railway in naming even the most humble tank engines after every town and village on the system. The system also included, indeed seems to have had its origin in, some of the least salubrious districts of south-east London through which Stroudley's immaculately kept yellow tank engines puffed their purposeful way out of the depths of the Thames Tunnel! So it also became on the Great Western for finding titles for 80 'Granges', not to mention 330 'Halls'. After living in Great Western territory west of Swindon for more than 50 years, I feel I know the country reasonably well, and yet if I was asked I should find some difficulty in pin-pointing more than a couple of dozen of the actual locations of these stately homes, 'Halls' and 'Granges' alike. To be frank, the names of these mixed traffic engines mean little to me, and they meant even less to the men who worked on them and serviced them.

On the fast-running sections of the line, the 'Granges' were not used in ordinary express passenger

traffic, but in emergencies they often did notable work. It was certainly the case when one of my railway friends was travelling on the 12.20 pm from Cardiff to Paddington one day after nationalization when a batch of the new 'Pacific' locomotives of the 'Britannia' Class had become the principal passenger engines at Canton shed, Cardiff. One of these was working the train in question, a heavy and crowded train of 445 tons tare, and got into such trouble that a stop had to be made at Swindon to get a fresh engine. The substitute eventually provided was a 'Grange', and what with the very bad running previously and the business of changing over, the Cardiff men with their new mount got away from Swindon 85 minutes late. My friend who clocked the run, a very experienced observer, told me that many passengers were standing in the corridors and that he judged the gross load behind the tender to be 485 tons. The start was rather slow, while the driver was taking the measure of his fresh engine, and the fireman was building up the fire for a major effort, but then they did splendidly as the log shows. The net time was 80 minutes and note should be taken of the magnificent speed from Uffington to Cholsey with an engine having wheels of only 5-ft 8-in diameter.

In the summer of 1954 I saw the working of a 'Grange' Class engine on the down 'Cornish Riviera Express' in a most interesting guise, on a summer Saturday. From the passengers' point of view the train was booked non-stop to Truro, with a 14-coach load. As this would have involved double-heading throughout from Newton Abbot, the eminently practical arrangement was made of changing engines completely, with two fresh engines running the train non-stop from Newton Abbot to Truro. The 'King' which had come down from London on the 10.30 am coupled on to double-head the immediately succeeding express to Plymouth. One of the most interesting points about this working was the closeness of the timetable margins ahead of the 'Cornish Riviera Express' in the Saturday timetable of that year. There was a train for the Torquay line leaving Paddington at 10.20 am, and providing this ran to time there would be no trouble from that source, although it had a clearance of only 5 minutes ahead of the 'Limited' at Newton Abbot; but then just look at the timetable just *before* the 10.20:

Train (am)		Arrival time in Newton Abbot (pm)
7.30	Birmingham-Paignton	12.28
6.35	Walsall-Kingswear	12.45
6.55	Wolverhampton-Paignton	12.56
8.50	Paddington-Paignton	1.10
9.30	Paddington-Newquay	1.16
7.30	Paddington-Newquay via Bristol	1.26
9.40	Paddington-Paignton	1.31
6.40	Leicester-Paignton	1.43
10.20	Paddington-Kingswear	1.55
10.30	'Cornish Riviera Express'	2.00

GWR: Swindon-Paddington

Engine No 6832 *Brockton Grange*
Load 445 tons tare, 485 tons full

Distance (miles)		Actual (min sec)	Speed (mph)
0.0	Swindon	0 00	
5.7	Shrivenham	9 32	58
10.8	Uffington	14 24	67½
13.4	Challow	16 43	70
16.9	Wantage Road	19 39	72
20.8	Steventon	22 53	73
24.2	Didcot	25 40	74
28.8	Cholsey	29 37	70
		pw check	40
35.8	Pangbourne	37 39	62
38.6	Tilehurst	40 14	64½
41.3	Reading	42 52	63
46.3	Twyford	47 45	60/65
—		sig stop	—
58.8	Slough	62 23	61
68.2	Southall	72 53	57
71.6	Ealing Broadway	76 23	62
76.0	Westbourne Park	81 24	—
77.3	Paddington	84 14	—

There were some intricate patterns of working even before Newton Abbot was reached, for the 7.30 am from Paddington (via Bristol) was booked to be overtaken by the 9.30 am while it was calling at Exeter, and similarly at Exeter the 6.40 am from Leicester was overtaken by the 9.40 am from Paddington. There was certainly plenty of scope for getting delayed, with such a complex procession of trains ahead.

I rode down from Paddington on the engine of the 'Cornish Riviera Express', No 6007 *King William III*, with a 500-ton train, and we passed Exeter on time, in $184\frac{1}{2}$ minutes, or 177 minutes net. But we caught up the last of the preceding trains at Dawlish Warren, and after a succession of checks reached Newton Abbot at 2.6 pm. There we exchanged the 'King' for two two-cylinder 4-6-0s, No 6873 *Caradoc Grange* and No 5964 *Wolseley Hall*, and I joined the driver and fireman on the leading engine.

The important point to appreciate when studying the table overleaf is that there is no opportunity for taking water immediately; that even with two engines the load was not greatly less than the maximum permitted with engines of these classes over the South Devon line. On this summer Saturday, however, the operating was excellent, and from the moment of leaving Newton Abbot, 5 minutes late, all signals were clear—even through the Plymouth district—until we reached the immediate approach to Truro station.

With a 500-ton train, both engines had to be worked very hard on the South Devon line. *Caradoc Grange* was opened out to no less than 55 per cent cut-off on Dainton bank, and 52 per cent on Rattery, and from the loud staccato beat of the engine behind us it was evident that she too was being pounded. Because of the permanent way check at Totnes—very awkwardly sited at the very foot of the Rattery incline—we lost a further $2\frac{1}{2}$ minutes to Brent, but with the aid of the miraculously clear road through the Plymouth area we had picked up 4 minutes on schedule when we crossed the Royal Albert Bridge into Cornwall, and passed Saltash. From there we went ahead in great style. The 1 in 60 gradient west of St Germans was taken at a minimum of 34 mph. Despite a bad permanent way check to 15 mph at Lostwithiel the train was 3 minutes early passing Par, and on the worst bank of all, up to St Austell, at 1 in 60, speed did not fall below $26\frac{1}{2}$ mph. On passing milepost 299 another $2\frac{1}{2}$ minutes should have seen us at rest in Truro; but we had caught up the 8.25 am from Paddington and were stopped for 8 minutes outside. Otherwise we should have completed this excellent and unusual run in $127\frac{1}{4}$ minutes from Newton Abbot, with a clear gain of 10 minutes on schedule.

Another conversion job, which originated in what can certainly be described as 'hole and corner' methods in the Swindon locomotive works, concerned the rebuilding of 20 4-4-0s of the 'Bulldog' Class with domed boilers of a similar but not actually the same design as used on the Dean Goods. The lines of the former Cambrian Railways—always in the plural when referring to pre-Grouping days—were subject to very severe axle-loading limitations, and in the 1930s a stud of the old Dean 'Duke' Class 4-4-0s were retained to cover

Left *A 'Grange' on the up 'Cornishman' climbing Hemerdon bank: No 6838* Goodmoor Grange. (M.W. Earley)

Right *No 6873* Caradoc Grange, *newly outshopped from Swindon in BR days.* (K.H. Leech)

GWR: 'Cornish Riviera Express', Newton Abbot–Truro

Engine No 6873 *Caradoc Grange* and no 5964 *Wolseley Hall*
Load 465 tons tare, 500 tons full

Distance (miles)		Schedule (min)	Actual (min sec)	Speed (mph)
0.0	NEWTON ABBOT	0	0 00	—
1.8	Milepost 216		4 07	43
3.8	Dainton box	8	8 45	18
—			pw slack	25
8.6	TOTNES	15	16 17	35
11.3	Tigley box		22 32	19½
13.2	Rattery box	25	26 47	28
15.5	Brent	28	30 36	44
25.1	Hemerdon box	41	42 17	—
27.8	Plympton		45 00	64
31.8	PLYMOUTH (North Road)	53	51 18	—
34.9	St Budeaux		56 35	—
36.0	Saltash	63	59 07	15*
41.1	St Germans		65 25	56
46.5	Menheniot		72 55	37/53
49.6	LISKEARD	83	77 00	38/54
52.9	Doublebois		81 38	34½
58.7	BODMIN ROAD	97	88 50	55(max)
—			pw slack	15
62.2	Lostwithiel		93 05	—
63.7	Milepost 279		96 58	32
66.5	PAR	109	100 57	55
71.0	ST AUSTELL		108 05	26½
73.4	Burngullow		112 15	58
77.8	Grampound Road		117 30	42
80.2	Probus		120 18	55/41
83.7	Milepost 299		124 42	50
—			sig stop 8 min	—
85.5	TRURO	138	138 15	—

Net time 124 minutes

* Speed restriction

the passenger services. No more modern 4-4-0s were then permitted to run westwards from Oswestry to the coast. Then one day early in 1936, engine No 3265 *Tre, Pol and Pen* was in 'B' Shop at Swindon for general repairs. The frames were in a bad way, and in the ordinary way the engine would have been scrapped; but because of the situation in the Oswestry Division, the demise of one of their passenger engines would have led to some awkward questions. In the shop Cook had a 'Bulldog' No 3365 on the very next pit to No 3265, and with the connivance of his chief, R.A.G. Hannington, he conceived the idea of building up the 'Duke' on the frames of No 3365, mounting the domed boiler, using the cab, smokebox and all the 'Duke' fittings, including the unbalanced crank, and its name and numberplate. The original frames were scrapped, and *Tre, Pol and Pen*, with 'Bulldog' frames, was returned to traffic, and apparently no one was any the wiser!

Some months later the Assistant Running Superintendent was planning to make a personal visit to the Oswestry Division, and the Assistant there, writing to agree the date, added a postscript to his letter: 'Bring up some more like 3265 in your bag'. As Cook says in his book, 'That started a hare—what was special about 3265?' Of course he and Hannington had to 'come clean', with the happy result that authorization was given for 20 more 'Bulldogs' to be rebuilt on the lines of *Tre, Pol and Pen* to form a new class, the '3200', to replace the ageing 'Dukes' on the Cambrian line. In the fashion of the day, they must be named, but not in using once again the 'Duke' names from the scrapped Dean engines. They must be named after 'Earls'. This had an amusing sequel. The names chosen naturally included those of certain directors of the GWR, and as these dignitaries expressed a wish to see some of the engines that had been named after

Above *The first of the 'Dukedogs' as originally turned out, No 3200* Earl of Mount Edgcumbe. (British Railways)

Right *Another of the '3200s' when named after earls: No 3209* Earl of Radnor. (British Railways)

Right *Two 'Dukedogs' on a heavy stopping train approaching Aberystwyth in 1947, No 9025 leading and No 9022 next to the train.* (E.D. Bruton)

them, Collett, rather with his tongue in his cheek, sent one to Paddington. The earls were not amused, that such inferior and antiquated-looking engines should be named after them, and Collett was instructed to take the names off. They were used afterwards on certain engines of the 'Castle' Class.

The '3200' Class 4-4-0s, or as one of my Birmingham enthusiast friends nicknamed them, the 'Dukedogs', were excellent engines. Shortly after the war I had some footplate rides on them on the Cambrian line and found them most enjoyable to observe. I wish I could say the same for their successors of the 'Manor' Class. These latter were intended to be a lighter version of the 'Granges', also using as many parts as possible from the 2-6-0s that were being withdrawn. The 'Manors', like the 'Granges', had new frames, and the wheelbase of the two classes was the same. But in the provision of a new and smaller design of boiler for the 'Manor', someone slipped up badly and produced one that was sadly deficient in steam-raising ability; how deficient was not revealed until some years after nationalization, as related in a subsequent chapter of this book.

20. Hawksworth's years—Phase 1

In January 1932, when Stanier left Swindon for the LMS, John Auld, formerly Chief Mechanical Engineer of the Barry Railway, and later Docks and Personal Assistant to the CME of the Great Western, was appointed Principal Assistant to the Chief Mechanical Engineer, and F.W. Hawksworth, who had been Chief Draughtsman from 1925, was appointed Assistant to the Chief Mechanical Engineer. Auld was older than Collett, but he was a charming personality, and rather against his wishes one gathered he was persuaded to stay while Collett, in his later years clinging on to office until he was over 70, was more often in London embracing the mists of spiritualism than of mechanical engineering. The running of the great department largely devolved upon Auld in the last years. At midsummer 1941 they both retired and Hawksworth stepped up to the chair so illustriously held by Churchward, though in circumstances as different as one could conceive from those facing former Chief Mechanical Engineers of the Great Western Railway.

Hawksworth was pre-eminently an engine designer. In his younger days as a draughtsman he had made the general arrangement drawing of *The Great Bear*, and it was not without very good reason that Collett resisted Stanier's recommendation, in the early 1920s, that he should be transferred for a time to the Locomotive Works, the management of which was becoming vacant. Collett could not spare him from the Drawing Office. When the overall parameters had been settled, Hawksworth designed the 'Kings', but in later years, when he saw what his former colleague was doing on the LMS, one feels sure that he must have had thoughts about the limitations of the 'Kings' in maximum sustained steaming capacity. In this respect they were undoubtedly 'over-cylindered'. When he took over from Collett the war situation was changing considerably. The Battle of Britain had been won. The night blitz on our cities had slackened to no more than an occasional pin-prick compared to its previous fearful intensity, and Hitler had thrown the might of his land forces against Russia. Even more important to us was the momentous 'Atlantic Meeting' between Winston Churchill and President Roosevelt which ensured us ample supplies of war material even before the USA became an active belligerent. On the Great Western Railway, while all the workshops were heavily engaged in war production, as well as maintaining the stock and plant in good order, in the main Drawing Office at Swindon there was time to give certain thoughts to the future, and we now know that Hawksworth from his long association with engine designing had his ideas already formed.

One day Mattingley, the Chief Draughtsman, came into the main Drawing Office with outline proposals for a new express passenger engine of the 'Pacific' type. One senior man was allocated the job of the boiler design, which would have a far higher degree of superheat than anything previously used at Swindon, while another senior draughtsman was given the task of modernizing the 'King' front end, internally streamlining the passages and ports as Stanier's men had so successfully done on the LMS 'Duchess' Class 'Pacifics'. The shortcomings of the 'Kings' in this respect were to be clearly shown in some post-war analytical trials to which reference is made in the final chapter of this book. No work was apparently done at this stage towards the design of the frames, but from what I learned some years afterwards, the cylinder sizes were to have been the same as those of the 'Kings', and with a boiler pressure of 280 psi, and coupled wheels reduced in diameter to 6 ft 3 in, the nominal tractive effort would have been nearly 47,000 lbs against 40,300 lbs on the 'Kings', and considerably in advance of the most powerful British passenger engine of the day, the Gresley 'P2' 2-8-2s of the LNER (43,462 lbs), soon to be vandalized by Gresley's successor. In war conditions, however, further work on a new express passenger engine could not be continued for a time, though Hawksworth took the opportunity to include two of the new features in his new 'County' Class 4-6-0s, as will be told later.

In the earlier years of the war, construction of standard mixed traffic engines of the 'Hall' Class had proceeded at intervals, though those built from 1941 onwards, numbered 6916 upwards, were at first unnamed to avoid using brass. These engines remained in every way a Swindon standard, retaining the medium degree of superheat, the unique form of front end construction and the bar-framed bogies that had been used from Churchward's early days. But when authorization came for more 'Halls', at the end of 1943, Hawksworth, from his long experience of the earlier engines, decided upon some considerable changes in design. He abandoned the built-up frame construction, which had cylinders carried on forged steel extension frames, and the saddle for supporting the front end of the boiler cast with the cylinders. In the new engines the main frame plates were carried through to the front buffer beam, with the cylinders cast separately from the saddle and bolted to the side of the frames with a fabricated stiffener between the frames. This stiffener was carried up to form the saddle for the smokebox, and within it were fitted the exhaust pipes from the cylinders to the blast pipe. Hawksworth also substituted a simple plate-framed type of bogie for the

Above *The first of the '6959' series of 'Halls' as originally turned out, painted black and unnamed.* (British Railways)

Right Witherslack Hall *during the 1948 Interchange Trials entering Manchester London Road (now Piccadilly) with a train from London Marylebone.*

rather elaborate design used hitherto.

The boiler was a new departure from the previous established Swindon practice, though outwardly there was nothing to suggest anything different. But the '6959' Class, as the new engines were at first referred to, had a three-row superheater, accommodated in 21 large tubes of 5-in diameter instead of the previous 14, and the superheater elements were of $1\frac{1}{4}$-in diameter, against 1 in. The heating surface, as compared to that of the standard 'Hall', was as follows:

Class	**'Hall'**	**'6959'**
Heating surfaces (sq ft)		
Tubes	1,686.60	1,582.60
Firebox	154.78	154.90
Total evaporative	1,841.38	1,737.50
Superheater	262.62	314.60
Total	2,104.00	2,052.10

The new engines, which like their immediate predecessors of the 'Hall' Class were at first unnamed, were widely welcomed in traffic, and on the slower schedules of wartime were frequently used on express passenger trains. After the war, however, with the improvement provided by some quicker timings, some modification to the draughting was found desirable.

When the three-row superheater was first introduced, no alteration was made in the draught arrangement, which had worked satisfactorily on the earlier engines, and indeed also on the 'Saints', for many years. The initial tests, however, indicated that a modification to this arrangement would make available a higher proportion of the potential capacity of the boiler. The alterations consisted of reducing the blast pipe orifice diameter by $\frac{1}{8}$ in to $5\frac{1}{8}$ in, in order to maintain the velocity of discharge, decreasing the taper of the chimney to 1 in 14, and increasing the length to 2 ft 4 in from choke to top to effect a more efficient ejection. The diameter of the chimney was left unaltered at 1 ft 3 in. Another slight change was to reduce the length of the superheater tubes, making the heating surface 295 sq ft against the 314 sq ft quoted when the engines were originally built. As thus modified the excellent steam rate of slightly over 20,000 lbs per hour was able to be sustained against a maximum demand for power.

Soon after the war, naming was resumed, though many of the titles adopted proved strange to West

Above *A celebrated engine bearing a name revered at Swindon: No 5930* Hannington Hall *as originally turned out.* (British Railways)

Left *An up West of England express (Saturdays only) approaching Whiteball Summit with engine No 6987* Sherrington Hall. (K.H. Leech)

Country, Welsh or West Midland ears. With the series beginning at No 6971, the first engine, *Athelampton Hall*, certainly savoured of Wessex, but then the nomenclature branched off to the Plain of York, to the Lake District and to other North Country names, including the last of that particular series, No 6990 *Witherslack Hall*, which from a variety of causes got such a raw deal in the British Railways Interchange Trials of 1948 and consequently gave a thoroughly unrepresentative performance. Referring to earlier days before the 'Hall' Class became so numerous as to exhaust the names of all the stately homes that could be thought of in Great Western territory, I was always intrigued that engine No 5930 should so frequently be chosen as the subject for an official portrait outside Swindon, not, it is true, in 'photographic grey' but in the full glory of the express passenger livery of the early 1930s. Hannington Hall is a noble old Elizabethan mansion in a fine park, in the village of that name near Highworth in North Wiltshire; but it was also the name of the much revered manager of the Locomotive Works at Swindon, R.A.G. Hannington.

I had a footplate run from Banbury to Paddington on engine No 5930 in 1952 in unusual circumstances. I was doing some articles for *The Engineer* on the working of the 'King' Class 4-6-0s, and had a pass to ride the 9.0 am up from Birmingham on a Saturday morning when I hoped the load would be at a maximum. It was; but neither my friends on the footplate nor I bargained for the news that greeted us when we arrived at Leamington. There had been a derailment at Bicester and we were going to be diverted via Oxford. The trouble was twofold: first that the 'King' Class engines were not permitted to run between Aynho Junction and Didcot; secondly, our driver, a top-link Wolverhampton man, did not know the road to Paddington beyond Oxford. So we stopped at Banbury and exchanged our 'King' for the first engine that could be spared, and at Oxford for our regular driver to retire to the 'cushions' and an Oxford man to take over. At Banbury the substitute engine, to my great interest, was No 5930 *Hannington Hall*, but at the moment in no state for heavy express running, with the fire anything but prepared to haul a train of 415 tons behind the tender. With some hard work by the fireman the situation was quickly improved, and from the restart at Banbury we covered the first 15.1 miles to Bletchington on a slightly favourable road in $18\frac{1}{2}$ minutes. But signal checks followed, and eventually our time for the 22.7 miles from Banbury to Oxford was $31\frac{1}{2}$ minutes.

At that time the fastest train from Oxford to Paddington was the 8.55 am from Worcester, which was booked to run the 63.4 miles non-stop in 73 minutes, an average speed of 52.3 mph over a road that is more or less level throughout. When the Oxford driver took over, the fire was in pretty good shape, but with a 415-ton train, this was no occasion to try and break records. The driver adopted the usual method of working with the 'Halls', a cut-off all the way of 25 per cent, and the main valve of the regulator just cracked. The regular Wolverhampton fireman obliged with a steadily maintained boiler pressure of 215 to 220 psi all the way to London, and without exceeding 60 mph at any point we passed Southall in exactly one hour from Oxford, 54.3 miles. Another 11 minutes should have seen us comfortably in Paddington, but signals delayed us, and the actual overall time from Oxford was $74\frac{1}{4}$ minutes.

Soon after the '6971' batch of 'Halls' was built, I had a run behind No 6972 *Beningbrough Hall* on the 12 noon express from Bristol to Paddington, which then ran via Bath and called additionally at Chippenham and Swindon. I was travelling with a colleague and we had much to discuss on our way up to town, and on joining the train at Chippenham we made straight for the restaurant car, ordered some drinks and continued with our discussion. But once into an express train I suppose it had become second nature to me to assess something of the locomotive work, and although I did not give it much attention on the run up from Chippenham I sensed that we were going faster than usual, and from Swindon, with the lunch about to be served and our documents cleared from the dining table, I began to log the run in earnest. I am glad I did, because we made a remarkable start out of Swindon, and even though we were soon pulled up, and held for just over a minute at Uffington, such was our subsequent progress that we still passed Reading in 45¼ minutes from Swindon, having almost achieved even-time from the Uffington restart!

Of course we were then getting wildly ahead of the leisurely schedule then laid down, and the pace was eased up considerably after Reading. Nevertheless, as the accompanying log shows, we covered the 58.8 miles from Swindon to Slough in 62 min 45 sec, and despite two more signal checks we clocked into Paddington 2¼ minutes early. As it was, the net time for the 77.3-mile run up from Swindon was only 79 minutes, and with a continuation of the former speed from Reading it could easily have been 76 minutes or less.

GWR: Swindon–Paddington

Engine No 6932 *Beningbrough Hall*
Load 390 tons tare, 420 tons full

Distance (miles)		Actual (min	sec)	Speed (mph)
0.0	Swindon	0	00	—
3.5	Marston East	5	50	60
5.7	Shrivenham	7	54	68
10.8	Uffington	13	23	sig stop
		14	30	
13.4	Challow	19	05	—
16.9	Wantage Road	22	23	67½
20.8	Steventon	25	55	eased
24.2	Didcot	29	06	65
28.8	Cholsey	33	38	62
35.8	Pangbourne	40	12	66
38.6	Tilehurst	42	47	69
41.3	Reading	45	15	64
53.1	Maidenhead	57	05	eased
58.8	Slough	62	46	—
—		sigs		—
68.2	Southall	74	09	60
71.6	Ealing Broadway	77	21	66½
—		sigs		—
77.3	Paddington	86	45	—

While it was a great disappointment to Hawksworth and to his enthusiastic supporters on the Board of the GWR that the 'Pacific' was not allowed to be built, at any rate for the time being, the project was certainly not abandoned altogether, and the two features that would have boosted the nominal tractive effort well above that of the 'Kings' and of the 'Pacifics' on the north-going lines were nurtured in another way. The coupled wheel diameter was to have been 6 ft 3 in and the patterns were actually made. As Bulleid had increased the working pressure on his boilers to 280 psi the same had been planned for the new Hawksworth 'Pacific'. While such a pressure was the highest that had yet been used on a British locomotive, and introduced problems from the temperature of the steam that brought metallurgical as well as structural design considerations in the boiler, it must equally be recalled that pressures of 300 psi were being successfully used on some of the largest American locomotives of the day. So, with orders for more mixed traffic 4-6-0s on the books at Swindon, opportunity was taken to make one batch a kind of guinea-pig for the proposed 'Pacific', which, far from being abandoned, thus remained in suspended animation. So authority was given for some mixed traffic 4-6-0s with 6-ft 3-in coupled wheels and boilers carrying a pressure of 280 psi. The original intention was to use the 'Castle' boiler, suitably strengthened to carry the much higher pressure, but the weight came out too heavy for the routes where it was proposed to use the new engines, so the design became a compromise as well as a guinea-pig.

The existence at Swindon of the flanging plates for the Stanier '8F' 2-8-0 of the LMS was turned to good effect, because on examination it was found that this boiler, with no more than slight modifications to suit the higher pressure, would come within the limitations of weight imposed upon the new class. It is interesting to see overleaf, alongside each other, the proportions of four well-known boilers, and from the table below the affinity between the LMS '8F' and the Hawksworth '10XX' is clearly apparent.

In the summer of 1945, enough leaked out from 'inside' at Swindon to set going a flood of rumours as to the nature of the new engines, including the probability of a 'Pacific'. To me it was reminiscent of Doncaster in 1920, when the new main-line engine turned out to be nothing more than an enlargement of the existing mixed traffic type—and that was all the more coincidental, because Hawksworth's 4-6-0 of 1945 bore the very same number, 1000, as Gresley's 2-6-0 of 1920! But both engines, despite their mixed traffic designations,

Left *No 1000, the first of the 'Counties', painted lined black, running on the stationary testing plant at Swindon.* (British Railways)

Above right *A controlled road dynamometer car test with engine No 1000* County of Middlesex *between Swindon to Stoke Gifford, passing Hullavington.* (K.H. Leech)

Below right *No 1018* County of Leicester *with the northbound 'Devonian' on the sea wall between Teignmouth and Dawlish.* (E.D. Bruton)

Class	**'Saint'**	**'Castle'**	**LMS '8F'**	**'10XX'**
Length of barrel (ft in)	14 10	14 10	12 $3\frac{9}{16}$	12 $7\frac{3}{16}$
Diameters outside				
max	5 6	5 9	5 $8\frac{3}{8}$	5 $8\frac{3}{8}$
min	4 $10\frac{5}{16}$	5 $11\frac{13}{16}$	5 0	5 0
Heating surfaces (sq ft)				
Tubes	1,686.60*	1,885.62*	1,479.0†	1,545.0†
Firebox	154.8	163.8	171.0	169.0
Superheater	262.62	262.62	245.0	254.0
Combined	2,104.0	2,312.0	1,895.0	1,968.0
Grate area (sq ft)	27.07	29.36	28.65	28.84
Boiler pressure (psi)	225	225	225	280

* Small tubes of 2-in diameter
† small tubes of $1\frac{3}{4}$-in diameter

caused a considerable stir in British locomotive circles.

Engine No 1000 was much more than an improved 'Hall' with an LMS '8F' boiler and 280 psi pressure. She had a twin-orifice blast pipe and a highly impressive double chimney, copper-capped in the best Swindon style. A new detail was the continuous splasher over the coupled wheels, while the tender was of an entirely new design, quite unlike any previous Swindon product. But what delighted supporters of the GWR perhaps more than anything else was the painting of the engine in the full prewar style, lined out, with the chimney cap and safety valve bonnet burnished as of old. At first the engine was unnamed. The framing and cylinder arrangement was the same as on the '6959' Class of 'Halls' with the standard $18\frac{1}{2}$-in by 30-in cylinders, and these, in conjunction with the 6-ft 3-in coupled wheels and 280 psi pressure gave a nominal tractive effort of 32,580 lbs, nearly 1,000 lbs more than that of a 'Castle'. The loading was 19.7 tons on all three coupled axles, and this, in conjunction with the use of only two cylinders, made the route availability slightly more restricted than that of a 'Castle', because of the hammer-blow effect on the track. So far as purely Great Western lines were concerned, the new engines had the 'red' route classification; but they were precluded from running over the LMS line between Yate and Standish Junction. They could not therefore be used on the Wolverhampton-Penzance trains, as between Birmingham and Bristol.

The pioneer engine, No 1000 *County of Middlesex*, was at first stationed at Swindon and was under observation from the testing section of the locomotive Drawing Office. She distinguished herself with some remarkable starts on preliminary test runs, but it was no more than natural from the most cursory study of the boiler proportions that such efforts could not be sustained for any appreciable time. A typical example of her early work was noted on the 7.50 am up from Bristol, after the engine had been transferred to Old Oak Common. Starting from Bath, and accelerating vigorously, Box was passed at 60 mph and on the 2 miles rising at 1 in 100 through Box Tunnel speed did not fall below 52 mph. On emerging from the tunnel, the quickening was such that Corsham was passed at 64 mph and a maximum of no less than 76 mph attained before the stop at Chippenham. The observer who noted this performance alighted at Chippenham and so could not tell how the engine continued on the non-stop run to London. The load was one of 12 coaches, about 400 tons gross behind the tender.

Apart from the early scrutiny of No 1000's work, the new engines seemed to have been allocated to the sheds with little in the way of briefing from headquarters as to what was expected of them, or how they should be used. There had been a degree of secrecy about their production, and the close liaison between the Drawing Office and the running inspectors which had characterized the introduction of new locomotive types on the GWR appears to have been lacking with the '10XX' Class. Some drivers, seeing a pressure of 280 psi on the gauge, seemed to think that they had a kind of 'Super-King' and tried to drive them accordingly. They were then surprised when they very quickly ran short of steam! At the time they were introduced, schedules were easy, even after the accelerations in the autumn of 1946, and on turns worked from Old Oak, for example, 'Kings', 'Castles' and 'Counties' were used indiscriminately. At Bristol (Bath Road), 'Counties' were used turn and turn about with 'Castles' and 'Stars', and not to the advantage of the new engines.

My first experience on the footplate with one of them came unexpectedly. I had an engine pass to ride the Penzance-Wolverhampton express from Plymouth to Birmingham. It was a Saturday in high summer, and from Exeter, after combination of the Torquay line and Cornish portions, we had a heavy train of 15 coaches and an ailing 'Castle' to haul them. We had a keen and experienced Bristol driver, but with a poor tool; a leak in the vacuum system that needed use of the big ejector to keep the brakes off caused us to make very heavy weather of it. The inspector who was riding with me was anxious to put up a good show, and threw out a message to have a fitter available at Taunton to try and get the vacuum trouble corrected. But expert attention was unavailing and it was decided to commandeer a new 'County' that was standing on the stopping train due to follow us to Bristol. My own pleasure was tempered by the long delay arising from the brake testing and eventual changing of engines. As our driver confided to me regarding the engine, No 5015 *Kingswear Castle*, when the inspector was out of earshot, 'even with this old crab I could have got to Bristol in an hour'.

However, by way of exchange we got No 1010 *County of Cardigan* to haul a train of 473 tons tare and 525 tons full with a great crowd of passengers. This run showed admirably what the 'Counties' could do, when expertly driven and fired. We got a bad permanent way check at Dunball, but then settled down to a steady 64 to 65 mph on level road. The engine was working in 20 per cent cut-off, with the regulator just far enough over on the quadrant to bring the main valve into operation. The boiler steamed well. Pressure was kept steadily at 275 to 280 psi first, but there was a slight falling off to 260 psi after about half an hour's running. We made a net time of 47¼ minutes over the 44.8 miles

from Taunton to Bristol, an excellent start-to-stop average of 56.8 mph and a complete negation of the commonly held idea at that time that the 'Counties' would not steam. Seeing that the engine was taken off a duty nothing approaching this for severity, with the fire not appropriately made up, this was a truly excellent performance. There was a sad anti-climax from the operating point of view. The inspector who was riding with me was a Newton Abbot man whose jurisdiction did not extend beyond Bristol, and, in making the substitution of a 'County' for the ailing 'Castle' at Taunton, he was apparently unaware of the embargo on 'Counties' over the Midland line between Yate and Standish Junction. Thus there was consternation on the platform at Temple Meads when we drew in with No 1010 at the head of the train. With such a load as 525 tons we should have needed assistance throughout to Wolverhampton, and a 'Star' was waiting to couple on ahead. but to find a third engine to replace the

'County' at a moment's notice on a summer Saturday afternoon posed its problems. It was nearly three-quarters of an hour before the train got away.

The 'Counties' were unusual engines in many ways. Looking back through the lavish documentation of British locomotive working, one can find many designs which, when first introduced, appeared to do very well and were the subject of much praise from those who took detailed notes of train running. Then, in not a few cases, the early reputations were not maintained, and to the outsiders it was difficult to understand why. The 'Counties' on the other hand got away to a bad start, for the diverse reasons discussed earlier. But when the regular express drivers got the measure of them and realized that just because they carried a pressure of 280 psi they were not a kind of 'Super-King', they settled down to some very good work. In my ordinary business travelling between Bath and Paddington I saw a good deal of their daily work, while on trips specially for the job of collecting data for literary assignments I made footplate journeys on them in Cornwall and north of Wolverhampton.

These were the three classes of service in which they were employed, and they brought out both the strength and weakness of the design in a variety of ways. The Bristol-Paddington runs demanded steady continuous steaming at a relatively high rate of evaporation if time was being made up, and it was in these circumstances that the engines could most easily be run short of steam. The Cornish road, with speed restricted to a maximum of 60 mph throughout and a heavily graded switchback to negotiate also, called for very careful handling with a locomotive of such high tractive power and relatively moderate steaming capacity to back it up. The maximum rostered loads for both 'Castles' and 'Counties' on the Cornish road were very high in relation to gradients and schedules, but I never personally managed to catch a 'County' with more than about 300 tons, and I have never seen a record of their work with anything approaching the maximum of 420 tons tare. The North main line from Wolverhampton to Chester was undoubtedly the scene of their most exciting and more spectacular work.

On the Bristol-Paddington run I had a number of good runs on the up 5.25 pm which I joined at Chippenham usually on Friday nights when the train was packed with passengers. The gross load was usually around 480 tons, and I had good runs with engines 1005 and 1007. On the non-stop runs up from Swindon on the midday train I also had some very fine runs, frequently attaining maximum speeds on level track of 70 mph with these loads of nearly 500 tons. And I had another unusual and exhilarating run about five years later on a summer Saturday afternoon with the 5.5 pm down non-stop from Paddington to Bath. It began normally enough, with No 1011 *County of Chester* hauling a 405-ton train. Schedule time was then 115 minutes to Bath, and after an early signal check the driver was not unduly hurrying, doing 63 to 66 mph from Slough onwards. Then we had to cut across the procession of Saturdays-only trains from the West of England coming off the Berks and Hants line at Reading, and we were practically stopped to let one of them cross our path. The recovery was vigorous, but then we came to a stand at Steventon, with all signals off. I feared the

Above left *No 1028* County of Warwick *at Paddington, having worked the 12 noon up from Bristol.* (O.S. Nock)

Left *No 1016* County of Hants *at Gobowen, working the 11.10 am Paddington-Birkenhead express.* (O.S. Nock)

worst—an engine failure. But no, it was a coach on fire! Looking back from the footplate the enginemen had seen what they thought was smoke coming from the second coach. When they stopped and went to look, their suspicions were confirmed, and once again the Great Western tradition of self-reliance in emergency came to our aid. Fortunately this was long before the days of 'route rationalization' and there were still goods sidings on the up side at Steventon.

While the guard and the signalman took all the necessary precautions to protect the train while we stood, the travelling ticket collector, having got the many passengers out of the suspect coach to other parts of a crowded train, went to assist the fireman in uncoupling, and a merry dance they had getting the heavy buckeye couplers clear. It speaks volumes for the energy and resource shown by those good fellows that the coach was parked in the siding, and we were coupled up and 'right away' once more in only 26 minutes from our first stop. Then *County of Chester* was driven hard. With a reduced load of 370 tons speed was worked up to 70 mph on the rise to Shrivenham; Swindon, 20.7 miles, was passed in 22 min 20 sec and the remaining 29.6 miles to Bath were covered in $26\frac{1}{2}$ minutes. The engine was eased a little down Dauntsey bank, not exceeding 74 mph, and speed fell away to 65 mph after the Avon crossing. But then the driver opened up again, and on the 1 in 660 rise to Corsham speed rose to $69\frac{1}{2}$ mph. So the 50.3 miles from Steventon signal box to Bath were run in 48 min 50 sec start-to-stop—a most enterprising piece of work.

Taking the story through to the year 1954, to the time when important improvements had been made to the 'King' Class engines, as will be told in the final chapter of this book, I had an engine pass to ride the 'Cornish Riviera Express' right through from Paddington to Penzance, and while a tender full of indifferent coal on the 'King' made the first part less good than it ought to have been, at Plymouth we exchanged the London engine for *County of Middlesex*. This engine was in excellent form, and although two heavy permanent way slacks were in operation, we arrived in Penzance a minute early. The working over the Cornish road is less familiar to those who compile logs of train running, and I have prepared a tabulation overleaf so that the details of our progress may be followed in relation to the steep and constantly changing gradients of the line. The load was one of eight coaches throughout, well patronized with passengers, even though it was late in October.

The stiff climbing to the summit at Doublebois station begins at the crossing of the viaduct over Lynher creek, about $1\frac{1}{2}$ miles before St Germans, but it is very broken, and in three stages: to milepost 258; from Menheniot; and finally from Moorswater Viaduct, beyond Liskeard, up to milepost 267. On the three stages the maximum cut-offs used, with the main valve of the regulator about $\frac{5}{8}$ full open, were 35, 30 and 27 per cent, though the engine had been eased on the second ascent to observe a permanent way restriction. The gradients are between 1 in 75 and 1 in 65. The engine was steaming freely and we topped the final ascent with a pressure of 270 psi. After a second perma-

Above right *No 1014* County of Glamorgan *at Ranelagh Bridge Yard, Paddington, having worked up on the 9 am from Bristol.* (O.S. Nock)

Right *The pioneer 'County', No 1000, on the 1.15 pm Paddington to Weston-super-Mare train passing Wootton Bassett.* (M.W. Earley)

GWR: 'Cornish Riviera Express', Plymouth–Penzance

Engine 1000 *County of Middlesex*
Load 8 coaches, 272 tons tare, 290 tons full

Distance (miles)		Schedule (min)	Actual (m s)	Speed (mph)
0.0	PLYMOUTH (NORTH ROAD)	0	0 00	—
2.2	Keyham		4 56	54
4.2	Saltash	8½	9 11	10
7.9	Milepost 255		—	60
9.3	St Germans		16 19	43
10.9	Milepost 258		19 34	28
14.7	Menheniot		25 04	53
—			pws	—
16.4	Milepost 263½		27 31	—
17.8	LISKEARD	28	29 47	52
19.9	Milepost 267		33 00	31
21.1	Doublebois		35 03	42/38
—			pws	15
26.9	BODMIN ROAD	41	43 45	60
30.4	Lostwithiel		47 33	51
31.9	Milepost 279		49 46	39
34.7	PAR	52	54 00	—
1.2	Milepost 283		2 47	41
4.5	ST AUSTELL	10	10 03	22½
6.9	Burngullow		14 51	60(max)
11.3	Grampound Road		19 43	41
13.7	Probus		22 27	65
15.7	Milepost 297½		24 45	41
17.2	Milepost 299		26 56	55
19.0	TRURO	29	29 35	—
0.6	*Penwithers Junction*	2	2 13	35
2.2	Milepost 303		4 55	31½
4.2	Milepost 305		8 47	31
5.2	Chacewater	9	10 20	47
6.2	Milepost 307		11 49	40½
9.0	Redruth		16 10	—
11.1	Carn Brea		18 45	54
12.7	Camborne	20	20 40	—
15.2	GWINEAR ROAD	24	23 50	—
3.4	Hayle		4 47	60(max)
5.0	ST ERTH	7	7 05	—
3.7	Marazion		6 10	56(max)
5.6	PENZANCE	10	9 53	—

nent way slack to 15 mph at Largin Viaduct, we reached 60 mph briefly on the downhill run to Lostwithiel, but for the most part speeds were much less than this. We passed Lostwithiel at 51 mph and so got a 'run' at the stiff 2 miles up to Treverrin Tunnel—1 in 72-64—on which the maximum cut-off used was 32 per cent. Because of the two permanent way checks we had dropped 2 minutes on schedule from Plymouth to Par, but the net time was no more than 51 minutes.

The climb from Par Harbour up to Trenance Viaduct is always one of the toughest parts of the westbound run through Cornwall, and here the engine was handled with skill. On the easy stretch from the start to the Harbour signal box we attained 41 mph, and we began the main climb, mostly at 1 in 60, with pressure at 275 psi and 30 per cent cut-off. Then for the most part we were working in 35 per cent. Pressure was at one time down to 255, but this was rallied to a full 280 as we neared St Austell, even though cut-off was advanced there to 38 per cent. Speed was mostly at 24 to 25 mph on the bank, though on one of the sharper curves we fell to 22½ mph. We topped the bank at Trenance with 270 psi on the gauge, and then took the downhill-biased switchback to Truro under easier steam.

The 3-mile climb at 1 in 80 from Penwithers Junction is another testing length. There, with cut-off advanced from 26 to 36 per cent, we did splendidly, not falling below 31 mph. No fast running is possible through the mining areas of Redruth and Camborne, and we ran easily downhill to Penponds Viaduct and into our stop at Gwinear Road. The subsequent steeply downhill piece to St Erth was taken mostly without steam, and at a speed not exceeding 60 mph. There is three-quarters of a mile of hard pulling from the restart, at 1 in 67, and the engine was worked in 50 per cent cut-off briefly; but then we ran easily down to Marazion, not exceeding 56 mph, and finishing into Penzance a minute early by the clock. The station allowance at St Erth was then 4 minutes, and that we did not need. The engine had steamed freely throughout and the working appeared to be economical.

To see the 'Counties' at their most thrilling, however, one had to ride the heavier of the Birkenhead trains between Wolverhampton and Shrewsbury. There one had the combination of a fast road, steep switchback gradients, and loads that were often near the 500-ton mark. The drivers of the Wolverhampton (Stafford Road) No 2 link became experts in the handling of the 'Counties', exercising the technique of building up a full head of steam, and then briefly using it at a rate that the boiler could not sustain for long. This technique was the only explanation for some of the almost phenomenal ascents of the Shifnal bank on the northbound run.

The gradients need a word of explanation. From Wolverhampton Low Level station the sharply curved line is downhill at 1 in 100 past Stafford Road sheds and Oxley sidings, and then it undulates with an upward tendency to milepost 148 (from Paddington via Oxford). Then comes the racing descent through Albrighton, followed by the formidable Shifnal bank—2 miles at 1 in 180 and then nearly 3 miles at 1 in 100 up to Hollinswood sidings. The rest is downhill into Wellington, but one can rarely attain any high speed, in readiness for making a particularly awkward station stop.

My first run on the 11.10 am from Paddington was on No 1029 *County of Worcester* with a 455-ton load. We got away with tremendous vigour, reaching 60 mph when no more than 3½ miles out; the engine was steaming so freely that the driver, using 20 per cent cut-off, was able to ease on to the first valve for the next stage, carrying the rise to milepost 148 at 53 mph and dashing up to 75 mph down Albrighton bank. Having passed Cosford, 9.2 miles, in the fast time of 11 min 10 sec, it was not until Shifnal station that the driver opened out on to the main valve of the regulator, and we topped Hollinswood summit at 36 mph. Despite a signal check at the finish we kept the 24-minute timing from Wolverhampton to Wellington. Then came a trip never to be forgotten on No 1016 *County of Hants*, with that master driver, Bert Griffiths, and a load of exactly 500 tons. There was a permanent way check right at the start which cost us about half a minute in running. We had some leeway to make up at once, and Griffiths set about it with a vengeance. Main regulator and 25 per cent cut-off with the engine quivering like a live thing took us up to 60 mph below Oxley, and over the summit at milepost 148 at 56 mph. But we were 1½ minutes down on *County of Worcester*'s time at Albrighton.

Down the bank Griffiths eased her on to the first valve, though no more than briefly; but at the very foot of the decline, when we were going at 73 mph, he changed over to main valve. The effect was terrific. The pulsation went right through your body; the exhaust sharpened into a roar, with the engine now developing over 2,000 ihp. The boiler could not stand such a demand for steam for very long, but Griffiths was magnificently backed up by his fireman. At the foot of the bank we had 270 psi on the gauge and when, passing Shifnal at 60 mph, the regulator was opened to the full we still had 250. But the 3 miles of tremendous pounding up to Hollinswood took their toll, and we topped the summit at 38½ mph with pressure down to 210. But we gained three-quarters of a minute on *County of Worcester* between Codsall and Hollinswood and would have kept our 24-minute timing to Wellington but for a signal check at the finish. Once over the top, pressure in the boiler rose rapidly, and was 280 psi when we were ready to leave Wellington. It was a tremendous and thrilling demonstration of the capacity of the 'Counties', doing a job for which they were ideally suited.

No 1029 County of Worcester *on the 9.20 am Bournemouth West to Birkenhead train near Hatton.* (R. Blenkinsop)

My appreciation of the sterling work of the 'Counties' on these trains was, however, slightly tempered one day when I was travelling up to Chester and joined the 9.10 am from Paddington at Birmingham. To my surprise our fresh engine, from Wolverhampton, was not a 'County' but a 'Saint', and this in the days of the nationalized railways: engine No 2926 *Saint Nicholas* with a load of 480 tons. I would dearly have liked to have been on the footplate on this occasion, but my authority only applied to the southbound run. For here was the engine design from which the whole Great Western two-cylinder 4-6-0 family was descended, and still in superb form. This old engine kept the 24-minute timing to Wellington, doing 75 mph down the Albrighton bank and topping Hollinswood at 38½ mph, the same as *County of Hants*. It left me wondering vaguely if any real progress had been made in the 30 years since Churchward perfected the design of his two-cylinder 4-6-0. The engine was in deplorable external condition, with hardly a vestige of any sort of painting showing through the coating of grime; but what a run—with a 480-ton load.

21. Hawksworth's years—Phase 2

It was in the last year of the Second World War that I made an entrée into the inner circles of the Locomotive Department of the Great Western Railway. By the introduction of a penfriend in Chicago I was asked by the editor of an American journal to write something about British locomotives in wartime, quoting from experience on the footplate. For me this was easier said than done. The time was midsummer 1944. My regular professional work at Westinghouse was involving at least six days a week, with a Saturday free about once a month, if I was lucky. As to the war itself, while following the Normandy landings the Allied armies were slowly fighting their way eastwards across France, London and the south-east of England were being plagued by the flying bomb attacks, and railway services were frequently disrupted. It was not likely that any railway would issue footplate passes under such conditions, and I could not spare the time to travel to the northern lines, and Scotland. Then it occurred to me that the West to North route of the GWR would provide a good example, particularly as I knew the Newton Abbot–Shrewsbury double-home turns were usually provided with 'Castles' in good condition. I wrote to Hawksworth explaining what I had been asked to do, and in a very short time a letter arrived saying, formally, that 'arrangements can be made . . .'

On the Friday evening before the first of the appointed days I went down to Newton Abbot full of apprehension. The war was still raging in all its fury; the blackout and the attendant security was as intense as ever. But when I walked over to the station next morning, and saw *Usk Castle* polished as though she was going to take a Royal special, and I met the men who were to be my companions for most of the day, I felt like a boy who has been let out of school! I wrote extensively of my experiences, judging that my American editor would want something for his money, and in due course the script that I had submitted came back from Swindon with no comment except approval. I was interested to see Hawksworth in his letter referred to it as 'The Paper', as if it were a technical treatise, rather

Above left *Series '5098' 'Castle' Class 4-6-0 No 7000* Viscount Portal *leaving Teignmouth with the 9.45 am up to Liverpool and Manchester.* (O.S. Nock)

Left *Another of the 'three row' engines, No 7003* Elmley Castle *on the 'Pembroke Coast Express' near Brinkworth.* (P.M. Alexander)

than a somewhat gossipy account of some personal experiences. Not till many years later did I learn that on receipt of my draft article he had sent a small team from the locomotive testing section of the Drawing Office to check up on what I had written on the two trains I had ridden. After that, apparently, anything I liked to ask for was agreed to immediately! It was not until many months later that I met Hawksworth personally, in the lounge of the Great Western Royal Hotel at Paddington, when I was engaged on another project. A much abridged version of the piece I wrote for the USA was published in *The Railway Magazine* in 1945.

In May 1946 Hawksworth turned out the first batch of 'Castles' with three-row superheaters, the '5098' Class as they became known. Their numbers ran from 5098 and 5099, and from 7000 to 7007, but the first two differed from the rest, and indeed from the subsequent engines in the '7000' series, in retaining the sight-feed hydrostatic lubricators that had been standard on the GWR since Churchward's time. The engines from 7000 upwards had mechanical lubricators, which at first brought problems of their own. In accordance with prevailing fashions elsewhere, it was intended to take the responsibility for regulating oil supply out of the hands of the driver and provide a carefully metered flow precisely to suit the needs of the engine. But the sight-feed lubricator was 'the breath of life' to Great Western enginemen; they had grown up with it, and were experts in its manipulation, and very soon there were complaints that the '7000' Class were sluggish in comparison. The constrast was perhaps worsened because the first two engines, Nos 5098 and 5099, were exceptionally powerful and free-running. Lubricators apart, however, the comparative boiler proportions of the new engines as compared to those of the original standard 'Castles' were as follows:

Class	**'4073'**	**'5098'**
Small tubes		
Number	197	170
Outside diameter (in)	2	2
Flues		
Number	14	21
Outside diameter (in)	$5\frac{1}{8}$	$5\frac{1}{8}$
Elements		
Number	84	84
Outside diameter (in)	1	$1\frac{1}{4}$
Heating surface (sq ft)		
Tubes	1,858	1,800
Firebox	163	164
Superheater elements	263	313
Total	2,284	2,277

By the time the '5098' Class was introduced, S.O. Ell had succeeded Roberts as engineer in charge of locomotive testing, and he, working on the principles established before the war by Roberts and elaborating them, carried out some of the most comprehensive trials to which British locomotives had ever been subjected, not only with the new three-row superheated 'Castles' but with a standard 'Castle', No 5087 *Tintern Abbey*, and with No 5046 *Earl of Plymouth* which had been fitted experimentally with a four-row superheater. Undoubtedly engine No 5098 *Clifford Castle* was the 'flower of the flock' among Great Western engines at the time, and once the Swindon tests were completed she was allocated to the Newton Abbot Division, and became much in demand for Ocean Mail Specials, non-stop from Plymouth Millbay Docks to Paddington. Before this, however, it is interesting to study some of the fascinatingly precise results that were obtained with this same engine on the stationary test plant in Swindon Works. It has often been considered that measurement of coal consumption by drawbar horsepower hour eliminated much of the variation in driving technique and effects of incidental delays, and reduced engine performance to a common yardstick by which direct comparison could be made between one locomotive and another. This was certainly not so, as clearly shown by the carefully controlled test results from *one engine*, No 5098 *Clifford Castle*.

With Hawksworth's approval Sam Ell gave me a number of graphs showing the performance of this engine in test house conditions, and from these I have prepared some tables that show the working results in different conditions of running. The maximum rate of evaporation that was determined with engine No 5098 was approximately 24,000 lbs of steam per hour. This is equivalent to a firing rate of 86 lbs of coal per sq ft of grate area per hour, comfortably inside the limit of 3 tons per hour which was the maximum firing rate agreed between British Railways and the Unions as the most any fireman could be expected to sustain. At a firing rate of 86 lbs of coal per sq ft of grate area per hour, Ell and his men determined the following performance figures for the '5098' Class on a rising gradient of 1 in 200:

Load behind tender (tons tare)	**Speed (mph)**	**Coal per dph hour (lbs)**	**Coal per train mile (lbs)**
254	60	3.6	45
326	55	3.3	49
399	50	3.15	54
472	45	3.0	60
544	40	2.8	67.5

One the Great Western main lines it is difficult to find any length of continuously rising gradients except on the Ashendon Junction–Aynho cut-off of the shortened main line to Birmingham, opened in 1910. The above details of coal consumption per drawbar horsepower hour are revealing of how the often-assumed 'common yardstick' varied.

The variations were even more striking in the case of a reduced rate of firing, 57 lbs per sq ft of grate area on level track, thus:

Load behind tender (tons tare)	Speed (mph)	Coal per dph hour (lbs)	Coal per train mile (lbs)
254	71	3.5	25
326	64.5	3.17	27.5
399	60.5	2.95	29.5
472	58.5	2.8	30.25
544	55	2.7	32.5

The speeds run on the 'Cheltenham Flyer' and the 'Bristolian' take on a new significance when it comes to relating the coal consumption to the speeds, as determined in Swindon tests at the maximum evaporation rate of 24,000 lb per hour on engine No. 5098, on level track:

Load behind tender (tons tare)	Speed (mph)	Coal per dph hour (lbs)	Coal per train mile (lbs)
254	86.5	4.3	37.5
326	82	3.8	39.2
399	78.75	3.5	41.8
472	73.75	3.2	45.0
544	69.5	3.1	45.0

Before the introduction of the 'Kings', engines of the 'Castle' Class, and sometimes even the 'Stars', were frequently to run the 'Cornish Riviera Express' with its full load of 14 coaches between Paddington and Westbury, a tare load of about the 472 tons quoted in the above table. With 'Castles' starting cold out of Paddington, the speeds on the level track to Reading rarely if ever reached such maxima as 73.75 mph, but if they did, in ordinary working conditions one could expect the coal consumption not to exceed about 45 lbs per mile—a remarkable tribute to the efficiency of the design.

Hawksworth also applied his higher superheater technique to the 'Kings' and the first time I was privileged to see the Stationary Test Plant in action, engine No 6022 *King Edward III*, recently fitted with a four-row superheater, was being put through some exhaustive trials. This was in 1947, and it was then that I first met Sam Ell and his men. I gathered from the enthusiastic attitude of all concerned that the project was proving a great success, but then the whole outlook of Great Western men was becoming overshadowed by the prospect of impending nationalization, which was to take place at the end of that same year. Overall responsibility for locomotive affairs passed away from Swindon, and there was instituted, early in 1948, the elaborate and far-reaching series of Interchange Trials between express passenger, mixed traffic and heavy goods designs of the former independent railway companies using the very hit-or-miss methods which the responsible engineers of the Great Western Railway had abandoned for ever in the 'thirties. It was small wonder that Swindon took so little interest in it, particularly when it was implied that if Hawksworth himself wished to accompany any of the trains he should apply to the boffins of the new Railway Executive for permission to ride in his own dynamometer car!

While the Interchange Trials had some psychological value in bringing together in a corporate national activity engineers of all the former independent railways, technically it was a monument of wasted effort. Later, when Riddles and his staff at the Railway Executive had time to examine the principles underlying the Great Western practice of locomotive testing, it was adopted in its entirety for British Railways, not merely at Swindon but at the new National Testing Laboratory at Rugby. In the meantime, after the somewhat indifferent showing the ex-GWR representatives made in the Interchange Trials, Hawksworth's engines were doing splendidly in their own right. I was given a footplate pass to ride the high-superheat 'King'

Left *The down 'Cornish Riviera Express' near Reading West in 1947, with engine No 6025* King Henry III *and the Author on the footplate.* (M.W. Earley)

Above right *Four-row superheated No 6022* King Edward III *ready to leave Paddington with the 3.30 pm West of England express in 1949; the author and Inspector Pullen with the crew.* (W.J. Reynolds)

Right *Later the same day, No 6022 with the 3.30 pm nearing Southcote Junction.* (M.W. Earley)

No 6022 *King Edward III* in 1949, going down from Paddington to Plymouth on the 3.30 pm and returning by the up 'Limited' next day. Although the running times were not as fast as they became later, the performance was most impressive. I wrote a long piece for my *British Locomotives from the Footplate*, which was published in 1950, and while the basic details were as there set down, it was the economical working of the engine that was the most lasting memory of the two-day round trip.

On the 3.30 pm down we took a 13-coach 450-ton load out of Paddington, and slipped the two coaches for Weymouth at Heywood Road Junction, 94.6 miles, in 96½ minutes. Castle Cary, 115.1 miles, was passed 4½ minutes early, in 116½ minutes, and despite a heavy permanent way check near Langport we reached Taunton, 142.9 miles, in 146¾ minutes. Restarting, still with the load of 375 tons which we had brought forward from Heywood Road Junction, we made a very fast ascent to Whiteball Tunnel, passing Wellington at 56½ mph and not falling below 41 mph in the tunnel. This driver seemed a specialist in hard uphill running, as was then necessary to keep the booked times, because of the restriction in maximum speeds still enforced by the Civil Engineer, as a result of wartime conditions of running, and of the exceptionally severe weather of January–March 1947. From Exeter, with the load reduced to no more than seven coaches, it was easy work as far as Newton Abbot, but then our driver opened the engine out with tremendous vigour for the formidable South Devon banks, clearing Dainton without falling below 31 mph, and Rattery at a minimum of 34½ mph on the steepest pitch. So we passed Brent 3½ minutes early, and could run easily down into Plymouth.

Next morning I went down to Laira shed to see the engine being prepared to work the up 'Cornish Riviera Express'. We were advised that the load would be 13 coaches throughout to Paddington, so that we should require a bank engine from Plymouth to Newton Abbot. Inspector Pullen, who had ridden down with me from Paddington, told me that in replenishing the tender they had put on roughly 4 tons of coal, and this including lighting up, represented our approximate consumption on the westbound journey. This was an inclusive figure of about 39 lbs per train mile. When engine No 6022 was requisitioned for further trials, after the main Interchange tests of 1948, with heavier trains than mine, the coal consumption was about 43 lbs per mile, when allowance was made for lighting up. If the same ratio of water to coal is taken as on the test trip of 1948, and the engine proved most consistent in

Below *The four-row superheater 4-6-0 No 6022* King Edward III *at Laira shed, ready to work the up 'Cornish Riviera Express'.* (O.S. Nock)

this respect, the consumption on my trip on the 3.30 pm with its most vigorous hill-climbing, works out at about 36 lbs per train mile—a very notable result.

On the up 'Limited' we had a 'Grange' as bank engine as far as Newton Abbot, and with the easy going round the subsequent coastal stretch there was little to record so far as engine performance was concerned until we left Exeter. The schedule then in force, allowing 191 minutes for the non-stop run of 173.5 miles to Paddington, with its average speed of 54.3 mph, may seem slow by previous standards; and although maximum speeds were still limited to 75 mph over much of the route, where there were not still tighter restrictions, the West of England main line was never as much of a speedway as certain sections of the Birmingham line were in pre-war years, as will be evident from Chapter 18 of this book. But as on the previous day, the driver of No 6022 did some splendid work uphill, passing Whiteball summit in 23 min 58 sec from the Exeter start, and equally in climbing the Bruton bank and from the Westbury district to Savernake. Here we were running 4½ minutes early, having climbed the 24.5 miles from Heywood Junction to Savernake in 25 minutes.

Down the Kennet valley we were in such good time that the maximum speed anywhere was 64 mph, though in the one place where a higher speed than 75 mph was permitted, from Whiteball tunnel down to Taunton, our driver gave us a pleasant little spin up to a maximum of 82 mph. Passing Reading in 144¾ minutes from Exeter, having dawdled down from Savernake in just over 35 minutes for the 34.1 miles, I could not help recalling my very first trip on the 'Limited', 25 years earlier, when *Malvern Abbey* brought us down in 29¾ minutes! On my run of 1949 we continued pleasantly, with no higher speed than 67 mph at Slough; and with 4 minutes recovery time in the schedule which we did not need we finished into Paddington 8¼ minutes early. Had we run from Reading in the style of *Malvern Abbey* in 1924, we could have cut a further 6 minutes off the time and been in Paddington in 176¾ minutes from Exeter! As it was, the performance data gave some striking figures. In making this run at an average speed of 57 mph from Exeter, the main valve of the regulator was open for only 32½ per cent of the total mileage, while for 147 out of the 173½ miles no more than 15 per cent cut-off was used. The water consumption, as given by careful readings of the tender gauge, was almost exactly 5,000 gallons, showing no more than 29 gallons per mile. Taking the same ratio for coal to water as indicated in the dynamometer car trials of December 1948, this suggests a coal consumption of no more than 32 to 33 lbs per mile.

Following this run Mr Hawksworth made arrangements for me to ride on some of the latest 'Castles' with the three-row superheater boiler, notably No 5098 *Clifford Castle*. It was not long after my trips on engine No 6022 that No 5098 made the notable runs with the Ocean Mail specials referred to previously in this chapter, and in sending the authority to ride on this very engine Mr Hawksworth was kind enough to give me copies of the Locomotive Inspector's reports on two very fine runs on those boat trains, reproduced on page 211. The first occasion, on which a load 303 tons tare was taken without assistance over the South Devon Line, was the first time since the war that a time of exactly 4 hours had been made between Plymouth North Road and Paddington. On the second occasion the load was heavy enough to need a bank engine over the South Devon line, but the one engine hauled the train of 338 tons tare over the 193.7 miles between Newton Abbot and Paddington in 195½ minutes, non-stop. The first train was delayed by signals between Castle Cary and Heywood Road Junction, resulting in an average speed of only 51.4 mph against the 61.8 mph of the second train between those two timing points.

My own trip with *Clifford Castle* was made on the 9.45 am from Newton Abbot to Shrewsbury, a double-home job for the crew, in this case a highly competent Newton pair. The long northbound run of 6 hr 7 min involved some hard work for engine and crew and a lot of notetaking for me. The day can be summarized thus:

Length of journey	216½ miles
Booked time, including stops	367 minutes
Left Newton Abbot	3 late
Arrived at Shrewsbury	6½ late
Actual time, including stops	370½ minutes
Booked running time	312 minutes
Actual running time	319 minutes
Net running time	295 minutes
Net average speed	44 mph
Water consumption	38 gallons per mile
Coal consumption (estimated)	40–42 lbs per mile
Coal per sq ft of grate area per hour of running time	56 lbs

The day's work could well be set down as a classic spectrum of the work allowed to the 'Castle' engines, including the high-speed running in which they excelled, and the slow grinding efforts on severe mountain gradients, on which they did not show up too well. The complete logs were published in the publication previously referred to, but now I have chosen portions of the complete story which show vividly both the strength and the weakness of the engines. Because of a

An up Bristol express east of Twyford hauled by engine No 7034 Ince Castle. (M.W. Earley)

comparison I wish to make with the performance of another engine of the class that I experienced on a later occasion, I am taking the less flattering part of the Newton–Salop journey first, that from Pontypool Road to Hereford. I must not be misunderstood in my strictures. The engine and crew dealt with this stage as competently as everywhere else. It was just that the engine did not seem able to climb a heavy bank as well as the basic dimensions would lead one to expect. The log of that part of the journey is shown overleaf.

The start, downhill on 1 in 104 to Little Mill Junction, was rapid; in less than 2 miles we were doing 59 mph, but after Nantyderry steam was shut off on the 1 in 80 descent, for the crossing of the Usk valley at Penpergwm. This slack, coming right at the foot of the climb to Llanvihangel, imposed a severe handicap with heavy trains; if the road had been suitable, the dip from Nantyderry could have been taken at 70 or even 75 mph, and the subsequent ascent taken much less laboriously. On this particular trip we reduced to 46 mph through Penpergwm, and although the driver opened out to full regulator and 25 per cent cut-off immediately we were through the station and on to the 1 in 150 grade that followed, the speed had fallen away to 40 mph when we passed Abergavenny and entered upon the really stiff part of the climb where the rise was 1 in 82. The point-to-point times scheduled over this section certainly took good account of this disadvantage, and there was no need to press the engine in order to keep sectional time. The driver had begun opening out before we passed Abergavenny Junction, and he went up, step by step, to 35 per cent. But the speed was already in the twenties before he started advancing the cut-off, and even his final increase, to 39 per cent, made no undue demand upon the boiler. At the top of the 1 in 82 pitch we were down to 17½ mph and with no change in the controls the engine recovered to 22 mph on the final 2 miles of 1 in 95 leading to the summit. Then we got away once more in characteristic style, and with 19 per cent cut-off and only the first valve of the regulator open, we swept down into the Monnow

BR(W): Ocean Mail Specials, Plymouth–Paddington

Engine No 5098 *Clifford Castle*

Date		26 August 1949		13 September 1949	
Load (tons tare)		303		338*	
Distance (miles)		**Time (min)**	**Average speed (mph)**	**Time (min)**	**Average speed (mph)**
0.0	Plymouth Dock Gates	0		0	
0.9	Plymouth North Road	3	18.0	3	18.0
24.0	Totnes	36	42.0	37	40.8
32.8	Newton Abbot	49	40.6	49 arr	43.8
				52 dep	
52.8	Exeter	73	50.3	76½	49.3
83.7	Taunton	104	59.6	110	55.2
111.2	Castle Cary	129	66.0	134½	67.4
131.8	Heywood Road Junction	153	51.4	154½	61.8
160.0	Bedwyn	179	65.0	182	61.5
190.4	Reading	208	62.9	209½	66.4
226.4	Paddington	243†	61.7	247½	56.9

* assisted by engine No 5060 from Plymouth to Newton Abbot
† Net time 239 minutes

GWR: Pontypool Road–Hereford

Engine No 5098 *Clifford Castle*
Load 13 coaches, 421 tons tare, 460 tons full

Distance (miles)		Schedule (min)	Actual (m	s)	Speed (mph)
0.0	Pontypool Rd	0	0	00	—
1.6	Little Mill Junction		2	42	59
4.2	Nantyderry		5	29	51/56
6.8	Penpergwm		8	29	60/46
9.5	Abergavenny	12	12	23	17
13.5	Llanvihangel	22	23	00	22
15.9	Pandy		25	54	74
21.0	Pontrilas	31	30	22	57
26.8	Tram Inn		36	20	63
30.1	Red Hill Junction	41	39	52	—
33.5	Hereford	47	45	15	

valley, passing Pandy at 66 mph and touching 74 half a mile farther on. At this point steam was shut off altogether, and No 5098 coasted freely down to the crossing of the river, where rising grades begin once more. Directly we were round the curve through Pontrilas the regulator was opened to the full; the gradually rising stretch past St Devereux and Tram Inn was taken fast, with speed rising to 63 mph, and then, with the usual cautious approach, we came into Hereford in 45¼ minutes from Pontypool Road, 33.5 miles. I have known considerably faster times over this section, even with loads of this magnitude, though these were made in days when Penpergwm curve was taken very much faster. Actually our tare load on this trip was 1 ton over the maximum of 420 scheduled for the 'Castle' class on the northbound ascent to Llanvihangel.

Although keeping the working times of the train, the performance of the engine on the ascent to Llanvihangel was not particularly impressive seeing how far the cut-off had been advanced. My assessment of the work at this stage of the run had been tempered by receipt of details of a wartime run over the same route clocked by Mr D.S.M. Barrie, later Chairman and General Manager of the Eastern Region of British Railways. Barrie was travelling in a train loaded almost as heavily as on my footplate run, 450 tons, but hauled not by a 'Castle' but by a 'Saint', No 2949 *Stanford Court*. The minimum speed on the 1 in 82 section of the Llanvihangel bank was 28 mph with an increase to 31 mph on the 1 in 95 leading to the summit. In all probability the boiler was being somewhat mortgaged to provide steam for such an effort, while on *Clifford Castle* pressure was maintained at 'sizzling point' throughout the ascent.

To show *Clifford Castle* at her most brilliant I have tabulated a little later the log of her running between Exeter and Taunton, and alongside are details of another outstanding run with the last but one of the '5098s', No 7036 *Taunton Castle*. The background to the run was that to supplement my footplate experiences on the 'Castles' which also included a successful run on one of the Wolverhampton–West of England trains, arrangements had been made for me to ride on one, *Taunton Castle*, on the 3.30 pm from Paddington to

The 4.10 pm Plymouth to Paddington express on Cogload Junction troughs, hauled by 'Castle' Class 4-6-0 No 5050 Earl of Berkeley. (K.H. Leech)

Western Region: 3.30 pm Paddington–Plymouth

Engine No 7036 *Taunton Castle*
Load 7 coaches, 241 tons tare, 260 tons full

Distance (miles)		Schedule (min)	Actual (m s)	Speed (mph)
0.0	Exeter	0	0 00	—
4.7	Exminster		6 50	62
—			pw check	15
12.2	Dawlish		16 05	56
15.0	Teignmouth		19 44	52
—			—	60
20.2	Newton Abbot	25	25 37	slack
21.3	Aller Junction		27 12	—
22.0	Milepost 216		28 05	56
23.0	Milepost 217		29 25	44
24.0	Milepost 218 Dainton box	32½	31 22	27½
28.8	Totnes	39½	37 06	63
30.0	Milepost 224		39 01	30
31.0	Milepost 225		41 24	24
32.0	Milepost 226		43 23	32
33.4	Rattery box	49	45 06	—
35.7	Brent	52	48 16	55½
—			pw slack	15
37.9	Wrangaton		51 55	—
41.2	Ivybridge		55 57	53/40
45.3	Hemerdon box	64	60 14	68
48.0	Plympton		62 27	82
50.5	Lipson Junction	71	65 19	—
52.0	Plymouth North Road	75	68 37	—

Plymouth. As far as Taunton the working had been immaculate, but then trouble began. The 'Devonian', which was running late, had her timing worsened by a freight train being allowed to precede her up Wellington bank. Both expresses were delayed, and we, running close behind the 'Devonian', reached Exeter 8 minutes late. Although the station staff there saved us a minute, the other train had left only just ahead of us, and had to make station stops at Dawlish and Teignmouth, while we were booked non-stop from Exeter to Plymouth—what a hope! Indeed, the Old Oak Locomotive Inspector who was riding with us forecast an arrival 20 minutes late in Plymouth.

But now fortune smiled upon us. The 'Devonian' was put into Dawlish Warren loop out of our way, and with this encouragement the men on *Taunton Castle* really went for it, and made the brilliant run tabulated above. Cut-off was advanced to a maximum of 40 per cent on Dainton bank, and to 35 per cent going up Rattery, but progress was hampered by a further permanent way slack after Brent, and after we had passed the summit of this part of the line, at Wrangaton, there was still the permanent speed restriction to 40 mph on the curve over Ivybridge viaduct, where incidentally a 'Star' running late took me, on the 'Cornish Riviera Express', at an unchecked 64 mph! Once past Ivybridge the line becomes straighter and is actually so down Hemerdon bank. On this exciting run I clocked a maximum of 82 mph before Plympton, but in the report I wrote at the time, because of the overall maximum enforced over most of the Western Region at the time, I originally stated the top speed there was briefly 77½ mph. There was no objection to this. Eventually we rode into Plymouth with the station clocks pointing precisely to 8 pm, right time, but by my watch our actual overall time from Paddington was 4 hr 30 min 27 sec, a trifling excess. Our net time from Exeter was 65 minutes, 10 minutes inside schedule. The driver and fireman who had worked down on the 3.30 pm were booked to take the 'Dutchman' next morning, 8.30 am from Plymouth Millbay. Usually, in deference to its normal load, it had a 'King', but our driver was so impressed with *Taunton Castle* that he asked for her again,

Below *No 7036* Taunton Castle *on a running-in turn from Swindon, at Chippenham,* (K.H. Leech)

Bottom *No 6001* King Edward VII *climbing Hemerdon bank with the 11 am ex-Plymouth to Paddington express.* (M.W. Earley)

Western Region: Exeter–Taunton

Train			9.45 ex-Newton		Up 'Dutchman'	
Engine No			5098		7036	
Engine Name			*Clifford Castle*		*Taunton Castle*	
Load (tons E/F)			421/460		460/500	
Distance (miles)		**Schedule (min)**	**Actual (m s)**	**Speed (mph)**	**Actual (m s)**	**Speed (mph)**
0.0	Exeter	0	0 00	—	0 00	—
1.3	Cowley Bridge		2 58	—	3 41	—
3.4	Stoke Canon		5 58	49½	6 45	48½
7.2	Silverton		10 17	56	11 05	55
12.6	Cullompton		15 51	60	16 45	59
14.6	Tiverton Junction		18 14	55/60½	19 16	50½/57½
18.9	Milepost 176		sigs	—	22 43	51½
—			pw			
19.9	Whiteball box	26	24 50	28	25 29	37½
23.7	Wellington		29 43	78	29 19	77½
26.9	Milepost 167		32 06	84	31 47	82
28.8	Norton Fitzwarren		33 38	70½	pw	15
30.8	Taunton	38	37 08		36 50	

even though he was warned that they would have a load of '14' from Newton Abbot. I travelled passenger by the train myself as far as Westbury, whence there was a convenient connection to Chippenham.

But now to the details of this up run as between Exeter and Taunton tabulated alongside that of *Clifford Castle* on the 9.45 am up from Newton Abbot. The latter engine made a really brilliant start from Exeter, as she had also from Teignmouth. From Exeter full forward gear and 75 per cent cut-off was used for the first 150 yards, then 45 per cent, and in half a mile from the start 35 per cent. By that time the regulator had been successively opened until at the half-mile point it was wide open. *Taunton Castle* with the 500-ton train was not hustled away as rapidly as this, and she was ¾ minute behind *Clifford Castle* by Stoke Canon; but making allowance for the difference in loads there was little difference in the running thereafter. *Clifford Castle*, which had been worked in 25 per cent cut-off from about a mile out of Exeter, was still doing 48½ mph within a mile of Whiteball summit, when signals and then the relaying slack delayed us. Not being on the footplate I did not know how *Taunton Castle* was being worked; but she kept the sectional time up to Whiteball and made merry down towards Taunton thereafter. *Clifford Castle* ran even faster, touching 84 mph below Wellington, and clipping nearly a minute off the sectional time from Exeter, despite the check at Whiteball.

On the 'Dutchman', when we arrived at Taunton the Traffic Department had yet another coach to add to the train and because they had been advised that a 'Castle' and not a 'King' was on the job, they had a bank engine ready to couple on and assist. But our driver and fireman disdained the idea of any such assistance, and we went on with the huge load of 535 tons. I recalled the occasion almost 25 years earlier when I was travelling on the 5.8 pm up from Newton Abbot, and our load was made up to *16* at Taunton, 514 tons tare, and this load was taken without assistance by the 'Star' Class 4-6-0 then named *King Richard*, as told in Chapter 14. The continuation of my

Western Region, Up 'Dutchman'

Engine No 7036 *Taunton Castle*
Load 15 coaches, 490 tons tare, 535 tons full

Distance (miles)		Schedule (min)	Actual (m s)	Speed (mph)
0.0	Taunton	0	0 00	—
2.4	Creech Junction	4	4 30	51
8.0	Athelney		10 18	62/59
11.9	Curry Rivel Junction		14 17	61½
17.1	Somerton		19 54	53
20.5	Charlton Mackrell		23 14	63½/67
22.7	Keinton Mandeville		25 26	66½
27.5	Castle Cary	31	30 03	58
29.1	Milepost 128		31 39	60
30.1	Milepost 127		32 42	56
31.1	Bruton		33 42	52½
32.1	Milepost 125		35 04	48
33.1	Milepost 124		36 21	46½
34.1	Milepost 123		37 45	40
34.35	Milepost 122¾		38 20	34½
40.4	Blatchbridge Junction	46	44 16	72
42.4	Clink Road Junction	48½	46 01	64½
45.7	Fairwood Junction	52½	49 01	72
47.2	Westbury	55	51 39	

run on the 'Dutchman' is tabulated herewith, and although I was not on the footplate the Inspector was kind enough to give me certain details in the few minutes we stood at Westbury. It was evident that the driver was conserving his efforts to make the maximum performance uphill, and while the running between Creech Junction and Curry Rivel Junction, across the Athelney marshes, was good though not unusual, there followed an astounding climb of the Somerton bank, where the minimum speed of 53 mph on 1 in 264 was steadily maintained for more than a mile. The equivalent drawbar horsepower rose from 800 at Curry Rivel Junction to 1,360 at the top of the bank.

After Castle Cary the engine was worked in 25 per cent cut-off with full regulator, and the ascent of the Bruton bank was a masterpiece in itself. It was here that my run of 25 years previously showed that the huge load was overpowering the engine, for while *King Richard* had covered the 15.7 miles from Curry Rivel Junction to Castle Cary in $16\frac{1}{2}$ minutes, it took all but 10 minutes to get up to milepost $122\frac{3}{4}$ and the speed fell eventually to 24 mph. With *Taunton Castle* on the up 'Dutchman' the 5 miles between posts 128 and 123 occupied only 6 min 6 sec and yet the average gradient between these two points is 1 in 122. Making careful allowance for the loss in kinetic energy in the train due to the deceleration from 60 to 40 mph, the average equivalent drawbar horsepower during that very strenuous 6 minutes works out at 1,600. The experimental section reported that the maximum they had noted with a 'King' when making up time in revenue-earning service was 1,440. *Taunton Castle* handsomely surpassed this, and it is probable that the actual cut-offs being used were slightly greater than those indicated on the scale and reported to me by my friends on the footplate. In any case the run provides yet another example complementary to those of the 'Kings' on the Birmingham route described in Chapter 18 of a steam locomotive being worked intermittently at far higher steaming rates than the boiler could continuously sustain. The practical result was that this enormous train was brought into Westbury $3\frac{1}{4}$ minutes early! It will be appreciated with what regret I left the train there to catch the local connection to Chippenham.

For-row superheater 'Castle' No 5049 Earl of Plymouth *on the 5.55 pm ex-Paddington South Wales express near Cholsey, with the Author on the footplate.* (M.W. Earley)

The last of the 'Castles', No 7037 Swindon. (British Railways)

22. Dissolution

After Hawksworth's retirement at the end of 1949, the entire organization of the former Chief Mechanical Engineer's department of the Great Western Railway was obliterated. The three sections into which personnel and workings were divided were not even placed under the same authority at the Railway Executive at 222 Marylebone Road, in London, or as most Regional men on the railways called it, 'The Kremlin'! Mechanical engineering work in the Western Region was henceforth separated between a Mechanical and Electrical Engineer, K.J. Cook, and a Carriage and Wagon Engineer, Hugh Randle, both with independent commands reporting directly to Riddles. On the other hand, W.N. Pellow, who had been Outdoor Assistant to the Chief Mechanical Engineer and Locomotive Running Superintendent, was consigned to the Operating Department and with him all the running inspectors, drivers and firemen and shed staff—reporting to Sir Michael Barrington-Ward. It was an exact replica of the organization set up on the Midland Railway after Cecil Paget had been appointed to the all-important post of General Superintendent in 1907.

Personnel-wise on the Western Region the new set-up lasted barely 18 months. In 1951 the last of the former CMEs, H.G. Ivatt, was retiring and the boffins at 'The Kremlin' seized this as a good opportunity to effect a general change-round of the most senior Mechanical Engineers in the Regions, and be it only whispered, to break up the solid core at Swindon who were steeped in the traditions of the Great Western Railway. Harrison, who had succeeded Peppercorn on the Eastern and North Eastern Regions, went to Derby as Mechanical and Electrical Engineer; Cook replaced him at Doncaster while Alfred Smeddle, who for a time had been Assistant to Swift at Brighton, was moved to Swindon. On the Carriage and Wagon side, Randle was appointed to the London Midland Region at Derby, while Charles Roberts succeeded at Swindon. The idea behind all these changes was doubtless to impose a kind of general cross-breeding of attitudes ready for the receipt of the new standard designs of steam locomotives, the first of which were due to enter traffic in the late summer of 1951. But things did not work out that way at all. The new much-publicized Class '7MT' 'Pacifics', after taking the road in various localities, sadly 'blotted their copybooks' with failures on the road, while the new Regional Mechanical Engineers at Doncaster and Swindon began lines of development quite apart from the policies engineered at 'The Kremlin'.

King George V *on an up West of England express in Sonning Cutting — the engine was then painted blue.* (M.W. Earley)

In my companion book *Great Locomotives of the LNER*, I have described the improved workshop methods that Cook introduced at Doncaster which resulted in what I called 'an Indian summer' for the Gresley 'Pacifics', but despite the resounding success he achieved in this field I always felt his deep-lying sentiments were elsewhere! I recall an incident some little time after he had left Swindon. After some signalling business at York I was travelling to King's Cross on the 'Heart of Midlothian', and just after we had stopped at Grantham I was surprised to see the down 'Yorkshire Pullman' also drawing in to stop. This latter train was normally hauled by an 'A4' non-stop from King's Cross to Doncaster. When it stopped, at the Pullman window immediately opposite were Kenneth Cook and his wife. Windows were pushed aside and we greeted each other. He said, rather ruefully, 'We're short of steam. Our driver's stopping for a "blow up".' Very soon we got the 'right away', but evidently our engine, a Peppercorn 'A1' 'Pacific', had stopped with the valves blind, and the driver had to set back a little before he could get away. As we passed, Cook was again at the window, his face wreathed in smiles, shouting across, 'Three cylinders don't start as well as four!'

On the Western Region, Keith Grand, first as Chief Regional officer and later as General Manager, was a worthy successor to Sir James Milne in the chair at Paddington. He was a vigorously energetic follower of all Great Western traditions, but when it came to accelerating the principal express train services back to their pre-war level, and perhaps even beyond that, he had come up against the stone-walling tactics of Gilbert Matthews, previously Superintendent of the Line and then responsible also for all locomotive running and footplate staffing. His fellow Superintendents in other Regions, influenced by the relatively poor showing made by the ex-Great Western engines in the Locomotive Interchange Trials of 1948, had apparently succeeded in convincing him that Swindon engines were past their prime, and for this reason he resisted all Grand's attempts to get accelerated services.

Smeddle attended these meetings, and while he knew that there were many engines in the combined fleet of 'Kings' and 'Castles' that were capable of top-class express passenger work, there were some that were definitely not. Recalling the established dictum of the Midland Railway Operating Department, faithfully followed by the LMS and now by BR itself, that any engine that could turn a wheel should be used on any train coming within the department's rules for loading and running schedule, whatever its mechanical condition, he became very interested in the tests Sam Ell was doing on draughting. At the same time Grand realized that in Smeddle he had a man after his own heart, who would give the utmost help in projects for train acceleration. At Swindon itself he may have brought with him two beautiful paintings of North Eastern Railway locomotives to hang in Churchward's one time sanctum, but Smeddle's enthusiasm quickened everything he touched, so that a delighted senior assistant of his could once exclaim to me, 'He's more Great Western than any of us!'

Modification to the front end of the 'Kings' had begun in Hawksworth's time with the fitting of a four-row superheater on engine No 6022. At that time there was no arrangement for self-cleaning in the smokebox; this was considered essential in British Railways days, and as the wire mesh would necessarily offer some resistance to the flow of flue gases from the tubes to the chimney it was evident that means had to be provided for sharpening the blast. This was done by removing the jumper ring on the top of the blast pipe, altering the height and reducing the chimney diameter from 1 ft 4 in at the throat to 1 ft 3 in, and from 1 ft 8 in at the top to 1 ft 5 in. These changes were made experimentally in the autumn of 1952 first to engine No 6017 and then to No 6001, and won golden opinions from the operating staff, though the news had not percolated upwards as far as Gilbert Matthews was concerned. When plans were announced in 1953 for the restoration of the pre-war 1¾-hour non-stop schedule of the 'Bristolian', he apparently advanced every conceivable reason why this could not be done. Smeddle told me how eventually at this meeting Grand lost his temper and shouted, 'Well double-head the bloody thing, Gilbert'! But by that time the memorable trials with engine No 6001 had been run and all the Western Region running people, from Pellow and his inspectors downwards, were all ready and waiting for accelerated schedules.

By Smeddle's kindness I was privileged to see something of the tests that were run from Reading West Sidings to Stoke Gifford yard and back some years before the construction of the new passenger station at Parkway. On the day that I travelled the load was made up to its maximum of 25 bogie coaches, 796 tons, and this had to be run at the full speed of the fastest ordinary express trains of the day. When I was crossing the line towards the test train, Inspector Pullen met me. 'Come to hear us make a lot of noise,' he laughed, but as the running cut-offs at 60–65 mph would not be much above 20 per cent I did not expect much. Climbing up into the dynamometer car, one of the assistant engineers whom I had met previously at Swindon was bubbling over with enthusiasm, and confided to me, 'You'll be thrilled to see what she (No 6001) can do now she's got one of Mr Ell's "Bob Martins" in her blast pipe'. I have had the privilege and the pleasure of writing up the magnificent results of these test runs in various publications, now more than 30 years ago, and for the present I must content myself with details of the log (overleaf) of the east-bound journey from Stoke Gifford, during which we covered the 73.5 miles from the East Yard box to a stop at Scours Lane Junction in 76 min 55 sec. We were working at cut-offs of about 30 per cent up the 1 in 300 to Sodbury Tunnel, down to 22 per cent on the ensuing descent to Little Somerford, and again at about 22 per cent through the fast running down the Vale of the White Horse.

On 30 April 1954 there was staged a kind of dress

Engine No 6001 with test fittings and indicator shelters ready for the Controlled Road Test in 1953. (British Railways)

Western Region: Dynamometer car controlled road test

Engine No 6001 *King Edward VIII*
Load 25 bogie coaches, 796 tons tare, 798 tons full

Distance (miles)		Time (m s)	Speed (mph)
0.0	Stoke Gifford East box	0 00	—
1.6	Winterbourne	5 45	—
4.3	Westerleigh Junction	10 18	40
6.9	Chipping Sodbury	13 58	45
11.5	Badminton	20 06	45½
17.3	Hullavington	25 58	72
21.8	Little Somerford	29 32	78
28.6	Wootton Bassett	35 43	58
31.5	Hay Lane box	38 48	56
34.2	Swindon	41 34	60
40.0	Milepost 71½	47 00	68
45.0	Uffington	51 24	69
51.1	Wantage Road	56 38	70½
55.0	Steventon	59 57	71
58.4	Didcot	62 48	71
62.5	Milepost 49	66 20	69
66.7	Goring	70 03	67
70.0	Pangbourne	72 57	67
73.5	Scours Lane Junction up home	76 55	

Western Region: 'Bristolian' test run, 30 April 1954

Engine No 6003 *King George IV*
Load 8 coaches, including dynamometer car, 253 tons tare, 260 tons full

Distance (miles)		Schedule (min)	Actual (m s)	Speed (mph)
0.0	Paddington	0	0 00	—
5.7	Ealing		7 26	68½
9.1	Southall	11	10 18	72
18.5	Slough	17½	17 51	75
24.2	Maidenhead	21½	22 14	80
31.0	Twyford	27	27 24	82/74*
36.0	Reading	31	31 23	75
41.5	Pangbourne		35 54	72
48.5	Cholsey		41 21	80
53.1	Didcot	48	44 44	84
60.4	Wantage Road		50 04	79½
66.5	Uffington		54 38	81½
—			pw slack	18
77.3	Swindon	67	65 44	72
82.9	Wootton Bassett		70 03	82
87.7	Dauntsey		73 20	96½
94.0	Chippenham	79	77 33	78
98.3	Corsham		80 51	80
101.9	Box		83 30	82
106.9	Bath	88½	88 17	35*
113.8	Keynsham		94 57	75
117.9	Dr Day's Bridge Junction	102½	99 19	—
0.0	Stapleton Road	0	0 00	—
3.2	Filton Junction	5	5 10	—
11.4	Chipping Sodbury		13 30	66
16.0	Badminton	18	17 47	63½
26.3	Little Somerford		25 25	93
33.1	Wootton Bassett	30½	30 22	65*
38.7	Swindon	35½	35 03	79
49.5	Uffington		42 51	89
55.6	Wantage Road		46 59	90
62.9	Didcot	56	51 52	92½
67.5	Cholsey		54 57	86
71.3	Goring		57 56	eased
80.0	Reading	68	64 31	82/77
91.8	Maidenhead	76½	73 01	90
—			eased	81
97.5	Slough	81	77 08	84
102.7	West Drayton		80 52	86
106.9	Southall	87½	84 13	73
110.3	Ealing		86 53	77½
—			pw slack	
114.7	Westbourne Park		92 55	
116.0	Paddington	101½	95 35	

* speed restrictions

The test train of 23 coaches approaching Swindon at 60 mph. (British Railways)

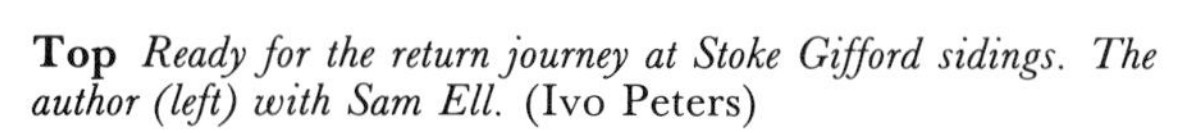

Top *Ready for the return journey at Stoke Gifford sidings. The author (left) with Sam Ell.* (Ivo Peters)

Above *Just after the start of the return run; the test train passing water troughs near Chipping Sodbury.* (Ivo Peters)

Top *'Dress rehearsal' for the introduction of the $1\frac{3}{4}$-hour 'Bristolian' in April 1954; No 6003* King George IV *passing West Ealing at 70 mph.* (J.F. Russell-Smith)

Above *The return journey of the 'Bristolian' dynamometer car trial, passing Hullavington at 86 mph.* (K.H. Leech)

rehearsal for the introduction of the $1\frac{3}{4}$-hour 'Bristolian' schedule which was to come into force in June of that year. But the out-and-home runs on that day provided the Locomotive Department with a much more strenuous exercise than they would have to face in ordinary working as can be seen from the accompanying table. On the outward journey in the approach to Bristol, instead of proceeding into Temple Meads they took the right-hand fork, stopped briefly at Dr Day's Bridge Junction to set down Mr Grand, who had been riding on the footplate, and continued to a second stop at Stapleton Road. Thence, after another stop and no more than $18\frac{1}{2}$ minutes after our first stop in the Bristol area, we were 'right away' on another 70-mph dash to Paddington. We arrived back there at 2.29 pm, having left at 10.55 am. The net times for the down and up runs were respectively 96 and $93\frac{1}{2}$ minutes, showing average speeds of 74.5 and 74.7 mph, and the 'Bristolian' went into regular service, together with other accelerated services, but not so sharply timed, in June. Other than the 'Bristolian' itself, all the others were hauled by 'Castles'.

More opposition from Gilbert Matthews came when it was proposed to accelerate the 'Cornish Riviera Express'. In 1954 the arrival time at Plymouth North Road was 2.45 pm, giving a non-stop run of 255 minutes over the 225.6 miles from Paddington. The fastest pre-war time had been the even 4 hours, and this Grand wanted to restore, with a maximum load of 12 coaches between Paddington and Plymouth with the addition of the two-coach Weymouth portion to be slipped at Heywood road Junction in the down direction. Ell was confident that with a 'Bob Martin' in the blast pipe the 'Kings' could comfortably manage the job, providing, of course, a bank engine was provided over the South Devon line. In early March 1955, dynamometer car test runs were made on the 'Cornish Riviera Express' working experimentally to the proposed accelerated timing, and some fine runs were made, with engine No 6018 *King Henry VIII*. Smeddle invited me to join him in the dynamometer car on the second down trip, when Gilbert Matthews also was a passenger. With a gross load of 490 tons to Heywood Road, and 420 tons onwards, I logged a time of 159¼ minutes (156 minutes net) passing Exeter, and the net time to our locomotive stop at Newton Abbot was only 178 minutes, an average from the start at Paddington of just over 65 mph. When Smeddle joined me in the car he said, 'Even old Gilbert's smiling now!'

My invitation had been extended to the final up journey on the following day, but unfortunately a business appointment on Tyneside necessitated my returning from Plymouth to London on the same evening, and I therefore missed the experience of witnessing the altogether extraordinary run that was made. I was told by someone who witnessed the arrival at Paddington that the train was practically on time, and when I was in London early the following week I was given a somewhat colourful account, by a friend in the Operating Department at Paddington, of how the crew were just about on their knees on arrival, and that there was no coal left in the tender. Later that week Sam Ell rang me up and invited me to see the dynamometer car rolls, and take any information I desired. I took the earliest opportunity to get to Swindon and hear the inside story of that memorable day. A tearing east wind had been scouring the West Country, and that 420-ton 'Cornish Riviera Express' had been pulling more like 500 than 420 tons. They had been double-headed between Plymouth and Newton Abbot, and over the coastal stretch there is not much opportunity for speeding; but after passing Exeter and meeting the full force of the wind, it was clear that they were beginning to lose time. Smeddle phoned from the dynamometer car urging them to step their efforts up, and then there began 2 hours of the most intensive coal heaving ever known on a Great Western locomotive.

In Coronation year, 1953, the down 'Cornish Riviera Express' with the special headboard passes Reading with engine No 6017 King Edward IV. (M.W. Earley)

The crew, Driver F. Bolt and Fireman E. Knapman, who I had previously ridden with on the footplate of one of the very fast Ocean Mail specials from Millbay Docks to Paddington, were a grand pair, and with them was Headquarters Inspector W. Andress. There was no stop at Exeter on this run, and no help from young cleaners with getting coal forward, and after Taunton, whenever Andress paused from doing his own job, he was taking the shovel to give Knapman a brief respite from the continuous labour of firing. What this meant can be realized from a comparison of the runs of 10 and 11 March, thus:

Down run: Paddington to Newton Abbot, start to stop

Running time, net	178 minutes
Average speed	62.5 mph
Average drawbar horsepower	
under power	978
actual	828
Coal per dhp hour	
inclusive of auxiliaries	3.33 lbs
exclusive of auxiliaries	3.21 lbs
Firing rate	3,245 lbs per hour
Net steam rate	29,560 lbs per hour

Up run; Exeter to Reading, pass to pass

Running time	127.6 minutes
Average speed	64.7 mph
Average drawbar horsepower	1,020
Coal per dhp hour	
inclusive of auxiliaries	4.13 lbs
exclusive of auxiliaries	4.00 lbs
Firing rate	4,210 lbs per hour
Net steam rate	29,835 lbs per hour
Total coal	8,240 lbs

The bare statistics of this heroic run, which I extracted from the actual dynamometer car chart, are shown in the accompanying table, and in studying the times and speeds it is very important to bear in mind that the train itself, because of the very strong headwind, was pulling like 490 to 500 tons instead of the actual load recorded.

Western Region: 'Cornish Riviera Express' Dynamometer Car Test Run, 11 March 1955

Engine No 6013 *King Henry VIII*
Load 393 tons tare, 420 tons full

Distance (miles)		Times* (m	s)	Speeds (mph)
0.0	Exeter	0	00	Pass slowly
3.5	Stoke Canon	4	13	52½
7.2	Silverton	8	22	58½
12.6	Cullompton	13	34	65
14.9	Tiverton Junction	15	40	60/66
19.9	Whiteball box	20	38	53½
23.7	Wellington	23	52	80
28.8	Norton Fitzwarren	27	49	71
30.8	Taunton	29	27	74
38.8	Athelney	35	45	71½
42.5	Curry Rivel Junction	38	40	75
48.0	Somerton	43	29	65/71½
53.5	Keinton Mandeville	48	15	67/75
58.4	Castle Cary	52	31	53
—		pw slack		17
61.8	Bruton	59	00	46
65.2	Milepost 122¾	63	32	42
71.2	Blatchbridge Junction	68	53	78
73.2	Clink Road Junction	70	29	73
76.5	Fairwood Junction	73	02	81
78.9	Heywood Road Junction	75	02	70
86.6	Lavington	81	28	76
92.1	Patney	86	41	64½
98.2	Pewsey	91	41	73
103.4	Savernake	96	20	61
107.1	Bedwyn	100	00	easy
112.0	Hungerford	104	35	62*†
115.0	Kintbury	107	19	70
120.4	Newbury	111	43	79
123.9	Thatcham	114	27	80
126.7	Midgham	116	52	58*†
132.3	Theale	121	46	74½
137.5	Reading	127	45	37*†
142.5	Twyford	132	52	68
149.3	Maidenhead	138	28	74
155.0	Slough	143	07	75
160.3	West Drayton	147	28	71
164.4	Southall	151	12	70
167.8	Ealing Broadway	153	51	71½
—		sig check		
172.2	Westbourne Park	159	38	
173.5	Paddington	162	04	

* From passing Exeter slowly
† Speed restrictions

I saw Bolt and Knapman a few days after I had been studying details of their great run, and their only complaint was not of the gale force headwind, nor of the appalling amount of coal they had had to fire, but of the concluding signal check at Old Oak Common which had prevented their clocking into Paddington in exactly the 4 hours from Plymouth. For Sam Ell, however, and those immediately concerned at Swindon, the technical details of the run included some very disquieting features, particularly the high back pressure when the engine was being fully extended, and this gave rise to the inordinate coal consumption. Thoughts of other locomotives to be tried occupied Smeddle and his men, though the 'BR8' 'Pacific' No 71000 *Duke of Gloucester*, which Ell had tested most exhaustively, was rejected at once. He referred to it as 'a coal scoffer', and it was not until the official British Railways Test Bulletin was published some little time later that I came to appreciate why. While the 'King' No 6013 on the last run up had used 4,210 lbs of coal per hour between Exeter and Reading, to provide a steam rate of 29,835 lbs per hour, the 'BR8', to provide 30,000 lbs in test house conditions had needed no less than 4,875 lbs of coal per hour!

Smeddle wanted to try a Peppercorn 'A1' 'Pacific', but conditions for the loan of one of these could not be agreed with the Eastern Region, and recourse was had alternatively to a 'Duchess', *City of Bristol*, from the London Midland Region, which was worked by Western Region men throughout the dynamometer car trials which Ell and his staff carried out. The weather was calm and fine in the four days concerned, but while the enginemen from Old Oak and Laira appreciated the engine and got some excellent work out of her, the train loads hauled, which were the same as those taken by the 'King', involved bank engine assistance between Newton Abbot and Plymouth on

The up 'Dutchman', the 8.30 am Plymouth to Paddington, rounding the curve on to the main line at Reading with engine No 6008 King James II. (M.W. Earley)

Left *The dynamometer test run on the 3.30 pm Paddington to Plymouth in May 1956 near Reading with engine No 6002* King William IV *having the twin-orifice blast pipe and double chimney. The author was riding in the dynamometer car.* (M.W. Earley)

Right *Engine No 6021* King Richard II *at Old Oak Common in 1962, having been fitted with a cross-stay bogie.* (Author's collection)

Below right *Last express duties for the 'Stars': No 4062* Malmesbury Abbey *on the up 'Merchant Venturer' at Thingley Junction, with the author on the footplate.* (K.H. Leech)

each of the four days. In the meantime, authority had been given to rebuild the front end of a 'King' with a twin-orifice blast pipe and double chimney. At the end of September 1955 Ell rode on the footplate of the engine concerned, No 6015 *King Richard III*, on the down 'Cornish Riviera Express'. They had no more than 10 coaches throughout from Paddington to Plymouth, but as he emphasized in a report to Smeddle: 'On stretches where high speeds of about 85 mph are normally obtained, speeds rose on engine No 6015 to over 100 mph with the same engine working'. Ell was so pleased with the results that he suggested that his Chief Assistant H. Tichener should also have a trip, and three days later, in company with Inspector Andress, they clocked one quarter-mile at $106\frac{1}{2}$ and one at $108\frac{1}{2}$ mph—the fastest authenticated speed ever achieved with a Great Western engine. The highest speed I have personally recorded was when I was travelling passenger one morning on the down 'Bristolian' behind engine No 6018 *King Henry VI*, and we attained $102\frac{1}{2}$ mph down the Dauntsey bank.

I was accorded the privilege of a footplate pass myself for the down 'Cornish Riviera Express' on Engine No 6015 in the late autumn of 1955, and although there were many delays, including a stop at Westbury to set down the Weymouth coach, on account of fog, we clocked into Plymouth on the stroke of 2.30 pm with a net gain of no less than 21 minutes on schedule. The load was 390 tons from Paddington and 350 tons from Westbury. I was also invited to some of the dynamometer car test runs made with another of the double-chimneyed 'Kings', No 6002 *King William IV*, made in May 1956; but in good weather conditions the enginemen had a relatively easy task compared to what was experienced on the final run up in the previous year with No 6013. Within my own experience in the dynamometer car, by far the hardest work demanded of No 6002 was on the 3 pm up from Birmingham Snow Hill. Through a piece of faulty operating we were stopped dead at Banbury Junction, and in trying to recover the lost time there were some significant features of the performance. On the descent from Ardley Tunnel, through Bicester to Blackthorn, when the speed reached 86 mph, the back pressure registered was only 2 psi while developing 900 drawbar horsepower. This was a marked improvement on previous working and undoubtedly contributed to the freedom of running at high speed.

At the beginning of 1958, however, the first diesels began to arrive from the North British Locomotive Company, and Swindon itself was already getting geared up to produce the first batch of '800' Class diesel-hydraulic units. These and the similarly-powered NBL locomotives were intended for top-class express service, and ultimately the complete replacement of steam traction on the Western Region. Few, however, foresaw the precipitous haste with which the change would ultimately be made. In 1958 a considerable life was envisaged for the 'Castle' and 'King' Class locomotives, if only from the amount of money that was spent in maintaining them. But in those later years the 'Kings' in particular fell victims to a number of troubles arising directly from their longevity. They were never anything but top-link engines. Apart from the brief periods when they were running in, after visits to Swindon for overhaul, they were consistently on the heaviest main-line express work, and after 30 years troubles of a purely mechanical kind were almost inevitable. At the time when the first engines were being fitted with the twin-orifice blast pipe and double chimney, some of them were also having part of their frames renewed with new cylinders. This had always been a source of some weakness in all the Great Western four-cylinder 4-6-0s, though in stating this it must be appreciated that it is said in a relative sense only. The design itself was very sound, but when locomotives were in continuous heavy service, such as the 'Castles' and 'Kings' rendered faithfully for so many years, any weakness, however relative, would begin to show up in old age.

When the question arose of renewing the cylinders of 'Kings', involving the making of new castings, Smeddle, with the knowledge of how the Gresley 'Pacifics' had benefited from the internal streamlining of their ports and passages, as exemplified by the advance in performance by the 'A4' Class as compared to the 'A3', had the drawings that had been made for the Hawksworth 'Pacific' examined. The cylinders were of the same nominal dimensions as those of the 'Kings', but the design would have entailed making new patterns and this was an expense that could not at that time have been justified. Another trouble that beset the 'Kings' was a crop of fatigue cracks that developed in the bogies from January 1956. Repairs had been made by welding from time to time, but at that period the failures were sufficiently numerous for the whole class to be temporarily withdrawn from service until additional stiffening strips had been welded to the bogie frames. They were not out of traffic for long. Engine No 6012 was returned to traffic in the first week of February and the others followed quickly.

While the repairs to the bogies were in the nature of 'patching up'—albeit a thoroughly good and lasting job—other modifications were considered which were intended to prolong the life of the class for a further dozen years at least; their early replacement did not appear to be foreseen in 1957–8. One of the most interesting developments was the proposal to fit roller bearings to all axles, and it went so far as the placing of an order with British Timken for complete sets of bearings for eight engines. The material was delivered at Swindon in 1957–8. Whether the substitution of roller bearings for the well-designed Swindon plain bearing would have increased the free-running qualities of the locomotives is a moot point; but it would almost certainly have reduced casualties from overheated bearings, which were becoming more frequent with the increased age of the locomotives. Unfortunately the work was never done.

When the diesels really began to get a hold on the West of England services, from 1959, the 'Kings' were transferred away from Laira shed, and their story until the withdrawal of the whole class for scrapping, in 1962, makes melancholy reading on which I prefer not to dwell. Instead I think back to some of the topmost highlights of Great Western locomotive performance

that I have been fortunate to record personally from the year 1921 when I first came to study engineering in London until the last of my trips with a steam locomotive in the Swindon dynamometer car in 1956—a fascinating and memorable 45 years. I like to recall that amazing fortnight in 1925 when I clocked two runs, timekeeping runs too, with 'Stars' and 500-ton loads on the West of England service; of *Lady of Lynn* on the Birmingham line, and of some very exciting runs on the 'Cheltenham Flyer'. Then there was that extraordinary run on the up 'Dutchman' when *Taunton Castle* and her men worked a 530-ton train from Taunton to Westbury and gained more than 3 minutes on schedule. Then of course there are the many test trips with the 'Kings' that I have been privileged to accompany, but last of all, constituting my last bow to the

Saturdays-only working for No 4061 Glastonbury Abbey; *a Wolverhampton to Weymouth express near Castle Cary.* (K.H. Leech)

memory of Swindon-built engines, is a run that has so far not been mentioned in this book.

Just after nationalization, with the help of my friends in the running department at Swindon, I was seeking out some of the last remaining duties of the 'Saint' Class. Some of these engines were working north of Wolverhampton, and I had an excellent footplate run with No 2930 *Saint Vincent* southbound from Chester. I was also given a footplate pass for the 10.50 am Swindon to Paddington, a heavy combined Cheltenham and Bristol express of 12 coaches, 375 tons tare and, crowded with passengers, fully 410 tons full. I was interested to see our engine was to be No 2934 *Butleigh Court*, for this was the residence of Neville Grenfell, one of Churchward's great friends. I understood that the engine had recently been through the shops for a light repair job, and while she had not been repainted, and was not exactly shabby, she was certainly not in that spanking condition with which one associated all Great Western express locomotives in days of yore. I was told that No 2934 had been fitted with new cylinders and outside steam pipes in 1938.

Driver W.H. Jones and Fireman T.J. Evans, of Swindon shed, were in charge, and on getting the 'right away' punctually, quite a gentle start was made; the regulator was not opened more than two-fifths and cut-off was quickly reduced, until at a point just beyond Highworth Junction, and about a mile from the start, it was fixed at 25 per cent. Under such easy steaming conditions acceleration was slow, by the usual standards here, and by Shrivenham, 5.7 miles out, the speed had not risen above 54¼ mph. Here the cut-off was further reduced, to 20 per cent. At this early stage in the run my interest was taken by the exceptionally smooth action and riding of the engine; she was almost as sweet-running as a 'Castle', and I can give no higher praise than that! On the gently falling gradients we gradually worked into a first-class stride: 64½ mph at Uffington, 68 at Wantage Road and 69½ through Steventon, where steam was shut off for Didcot. We had then covered 20.8 miles from the start in 24½ minutes, but adverse signals checked us into Didcot.

Many more passengers joined the train at Didcot, and with the road now level the driver worked the engine slightly harder on the run to Reading. 30 per cent cut-off was used throughout this stage, though again with only a moderate opening of the regulator. The 17.1 miles were covered in 21¾ minutes start to stop, with a maximum speed of 66 mph. Up to this point the going had been much as I would have expected from this veteran locomotive; the steaming was excellent, and the speed comfortably within scheduled requirements. Water consumption was low—a little under 30 gallons per mile. But now, on the concluding stage, there was a relaying slack to 15 mph in operation near Southall, and in addition we left Reading slightly behind time. Still more passengers joined the train, and with the 12 coaches now filled almost to capacity, the gross load behind the tender was little, if anything, short of 420 tons. It was also very soon evident that Driver Jones intended us to be in Paddington on time. Almost at once the regulator was opened much wider than I had previously seen on this engine, to rather more than three-quarters full, and linking up was more gradual: 35 per cent when ¾ mile out; 30 at 3 miles, 25 at 5 miles; and 20 at 8 miles. Our exploits are best summarized in the accompanying log:

Distance (miles)		**Time (m s)**	**Speed (mph)**
0.0	Reading	0 00	—
3.0	Milepost 33	5 42	52
5.0	Twyford	7 51	61½
8.0	Milepost 28	10 37	68
11.8	Maidenhead	13 48	74
15.0	Burnham	16 21	76½
17.5	Slough	18 23	72½
21.25	Iver	21 33	70
25.1	Hayes	24 17	72½

In Chapter 16 of this book I have told how my friend E.L. Diamond extolled the running of the 'Saint' Class 4-6-0 based at Landore on the heavily loaded double-home turns between Swansea and Paddington. He was a highly qualified professional engineer and had been a pupil of Sir Henry Fowler; but while he had plenty of opportunities for riding Midland engines during his training, I do not believe that he rode on any Great

Right *The maker of a record climb to Llanvihangel in the war years: No 2949* Stanford Court *in BR livery at Wantage Road in 1950.* (J.F. Russell-Smith, National Railway Museum)

Below right *One of Churchward's favourites, No 2934* Butleigh Court, *before the fore-end had been renewed.* (M.D. England, National Railway Museum)

Bottom right *A fitting tailpiece — engine No 7017* G.J. Churchward, *as first turned out in 1948.* (British Railways)

Western types subsequently. In submitting his logs to *The Railway Magazine* he commented that the 'Saints', and I quote, 'were obviously being worked at their limit for hours on end, and the marvel is that the engines stand such apparently merciless driving without ill effect'! On my run with *Butleigh Court*, the engine developed this superb piece of running with complete equanimity, if one may apply one more human trait to the steam locomotive. While 20 per cent and more than three-quarter regulator is not *easy* going at over 70 mph, it is certainly not 'merciless driving'; in fact, for 10 miles east of Maidenhead she was linked up to a little under 20 per cent. And still the riding was delightfully smooth and comfortable. I estimate that the drawbar horsepower was over 1,300 from Maidenhead onwards, and all the time the boiler pressure remained quite steady at 220 psi.

After Hayes we reduced speed for the relaying slack, right down to 10 mph; but with yet another fine acceleration, and a clear road into Paddington, we were able to cover the last 9.1 miles from Southall in 11 minutes. Thus, despite this heavy slack at Southall West we ran the 36 miles from Reading to Paddington in 38 minutes 35 seconds start to stop, and so finished the journey a minute or so ahead of time. The water consumption on this last stage hardly suggests thrashing, the gauge on the tender indicating 1,300 gallons from Reading—a very modest 36 gallons per mile. The normal coal consumption of these engines is about 1 lb per gallon of water, and certainly the fireman's work could not at any point in the trip have been called arduous, even when we were working into so exhilarating a speed east of Reading. So, with this magnificent performance of *Butleigh Court*, an engine then 37 years old, I end my account of the Great Locomotives of the GWR.

Appendix I: Preserved locomotives of the GWR

Historic units in museums

0-6-0 No 2516 (Dean Goods); GWR Museum, Swindon
4-4-0 No 3717 *City of Truro*; GWR Museum, Swindon
4-6-0 No 4003 *Lode Star*; GWR Museum, Swindon
4-6-0 No 4073 *Caerphilly Castle*; The Science Museum, London.
2-8-0 No 2818 (Standard goods); National Railway Museum, York

Others
'King' Class
No 6000 *King George V*; Bulmer Railway Centre, Hereford
No 6024 *King Edward I*; Quainton Railway Society, near Aylesbury

'Castle' Class
No 4079 *Pendennis Castle*; Australia
No 5029 *Nunney Castle*; Didcot Railway Centre
No 5043 *Earl of Mount Edgcumbe*; Birmingham Railway Museum
No 5051 *Drysllwyn Castle*; Didcot Railway Centre
No 5080 *Defiant*; Birmingham Railway Museum
No 7027 *Thornbury Castle*; Birmingham Railway Museum
No 7029 *Clun Castle*; Birmingham Railway Museum

'Hall' Class
No 4920 *Dumbleton Hall*; Dart Valley Railway (Buckfastleigh)
No 4930 *Hagley Hall*; Severn Valley Railway
No 4942 *Maindy Hall*; Didcot Railway Centre
No 4983 *Albert Hall*; Birmingham Railway Museum
No 5900 *Hinderton Hall*; Didcot Railway Centre
No 6960 *Raveningham Hall*; Severn Valley Railway
No 6989 *Wightwick Hall*; Quainton Railway Society
No 6990 *Witherslack Hall*; Great Central Railway
No 6998 *Burton Agnes Hall*; Didcot Railway Centre

'Manor' Class
No 7808 *Cookham Manor*; Didcot Railway Centre
No 7812 *Erlestoke Manor*; Severn Valley Railway
No 7819 *Hinton Manor*; Severn Valley Railway
No 7820 *Dinmore Manor*; Gwili Railway, Carmarthen
No 7822 *Foxcote Manor*; Cambrian Railway Society, Oswestry
No 7827 *Lydham Manor*; Dart Valley Railway (Torbay section)

'1400' Class (formerly '4800' Class) 0-4-2 tank
No 1420; Dart Valley Railway (Buckfastleigh)
No 1450; Dart Valley Railway (Buckfastleigh)
No 1466; Didcot Railway Centre

'2251' Class 0-6-0 mixed traffic
No 3205; Severn Valley Railway)

'2800' Class 2-8-0 heavy freight
No 2857; Severn Valley Railway
No 3822; Didcot Railway Centre

'4300' Class 2-6-0 mixed traffic
No 5322; Didcot Railway Centre
No 9303; Severn Valley Railway

'45XX' Class 2-6-2T light tank engine
No 4555; Dart Valley (Buckfastleigh)
No 4561; West Somerset Railway
No 4566; Severn Valley Railway
No 4588; Dart Valley (Torbay section)
No 5521; West Somerset Railway
No 5541; Norchard Steam Centre, Lydney
No 5542; West Somerset Railway
No 5572; Didcot Railway Centre

'5101' Class 2-6-2T heavy passenger tank
No 4141; Severn Valley Railway
No 4144; Didcot Railway Centre
No 4150; Severn Valley Railway
No 4160; Birmingham Railway Museum
No 5164; Severn Valley Railway
No 5193; Steamport, Southport
No 6106; Didcot Railway Centre

'5200' Class 2-8-0T heavy South Wales type
No 5224; Great Central Railway
No 5239; Dart Valley Railway (Torbay section)

'5600' Class 0-6-2T South Wales tanks
No 5619; Telford Horsehay Steam Trust Railway
No 5637; Birmingham Railway Museum
No 5643; Steamtown, Carnforth
No 6619; North Yorkshire Moors Railway
No 6695; Swanage Railway Centre
No 6697; Didcot Railway Centre

'5700' Class 0-6-0T standard domed pannier
No 3650; Didcot Railway Centre
No 3738; Didcot Railway Centre

Above *No 4003* Lode Star *in service on the GWR.* (Real Photos Co Ltd)

Right Caerphilly Castle *in Great Western days approaching Patchway with an up South Wales express.* (A.V. Goodyear)

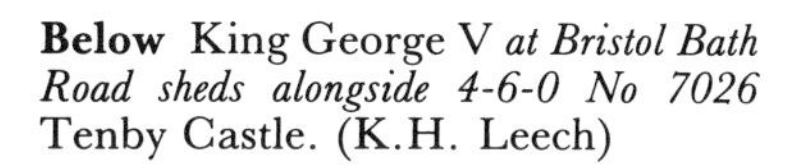

Below King George V *at Bristol Bath Road sheds alongside 4-6-0 No 7026* Tenby Castle. (K.H. Leech)

No 5764; Severn Valley Railway
No 5786; Bulmer Railway Society
No 7714; Severn Valley Railway
No 7715; Quainton Railway Society
No 7752; Birmingham Railway Museum
No 7760; Birmingham Railway Museum
No 9600; Birmingham Railway Museum
No 9681; Norchard Steam Centre

'6400' Class 0-6-0 small pannier
No 6412; West Somerset Railway
No 6430; Dart Valley Railway (Buckfastleigh)
No 6435; Dart Valley Railway (Buckfastleigh)

'7200' Class 2-8-2T heavy main-line tank
No 7202; Didcot Railway Centre

'9000' Class 4-4-0 'Dukedog'
No 9017; Bluebell Railway

'9400' Class 0-6-0T pannier tank, domeless
No 9400; GWR Museum, Swindon
No 9406; Quainton Railway Society

Appendix II: Out of the shadows—the 1952 saga of the 'Manors'

After my somewhat curt dismissal of the 'Manor' Class 4-6-0s in Chapter 19 of this book, it could appear a little strange to see, in Appendix I, that no fewer than six of them should have been preserved, and kept in full working order. On footplate journeys made not long after the war, mainly on the former Cambrian Railways line, I found them indifferent performers, but I do not think that anyone at Swindon realized how bad they were until Smeddle, in answer to repeated remonstrances from the Running Department, instructed Sam Ell to take one of them on to the stationary test plant and find out what the trouble was. The engine selected was No 7818 *Granville Manor*, and it was in first class condition mechanically. The report subsequently prepared, which was one of the most comprehensive ever presented to British Railways, was not one of those publicly issued to the technical press. But Mr Smeddle was kind enough to give me a copy, and the initial findings were startling, to say the least of it. As designed and put into traffic in 1938, the 'Manors' compared with the 'Halls' as follows:

	Manors	Halls
Cylinders, diameter × stroke (in)	18 × 30	$18\frac{1}{4}$ × 30
Coupled wheel diameter (ft in)	5 8	6 0
Total heating surface (sq ft)	1,585.5	2,104
Tractive effort (lbs)	27,340	27,275

Against the measured maximum output of considerably over 20,000 lbs of steam per hour, recorded in tests on the Swindon stationary plant with one of the 'Halls', the best that could be got out of No 7818, as first received for test, was barely 10,000. No wonder the Running Department complained.

Following the initial tests, Ell immediately put in hand a fairly drastic modification to the draughting. On the blast pipe the jumper ring was taken off, and the orifice reduced to a $4\frac{3}{4}$-in diameter. An experimental fabricated stove-pipe chimney, having a taper of 1 in 14, was fitted, and when it was clear that these changes were giving a greatly improved performance, a series of full dress trials were commenced with the engine being indicated. It was found that a still greater improvement could be made by a further slight reduction in the diameter of the blast pipe orifice, to a $4\frac{5}{8}$-in diameter, while to effect more even combustion the free grate area was increased by removal of both sections of one of the firebars. The free air was thus increased from 39.9 per cent to 41.9 per cent of the nominal grate area.

No 7818 Granville Manor *on the test plant at Swindon.*

With the new draughting arrangements the engine steamed freely, and when fired with Bedwas coal, a Grade 2A soft Welsh, reached a maximum evaporation of 20,400 lbs per hour—more than double that which was attained with the original draughting. One may certainly express a little astonishment that, with so little in the way of alterations in the smokebox, a class of very lame ducks like the 'Manors' could be made into a superb medium-powered locomotive. It is a sobering thought that many other lame ducks of locomotive history might have been similarly improved if the principles of draughting had been more thoroughly understood and skilfully applied.

Bibliography

Technical Papers

Institution of Mechanical Engineers

1902 Large Locomotive Boilers, G.J. Churchward
1904 Testing Locomotives, G.J. Churchward
1914 Combined Automatic Train Control and Audible and Signal System on the GWR, W.A. Stanier

Swindon Engineering Society Transactions

Numerous papers read by members of the GWR Mechanics Institution

Institution of Locomotive Engineers

1950 The Late G.J. Churchward's Locomotive Development on the Great Western Railway, K.J. Cook
1953 Developments in Locomotive Testing, S.O. Ell
1955 Presidential Address: 'A Machine of Precision', K.J. Cook

Journals

The Engineer, The Locomotive , The Railway Engineer, The Railway Gazette, The Railway Magazine

Books

Armstrongs of the Great Western, H. Holcroft, Railway World, 1953
Vol 1 1825–1925, E.L. Ahrons, Ian Allan, 1960
Vol 2 1925–1965, O.S. Nock, Ian Allan, 1966
British Locomotives of the 20th Century
Vol 1 1900–1930, O.S. Nock, Patrick Stephens Limited, 1983
Vol 2 1930–1960, O.S. Nock, Patrick Stephens Limited, 1984
Vol 3 1960– the present day, O.S. Nock, Patrick Stephens Limited, 1985
Classic Locomotives – 'Saint' Class, O.S. Nock, Patrick Stephens Limited, 1983
Engine 6000, O.S. Nock, David & Charles, 1972
Great Western Railway – An appreciation, O.S. Nock, Heffers
Great Western Railway in the 19th Century, O.S. Nock, Ian Allan, 1962
Great Western Railway in the 20th Century, O.S. Nock, Ian Allan, 1964
Great Western Locomotive Practice – An outline, H. Holcroft, Loco Publishing Co, 1957
Great Western Steam, O.S. Nock, David & Charles, 1972
History of the Great Western Railway
Vol 1, E.T. MacDermot, Ian Allan, 1964
Vol 2, E.T. MacDermot, Ian Allan, 1964
Vol 3, *1923–1947*, O.S. Nock, Ian Allan, 1967
Locomotive and Train Working in the latter part of the Nineteenth Century
Vol 4, E.L. Ahrons, Heffers, 1952
Mixed Traffic Types of the GWR, O.S Nock, David & Charles, 1978
Sixty Years of Western Express Running, O.S. Nock, Ian Allan, 1973
Speed Records on British Railways, O.S. Nock, David & Charles, 1971
Stars, Castles and Kings of the GWR, O.S. Nock, David & Charles, 1967
Standard Gauge Great Western 4–4–0s
1. 1894–1910, O.S. Nock, David & Charles, 1977
2. 1904–1961, O.S. Nock, David & Charles, 1978
Swindon Steam 1921–51, K.J. Cook, Ian Allan, 1974
Tales of the Great Western Railway, O.S. Nock, David & Charles, 1984

Index

Authors:
- Ahrons, E.L. 4, 6 et seq, 21, 191
- Allen, C.J. 43, 129, 136, 144, 177
- Charlewood, R.E. 14, 169, 174
- Gairns, J.F. 72
- Goodyear, A.V. 60, 80, 169, 177, 185
- Maskelyne, J.N. 24
- Rouse-Marten, C. 10, 12, 27, 37, 45, 47, 52
- Scott, Rev W.J. 43, 47
- Sekon, G.A. 42

Boiler design:
- large loco 34, 66
- superheater 72, 73
- taper, first used on *Mauritius* 64

Broad gauge 4, 6 et seq

Dynamometer Car trials:
- Engine No 3435 38
- Engine No 4013 58, 59
- Engine No 4074 121, 122
- Engine No 6001 218
- Engine No 6013 221

Engineers:
- Anderson, J.E. (LMS) 131
- Armstrong, J. 22
- Auld, J. 163, 196
- Bowen Cooke, C.J. 4, 78
- Burrows, G.H. 72, 113, 132
- Churchward, G.J. 4, 20, 25, 70, 135
- Collett, C.B. 5, 113, 117, 134, 153, 163, 170, 196
- Cook, K.J. 5, 49, 136, 155, 160, 191, 194, 216
- Dean, W. 5, 7, 11, 17, 23, 25, 34
- Deeley, W.M. 55
- De Glehn, A. 38
- Diamond, E.L. 141, 144, 172
- Drummond, D. 4, 41, 71
- Dymond, A.W.J. 132, 154, 170
- Ell, S.O. 5, 171, 217 et seq
- Gooch, Sir D. 4, 6, 25
- Gresley, Sir N. 114
- Hall, F.C. 135
- Hannington, R.A.G. 113, 194, 198
- Hawksworth, F.W. 5, 66, 113, 132, 154, 190, 196, 206, 210, 216
- Holcroft, H. 82
- Holden, J. 7, 25
- King, H.C. 36
- Lloyd, J.C. 153
- Pearce, W.H. 55
- Pellow, W.N. 115, 216
- Roberts, C. 169, 171
- Smeddle, A. 5, 186, 216 et seq
- Stanier, W.A. 49, 70, 73, 113, 155, 163
- Stroudley, W. 7, 38
- Webb, F.W. 4, 49

Interchange Trials:
- with LNWR 75
- with LNER 124
- with LMS 130

Locomotive Classes (GW):
- Tender engines:
- 'Aberdare' 62
- 'Atbara' 29, 33, 46
- 'Atlantic' 50, 77
- 'Badminton' 25 et seq
- Broad Gauge 4-2-2 6 et seq
- 'Bulldog' 20, 26, 63, 71
- 'Camel' 26, 33
- 'Castle' 114 et seq, 161 et seq
- 'Castle' (improved) 207, 210
- 'City' 36 et seq, 61
- 'County' (4-4-0) 49 et seq, 86
- 'Dean Goods' 20, 190
- De Glehn 4-4-2 38–50, 54, 89
- 'Duke' 17 et seq, 64
- 'Dukedog' 194
- 'Flower' 70 et seq
- 'Grange' 135, 192
- *The Great Bear* 66 et seq 117
- 'Hall' 134 et seq
- 'Hall' (improved) 196 et seq
- 'King' 153 et seq, 170, 176 et seq, 208, 217
- 'Manor' 195
- 'Saint' 34, 49, 76, 140 et seq, 170, 172, 224
- Standard gauge 'singles' 7 et seq, 42 et seq, 79
- 'Star' 55 et seq, 73 et seq, 92 et seq, 140
- '22' 0-6-0 190
- '28' 2-8-0 49, 86
- '43' 2-6-0 83 et seq, 133
- '47' 2-8-0 112
- '1000' 4-6-0 200 et seq
- Tank engines:
- 'Metro' 22 et seq
- 2-4-2 82
- 'County' 49 et seq, 82
- '31' 49
- '42' 85
- '45' 98
- '48' 188
- '56' 132
- '57' 188
- '72' 190
- '94' 188

Locomotive types, typical express of the 1880s 6

Logs of runs, detailed:
- Birmingham route, via Bicester 145, 147, 178–9
- Birmingham route, via Oxford 15, 86
- Bristol main line 91, 138, 139, 161, 168, 174, 175, 192, 199, 218, 224
- Cornwall main line 194, 204
- Ealing–Paddington 82
- South Wales, via Badminton 140, 142
- West of England, via Bristol 12, 13, 14, 25, 31, 32, 53
- West of England, via Westbury 52, 58, 59, 61, 110, 112, 125, 127–8, 148–9, 150, 184–5, 213, 214
- Worcester, to and from Paddington 80, 81

Ocean Mails, logs 41, 43, 44, 45, 211

Personalities:
- Antrobus, G.P. 177
- Brocklebank, Sir Aubrey 153
- Cawdor, Earl 27
- Flewellyn, G.H. 43, 46, 130
- Grand, K.W.C. 216, 219
- Granet, Sir Guy 130
- Grenfell, Neville 76, 135, 224
- Hungerford, Ed 155
- Inglis, Sir James 68, 113
- Kay, J.A. 176
- Malan, Rev A.H. 7 et seq
- Milne, Sir James 160, 216
- Pole, Sir Felix 113, 123, 129, 134, 155, 160
- Yorke, Sir Arthur 64

Royal trains 31, 116

Testing of locos, methods 117 et seq

Trains:
- 'Bath Spa Express' 91, 109
- 'Bristolian' 174, 218
- 'Cheltenham Flyer' 161, 168, 175
- 'Cornishman' 7, 46
- 'Cornish Riviera Express' 31 et seq, 52, 84, 110, 112, 123, 125 et seq, 156, 159, 184, 194, 204, 221
- 'Dutchman' (Up) 123, 214
- 'Flying Dutchman' (Broad Gauge) 7
- 'Flying Welshman' 11
- 'Irish Mail' (via Fishguard) 142
- 'Ocean Mails' 40 et seq, 211
- 'Shakespeare Express' 143
- 'Torbay Limited' 148
- 'Zulu' (Broad Gauge) 6, 7

Of further interest...

The 'Great Locomotives' Series

by O.S. Nock

Volume 1: Southern Railway

'Jubilees', 'Schools', 'King Arthurs' and many other familiar names will be found among the *Great Locomotives of the Southern Railway*, all described in O.S. Nock's customary authoritative and entertaining style. Here are not only the histories and technical details of every major class of locomotive to run on the rails of the Southern Railway, but also the stories of the designers and their philosophies. A wealth of the author's personal recollections of the era and a fascinating collection of photographs make this book a must for the shelves of every railway enthusiast.

Volume 2: LNER

With a network covering the mountain lines of Scotland, the great industrial belt of the North of England and the rural reaches of the Fens, the London and North Eastern Railway and its constituents carried a huge variety of traffic and developed some of Britain's finest locomotives to do the job. O.S. Nock describes the men and the machines, from Patrick Stirling's graceful '8-footers' to Sir Nigel Gresley's East Coast 'Pacifics'. Containing many personal recollections and details of remarkable runs behind LNER steam, this book continues his account of landmarks in British locomotive development.

Volume 3: LMS

The constituent companies of the LMS produced many powerful and innovative designs, notably the great rivals the LNW and Midland Railways, and these are described in detail in this third volume. But following the Grouping of 1923, the traditional inter-company rivalries died hard, and it was not until W.A. Stanier was appointed Chief Mechanical Engineer in 1932 that the golden age of LMS locomotive power dawned, bringing with it the legendary 'Black Fives', 'Princess Royals' and 'Duchesses'. The background stories of the design and development of all the great locomotives of the LMS are told here with the same detail, authority and humour that characterizes the previous volumes covering the Southern Railway and the LNER.

No 6011 King James I *(left) overtaking No 4085* Berkeley Castle *on a stopping train in Sonning Cutting*. (M.W. Earley)